A Love Song

FROM THE ALPS TO THE CAHILL AND BEYOND

A Life Journey of Romance
Resolve & Redemption

MY LIFE STORY
by John M. Souder

A Love Song
From the Alps to the Cahill & Beyond

by John Souder

Library of Congress Number: 2013911293
International Standard Book Number: 978-1-60126-390-2

Printed 2013 by

Masthof Press
219 Mill Road
Morgantown, PA 19543-9516

Table of Contents

Prologue vii

Dedication viii

Acknowledgements.. ix

About the Author xi

Foreword... xiii

CHAPTER 1—Beginnings of Romance.................................... 1

CHAPTER 2—Our Genealogies 8

CHAPTER 3—Grammy Landis 13

CHAPTER 4—Grammy and Grumpop Souder........................ 16

CHAPTER 5—Anabaptists—Who Are They? 20

CHAPTER 6—John Derstine Souder, "Local Historian" and

              Folk Artist (1865-1942) 25

CHAPTER 7—My Dad.. 30

CHAPTER 8—Farm Life in Telford 34

CHAPTER 9—Creative Fun Growing Up 37

CHAPTER 10—Trap Lines of the '50s...................................... 43

CHAPTER 11—Following the Path of Jesus.............................. 47

CHAPTER 12—Huts and Rafts at the Duck Pond.................... 49

CHAPTER 13—Pigeons, Rabbits and Guinea Pigs 53

CHAPTER 14—The Market Truck 55

CHAPTER 15—Winter Entertainment—a Few Generations Ago 60

CHAPTER 16—Uncle Raymond 63

CHAPTER 17—Famous Fruit Trees on the Farm 67

CHAPTER 18—Dogs of the '40s and '50s 71

CHAPTER 19—Strawberry—the Tramp and Other Hobos 74

CHAPTER 20—It Was an Accident 80

CHAPTER 21—Schoolteachers.. 82

CHAPTER 22—Our High School Days..................................... 91

CHAPTER 23—One Foggy Night in 1960 96

CHAPTER 24—Road Trips While Dating 98

CHAPTER 25—Centereach, Long Island, N.Y. 101
CHAPTER 26—Stargazers 103
CHAPTER 27—Susan Landis Souder, LPN 105
CHAPTER 28—Wedding Bells 110
CHAPTER 29—Honeymoon—Early Married Life...............................115
CHAPTER 30—Alternate Service 118
CHAPTER 31—Our Calling, Commitment and a Little Bridge 121
CHAPTER 32—Sullivan County 127
CHAPTER 33—Four Precious Treasures 136
CHAPTER 34—Back Pains..149
CHAPTER 35—Learning to Lead 154
CHAPTER 36—Farming in Sullivan County 161
CHAPTER 37—Rocks, Rocks and More Rocks 169
CHAPTER 38—Real Mountain People . . . Like Ellery 171
CHAPTER 39—Dirt Bikes, Snowmobiles and Four-Wheelers 180
CHAPTER 40—Holiday Traditions 188
CHAPTER 41—Hayfield Surprises 195
CHAPTER 42—Memories of DarWay...199
CHAPTER 43—My Building Career 203
CHAPTER 44—Twenty-Four Thousand Tiny Yellow Puffs...................207
CHAPTER 45—Introducing . . . the Berkes..225
CHAPTER 46—Beaches, Boardwalks, and Sand Castles 229
CHAPTER 47—Dad, Can We Use . . . ?..234
CHAPTER 48—Grand Marais...237
CHAPTER 49—Honduras Calling..241
CHAPTER 50—Brothers 251
CHAPTER 51—The Hunting Tradgedy 255
CHAPTER 52—Cars and Trucks 264
CHAPTER 53—The Applesauce Factory Affair.......................................269
CHAPTER 54—Hope Deferred . . . With Grammy Souder 273
CHAPTER 55—The Half Pipe 280
CHAPTER 56—A Second Chance...283
CHAPTER 57—Piccalilli Parties 288
CHAPTER 58—Twig Art...292
CHAPTER 59—Rudy's Place 294
CHAPTER 60—Westward Bound for Six Weeks.....................................303

CHAPTER 61—2003 322

CHAPTER 62—Signs of a Tsunami 323

CHAPTER 63—Five-Star Kindness...331

CHAPTER 64—Angel in the Crowd..334

CHAPTER 65—Epilogue...339

CHAPTER 66—Other Places We've Explored............................340

CHAPTER 67—Ebenezer, Our Rock of Hope 349

CHAPTER 68—LHF's Centennial Celebration............................354

CHAPTER 69—40th Wedding Anniversary 355

CHAPTER 70—A Treasure in Jars of Clay 356

CHAPTER 71—Short-Term Missions...367

CHAPTER 72—Renee's Tribute 370

CHAPTER 73—Williamsport ICU...372

CHAPTER 74—The Gatehouse (Inpatient Hospice) 376

CHAPTER 75—Brenda's Tribute..381

CHAPTER 76—Lori's Tribute...383

CHAPTER 77—Mike's Tribute 385

CHAPTER 78—Grandkids' Tributes—Three Oldest 387

CHAPTER 79—My Grateful Tribute 389

CHAPTER 80—Bowery Mission Trips.......................................392

CHAPTER 81—Pink Knit Gloves...394

CHAPTER 82—"Mom's Clothes" 396

CHAPTER 83—I hugged her last night 399

CHAPTER 84—What's It Like, Honey? 400

CHAPTER 85—Now That You're Gone......................................404

CHAPTER 86—Thinking, Pondering, Wondering 409

CHAPTER 87—Light Will Rise..411

CHAPTER 88—Full Moon Rising..413

CHAPTER 89—Peace in Prescot Valley.....................................416

CHAPTER 90—Officially Welcomed —Marliss Ann Berke.................420

CHAPTER 91—Hurricane Ponderings 422

CHAPTER 92—Beauty for Ashes..425

Afterword..434

v

Prologue

Can I do this?
2010

All my life I have worked hard with my back and hands on the farm and construction. It energized me. College did not interest me. Most of my life, I kept some form of a diary or journal to record daily events. Writing my life story or publishing a book never entered my mind until later in life. Authors were held high on a pedestal far beyond my reach. In my mind no one would ever print my simple writings. Would they even want to read them?

A large portion of my fears and inhibitions to write stemmed from my limited vocabulary. Didn't all writers have a college education and the ability to use words we ordinary people stumbled over? How could an old farm boy write something people would actually read? Well, after a few years of writing and emailing "Dad's Weekly" to my children and grandchildren, they began telling me I should write a book. That ignited a spark in me.

I enjoyed, (and still do) writing about our farm life, our church and family life, the wildlife in our county and more.

A popular contemporary Christian song writer gave me new hope and perspective. He had similar fears about people accepting his music. Here is a small portion of one of his songs which helps me:

"Why should I fear man when You made the heavens? Why should I be afraid when You put the stars in place? You shine . . . Filling us with courage and strength to follow You."

-Contemporary song written by Brian Doerksen

So with some trepidation and fear of coming up short in the end, I'm committed to "following" my heart to write my story. A huge thank you to Eva Shaw, my online writing instructor, for your tips, critique, and encouragement. You were a channel of God's blessing.

Dedication

All the Glory and Praise belongs to God, My Heavenly Father.

I dedicate this book to the following people:

To my sweet Susan,
who journeyed with me and now enjoys the lavishness of Heaven.

To my wonderful children,
Renee, Brenda, Lori and Mike
and their respective spouses, Rod, Eugene, Mike and Mercy.

To my twelve treasured grandchildren,
Ciara, Rachel, Bekah, Tyler, Rayah, Kaiti, Rissa, Leah, Bethy,
Emmett, Jude and Eva.

To my special sister, Joan.

And to my second love and cherished wife,
Marliss.

Acknowledgements

I owe my being to the God of the universe in whose image I was created, to the Lord of Lords who paid a debt none of us could pay, and to the Holy Spirit who gives comforting guidance each day. Without God in my life, it would have been meaningless. Thank You.

I want to thank my parents and grandparents for the rich Christian heritage they gave me as a young child. They helped me build my life on a solid foundation with Biblical principals to guide me. They also instilled in me and mentored for me great work ethics, allowing just enough time for fun and socializing. I now can appreciate their resolve that I finish high school. Thank you.

I am ever so grateful for teachers like Pearl Schrack who taught me the importance of reading and literature. In high school I loathed reading. Now I cannot read enough. Miss Schrack, I owe you big time for your persistence and patience with me. Thanks.

John Ruth receives the credit for detailing our geneologies. His help and wealth of knowledge about our ancestry and Mennonite history was extremely valuable. Bless you.

Henry Goshow, thanks for following God's call to Sullivan County and hearing God's voice on behalf of Susan and me and our calling. Thanks for being second parents to us in our early parenting life.

To my sister, Joan, for being a constant encouragement and supporter of our ministry in Sullivan County. Thank you.

To my four children, Renee, Brenda, Lori and Mike; I cannot thank you enough for supporting and encouraging me to follow my writing dreams. Renee, it was you who first mentioned that I use my "Dad's Weekly" to write a book. That was the spark that ignited my fire. You all are my most precious treasures and I am ever so grateful for each of you and your dedication to following God's call in your lives. Bless you.

Susan, my wife of 47 years, how can I ever thank you for believing in me? Your little "sticky notes" kept me alert, on time, and helped me *remember not to forget*. Thanks for proofreading every "Dad's Weekly." Thanks for loving me and the opportunity to really love you. Your grace and generosity is unsurpassed. This book will tell much more. I love you "big much."

A big thank you to Susan's siblings and many others for enjoying my writings and helping to boost my confidence as an author.

It was providence that connected me with Eva Shaw, my online writing instructor, who deserves much praise and gratitude. It was you, Eva, who gently critiqued my writing attempts and skillfully showed me how to write my voice and use words. I am forever grateful for your expertise.

Last but surely not least is my second love, Marliss. Our God always knows how to produce light in the darkness, bring joy after weeping and turn our mourning into dancing . . . literally. After the great loss of our first spouses, God brought us together. You, hon, have been so gentle, so patient, so helpful in processing my thoughts. You have endured many lonely hours on the couch with our pups while I wrote long into the night. You gave me all the space and time I needed to complete this. You have even been *my* counselor. Thanks for being so supportive and unselfish as I wrote about my family, my first love, my life. Never once did I hear you say . . . "Stop talking about Susan." And now, it's our life. Bless you. And to God be the Glory.

About the Author

John Merrill Mittman Souder was born in Sellersville, Pa., on January 15, 1943, to John and Margaret Souder of Telford, Pa. He grew up on a poultry and crop farm. He attended Rockhill Mennonite Church, a fairly conservative church, from childhood until moving to Sullivan Co., Pa. He graduated eighth grade from Franconia Mennonite School, now known as Penn View Christian near Franconia, Pa. He graduated from Christopher Dock Mennonite High School in Lansdale, Pa.

He married Susan Alderfer Landis, his high school sweetheart and daughter of Sally and Pastor Elias Landis of Harleysville, Pa., on November 10, 1962.

John Merrill, better known as "JM" or John later in life, intended on taking over the home farm established in the 18th century. But God called him and Susan to move north 150 miles to assist in establishing Estella Mennonite Church, started by his home church, Rockhill.

In 1964, Susan and John moved to Sullivan County and remained there until Susan's death in 2010. John and his second wife, Marliss, continue to live and operate the home farm in a retired mode . . . when they are not traveling.

John operated a veal and chicken farm and also began a construction business in 1979 with his second cousin, Rod Goshow. They named it Brotherhood Builders and were partners for 15 years after which JM started his own construction business.

Susan was a Licensed Practical Nurse (LPN) and practiced for 13 years at DarWay, a local nursing home.

JM and Susan devoted many years to Christian service. In 1999 and 2000, they served three months in Honduras with MAMA Project.

Together they raised four children. College and friends were the catalyst in moving three of them, Renee, Brenda and Mike to Virginia. Lori lives just four miles from home.

It was during the late 1990's that JM started writing weekly letters on Sunday night to his children. Those letters became known as "Dad's Weekly" and were basically newsy letters of what was happening around the homestead. News of church life, the neighborhood, farm activity, wildlife sightings, gardening, and our personal life was recorded. Each letter concluded with encouraging scripture, prayers and Christian quotes or even a synopsis of the Sunday sermon. It was intended to jump start the week with encouraging words and exhortation.

Renee saved almost every weekly and stored them in a binder which became a rich source of material to draw from for the book.

While Susan was battling cancer the last two years, JM began to pursue writing their life story with the encouragement of their children. And so it all began.

Foreword

I equate this book endeavor to the renovation of a house which most sane people would have demolished. There were ideas in my head about what to do with it. So I drew up plans on the computer and began the long process of reconstruction. I set no time limit hoping to minimize frustration. Other jobs and commitments needed attention as well. It took three years to complete with some outside help, laboring full time the last six months.

Over the past ten years hundreds of families, friends and people we had not known have enjoyed the hard labor of love put into our vacation rental. I've never been sorry for starting the project. However, at 67 I doubt that I'd ever tackle something that involved and intense again. Or would I?

All that to say . . . writing our life story feels a lot like that project. Daunting, I must say. I feel like if I could have done it with a hammer, saw, level and square, it may not have taken as long. Those skills were already sharp. Since I didn't have a website to demonstrate or explain writing with those tools, here's the trail I traveled.

I dug up all the "Dad's Weeklys" written over a period of 15 years. Fortunately, I filed them where they could be found. But that would only cover that period of time.

I recorded an interview with a historian, John Ruth, who knew our families well. He gave me some valuable information regarding our ancestors—where they came from; their life styles; when they came to this country; and how they arrived at our homesteads.

You'll read about our growing-up years, our schools and churches and when I first noticed "her." That was in seventh grade. Standing in the second row in chorus in the alto section, she saw me looking at her through the small window in the classroom door. I smiled at her and she smiled back. My heart skipped a beat and I floated down the hall to my next class. The only thing I could see the rest of that day was that beautiful smile and her dark brown wavy hair curled into long pig tails. Puppy love you say. Guess what. I married her and had 47 wonderful years together. We vowed . . . "for better or worse, richer or poorer, in sickness and in health, till death do us part." And it has.

High school and the dating days were fun to remember. My life on the farm at home. Neighborhood ball teams, ice hockey on our pond, building huts and tunnels in the hay mall. Oh, my, so many bubbles rising. Yes, I had to sort them out.

Engagement, nurses' training, our marriage. Our honeymoon. Our kids. You will read about the big decision and our move 150 miles north to help establish a church . . . seeing our family grow and mature on the farm we called home the rest of our days. Struggling to make ends meet on the farm. Starting a construction partnership with my cousin. Church life and its challenges. Soccer games, college life. An unwed pregnancy transformed by God's grace. The death of my only brother at 29 struck by a bullet behind our barn in the early morning darkness by a random deer hunter. The changes that brought.

Family camping vacations, the trip west, Alaska, Europe, Hawaii, and many more. Graduating from sand castles to sand houses and steepled churches on the beach.

The discovery of cancer the same year we moved to Virginia to build a house for my oldest daughter. Alas . . . the death of my beloved soul mate—mother of four and MawMaw of twelve grandkids, my sweet Susan. The tears and grief. Then what? Well, if you stay tuned, you'll find out. Actually, death is not the end. It's the beginning of our eternal life. But since I'm still here, there is more to write and read.

I mixed it up a bit straying from chronological order. My apologies for any repetition of scripture or overlapping story portions. All stories and chapters were written over a three-year period.

Often the memories would rebound late into the wee hours of the morning as I sat tapping the keys while sitting in my chair next to our bed trying to capture this wonderful and challenging life. Then came those last years . . . so much suffering and pain for Susan and her graceful patient attitude through it all, and the horrific experiences with cancer. I called for God's help and the expertise of my online writing instructor, Eva Shaw. I tapped the memory of family members and relatives.

Since I have many other interests, and family to love, time management was crucial. Morning and evenings were generally my best writing moments. TV took a far back seat. Finding the words for these pages took over three years and many mugs of coffee. The title, "A Love Song" stems from my love for good music, my family and God. In its entirety, the making of my life feels like a song of love complete with extreme emotions expressed there-in. It began in Switzerland and extends to our mountain, the Cahill and beyond.

Now I wonder, am I finished? What did I leave out? Will there be another book? Oh, my . . . good grief. Now, *that would be the limit!*

CHAPTER 1

Beginnings of Romance

"The future lies before you, as a field of new-blown snow.
Be careful how you tread it, for every step will show."
Quote from the Schul-Andenken - 1961

She was a "cool babe" and her shy smile could melt a stone. She never wore jeans or slacks, always a skirt and blouse; mostly a practice of belief and conscience motivated by the church. A small, white netting covered part of her dark brown hair with gentle waves in front and pigtails secured by barrettes. Her dark brown eyes, long eyelashes and dark eyebrows, her short shapely nose, rosy cheeks and heart shaped lips, together screamed, *I'm beautiful!* She always was! Girls in this time period wore ponytails, poodle skirts, pedal pushers and scarves, if they were cool ckicks. Susan *was* except for the short skirts and pedal pushers.

Susan (better known to family as Mom or MawMaw) and I were attracted to each other when she was in seventh grade and I was in eighth grade at Franconia Mennonite Day School, near Telford, Pa. Today it is known as Penn View Christian School.

For me, it was purely physical attraction. I wasn't the only one interested in her and rightly so. I was average height, thin, tanned skinned, a large head of wavy dark brown hair and usually, neatly combed. Popular hairstyles for boys were; flattops and DA or ducktail slicked back with grease, and sideburns. I had none of them. "Cool cat" guys wore wranglers, leather jackets with collars turned up—which I did. I think I was a fairly sharp dresser, thanks to my mom and sister. I envied larger built boys like my friend, Lowell. But I never let any work, project or 100-lb. sacks of feed intimidate me. My passion, up until I met Susan, was farming, biking, trapping, skating, fishing, building and sports of any kind.

Please keep in mind now, that the culture we grew up in, people dated and married much earlier than towards the end of the 20th century or the beginning of the 21ˢᵗ century. Particularly in our religious circles, mid-teenage dating was not frowned upon. Late teens and early twenties were normal for marriage. That said dear ones, maybe you will better understand our story.

We wrote notes to each other, sending them back and forth via friends in school. We were both too shy to approach each other and talk other than to say "Hi" in the hallway. At the end of that school year, we lost track until two years later when she joined me at Christopher Dock High School (CD).

I met Susan's cousin, Merrill Landes, at CD and we became best friends. He had a great sense of humor, and we liked all the same sports, especially ping pong. Since he attended the same church as Susan, he had an inside track with her family and kept me updated. When he found out that I had a "crush" on Susan, he said, "Suz, she's a hot chick." I already knew that, but appreciated his taste and affirmation.

Susan was a freshman and I a sophomore. It was an opportunity to get re-acquainted. Merrill rode to school with Emma, Susan's oldest sister. Emma was the head cook and drove a 1953 Ford station wagon with imitation wood siding all four years we went to school. She always had a car full of students gladly paying the 25¢ taxi fee. Riding to and from school, Merrill would tease her and find tidbits of information to tell me. Some of it she intended for me and other info. she didn't. But I was always interested in anything he had to report.

One day, in her freshman year, she didn't show up for school. I soon learned that her father had died. I never got to know him personally but had heard wonderful things about him. He was a preacher, butcher and farmer and a wonderful husband and father to 12 children.

He raised cattle, sheep, chickens and turkeys; and grew lots of potatoes and vegetables for market. The butcher shop was his main income.

At 58, he lost his battle with throat cancer. Pop (as they knew him) was not a smoker, was a man of integrity, strong in stature, soul and spirit. Pop was a very kind and tender loving man, well respected at home, in the community and in church. He was conscientious and ethical in all his business dealings. Every summer, he took some of the family deep sea fishing to help feed his large family. Those were fun and festive times providing lots of fresh fillets for the freezer.

With Pop's passing, Susan's mom had good reason to be devastated, but her strong faith and large family pulled her through. I remember going to the viewing at the funeral home. There were so many friends and family that the waiting line stretched way out along the street. I spotted her as soon as we entered. She sat in the front row between Ruthie and Jim (the three little ones) as they were called. Her face was sad and eyes swollen. Our eyes met and she offered a brief but sad smile. I had no words, nor did she. To our human minds, Pop was too young and would have had so much more to offer life had it not been for cancer. But then, who can understand the mind of a loving God whom we trust? Not that that made it any easier to accept. It's the hope of seeing him again some day.

Mid-teens

Days later, I found her after school by the stone wall at Grebel Hall. She stood with one foot up against the wall behind her. She wore a plaid wool skirt and white blouse, a grey scarf around her head and as usual, was holding a stack of homework. A couple friends stood nearby talking. I walked up to her searching for comforting words to say but she spoke first.

"I like that jacket, did you just get it?" Of course my collar was turned up.

"Yeah, was time for a new one I guess," I said, still thinking of what to talk about. I knew her tender heart was broken just having buried her Dad.

"Wow, looks like you got lots of homework," I said.

"You know Miss Schrack. She loves reading assignments," she said. "And Mr. Reinford loves to give big assignments for German class. German is so hard. He's so nit-picky, every pronunciation has to be just his way. You'd think Pennsylvania Dutch would help, but no, we have to use perfect *high* German."

"I'm sure you'll figure it out. You're smarter than me. Glad I don't have to take it," I said. "That's why I took Commercial instead of the Academic course."

Emma pulled up and she had to go.

"Call me if you can," she said smiling.

"Ok. See ya," I said.

"I keep a close watch on this heart of mine
I keep my eyes wide open all the time
I keep the ends out for the tie that binds
Because you're mine, I walk the line . . . "

-Johnny Cash

Most families have some rules and guidelines regarding dating. So did we. Phone calls were to be short and not every night. No dates until you were 16 years old and then only weekends. At that age curfew was 11:00.

Really, we had no problem with these rules. We could see each other every day at school. And I had great respect for her mom (Mom) as we called her and (Grammy) as grandchildren called her. Sally was a widow, with 12 children. The three youngest were unmarried. Emma and Kass were also single and lived at home including Aunt Lizzy Etta. They all shared responsibilities with household chores.

Once a month, there was a school social event held in the gym. It could be one class or a combination of classes. Group games and various competitions were scheduled. We looked forward to those fun times together. You wouldn't believe how animated and excitable Susan was then. Her grade had lots of talented singers and drama students. She was among them. She escaped her shy shell at socials, games, skits, plays or in chorus practice and tours.

I loved watching her whoop and cheer, and act out her drama parts. Boy was she good . . . stunning and attractive. But I had a hard time with how comfortable and buddy-buddy she acted around certain boys. They were too friendly with her and she seemed too happy with them. I was jealous. Yes, jealous. I had some maturing and growing up to do. Susan had a hard time understanding why it bothered me. So did I. So we wrote notes to each other trying to work it out and talked about it often. It was the only area we struggled with in our relationship. It was the area I struggled with most throughout high school. Maybe it's because girls mature much earlier than boys. At least, that makes me feel better.

16 – LICENSED TO DRIVE AND DATE

In the 50's, if you wanted a car that looked and sounded tough, a '55 BelAir Convertible with dual glass pack mufflers would be a good set-up. Or a semi-custom '56 Merc, chopped and lowered, with lake pipes, was also a good machine. So slick back the DA, put the top down, tune in the top 40 DJ and take a ride. Now that was groovy and sharp!

I was one of the younger kids in my class having started first grade at five years old. It was mid January in my junior year before I turned 16. Susan turned 16 the end of March in her sophomore year. That meant I could take her out on a date. Yippy! I think the first time she had permission to ride with me was home from a school social. For the first half of that year, I drove my dad's 1954 black Chrysler New Yorker. It was more like a big boat, but it had wheels, lots of power and I had the keys and a license to drive. The social was fun but what I looked forward to, and I know she did too, was riding home alone together. I opened the passenger door for her and she *scooched* over to the middle to sit closer to me. Unless it was a super sports model, cars all had bench seats in front instead of bucket seats. No seat belts. If only I could remember our conversation, but I don't. It was most certainly small talk and too soon we were driving in her long gravel lane. Being a school night, I couldn't stay but I could walk her in to the house. No kiss. No hug. Just smiles.

"Thanks, it was fun. See you tomorrow sometime," she said opening the house door with an armload of books. I affirmed our fun evening and walked back to the car thrilled as though riding a 10-foot wave.

Early on, most of our dates were double dates, at least every other week until the end of school and into the summer. Near the end of the summer before my senior year, Daddy bought my first car, a slightly used '57 Chevy. It was a black, four-door hard-top Bel-air with red interior and large white walls on the tires. If only I had the foresight to keep it instead of trading it a few years later. Wow! I must admit, I was way too big and proud for my britches driving that car. Yes, I was grateful. And yes, I was blessed to have a Dad who could pay for it.

My best friend, Merrill, was the only other guy in my class who had a newer car than me. His Dad bought him a brand new '57 Ford Fairlane 500 soon after he turned 16. We both kept our cars clean and brilliantly waxed. By our senior year, lots of my buddies had sharp-looking cars. Even a brand new VW Bug or Beetle, as you may know it, was envied. One of my friends had one. Another friend, after working part time nights stacking grocery shelves to earn money, took out a bank loan to buy a new 1960 Plymouth; one of those muscle cars with big fins and push buttons to shift gears. The girls loved it.

A favorite hangout on a Saturday night after a youth meeting was the "Big Pixy." It was one of those drive-up, eat-in-your-car hamburger joints. Good-looking girls dressed in mini skirts came out to take our order and then served us in our cars. Lots of our friends often showed up and we'd sit in our cars, radios tuned to WIBG listening to "Dream, dream, dream" by the Everly Brothers while eating and laughing and watching other people come and go including the serving girls.

Even today, 2011, there is one of those "eat-in-your-car" restaurants still active in Staunton, Virginia. I recently ate there with my kids and grandkids. They play '60s music from a juke box, believe it or not. The last time we went, I punched in my own number, "Wake up, my little Susie, wake up . . ." Nostalgia, good ol' days, it's great.

Another favorite dating place was miniature golf. There were two in particular that we liked; Twin Oaks and Twin Lakes. Both were 20 miles from Susan's home but lots of fun. Usually, four or five couples would be there together. As in most sports or competition, Merrill was the one to beat. We were great jolly competitors. Susan and Nancy, his girlfriend (now wife), were just happy to be with us and thoroughly enjoyed our entertainment. I can still hear Merrill laugh when a ball overshot the hole.

"Ha, ha, ha. What happened John Merrill? Suz makin' ya nervous?"

I shot back with, "Hey man, get over it. Maybe you got a hole in one this time but it doesn't mean you're gonna win."

He kept laughing his hearty ol' laugh.

Sometimes it got quite cool in late autumn, all the more reason for Susan to stay close to me. I loved it!

Affirm every opportunity to be close to your lover. Boy, do I treasure those memories.

FACTS AND FAVORITES OF THE '40S AND '50S

Prices when I was born in 1943; Average house—$3,600. Annual wages—$2,000. Gallon of gas—15 cents. Average car cost—$900. Bottle of Coke—5 cents.

By 1960; House—$12,700. Wages—$5,312. Gas—25 cents. Car—$2,600. Coal—$15/ton.

- World War II
- The Pentagon is completed—the Great Depressions ends—U.S. one-cent coin is struck in steel due to copper shortages.
- Bengal; India famine leaves up to 3 million dead.

POPULAR FILMS OF THE '40S:
Heaven Can Wait/Lassie Come Home/The Titanic—1943

POPULAR MUSIC
Frank Sinatra "In the Mood" by Glenn Miller/Oklahoma Musical opens on Broadway

POPULAR INVENTION
The Slinky

MAJOR WORLD POLITICAL LEADERS
> U.S.—President Franklin D. Roosevelt
> Russia/Soviet Union—Joseph Stalin
> Germany—Chancelor Adolf Hitler
> Italy—Benito Mussolini
> U.K.—Winston Churchill

Baseball Hall of Fame in the '50s include—Willie Mays, Hank Aaron, Mickey Mantle, Yogi Berra, Whitey Ford, Frank Robinson, Jackie Robinson, Roy Campanella, and Ted Williams.

In 1951, the first nationally televised game featured the Brooklyn Dodgers and the New York Giants.

Basketball favorites were—Michael Jordan, Bob Cousy, Bill Russell, Wilt Chamberlain, Doc Rivers to name just a few.

1969—The U.S. landed Neil Armstrong and Buzz Aldrin on the moon and returned safely back to earth. Many recall the immortal words first spoken from the moon to earth—"ONE SMALL STEP FOR MAN, ONE GIANT LEAP FOR MANKIND."

Segreation and racism was still a real part of our lives.

My favorite snacks growing up and to this day are:
> Juicy Fruit Gum, Snicker Bars, Strawberry Ice Cream, Vanilla D.Q.
> I love dunking most any cake or cookie in coffee, especially Shoofly Pie, Hard Cake, Erma Cakes, and all cookies.
> If I have my choice of coffee—it is Dunkin' Donuts!

CHAPTER 2

Our Genealogies

Yes, please take time to read the ancestry of our family. It's actually quite interesting knowing these were real people who struggled to make ends meet like you and me. Knowing about our roots helps us better understand who we are and where we originated. Thanks for reading this history.

We'll start by listing the first immigrant of each side of both families. Beginning with Susan's father Elias N. Landis' line. Next will be Susan's mom's line, Sallie A. Landis. Next, my father, John R. Souder's line. Next, my mom's line, Margaret D. Mittman Souder.

All data was obtained from websites and historian John L. Ruth of Salford Mennonite Church.

ELIAS N. LANDIS FAMILY ANCESTRY

1727 – JACOB LANDIS [THE IMMIGRANT] came to Philadelphia from Zurich, Switzerland, and settled along the Branch Creek near Harleysville, Pa. We have no record of his wife's name.

JACOB LANDIS II married MARY CASTLE.

YELLIS LANDIS married ELIZABETH KULP and settled along the Branch Creek near Salford.

JACOB LANDIS married SUSANNAH DETWEILER and lived on a farm which is now the property of the Graterford Eastern Pennitentary in Graterford, Pa.

ABRAM D. LANDIS married ELIZABETH REIFF.

ELIAS [pronounced "A"lias] R. LANDIS married _____ METZ.

ABRAM LANDIS married EMMA NICE.

ELIAS N. LANDIS married SALLIE ALDERFER.

The homestead where Susan was raised was originally owed by a Gerhart Clemens [690 ac]. It was later divided into three parcels—one parcel to

Front row, left to right: Kass, Mary, Mel, Betty, Emma, Curt. Second row: Susan, Ruthie, Jim, Doris, JR, Abe.

each son. Sometime in the 1880's, the property was sold to Elias R. Landis and passed down to Susan's father, Elias N. Landis. The Landis name was spelled either with an "i" or an "e" but both spellings came from the same root family in Zurich, Switzerland.

SALLIE M. ALDERFER LANDIS

1732 – HANS CLEMMER married ANNA DETWEILER then came to Philadelphia from Steinsfurt, Germany. According to John Ruth, the historian, Hans was not Mennonite, but Lutheran and he did not have enough money "to get off the boat." Someone obviously paid for him to enter America. "Oral tradition" has it that "Hans was killed in a freak accident when a horse ran him against the post."

FRIEDRICH ALTDÖRFER married Hans' widow, ANNA DETWEILER, because he was "an indentured servant, slave."

JOHN D. ALDERFER married ELIZABETH ROSENBERGER.

ABRAM R. ALDERFER married ANNIE KEELEY.

JACOB K. ALDERFER married SUSANNAH SWARTLEY.

It's recorded that Susannah sent a sampling of her needlework back to Switzerland for display.

PHILLIP GRANT S. ALDERFER married KAITIE MOYER.

My Grammy Souder & me with about 120 eggs.

Phillip grew up on the John Ruth farmstead. He was known later in life for his famous scrapbooks and coke.

Kaitie's father, Jacob C. Moyer was a preacher. When I asked if it was the Jacob Moyer who worked at Moyer and Son feed mill in Telford, John was adamant to say, "Oh my, there are many, many Jacob Moyers; there's Jacob D., Jacob Dinn, Jacob L., Jacob C.M. (that stands for cow manure, he said ☺)." No, it was Jacob C. Moyer, the preacher.

SALLIE M. ALDERFER married ELIAS N. LANDIS.

All the above and much more can be found in the book ALDERFERS OF AMERICA *and on the website rootsweb.com.*

JOHN MERRILL M. SOUDER

1736 – IMMIGRANT CHRISTIAN SOUDER and MARGARET SOUDER came into Philadelphia, Pa., from Zurich, Switzerland, on the ship called *HARLE* with 388 people on board. They bought land in New Britain, Pa., and built a farm. In 1755 they bought the land and farm on Church Rd., Telford, Pa., and moved there.

JACOB SOUDER married BARBARA FUNK.

CHRISTIAN SOUDER married KATHERINE NICE.

JOHN N. SOUDER married MARY DERSTINE.

JOHN D. SOUDER married SALLIE ALDERFER. Sallie lived on the John Ruth farmstead.

John D. Souder is a noted historian of Montgomery Co., Pa. He created 500 fraktur drawings during his lifetime, many of which are preserved at the Mennonite Heritage Center in Harleysville, Pa., and his "BEEHIVE" is preserved intact at the Schwenkfelders Historical Library in Pennsburg, Pa. Much more can be learned by going to the website rootsweb.com.

PRESTON A. SOUDER married EMMA RUTH (preacher Joe Ruth's daughter).

JOHN R. SOUDER married MARGARET MITTMAN.

JOHN MERRILL SOUDER married SUSAN A. LANDIS (preacher Elias N. Landis' daughter).

John L. Ruth, the historian, says that the Landis, Souder, Alderfer and Moyer families all immigrated from a 20-mile radius near Zurich, Switzerland.

GRAMMY SOUDER – EMMA RUTH SOUDER

1717 – IMMIGRANT HENRY RUTH married MAGDALENA.

JOHN RUTH married _____.

HENRY RUTH married ANNA YELLES.

JOSEPH RUTH married ANN PRICE.

NOAH RUTH married MARIA GEHMAN.

JOE RUTH (bishop) married MARY KRATZ.

EMMA K. RUTH married PRESTON A. SOUDER.

JOHN R. SOUDER married MARGARET D. MITTMAN.

JOHN MERRILL M. SOUDER married SUSAN A. LANDIS.

THE DELPS – MARGARET DELP MITTMAN SOUDER

JOHANN PETER DELP lived in Germany and was the father of IMMIGRANT HANS GEORGE DELP b. 1718, d. 1789.

JOHN DELP married ELIZABETH KRUPP.

ISAAC DELP married RACHEL FRETZ.

EPHRAIM DELP married ANGELINE BAKER and lived in Hatfield.

CHARLES DELP married ANNA PRICE. He was an influential man in the Hatfield and Lansdale area.

CHARLES DELP JR. became Mayor of Lansdale during 1960s to 1970s. Also owned a large trucking company.

ANNA P. DELP wife of Charles and mother of MARTHA.

MARTHA DELP married ELMER MITTMAN. Her husband died when my mother, Margaret, was only 7 years old.

ANNA MARGARET MITTMAN married JOHN R. SOUDER.

JOHN MERRILL M. SOUDER married SUSAN A. LANDIS.

Grammy Souder, 80th Birthday

CHAPTER 3

Grammy Landis

"Children are a heritage from the Lord . . .
Blessed is the man whose quiver is full of them."
Ps. 127: 3 & 5

Obviously, the size of the quiver varies a lot from family to family. Ours was full with four. Some claim theirs can only handle two. Others keep stretching it so it can hold a happy dozen or more. Guess it's partly a matter of desire or could it be . . . God's plan. Family size in the Bible varied considerably.

I came from the middle of a quiver of three. Susan was number eleven of twelve. Her parents' quiver had 25 years to expand to include all 12.

Sallie Alderfer Landis was married at 18 to Elias Landis from Harleysville. All of their children were born at the homestead just below Salford Mennonite Church. Jim, the last of the twelve children was born when Sallie, better known to us as *Mom* or *Grammy*, was 45 years old. All siblings were born at home and healthy, praise be to God.

In this day and age, many people may think of a family that size as a "childrens' home." In many ways, that's just what it was. The chatter and laughter of children was a very normal sound in Grammy's house as I knew it. With twelve children of her own, over thirty grandchildren and about that many great-grandchildren, what would one expect? It was a special treat to visit Grammy Landis.

"Well how are you? I'm so glad you came to see me," she'd say holding and patting your hand with both of hers. It was a rare sight if she didn't have a huge smile. "What a nice surprise. Come and sit for a while. How 'bout we play memory?" she'd say pulling out some chairs at the table. Who could refuse a game of memory with Grammy? Grandchildren learned it at 3 years old and some played till they were married. What fun. Such a bonding time for all.

13

Grammy Landis was raised Conservative Mennonite. She wore a white mesh covering with white ribbon strings long enough to tie them together when gardening. This was in accordance to the Mennonite doctrine based on I Cor. 11. Her normal attire included a long dress with a secondary top piece called a "cape." Its purpose was to give cover and modesty. Never would a conservative woman be seen wearing low-cut dresses or with trousers indicative of men's apparel. Black stockings and black shoes were also necessary even out in the garden. No jewelry was allowed or worn by Grammy. No makeup of any kind. Simplicity and modesty according to I Peter 3 was religiously practiced.

Grammy was no slouch around work. She cared for a large vegetable garden growing string and lima beans, corn, various squash, potatoes, lettuce and herbs. With the help of her children, her sister-in-law, Lizzy Etta and great-grammy, they canned and froze hundreds of quarts for the family. Grammy cultivated her garden with a one-wheeled push cultivator until she was 91.

For extra family income, she made several hundred pounds of cornmeal mush in the back kitchen for their weekly market in Philadelphia. She continued that business into her 80s.

Baking was also a specialty not only for the family but for market. Shoe-fly pies, funny cakes, fruit pies and cookies in mass production were baked each week.

Encouragement was her gift. Anyone who met Sallie (Grammy) would surely leave encouraged no matter the occasion.

If you happened to come to Grammy's house in the morning, you would find her at the end of the long dining room table with a stack of books, cards, Bible, and pencil where she read, wrote and prayed for many people. She faithfully sent cards to her family, the sick and those in prison. She had a passion for prisoners and even visited them at times. An unforgettable headline in the *North Penn Reporter*, local paper, read: "Eighty-Year-Old Grammy Goes to Prison!" She loved everyone. It had to be the consistent faithful prayers of Grammy and my mom that kept all of us on the "narrow" road. Thanks Grammy. Thanks Mom.

The verse most quoted by Grammy Landis in regards to her offspring was III Jn. Verse 4, *"I have no greater joy than to know that my children walk in truth."*

And in keeping with the training of these Godly women, all of their children followed after God's heart. It's a principal of God's word, that "If we train up a child in the way he should go, when he is old, he will not depart from it." That's what God says. I cannot explain why it doesn't seem to hold true for everyone. Somehow, it has to be true because God does not, never did and never will lie.

Grammy lived a long productive life, dying of heart failure at age 93. Susan was caring for her at the time of her death. In her grief, she counted it a privilege to witness her Mom's last breath on earth and be transported to her eternal home. Bless you Mom, for the legacy of love you lived and for giving me Susan.

CHAPTER 4

Grammy and Grumpop Souder

There are advantages to growing up in a double farmhouse. Grammy and Grumpop, well, that's what we kids called him, lived on the other side separated only by two inside doors which were never locked. Not sure why we called him Gumpop but that's how I always addressed him. It was Grumpop who first let me steer the Model B John Deere tractor as I stood between his legs in front of the seat. I was five years old. He was the one who did most of the corn cultivating and I was lucky enough to ride along. As we headed down the dirt road to home in 6th gear, he would randomly lift one leg to wave as he said, "Hi Jake." There was no one nearby but he did it just the same. Grumpop had his own style of humor.

We found him in the feed room downstairs in the hay barn. "Grumpop, is it Saturday today?" I said.

We liked Saturdays. That was the end of the work week and the day he would give us an allowance. I can still see him reaching into his blue bib overalls, smelling like a mixture of pig and chicken manure with a wad of tobacco tucked in his cheek. "Come here boys," he said in his Pennsylvania Dutch accent and pulled out a very old tattered black pouch with coins in it. "I guess you both finished your chores today, huh?" he asked.

"Yep, Grumpop, we did," David and I both chimed in quickly, knowing what comes next.

"Well then, I guess you deserve to be paid," he said as his old wrinkled fingers found two shiny dimes. "Here ya go," he said with a grin, "now don't spend it all on candy."

"Thanks Grumpop," we said and off we ran with big smiles and talking to each other about what we would get with it. A 10 cent piece back in the '50s would buy a glass bottle of Coke at Frank Keller's store across the field. We could walk there or ride our bikes and be there in five minutes. Usually, we'd pick up Harry and a few other neighbors on our way past their houses. Up the road to

Fourth Street and down the hill alongside the cornfield past the ice dam and just beyond the squirrel woods was the store.

Old Frank must have been 85 years old, or so it seemed to us. As we opened the squeaky old screen door, there he sat in his worn-out stuffed chair smoking a cigar. He stood slowly to his feet and said, "What would you like today?"

"Ah . . . I'll have this pack of gum," I said softly.

"That'll be 20 cents for the pack of baseball cards and gum," he said.

"Shucks, I only have 10 cents. Let's see . . . how 'bout a Coke then?" I said.

"Yep, but don't forget to leave the bottle or I'll have to charge you 5 cents deposit," he grunted as he stumbled up the stairs to the soda ice chest. "Here ya go. Now what'l it be for you, youngster?" speaking to David.

"I'll have a pack a those wax bottle drinks," he said kinda shyly.

"Do you have 5 cents?" the old man asked.

"No, but here's a dime."

"That'l work," he said exchanging the dime for a nickel. Five little wax bottles in a pack filled with liquid in different colors and tastes. You'd bite the top off and drink it. Yuuummmy. And with that we were outside sitting on our bikes enjoying our snacks.

"Better get home," David said as he booted the bike's kickstand. After returning the empty Coke bottle, we were off to see who could get home first.

When we had time, we would look for empty bottles in the ditches along the road. We'd save them up and return them to Frank's store for a nickel a piece—good spending money.

Back at the house, (I forget who won the race riding back home), Grammy was at the porch side window singing hymns as she hung up the wash. There was a long wash line attached to a pulley at the ol' walnut tree on the other side of the garden. She could reach out through the window, which was on hinges, and hang up the wash from inside the sun porch. How great is that! Of course she had done the wash in an old wringer washer down in the basement and then had to carry it up the steep winding stairs to the kitchen and out onto the sun porch. Grammy was a short and somewhat stout woman with high blood pressure and eventually, diabetes. To me she seemed pretty old but was likely only in her early 60s.

"Hey John Merrill, listen to this," she said as she began to tell me one of her many memorized poems. "Said the sparrow to the robin, I wonder why it is, that these anxious human beings run about and hurry so? Said the Robin to the sparrow, I think that it must be, that they have no heavenly Father like who cares for you and me." Then she'd laugh. She was a "jolly good fellow" of a Grammy to us. Never saw her looking worried or acting like it. When suppertime came, I remember sneaking over to their side of the house and would stand at the table till she told me to sit down. The table was set with food and the old tattered black Bible was opened. Grammy would look at the daily devotions guide and read the portion for that day. "As it was in the days of Noah, so shall it be when the Son of Man comes back to earth . . ." as she finished reading she closed the Bible and bowed her covered head to pray. The whole while, Grumpop had his head cradled in his wrinkled, dark, tanned hands with elbows propped on the yellow-topped table, sleeves rolled up, listening . . . I guess. Grammy would pray, or sometimes Grumpop and then they'd eat. Most of the time Grumpop would quietly eat, very slowly with eyes closed, occasionally opening them to make a brief comment. I still don't know why. Just his habit I guess.

When supper was finished and the dishes washed and put away, it was time for a game or listen to the radio. Games, what fun playing with Grammy. Grumpop would listen to the radio while we played Parcheesi. I can still hear Preacher Oral Robert's forceful voice proclaiming healing in Jesus' name if you would only believe. After that program he might listen to the "Amos and Andy"

My Dad, Mom, Dorothy, Grammy Souder, Lester, Sally and Grumpop (circa approximately 1938).

show or if it was after 8:00, he'd say, "Guess I'll go up the wooden hill . . . time to hit the hay." And off he'd go shuffling through the kitchen and up the winding wooden stairs to bed.

If it wasn't too late, Joan, David and I would challenge Grammy to one more game of Parcheesi. It was a board game for only four players. It had four black, round cardboard shakers to shake the green or red dice and a home base on each corner with a final home area to get your four buttons in. You needed a five to get out, a double would give you fourteen, and chasing someone home would give you ten more. Safety, was landing on the red blocks. No one could chase you home on safety. "Double," she said. "One, two . . . fourteen, got you," Grammy would say with a belly laugh as she chased me home.

"No fair," I'd say. But it didn't matter, she was hard core. She'd just laugh and say, "Just wait, you might get to chase me home . . . if you don't quit." I soon learned some of her tricks and came to be a pretty good competitor.

The next night would find me back at the dining room table ready for more Parcheesi, if it wasn't too late. I actually still have most of that Parcheesi game intact in our closet.

Oh my, what a fun game and a fun Grammy she was. My advice to you— turn off the TV, turn off the phones, turn down the lights, turn on the radio and get out a board or card game—one for most ages. Learn to be a good sport if you win or lose and play just for fun. Let someone laugh at you when they chase you home or win, but watch how they win and learn the game. Eventually, you will beat them. You'll be surprised at how much fun you can have without all those electronic gadgets or just being a spectator in front of the screen. DO IT.

CHAPTER 5

Anabaptists— Who Are They?

"**D**o you, John Merrrill Souder confess your sins and repent thereof?"

"I do."

"Have you accepted Jesus as your Savior?"

"I have."

"Do you desire to join this church, Rockhill Mennonite Church and be a member in good standing according to the confession of Faith?"

"I do."

"Do you believe in the one and only true God and the Holy Trinity— Father, Son and Holy Ghost?"

"I do."

"Upon these confessions of faith, and your desire to be a member of this congregation, I now baptize you with water in the name of the Father and the Son and The Holy Ghost."

With my head bowed and kneeling next to some of my buddies in front of the congregation in 1953, I was baptized. Water dribbled off my head, down across my suit coat and onto the floor. Bishop Arthur Ruth, a distant relative of mine, (appearing to me about 80 years old but probably 50), reached into the silver bowl of water held by his wife clothed in black, cupped his hands and transferred water from the bowl to my head in the tradition of baptism by sprinkling. He then reached out his hand indicating that I should "rise" which I did. He greeted me with "a holy kiss" and his wife shook my hand as they said, "We receive you into the fellowship of the body of Christ and Rockhill Mennonite Church."

Oh, the "holy kiss?" You know what a kiss is but . . . what's a "holy kiss?" Well, it's commanded by the Apostle Paul in some of his writings, specifically I Thessalonians 5:26, II Corinthians 13:12, and Romans 16:16. So in my growing-up years, if you were a baptized believer church member, you were "supposed" to greet each other (men to men, women to women) with a "holy kiss." Yeah, I know you think it's gross! Well, it was a bit strange and often, I tried to avoid the lips, but most older men were well trained and didn't let you avoid the lip on lip kiss . . . the "holy kiss." Yeah, I know, me too . . . glad that tradition never stuck. But it actually has stuck in the very Conservative Mennonite and Amish traditions who continue to practice the "doctrine" of the holy kiss, even to this day.

So, Believers Baptism is obviously stated to mean that one has personally accepted Christ's gift of Salvation and has chosen to be baptized. This is in opposition to the Roman Catholic tradition of baptizing infants into membership, entrance into the church and its faith.

In order for you to understand our Mennonite faith more clearly, I am including some information from the internet.

Let me preface this by saying that during the early years of the 16th century, the Reformation broke out in Europe among three groups of peoples—the Roman Catholics, the Protestants and the Anabaptists.

"The Anabaptists and other groups originated in the Protestant Reformation of the 16th century. Martin Luther, a Roman Catholic priest, initiated a series of events beginning on October 31, 1517, which shook, divided, and in some instances revitalized Christianity in Western Europe and which are collectively known as the Reformation."

"At the first organized congregation of Swiss brethren or Mennonites, (that at Zurich in 1525) it is known that the leaders and at least some of the members had formerly been Catholics. The same is true also of Menno Simons and some of his coworkers in Holland. Among the more prominent issues which brought upon them the wrath and persecution of the state churches, both Catholics and Protestants, were *their rejection of infant baptism, their insistence upon a freedom of conscience, their refusal to have any part in carnal warfare, their discipline requiring faith in the Lord Jesus Christ and repentance for sin as requisites for baptism and a holy life as a requisite for continued fellowship, their zeal in not only contending for the tenets of faith which they espoused but also in turning the light of truth upon the shortcomings of their opponents, and their contending for a complete separation of Church and State.*"

The following is copied from the internet site History.com:

October 6, 1683 – First Mennonites arrive in America

"Encouraged by William Penn's offer of 5,000 acres of land in the colony of Pennsylvania and the freedom to practice their religion, the first Mennonites arrive in America aboard the *Concord*. They were among the first Germans to settle in the American colonies.

Seeking religious freedom, Mennonite Francis Daniel Pastorious led a group from Krefeld, Germany, to Pennsylvania in 1683 and founded Germantown, the pioneer German settlement in America and now part of the city of Philadelphia. Numerous other German groups followed, and by the American Revolution there were 100,000 Germans in William Penn's former colony, more than a third of Pennsylvania's total population at the time."

All of Susan's family and all of my family descended from Swiss/German Mennonite roots. That includes both sides of our families; Landis and Alderfer for Susan, Souder and Mittman for me.

In November of 1987, our 25th anniversary, we took a trip to Europe (Germany, Switzerland, Austria and France) to trace our roots and actually visit a second cousin, Mary Jane (Kolb) and her husband, Pierre Goldschmidt and her family. Both of our families came from towns near Zurich, Switzerland. It was interesting to visit actual locations where our forefathers were martyred for their faith, a sobering memory. We visited a very old cathedral where some of them were arrested and hauled away to be burned at the stake or tied and drowned in the river.

As part of our plan on that trip, we used "Mennonite Your Way," an organization that provides for people to stay in private homes while traveling. We stayed with a Mennonite couple. An interesting side note; when we signed their guest book, we noticed other people from "the States." One name was that of my high school English teacher—Ms. Schrack. What a shock to find her name there.

The wife drove us up into the Alps following very narrow and steep roads. We were fortunate not to meet anyone on dangerous turns. Upon arrival to the destination she spread out a linen tablecloth for a picnic with homemade bread, cheese and fruit. The setting was on a wildflower speckled meadow dwarfed by the towering snowcapped Alps. It was heavenly. The woman, I forget her name, was 60 years old but by the speed of her hiking stride, was obviously in great shape. She led us to a spot way back into the Alps where, according to her, was one place where our Anabaptist forefathers and their families worshiped in secret.

The site was an abandoned cave and the opening overlooked a huge valley. We stood there feeling like it was Holy ground as we sang in harmony,

"Faith of Our Fathers" living still, in spite of dungeon, fire and sword; I shall never forget that day as we sang, observing and pondering the setting, old worn stumps, rocks, and hand hewn benches, retaining the memory of what actually happened in that place, centuries ago.

Unless we could have lived through those horribly difficult times, we cannot appreciate the freedom of worship we enjoy. And oh, how we take for granted our freedom. Dear God! But for His grace and longsuffering, we would not have freedom at all . . . like our forefathers.

But . . .

> "Praise be to the God and Father of our Lord Jesus Christ;
> In His great mercy, he has given us new birth into a
> living hope . . . into an inheritance
> that can never perish . . . kept in heaven for you . . ."
> I Peter 1:3-4

My spiritual foundation growing up took root at Rockhill Mennonite Church along a railroad track behind Telford, Pa. It was my home church, my dad's, my grandfather's, great-grandfather's and back generations.

The first deed recorded for Rockhill Church was in 1730 for ¼ acre of ground in Bucks County and for three pounds, given to Jacob Kolb. The first building was built of logs and planks and was used for 65 years before being torn down. It was replaced in 1838 with a stone structure 40' x 52' with a slate roof and housed up to 300 people.

It was the practice of the Mennonite church to "draw lots" for pastors and ministers as is recorded in Acts 1:24-26. None of the ministers in the early days of the church were paid salaries. They were basically farmers and volunteered as ministers while receiving free will offerings to help with their income. From 1733 to the end of the 19th century, about nine ministers were recorded as serving, some as many as 47 years.

Names like Derstine, Souder, Alderfer, Allebach, Fretz, Bechtel, Gehman, Detweiler, Wenger, and Landis were all common Mennonite names of men in church leadership. My great-grandfather, John D. Souder, was a renowned historian in the 1930's and wrote many documents, and created many fraktur paintings, many of which can be found at the Mennonite Heritage Center in Harleysville, Pa. In fact, that's where you can find most any historical facts regarding our church history. I would highly recommend a trip to that facility some day.

My earliest recollection of attending church at Rockhill is around 5 years old. Daddy would drop us off with Mom at the side basement door and he'd go park the car. We hung our coats on racks, men and boys on one side of the basement and ladies and girls on the other.

Daddy would help us, making sure we used the bathroom and then we'd go up the steps to the sanctuary, men up one set of stairs, women the other. Until I was about 12 years old, it was tradition to be segregated, women on the right, men on the left. It was a big deal when the ministers reluctantly agreed to allow integration. First, the brave and more liberal families sat together, then slowly but surely, most followed suit. There were a few older ones that never agreed to it and sat separately.

When you became a teenager, it was expected that you were old enough to sit with your friends in the back of the church. Well, for most. I had to wait a few extra years before Mom and Daddy allowed us to sit back there. But eventually, we did. The older you were as a teen, the further back and finally, the optimum was attained . . . the last bench. Oh, yeah, they were benches, hard no-cushion benches with racks for hymnals. *The Life Songs* and *Mennonite Church Hymnal* were our song books. We never sang choruses in church. They were for kids and Bible school. The neat thing about singing those hymns was, I learned to memorize many of them from repetition. We sang only hymns at every service, many times. I used to complain about some of them, but now, oh, how I love them. The authors were certainly inspired. The harmony was wonderful although, at the time, I didn't appreciate it as I do now.

Today, I can start with the first letter of the alphabet for the first word of a hymn and go all the way to z several times over and sing at least one or more verses. Can you do that with your choruses? It's okay, just asking.

During the seat rearrangement came many other changes at church. There was the issue with new translations of the Bible. Some ministers thought it was "just plain wrong" to read from any version other than the King James version. I remember when my cousin, Harold, came to church with "the Revised Standard Version." How could he do that? He must know Clint (our minister), wouldn't read from it. Harold was a scholar if there ever was one and he was always on the cutting edge of education.

When television was invented, Mennonite and other conservative churches labeled it, "a tool of the devil," one not to be used or owned by church members. Actually, there is some wisdom to that thinking. Stop and think . . . how many hours of our lives are spent watching others do something on TV? It could be an astounding discovery.

CHAPTER 6

John Derstine Souder, "Local Historian" and Folk Artist (1865-1942)

John L. Ruth

Excerpts of the entire document.

John, Jr., fourth of John N. and Mary Derstine Souder's many children, was born on March 4, 1865, five weeks before the end of the Civil War. The farm on which he opened his eyes was "in the hills of Rockhill" near Almont, just west of Sellersville, amidst a declining Mennonite community of Detweilers, Freeds, Kinseys and Landeses.

Mother Mary, from a farm at present-day Church Road and the Route 309 bypass (residence of Russell Detweiler), was of the Derstine mill lineage in the Rockhill congregation. She would have seven more children before she died in 1873, when John, Jr. was eight years old. John, Sr. then married her sister Esther, who bore him another four. The Derstine sisters had come from a family of 15 siblings.

In 1869, when John, Jr. was four years old, the Souders moved their family from Rockhill to Franconia Township to the 1755 Christian Souder homestead across the road from the Indian Creek Reformed Church. This would be the center of the future historian's memory. Only one image from "the hills of Rockhill" stayed in his mind: the sight of a fox running off with a chicken into the nearby woods. To that he would add his family's memories of the wartime tensions they had experienced in the years before his birth. Known to be Christian pacifists by their non-Mennonite neighbors, the Souders had seen their children taunted in the local school, and they had felt "humbled" during the Battle of Gettysburg, which occurred during the wheat harvest of 1863. In those solemn weeks, young John learned, there had been "not much laughing and jesting."

Growing up along the Indian Creek, John thought and spoke in German as he learned hymns on his Rockhill-born mother's lap. He would remember his Franconian father, a man never known to use profane language, quoting from the old German devotional book *The Wandering Soul*. Grandfather Christian Souder, who had been born on the homestead in 1797, was even more German in speech, as he explained to the little boy the meaning of some stones in the Souder meadow. There had been an old road there, he said, leading to the "reffer." As the grandson grew up, he would decode this statement to understand that a road had gone from the Indian Creek to Easton on the Delaware River. And his sense of the mystique of history would grow another notch.

Near the Franconia homestead was a schoolhouse, so jammed with students that by John's second year it was replaced with one on the Cowpath Road. John never forgot the thrilling moment when teacher Enos C. Beans brought a violin to lead the singing. With other pupils, he brought his own copy book; at the top of the page the teacher placed an example of writing for the student to imitate. As to reading books, there were all kinds—"Some had the Sanders, some the Monroe and some dating way back to their grandfather's days."

Chaotic as it was, John loved school, and would recall these years as the happiest of his life. He wrote several unassigned but very interesting "dialogues," in which he cast himself and schoolmate Horace Bergey as Franconia farmers discussing issues of the day. At the end of one term he wrote, "I must say that I am sorry . . . For I am just in a good condition for learning, and I just wish there would be longer school." Watching the other pupils take their books home and put them away, John called this "wrong." He himself looked in one or another of his schoolbooks every day during the long summer.

A person could never get too much education, he thought, and predicted that youthful neglect of study would bring regret in adulthood.

Church, for the Souders, was all in German, whether at the "little meetinghouse in the woods" beside the North Penn Railroad tracks at Rockhill, or at Franconia, where "a large crowd" assembled for his mother Mary Souder's funeral when John was eight years old. "Not a word of English" was heard. In fact, when a preacher from Vincent across the Schuylkill, or from the Midwest, did hold forth in English, John's father called them "no right Mennonites anymore."

Even before marriage, John had taken an interest in raising various kinds of poultry. While this was his first business, a few years later his mother-in-in-law collapsed and died on a sidewalk in Telford. In 1893 the young couple moved into town and went into the store business themselves. Here they did well enough, especially when John was named postmaster, and served thus for about five years. He was also a rural postman for a longer time.

When a trolley line passed through Telford in 1899, John's poultry business gained a new advantage. "Mr. Souder," announced a local paper, "is the pioneer poultry breeder of Eastern Pennsylvania, but now has many imitators. His business extends to every state in the Union and to many foreign countries. He . . . also . . . takes an active part in the Farmers' Institutes of the county."

The Poultry tribune

John had a catalog printed, complete with his own portrait and photos of various local scenes. It described both product and philosophy:

"We have six daily mails, some of them run on the fastest schedule known to mail service, so that we are brought in direct communication with our customers over the whole Union. All letters are answered the same day received."

"We have often shipped eggs for hatching within an hour's notice."

"We have sent eggs to the Pacific slope and hatched every egg out of 15."

"Visitors are always welcome except on Sunday; this is our day of rest. Our yards are located only a few squares from the depot."

As John D. Souder approached his 70th birthday, the thought that he had been collecting local history for 50 years brought him much pleasure. The work in his bulging "Bee Hive" had been brought to harvest by "a school boy," John C. Wenger. Now that young helper was preparing to study in Europe. That too was a fascinating thought, since 30 years earlier John had been told by Governor Samuel W. Pennypacker that much Pennsylvania history was "still stored in the archives of Germany, Holland and England and should some time be brought in by competent scholars."

John was sad to observe that, to put it mildly, "not all are interested in history." Of his three surviving sons (five had died young), Raymond was incompetent; Preston was occupied with the family farm which he had taken over (without mother Sallie being informed of the finances involved); and the youngest son Mahlon was certainly bright enough, John thought, "to take my place in history, and do a better job, but he says, 'Pop, your history is like antique to me. I like new things.'"

Souder's 75th birthday brought more newspaper accolades, the news that his fraktur output had now reached 400.

PHOTO FROM THE METROPOLITAN MUSEUM NEW YORK 1940.

My work is symbolical as found in the Pennsylvania
German Manuscripts; emblems, precepts, allegorious and sim-
-litudes:: ""I have spoken to you after the similitudes
of God. James 3-5.""
            Consider the Lilies how they grow. (Christ).
            I am the Rose of Sharon. Christ).
            The Heart and Dove. the Holy Spirit).
            I am the bright and morning star. (Christ).

This is the product of the early School Master, a holy
manifestation is found in the same. They confer Im-
-mortality on saints of old and have been a blessing
to millions of people, their fine Christian virtues
engraved on the hearts of man hard to forget. He
lives, yea he lives for ever more. They are Bible
symbols, and can be traced back to certain Christian
sects of early Pennsylvania. I have collected and
reproduced over 400 specimens of Frakture, and it is
believed am the only one in the land that has under-
-taken to revive this kind of writings.
            John D. Souder
            Telford pa. ,

My great-grandfather at his desk at his farmhouse on Church Road, Telford, PA.

At Christmas of 1941 the note of parting and death, already evident, became stronger. "Then cometh the end, a statement by the Apostle Paul regarding the Last Things" (I Cor. 15:24) was a phrase that John liked. But he yoked to it a statement of Jesus: "Nevertheless I must walk today and tomorrow and the day following" (Luke 13:13). The end was coming, but until then, there was work to do.

A truly amazing burst of creativity flared on the old man's 77th birthday, March 4, 1942. At least seven sizable frakturs, dated on that day, are known to survive. Most of them include words such as, "Here Lord, Take this as something I have done for Thee, It's the best I can do on my 77th birthday." This was followed by several wonderful pieces, all on a kind of yellow paper. Then, on June 1, on a fraktur dominated by words rather than ornamental motifs, comes the touching—and revealing—"Evening Prayer":

O Thou Great Spirit
  As I close my eyes in slumber
   this night
  Do you think I have done
   Enough to-day
   To earn the right
   To live to-morrow
    Made by John D. Souder
    June 1st AD. 1942

In this, as in all previous pieces, there is no sign of a trembling hand.

In mid-August 1942 John D. Souder became bedfast, and on September 14 he died.

To read the entire document written by John Ruth, historian, find it in the archives of The Mennonite Heritage Center, Harleysville, Pa.

CHAPTER 7

My Dad

"How long you gonna sleep, it's 7:00 . . . time to get up." His words were easily audible coming from the bottom of the long stairs. "I finished seeding clover in the back field already, come on, we got work to do."

Later I discovered he'd been up at daybreak—5:00, to get the field seeded before chores. His heavy footsteps echoed down the cellar steps and the clanking of iron and chattering pipes got me up with a start. "I'm coming," I muttered as I pulled on my wranglers and yesterday's socks. It was my job to fix the fires and take out the ashes.

The old coal stove which looked like a metal octopus with heat pipes coming out at all angles on top, needed to be filled with coal from the bin and then the ashes needed shaking down. By the time I got there Daddy was on his way to the garden carrying a bucket of ashes. Sitting down on the bench next to our shoes and boots, I found mine, grabbed a hat and coat hanging behind the bench and hurried outside.

"Here," I said, "I'll do that."

"Okay," Daddy said, "but be sure to save the unburned coals. Don't throw them out." (It was our practice to pour the ashes into a big sieve with a handle on it and shake it until there were just the unburned coals left.) With that he was off to the barn to feed the chickens . . . 500 layers. Daddy would be expecting me and my brother David to be right behind him to help with the chores.

After an hour of feeding and watering the chickens, several hundred turkeys, 30 to 40 pigs and several hundred ducks and geese it was 8:00 and time to wash up for breakfast. School started at 9:00.

Daddy was tall and muscular. His large hands and dark tanned arms revealed scars here and there from years of hard work. A hat of choice for the occasion at hand generally covered what little hair was left on his head, though only in his 30s. Sometimes it was an old sweat-stained straw hat, sometimes a tattered baseball type or a dressy full rimmed hat. There would be dark smiling eyes behind dark rimmed glasses with a clean shaven face but never a beard or a mustache for Daddy. His quick step and sharp mind left no grass growing under him.

Always going somewhere, working, selling or buying, reading or studying his Sunday school lesson, he was an active man but never bored. You knew where he stood with his convictions and belief. Just get him started.

When he was 19 years old, the doctors told him he probably would never work again. Rheumatic fever had put him in bed for weeks. His heart was damaged beyond repair, but with an attitude and determination to match his stature and God's grace, he survived and walked out of the hospital. After months of rest and his fiancé helping on the farm, he was soon back on his feet and working. They married soon after his ordeal with the fever and they bought a small house on Hamilton Avenue in Telford, Pa.

A few years later, their first child was born, a darling little girl. Well, not all that darling according to Mom. She said there were many nights when she felt like throwing the little tot out the window because she was screaming so badly. Seems Joan had something called "colic" which gave her terrible stomachaches.

Mom worked in the clothing factory down the street while Grammy Souder babysat. Daddy worked the farm and started a market route in his early 20s in the suburbs of Philly selling produce from the farm, poultry, eggs, butter, meat and frozen foods including ice cream. It was his "bread and butter" during the years just after the Depression.

David and I were born within the next five years completing the family. They had wanted more children but the doctor made it clear—Mom would need a hysterectomy. She was only 26. The news was not what they expected. They had hopes of having four children. But God had other plans. The next five years would be financially and emotionally challenging due to the Depression. Gas was rationed, money was tight but God was faithful. Mom told about digging to the bottom of her worn-out purse to find a little change to buy bread from the baker.

As David and I grew older, our muscles became stronger from lifting 100-lb. bags of feed and carrying 5-gallon pails of water doing chores. Daddy expected the eggs to be gathered from the three pens upstairs in the barn, one downstairs and five pens in the long chicken house facing the large pond. Twice daily this had to be done. Two to five baskets a day containing 100 eggs each had to be washed in the washer one basket at a time and then hung up to dry in the walk-in cooler. Every Wednesday morning Daddy and Mom would be found grading and candling eggs downstairs in the barn getting them ready for market.

The egg grader was a machine about 3' x 2' and had 4 separate trays. Eggs were set on an incline with light shining up through a hole so you could see any blood spots and manually remove those eggs. The eggs rolled onto the electric conveyor and traveled over a weight mechanism tipping the egg onto the correct tray according to size. As I walked into the barn I could hear Daddy sharing his problems or joys with Mom.

"I just wish we could get that fence finished at the cemetery," Daddy said. "Seems like someone on the committee always has an excuse when we have a work bee . . . winter's coming and we're only half done."

"Now don't be so hard on them," Mom said. "Everyone has plenty to do besides getting that fence up." She always had a way of calming Daddy's nerves when he got in a stew.

"I guess," he said. *"Auch du leva, nuch-a-mul,"* he said, reaching for a rag to wipe up the spattered yoke on the floor. Daddy and Mom were from German-speaking families and would use the Pennsylvania Dutch language at random. Translated, it meant, *"Oh my goodness, another one."*

"Du bisht venich shuslich," Mom said with a chuckle. Meaning "You're getting a bit careless." They both laughed and kept working.

Thursday and Friday were market days. Daddy had a large truck with a small freezer on board and shelves packed with produce from the farm or a local wholesale store. Eggs were packed in 30 dozen crates and boxed into one dozen cartons when sold to his door-to-door clients. "Gotta go Margaret," he said. And with a kiss he squeezed her saying, "See you around 8:00 tonight honey, if all goes well." Out the drive he went beeping the horn on the old green and white Dodge van.

The years flew by and before you know it, I was 14 and David, 12. Summers were crammed full of work. Planting and harvest were added to Daddy's already full schedule. But we were no strangers to hard farm work. In fact we thrived on it. If we had a choice, we would rather have skipped school all together and just help run the farm.

"When do I get to plow with the 3010? You got to plow when you were 12," David said in a depressing tone.

"Guess you'll have to ask Daddy when he gets home. I'm supposed to do the back field before it gets dark," I said. "You mi'-as-well get the eggs till I get home," I shouted above the rumble of the John Deere diesel. And off he went to the barn for a couple of empty baskets muttering to himself. But soon after, I do remember him sitting on the tractor's fender while I plowed and he learned to plow very straight furrows himself.

It wasn't long till the wheat was ready to harvest. One day Daddy whispered to me and David, "Come out in the garage, I want to show you something." Now we knew there must be something special to see if Daddy said that.

Daddy, Jay Shisler, David, myself and a neighbor boy eating watermelon.

With our excitement building we walked toward the large cement block garage which housed most of the farm machinery. Daddy was a thrifty man and knew how to save money. He only spent money on things which helped him make money—like good machinery. It seemed like he had a built-in calculator under those hats he wore. He could add, subtract, multiply or divide many figures without paper and pencil. "You gotta do better than that," he'd say to a dealer trying to sell him new machinery or something. "I'll give you this much and no more, take it or leave it." Then there'd be a long dialogue with the salesman and they'd get sidetracked discussing farming, religion or politics quite a while before making the deal. Daddy would usually get a bargain before it was all over.

Lifting the heavy 12-foot overhead wooden door with his strong arms, he grinned at us as we stood dumbstruck. There before our bulging brown eyes was a huge brand new self-propelled combine, the first one like it in the area. The big garage door had to be propped with a long board for the combine to clear the opening. "When did you get this? Is it ours? I can't believe it," we both said at once jumping up the steps to the platform and sitting in the seat. Daddy chuckled, smiling real big and proud as a peacock. "You'll get your chance to try it out next week," he said. "Come on down, I hear Mom calling for supper," he added. He closed the big door and said as a challenge, "Let's go, I'll beat you into the house for supper." And off he ran up the long pavement and two sets of concrete steps, with me and David close behind.

CHAPTER 8

Farm Life in Telford

(A Short Summary)

During my teen years at home, the farm grew and changed rapidly. As Daddy's income from the farm and market route increased, so did his machinery. The John Deere Model Bs and As gave way to two brand new 520s. They actually had power steering and 3-point hitches and could handle a 3-bottom plow. Wow!

The 520s were much more stylish but the putt-putt sound from the two-cylinder gas engines was still the same. That was 1958. In 1960, John Deere came out with a whole new "generation" of tractors. Four cylinders replaced the smaller two cylinders and the putt-putt tractors were doomed for antiquity. Diesel engines were now dominant and more powerful.

I. G. Rosenberger had an annual open house. The large garage was converted into a theater where the latest new machinery was shown on film. Daddy, David and I always looked forward to those events. It was there that seeds of desire for bigger and better machinery took root.

"Daddy, we should get one of those new 3010 tractors," I said. "They can pull 4-bottom plows and much bigger equipment. We could farm more ground and grow more corn. What do you think?"

His big smile and chuckle said it all. I think we were on the same page.

"Guess I'll have to talk with Roland and see what he can come up with," he said. But Roland couldn't come close enough in price to suit Daddy. So one day while working in the machinery shed, a truck pulled in the drive with large lettering on the door—"Robert E. Little – John Deere."

David and I looked at each other and grinned.

"Maybe we'll be able to make a deal with this guy," one of us whispered.

Daddy and Bob stood at the work bench trading farming stories for some time before getting down to business.

"Well, John, how 'bout giving me a chance to deal with you? I know you've been a longstanding customer with I.G. but I think I can do better. How 'bout trading those 520s for two 3010s? With these new generation tractors, you'll go from the putt-putting 32 hp to the four cylinder purr of 72 horse power diesel. You won't believe the huge difference that will make for your farm. I'll even bring one down for you to try out. What-da-ya think?" Bob said with a grin.

Now even though Daddy was anxious to try one out, he didn't let on.

"I'll tell you what. Give me your best price, you've got to do much better than I.G.'s price and we'll talk about it," Daddy said.

About an hour later, Bob had the okay to bring a 3010 to try out. Yip-piti-yi-ya! David and I were ecstatic. But we would have to wait till the weather got warmer.

Spring came early in 1960 and so did Bob. As soon as the ground was ready to plow, a large truck pulled into the barnyard. Robert E. Little – John Deere farm machinery dealer was painted on the side of the truck. On it, stacked facing each other were not one, but two 3010 diesel John Deere tractors, and one had a 4-bottom plow attached.

It was a Saturday morning. David and I came flying out the pavement to get a closer look. Daddy was right behind with a big grin. Apparently, Bob and Daddy had agreed on a price and made a deal. We had just made a serious upgrade in tractors. I remember the elation of sitting behind the wheel as we plowed, diesel smoke trailing up and over us as the tractors purred along the fresh furrows. Bob made the proper plow adjustments and without a doubt, we were all hooked. A neighbor came across the road to watch and comment. He'd never seen such big farming equipment in the neighborhood. In no time at all, the 15-acre field next to our house was plowed.

Then came a new and larger disk and cultipacker, 4-row corn planter and later on, a large model 55 John Deere self-propelled combine. Dad picked up many new customers for custom combining. We went as far as Line Lexington, 8 or so miles away for business. Between the ages of 15 and 20, I ran that combine over hundreds of acres before Dad traded it for a larger and better 4400 model. David ran that one until the time of his death in 1974. By that time, the farm had a fully-automated grain drying setup with several large storage bins. The farm was very productive in small grains as well as a large hog finishing yard big enough for several hundred hogs. All that besides the poultry aspect which produced thousands of starter pullets semi annually. The meadow next to the pond and the orchard across the road were each neatly arranged with a dozen or more chicken shelters for free range.

This setup was about perfect for two full-time people plus a couple hired hands. And so it was until God called one . . . and then the other . . . home;

David in 1974 and Daddy only three years later, leaving Mom and Joan . . . and me, 150 miles north, to cope with the farm. I spent the Summer and Fall of 1977 and 1978 running back and forth weekly to run the farm, planting, harvesting, selling and maintaining the machinery. Mom and Joan did the paperwork. Mom gathered, cleaned, graded and sold the eggs, hundreds of them weekly. By the end of 1977 we knew we had to sell the machinery. I could not run two farms 150 miles apart and Mom and Joan couldn't either. So after many months of preparation, we held a huge farm auction and sold it all. It was a sad, and historic day, dispersing of a century or more of stuff. We all parted with many antiques and things we'd have loved to keep but for what? So we sold it.

The farm was now void of its tools to be run as a real farm. Buildings stood starkly bare and empty, unused but still needing maintained, which I did with the help of neighbor Harry.

Mom went through her own depression and ended up at Phil Haven Hospital for a few months. All this happened around 1995. I was in Virginia building Renee and Rod's house. We were having Mom's farmhouse renovated extensively by adding a new kitchen. It eventually got the best of Mom. When she finally recovered, she lived in the new addition for the remainder of her life. During that time, the entire farm was developed by a local builder. Large beautiful houses now fill the fields where I once drove tractors and combines. It's a shame to see such productive flat farmland destroyed and replaced by developments. But that's called "progress." Though it's partially my doing by agreeing to it, I have to question that theory.

CHAPTER 9

Creative Fun Growing Up

I don't know where they came from but our first roller skates got lots of hard use. There was no concrete or blacktop on our farm at that time to skate on. Daddy concreted the basement floor when we were still in grade school. That's when the roller skates showed up. We would strap the skates onto our shoes. There was a special key to tighten the skates so they would stay on. "Don't lose that key!" Daddy said. Round and round the basement we went, playing tag. "You're it," someone said and off we went. Sometimes too fast around the corner and "splat" we'd go sliding on the concrete, into the stone wall usually through a water puddle from the last rain that leaked in. Boy did we have fun skating.

PING-PONG

The homemade ping-pong table set on wobbly saw horses at the bottom of the cellar steps. Whitewashed beams above us barely cleared our heads. Daddy always had to "duck" when walking in the cellar. After some practice pong, I'd say, "Let's volley." Whoever won the volley served first. David and I played a lot. But I loved the game more than he. At least one night a week I'd ride my bike to a neighbor's house to play. He was about 23 years old, more advanced than me and taught me how to slam, put spins on the ball and return them. Eventually, at age 14 or 15, I could beat him 2 out of 3 games.

The competition proved so discouraging for David that the overhead beams and the poor ping-pong table received many dents from his paddle. But he kept trying and beat'n the table. That table, with its scars, still gets used at Rudy's Place supported by the same old wobbly saw horses.

BUMSOCK

That's what we called it—a burlap feed bag tied into a big knot. We used it to throw at someone playing tag up in the haymow. Neighbors and cousins would show up to play. Running along the beams 12 feet and higher off the floor, jumping into the bales of hay to avoid a "hit" was big time fun. "I got you," Cousin Jay would shout and disappear into a hay tunnel. Against Daddy's better judgment, he let us build tunnels in the haymows with small square bales. We would rearrange the bales using boards creating tunnels into the large dens way down under the bales. We'd have to crawl on our bellies through the long, dark tunnels hoping to find someone to hit with the bumsock and then disappear. What fun for us . . . until Daddy discovered all the open bales. He was not happy. Then we would have to try to retie them. But it was well worth it.

KICK THE TIN CAN

Yes, it was a game we made up. At least we thought we did. Here's how to play: Set up a large empty tin can where all could see it. The "it" person would stand with one foot on the can as he counted to 20. "Ready or not, here I come," he or she would shout. All the players would be hiding, hoping to outsmart the "it" person while he was searching for someone, by running and kicking the can and then go back to hiding. If the "it" person saw someone first he would run back and kick the can shouting their name as he ran off to hide. Then it was that person's turn to count and hunt. "Sorry, chore time, gotta go." Then the neighbors would leave.

HALF BALL

What a crazy idea but it was fun. We would find an old worn-out water hose (hopefully worn out) and cut it into pieces about 6" long. Then find an old broomstick for a bat and set up bases like for baseball. Divide into teams and play ball. Or you could just play that each person gets three outs and he goes to the outfield as the others all move up. See who could hit that piece of hose the furthest or get the most runs. Good fun for an hour or so.

PLAYING FARM

Soon after we could crawl, David and I began to imitate Daddy by playing "farm." The closed in sun-porch was our barnyard. With our new toy farm machinery we got for Christmas presents and a large box of wooden blocks we were all set. For our barn, we'd line up the toy tractors, combine, baler, wagons, plows, disks, you name it, along one wall. There were plenty of homemade throw rugs scattered throughout the downstairs rooms on both sides of the house. All we needed was a wooden ramp to get up into either room. The rugs were given names like: the back field, behind Lawells, the back meadow, Ratsells, the orchard, 4th street or Vandykes. Cornfields would be dotted with corn kernels. Grain fields with oats or wheat. Hay fields were our favorite. We would load up the little wooden blocks on the toy wagons and pull them up the ramps with our toy John Deere tractors making that putt-putt-putt sound as we went.

One of us would go ahead with a tractor and baler as the other set the blocks down behind the baler in circles around the field (rug) to be picked up later. Then back out to the field to gather up the bales and bring them back to the barn. Daddy bought a sheet of thin plywood one day having decided we needed a *real* barn. We helped him build this nice big barn with half the roof opening on hinges to store our equipment and our blocks we called hay bales. It was actually big enough to hide inside when we played hide and seek. Many hours and days were spent crawling around the floor "playing farm." We constantly devised new ideas as we played. You can imagine. Yes, *these* were good old days.

PLAYING CHURCH

Going to church was a big part of our lives growing up. It wasn't just Sunday mornings, but Sunday night young people's meetings or hymn sings, Tuesday night winter Bible study, and Wednesday night prayer meeting. Several times a year there were weekly revival services with special speakers. So it should be no surprise that on Sunday afternoon when we had company for dinner (lunch), that we kids would gather on the steps in the hallway to "play church." If you weren't part of the "congregation" sitting on the stairs as pews, you probably had a leadership role. That would mean you were a song leader with a hymn book in one hand and waving the other hand to direct the congregation. We would sing old hymns or Bible school choruses.

You may be an usher passing a soup bowl around to collect the make-believe offering. Maybe you volunteered to make the announcements or do the prayer. If you volunteered to preach, then you would need a Bible in one hand as you told the people that Jesus died for them and loved them and they needed to repent of their sins and come kneel at the bench that you were standing on to be saved. The preacher needed to shake the Bible, talk loud and keep telling them to repent until someone came down the stairs.

Then you would put your hand on them and help them get saved. Of course the girls needed handkerchiefs or tissues to pretend to wipe their tears as they cried.

I know this sounds a bit sacrilegious, but we were dead serious and didn't mean to make fun of church. It was our way of having fun and "doing church." Seems like the traveling evangelists who came to do week-long revivals had quite an impression on us, seeing how we played church. At least it had a good impact.

PASTOR WILLIAM JENNINGS

Speaking of evangelists, let me tell you about Preacher William Jennings. Pastor Jennings was from Tennessee. Seemed like he came to our church every other year for revival services. For me growing up, revival services meant that a preacher from faraway would come and preach loud and long every night for a whole week. Their goal was to see people change their ways, accept Jesus and get saved or hope they would commit to live better lives. Usually, those services were boring for little boys and girls so we would be sure to take paper and pencils along to draw while the preacher did his thing.

But Pastor Jennings was different. He seemed old to us back then. He was probably only 70 years old, maybe younger. Oh, you think that's old too? Nevertheless, Pastor Jennings would do it all; lead singing, pray, tell stories and preach. Our favorite part was the little meeting he did specially for children. He would call all the children out of the congregation to come down to the front of the church. We'd come and sit in the front benches. Some were too shy so their Mommies would bring them and sit there too. Pastor Jennings would come down off the big high pulpit and stand real close to us telling us Bible stories mixed in with other stories. He made it feel like we were the only ones in the room listening. We had no trouble listening and understanding him. Pastor Jennings seemed to know how children thought and how to make Jesus real to us.

One Sunday after church Mom and Daddy invited Pastor Jennings to our house for dinner. He and his wife, about half his size, came to dinner. It felt like having Jesus' brother at our house, because he was such a wonderful man, so kind and caring. Little people like us kids felt special around him. He paid attention to us. Most other older people kinda ignored us or didn't talk with us like he did.

According to tradition, after the meal, we had dessert and then "returned thanks." That meant we would pray again at the end of the meal. Then us kids could go play. But before we went out to play, Pastor Jennings asked us if we would like him to show us how to make a whistle. Of course we wanted to know how. "Get me a fresh clean empty tin can," he said. "And I'll show you how."

My first bike.

The Telford Farm in its prime, circa 1970.

Mom gave us an empty can she had just thrown away and off we went out to the milk house—Daddy, David, me and Pastor Jennings. "Now, do you have a tin shears?" he said. Daddy got him one and he began carefully cutting a wide strip around the can. "How 'bout a pliers?" he asked. Daddy gave him an old pliers. "Now, boys, watch carefully and you'll see how to make one," he said as he began to bend it into shape. Before we knew what happened, he was whistling loud enough to make ol' porky begin to yap and whine.

"Wow, that is so neat, can we try it?" we both said at the same time. I wish we had paid better attention because we never could quite make our creation work like his did.

You see how great an impression Pastor Jennings made on us. Just like Jesus made an impression on the little children He called to come and sit with Him when He was here on earth. Giving special attention and recognition to people makes them want to listen and believe what you have to say. God's word, the Bible, is believable because He cares so deeply for us and shows it in many ways everyday. But too often, we don't pay attention and then we get it wrong and we wonder why.

I will never forget humble Pastor Jennings, his smile, his stories, his creativity, and his love for children. But I did forget how to make a whistle out of tin cans.

CHAPTER 10

Trap Lines of the '50s

"Well son, how many do you have this week?" asked the man dressed in a dark fur coat and smelling like a skunk.

"Seven brown ones and one pure black one," I said as we stretched them out on the truck tailgate for him to see. David helped me get them lined up. He methodically checked each one out and said, "They look good, no holes and nice size. This week I can pay $2.50 a piece for the brown ones and $4.00 for the black one."

David grinned at me and I grinned back trying not to act too excited. I said, "Sounds good to me."

The fur trader's helper picked them up and threw them on top of the pile into the back of his pickup covered with a homemade wooden cap. Meanwhile he pulled out a large billfold and paid us in cash. "That'll be $17.50 plus $4.00 for the black one. Here's $21.50" he said as he handed us the cash.

Together we jumped back in the pickup and Daddy drove us back home. Trapping season opened the Saturday after Thanksgiving. Since we were only 10 and 12 years old, we didn't need a license to trap. The year would have been 1955 or '56. Muskrats dug holes and made trails all around our farm pond as well as along the streams leading into and out of the pond. What's a muskrat? It's a rodent that looks like a very large rat or a small beaver and lives in and along stream backs and ponds. I can still see their trails leading from the "crick" to the cornfield and nearby meadows where they fed at nighttime. They were easiest to find when it was frosty or snow covered. Then their fresh trails stood out like pepper on mashed potatoes.

We would attach wooden stakes and a name tag to a small chain on our traps the week prior to "mushie" season. That's what we called them, mushies. Daddy had lots of traps and we bought some new ones at the hardware store. Daddy showed us how and where to set the traps to be successful. He went along with us the very first time to set and to check them the first morning. After that, it was all up to us. Knowing how to make a good set was an art and a challenge to learn. It was important to wear gloves and rubber boots to keep them from smelling human scent. To open and spread the jaws of a #1½ Victor trap, you needed strong, steady hands so when you set the little trigger which held the pan, it didn't accidentally snap closed on your fingers. At our young age, we used our feet to hold the trap while setting the trigger. I don't ever remember getting caught myself, thank goodness.

"What about this hole?" David said pointing to an old tree stump along the crick.

"Yeah, that looks pretty fresh, like it was used last night," I said as I pounded a stake in the ground next to the hole. Carefully setting and positioning the trap in the hole underwater, we made a mental note of where it was. All around the pond, up and down the crick we went with traps slung over our shoulders and carrying a hammer looking for good signs to set our traps. "Wow, look at this fresh trail. It goes all the way to the cornfield." I said.

"And look at the mud on the trail and the muddy hole it leads to," David said all excited about our possibilities for a good catch.

"Here," I said, "is the last trap we have for now."

"There's more in the milk house if we need them," David said.

Just then I noticed someone at the edge of the field next to the ice dam carrying a hammer and traps. We hunched down low along the crick bank so he wouldn't see us as he walked on around the dam setting his traps.

"He better stay off our land," I whispered to David. "We'll have to get out here early in the morning in case he wanders down here and sees our traps."

"He could steal our mushies if he gets here first," David said, feeling a bit uneasy. "Maybe we should tell Uncle Charlie?"

"Well, let's get on home," I said. "But first let's backtrack and be sure we know where all the traps are set."

With that we followed our trapline back to the pond. Forty-three traps is the number we agreed on. It was getting dark by now and time to get back for supper. Monday after school, we would take a dozen or so traps and ride our bikes up to Fourth Street. There was a small, muddy mushie steam behind Mr. Forest's, Rider's, and Mr. Alderfer's house. They gave us permission to trap. All told, we would have 56 traps set.

"Early to bed, early to rise, makes a man healthy, wealthy and wise." At least that's what Ben Franklin says. Our version went like this, "Early to bed and get up early is wise, but get to the trapline before sunrise." Actually, if you didn't get to the traps before the sun was up, you may lose a mushie or two.

If they were caught in the trap for too many hours, they would chew their own foot off to free themselves and save their life. They are not dumb animals. So no matter how cold it was, David and I would get up and dress real warm before heading down to the pond with our flashlights and weapons. Yes, weapons, you can't sell live muskrats.

No offense, please, animal rights people. I love animals too. God made everything for a purpose and back in my day the purpose for some animals was to provide coats to keep humans warm.

Some mornings we would come home with nothing. Other mornings we may have four or five. "We got one up here," David or I would whisper as loudly as possible but quietly enough so as not to warn a trapped muskrat. After it lay still, I would open the trap, take our prize and reset the trap. "None here . . . or here. But, hey, this one's snapped," I said excitedly. That would at least tell us that the trail or hole was active.

When we got to be 12 and 14 years old, Daddy let me drive the 1954 Ford pickup back to Fourth Street in the early morning darkness. It made us feel pretty proud and all grown up to be able to drive on the road, albeit only ½ a mile.

Occasionally, while checking the trapline, we'd smell a skunk. Sure enough there it was, in one of our traps. We'd take care of it with Daddy's Winchester 22 rifle and quickly run for the truck or home. A day or two later, we'd be able to get it out of the trap without stinking so badly. If it was mostly black with a little white, it was worth some money. If it was mostly white, it wasn't worth much.

There were other animals we wanted to catch. If we happened to catch a mink, you'd think we'd won the lottery. The fur trader would pay us $25.00 for a mink. But I can't remember catching any. Mink coats were very expensive. Once in a while, a weasel would get caught. They were vicious little suckers if they were still alive. They were worth as much as black mushies. Opossums were rarely worth saving for some reason. I remember catching a raccoon one time. He was as mean as a wild boar backed into a corner. He spat and hissed and pawed at us until the ol' 22 barked just once. He was history and worth about $4.00. Not really worth the trouble but once they're caught there's not much else to do with them.

We were quite proud of our catch and the sight of mushies hanging from the overhang in front of the barn. There they were safe from predators like dogs, cats, and hawks. Generally it was cold enough to keep them there for a week.

One morning toward the end of our trapping days, we were rudely surprised to find a bunch of our traps missing. We had them tagged so no one could claim them but they were gone. We never really found out who stole them but we had a good idea. That guy who was setting traps around the ice dam was a suspect but we never could prove it. Guess there are risks to everything.

Our best year ever as I recall was close to 70 muskrats besides a few other furs. David and I got to split the money. It was nice to have extra spending money and some to save.

The last couple of years we trapped, I was allowed to drive the pickup a mile and a half to Gettys' gas station on the Telford Pike and Rt. 113 where the fur trader made his weekly stop to buy furs. It was always fun to see what other trappers caught and what the trader had in his truck. At school, there were a few other boys who trapped as well. We would tell our stories and compare our luck and see who ended up with the most.

I saved a few traps and they hang in my wood shop today. Actually, a few years ago, there was a family of muskrats in our pond in Sullivan County. I eventually caught all of them before they drained the pond. They were tunneling from the pond to the swamp and would have drained the pond. Oh, yes, the wonderful memories of trapping when I was a boy. Thank you God for experiences like this. Maybe there's a reason why I liked Jack London's paperbacks like *Call of the Wild*.

CHAPTER 11

Following the Path of Jesus

The old hymn takes me back to a hard wooden bench in a church by the railroad tracks near Telford, Pa.—Rockhill Mennonite Church, my childhood church. The four-part harmony filling the church, men sitting on the left of the aisle, women on the right, was almost heavenly. It never entered my adolescent mind that we were missing a piano and other instruments until later in life. That's the way it was in plain Mennonite traditions.

Number (whatever it was) . . . the chorister called out twice before blowing on a little round toy he took out of his pocket. A pitch pipe, they called it. "Ummmummmum . . ." hummed the chorister going up the musical scale as he raised a hand in the air. Then he began to sing and wave his hand in some kind of pattern that was supposed to help people keep in rhythm. "Follow the path of Jesus, walk where his footsteps lead" . . . Daddy's deep mellow voice on the melody, Mom singing alto across the aisle . . . "keep in his beaming presence . . . every counsel heed . . . watch while the hours are flying" . . . Who was that? Some guy singing louder than the rest . . . "ready some good to do" . . . *He's sure not bashful, holding on to the last words longer than anyone else,* I thought . . . "Quick while his voice is calling" . . . "yield oohh-bee-ddi-annnce . . . ttrrrruuuu-a" he sang dragging it out longer and still louder.

David looked at me and grinned slightly as I leaned into Daddy and whispered, "Why does he do that?" Daddy kept a straight face as he leaned toward me and said softly, "Tell ya later." Years later, when church rules changed and ladies and men could sit together (a big deal), I learned who that was . . . Brother J. I admired him and felt sorry for him at the same time. Guess that's from my mom's genes. She was so tenderhearted and taught us never to look down on others. I didn't laugh or make fun of Brother J. but wondered what made him do that? Our church was by no means related to the Pentecostals and we had no clue what a Charismatic was. But I knew Brother J. was sincere. Maybe he had some kind of epilepsy. Other hymns like "Wonderful Grace of Jesus" and "It Is Well with My Soul," seemed to put him in rare form. Sometimes he would hold those last notes so long and loud that his voice would tremble. His petite Mennonite wife sat quietly beside him without flinching when he did that.

One Sunday, having grown older, I pondered (like I often daydreamed in school to avoid studying) the words to that hymn. The long freight train had gone by blowing its loud whistle and all the little pre-school kids got to stand on the bench to watch while the preacher waited . . . (an interruption momentarily enjoyed by most kids . . . and teens). Time to end the service. The chorister stood and announced a favorite hymn of Brother J. "Follow the path of Jesus" . . . "walk where his footsteps lead." *Where are they leading?* I wondered . . . "every counsel heed." Everyone? How is that possible? . . . "watch while the hours are flying . . . ready some good to do." Hours flying? Seems to me they creep by here at church.

I'm watching and listening to Brother J. sing in the bench in front of me. He sure sings like he means every word! "Hummmm. But I think I'm always ready some good to do." Now, Brother J. has his eyes closed.

His head is lifted slightly, singing with passion, his voice and the hymn book shaking as he holds on to those last words . . . "quick while his voice is calling, yield obedience true."

It was very likely this hymn and others like it (and maybe watching Brother J. sing) that spoke conviction to my tender heart persuading me to accept Jesus as my personal Savior and to join the church. I was only 10 years old but I felt an urging to do it. Sometime that year in 1953, I was sprinkled in baptism by Bishop Arthur Ruth, a relative of my grammy, along with some of my buddies. Though I strayed from my early commitment to God and the church, it was the guiding words of those old hymns and childhood choruses that spoke deeply into my heart. Fifteen years old and sitting on the rear bench of that church with my buddies, God spoke powerfully to me through another old hymn, "I'll go where you want me to go dear Lord . . . over mountains, rough plains or sea . . . " With tears falling on my lap, I vowed to God to do just that when the time was right. It was one of those turning points in life when God gets our attention and shows us which path to follow. I pray that my children and their children's children and anyone who reads these words, guard their hearts and keep them soft for the seeds of God's word to take root in. A fertile seed bed and a good foundation is critically important early in life to make you strong and spiritually healthy as you follow the path of Jesus.

CHAPTER 12

Huts and Rafts
at the Duck Pond

"Hey Jack!" I yelled across the pond. "Ya got any extra drums?"

"Nope . . . used the last one from our barn, sorry," he hollered back and went on pounding nails.

Jack was the eldest boy in the family. Jamie was a couple years younger and, as many younger brothers, walked in his shadow. Not that it's wrong or bad to do so, that's the way it happens. Just as my brother, David, often followed my lead in his younger years. As neighbors, we had that in common.

His father bought the farm across from our pond on the hill along the cowpath road. That was around 1950 after the Richardsons decided to get out of the dog business. That's right, dog business. Well, here's the scoop; the Richardsons raised Great Danes. They built a very large kennel along one of the cornfields we farmed. It was built with 6' high link fencing creating 5 or 6 pens to contain the Great Danes. Occasionally, one would escape and be loping through the fields and we'd call and tell them. The barking from those beasts was rather easily heard at any hour of the day or night. Rather annoying to hear them at nighttime.

So when the Richardsons moved, we were pleased that the dogs went with them. We were also happy to find some kids our age on the other side of the pond fishing one day. But even little boys can be possessive and protective of their dad's property, especially when strangers show up on it and acting like they own it. At first sight, we were excited thinking of the fun we could have playing with them. But when they acted like the other side of the pond was theirs, well, that was a different story.

"Daddy, guess what? We saw some boys fishing on the pond today from the other side. Are they allowed to do that? Isn't that our land?" We were full of questions and figured we knew the answers but wanted Daddy's affirmation.

"Well boys, yes, the pond belongs to us and part of the land over there too. But their boundary comes down the hill to the center of the dam breast and goes straight to the cowpath bridge," Daddy explained to us. We didn't quite get it or maybe we didn't want to get it because we always trapped muskrats down the creek from the dam breast to the road. We were trying to justify our plan to set more traps that coming season. Maybe that's why last year someone was snapping our traps and a few actually came up missing. Our tender minds were very curious and beginning to find those culprits guilty of stealing.

Now just a minute here, let me explain something. I jumped from seeing Jack and Jamie down at the pond, to accusing them of stealing traps. Let me fill in some gaps.

Our first association was early summertime just after school was out. David and I were building a "hut" with old used boards from the farm. Daddy saved every used board from building projects and to help shed rain water, leaned them up against the old mulberry tree and two pear trees between the chicken houses. He said we could use a few of them for our hut.

There were piles of old used tin roofing that we used for our roof. A roll of tar paper tacked to the outside made it semi-waterproof. Recycled nails were all we were allowed to use on the hut. Of course, we had little money to buy new material and were happy just to have access to used materials. We cut every board by hand, designed it as we built and nailed each recycled nail with whatever old hammers we could find. We finished it by mid summer between morning and evening chores. We had chosen to build it next to the big ash tree about 6' from the pond's edge where daily we fed about 200 geese and ducks. The hut had a slightly split level, was about 4' wide, 8' long and about 4' high with a shed roof, one window and one door hinged with old leather strapping and a homemade wooden lock. We draped the window with an old burlap bag, and found an old carpet in the garage no one was using for the floor. It wasn't high enough inside to stand up but then we hadn't used ladders to build it. At the ages of 8 and 10, David and I had not been educated about levels, squares or transits but we were proud nonetheless of our accomplishment.

While we were building our hut, guess who was watching? You guessed it, Jamie and Jack. They came over now and then to talk about it and ask questions. Now Jack, being the oldest, about 12, took the lead as he and Jamie decided they wanted a hut on their side of the pond. It was actually our land, but Daddy didn't care. This was just kids' stuff and he likely figured we'd soon enough grow out of it and what could it hurt anyhow? So they dragged old lumber down to the pond from their barn and within a few weeks, they had a hut too. It wasn't as big as ours but it was a hut.

Each of us built a fire pit with rocks from the pond bank. They invited us over and I soon learned to enjoy roasting apples on the end of a twig sharpened with a dull pocket knife.

"You keep turning the apple till its black and when you hear it sizzle and see it hiss steam, that's how you know it's ready to eat," Jack instructed us.

He was right, it worked and to this day, I like doing apples roasted over a campfire. Only, it's been about 20 years since I've tried it. I remember showing Mike and Lori down by our pond a long time ago. No, not building a hut, roasting an apple. ☺

After the huts were built and summer was hot, we'd swim in the pond with the ducks and geese. The pond was only 4' deep at the deepest end. When we stood on the bottom, our feet sank above our ankles in stinky mud causing the water to bubble even darker.

I think it was Jack's idea to try building a raft to ride and jump from.

Jack, being the crafty one, decided to build their raft on tin drums. No idea where they came from but he had them.

David and I thought a few old barn beams should work so we lined them up, dragged more old splintered boards down to the pond and nailed them on across the beams. We nailed four boards upright around the perimeter to give us a railing effect, about 8" high, slapped a couple across the corners for seats and called it "our raft."

By this time, Jack and Jamie's raft was already floating and ready to go. They jumped on and with a long stick pushed away from the bank singing some campfire song as they went. They were proud and also anxious to see how ours floated. David and I pried and pulled, pushed and heaved until finally it slid into the muddy water with a splash. The barn beams sank leaving the deck boards just barely above the water, but it was floating. We stepped gingerly on one at a time, pushed away with a long stick and we were rafting, albeit slowly and taking on water. But we didn't tell Jack and Jamie. We stayed fairly close to our side heading for the far end of the pond as we polled our way along.

Jack's design with the drums kept theirs afloat much better than ours so we looked around the farm for some of our own. It took some work but we revamped our raft with a few 5-gallon cans tied alongside which gave it more buoyancy.

We spent many days and evenings that summer down at the pond, after chores and whenever possible, swimming, rafting, fishing, working on the hut and sitting around the campfire roasting apples, hotdogs and marshmallows. I hadn't yet heard of Huck Finn and his motley crew, but there we were imitating them anyhow. If only we had a video of those days.

With all the construction going on at the pond that summer, back to school came way too quickly. The hut stood through many seasons until we were all too big to enjoy crawling around in it. Like all good things, sooner than later, it was recycled.

Sometime in the next few years, we began trapping. That's when the boundary dispute surfaced. I remember Daddy talking to Mom about it and actually talking it over with the neighbor down by the dam wall. Seems like they figured out that the boundary line was as written earlier in this story. But from then on, they kept more to themselves. Of course, we all were older and no longer took interest in rafting and crawling around in 4' high huts. But hey, for 8- and 10-year-old entrepreneurs, it was history well lived. Nothing beats creativity for young kids. It defines skills that may stick for a lifetime. It did for me. I'd recommend it to my grandkids, any kids, any day if the occasion and opportunity presented itself. But use plastic or steel drums for floating devices. One more suggestion . . . keep your mouth closed when swimming in duck ponds. ☺

CHAPTER 13

Pigeons, Rabbits and Guinea Pigs

"**R**eady, set, GO." And with that, as fast as possible, we shoved the wooden overhead door up, ran under and pulled it back down behind us. Up the wooden ladder we scrambled so fast you'd thought our pants were on fire. "Why, you ask?" Good question. Well, sit back and listen to the story.

On the farm growing up was a double-sided corn crib with a little attic in it. Between the two outside cribs filled with corn was a large room with a perforated steel floor. Around 1959, Daddy had installed a false floor that looked like a big screen so that hot air could be forced up through it to dry shelled corn. Then the corn was moved by an auger and shovels from that floor to the cribs. There was an area overhead with a floor to store whatever. At each end of that room was a window for light and ventilation. David and I noticed that whenever we went into the crib to help bag or move corn, besides lots of mice and some rats scurrying around, pigeons were flying around upstairs trying to get out. They would come in regularly for a snack.

One of our hobbies was raising rabbits and guinea pigs. Under the overhang of the barn stood a four-tier-high hutch big enough for 12 pair of rabbits and boxes for their bunnies. Since the barn faced southeast, the front was always warm but in wintertime, we'd cover the sides with burlap bags for protection on snowy days.

Next to that, just inside the barn entry was my guinea pig hutch. We had four Mammas and one Papa, enough to raise plenty of guinea pigs. Leftover vegetable greens from Daddy's market route provided a daily healthy feast. The kind of breed was not important. Quantity was. On a regular basis, a man would stop by the farm to buy rabbits and guinea pigs. It was a little enterprise which made some spending money for us.

So . . . , here's where the pigeons come in. One day when the "rabbit man" was making his rounds, he saw pigeons flying in and out of the corn crib. As he took out his roll of cash to pay us for some bunnies, he said, "You know, those pigeons are worth some money if you can catch 'em."

Well, that's all we needed to hear. More spending money if we can catch 'em. So we came up with a plan. "Hey, if we tilt the windows open so they can easily get in, set up a ladder to the upstairs and have a broom and a feed bag ready to go, we can do it," I said. "If we get up the ladder really fast and surprise them, we can close the windows and we got 'em." Next day after school, we quickly changed our clothes, grabbed a couple peanut butter crackers and a glass of milk and ran out to the corn crib. The overhead door was closed but the windows upstairs were still open. Good.

"Now," I said whispering to David, "when I open the door, you grab a broom and get up the ladder. I'll be right behind you after I close the door. When you get upstairs, close the window as quick as you can and I'll get the other one."

"Okay," David said all set and ready to go. Upstairs, pigeons were flying everywhere trying to escape. Some got away but about 10 or 12 didn't. With our brooms, we would, as carefully as possible, swat them out of the air and bag them. Sometimes they would fly down into the crib and we'd jump into the corn sliding after them. "Gotcha!" Probably half of them escaped but hey, we had some to sell.

We found out that they were bringing good money at the Harleysville auction, held every Wednesday. So Daddy agreed to drive us there to sell them. We'd put them into a wooden chicken crate to haul them to the auction. Then they would put them into their crates tagged with a number designating David and John Merrill Souder as owners. In a few days, we would get a check in the mail made out to us. If I remember right, we got about $2.00 per bird. Can you believe it?

People think they are a delicacy to eat. Can't be but a few bites on 'em. Yes, pigeons are worth catching if you can connect a couple of creative, energetic kids with a buyer for their catch. Hmmm . . . I think I just heard a flutter of wings and a familiar cooing. Better check it out.

CHAPTER 14

The Market Truck

"Hey Daddy, Kenny's here . . . and Uncle Abe is right behind him!" I yelled coming into the barn with two baskets of eggs to wash. Daddy was in the back part of the barn downstairs grading eggs with Mom. It was Wednesday, the day to prepare for the market route which was Thursday and Friday. The Christian radio station and the rhythmic sound of the egg grader gently dropping eggs onto one of four trays trumped any sounds coming from the outside.

There they stand, Daddy on the left, with a basket of washed eggs next to him (ten more hanging from the ceiling waiting to be done), the grader straight ahead. He is methodically putting the eggs onto the rubber sloped runway. A light bulb shines though the grader's runway revealing any blood-spotted eggs which he removes before they continue across the grader. Mom stands to the right boxing the eggs, with 30-dozen-size egg crates on either side and two behind her.

"Opps, another one for the cats," Daddy said matter-of-factly." Mom just continued on with her boxing job careful to put the correct sizes in the right crate. Extra large, large, medium and pullets and even "cracks" were loaded on the market truck.

Meanwhile, Kenny and Uncle Abe were waiting outside. "Daddy, didn't you hear me? Kenny and Abe are here. They're waiting for you," I said putting my basket of dirty eggs into the washer.

"Sorry, I didn't hear you. Be right back," he said to Mom running out to meet them.

"John, you're a busy man. Do you ever take time to rest?" Kenny said joking but also aware how hard and long Daddy worked. Kenny was from the family of Zeigler's fruit farm, later better known as Zeigler's Apple Cider business. He was a big joker, a great salesman and loved to debate Christian theology with Daddy. He sold Daddy apples and peaches in the summertime for resale on the market truck. There was always some bargaining going on between them but all in good fun.

Uncle Abe stopped by with Keller's Creamery products, basically butter and cream. Then there were the wholesale trucks from Alderfer's Bologna, Moyer's Meats, Lehigh Valley ice cream truck, and sometimes, the ice man. Ice was needed to keep Daddy's coolers cold and to ice down freshly killed poultry that he sold on his market route. It was delivered in large blocks of 50 and 100 lbs.

As much as possible was raised on the farm . . . chickens, eggs, turkeys, geese and ducks. In the summer, we raised sweet corn by the acre, string beans, lima beans, red beets, tons of tomatoes and rhubarb. Everything had to be washed, or cleaned and loaded on the market truck for the route or stored in the cooler until those days.

There even was a chest freezer on the truck loaded with ice cream and other frozen items he purchased for sale. Ice cream was either in half gallon boxes or pint boxes. I loved the assortment of pints because we would occasionally get to cut them in half and eat out of a box of our choice. A real treat for us kids.

When I was 8 or 9, I was allowed to go along to market. By 6:30 a.m. the truck had to be ready to go. We ate breakfast and were off by 7:15 for the Philadelphia suburbs. Down the cowpath we rumbled, through Hatfield, past Lansdale on to Montgomeryville Square.

There we took Route 309 on down to Springhouse where our first stop would be Rotelles—sounds like rowtellies. We would back our truck in alongside many other "hucksters" parked there to buy produce. Rotelles was an Italian run wholesale produce outlet where Daddy bought (bargained if he could) fresh produce. For a young boy like me, the men that ran it looked and seemed more like mafia. They were rough, foul mouthed, and obnoxiously loud.

"Bananas, get your bananas right here. Ten cents a pound today just for you, John," a big dude would be yelling as he strutted by on the cruddy concrete floor.

The dirty bathrooms had naughty words scribbled all over them except where a few photo calendars hung of nude girls. Boxes of produce were piled high all through the warehouse. I generally stayed pretty close to Daddy and kept my mouth shut . . . at least until I was "of age" and had to buy produce myself when I took the route on occasion. Yes, Rotelles . . . whew . . . quite an impression.

Back in the truck, we headed down the pike as Daddy commented about the high price of lettuce, cabbage, peas or whatever. He was happy and as friendly as a huckster should be when he knocked on the first door that morning.

"Knock, knock—FARMER," he said in a smiling voice. Often a bath-robe clad woman would appear at the door rubbing her eyes in the morning sunshine. "Oh, it's you, Mr. Souder. Ca-mone in," she'd say. Or he may just stand at the door with his pad and pencil to take her order. Back in the truck, he would tell me what to get for him while he filled the order. It may mean cutting pork chops on his chopping block with the big cleaver, sometimes also using the meat saw. It wasn't too many years before he would teach me to take orders (only small orders) and learn to make change. We never had a calculator on the truck. No adding machine, no computer, just pencil and paper and your trained brain to add and subtract.

While Daddy took their orders, I was supposed to be bagging and weigh-ing up various produce to help speed up processing the orders. My reward was a popsicle or half of a pint box of ice cream on the way home.

House by house, through Glenside, Jenkintown, neighborhood by neigh-borhood we went in a systematic pattern each week. I began to learn the stops and the ladies. Some nice, some not so nice. Some with screaming kids and some widows. When midday came, we stopped at the Glenside Diner for lunch. They bought eggs, bacon and butter from us and in exchange, we bought lunch. My treat was usually meatloaf, mashed potatoes and succotash (peas, carrots and lima beans). If I was lucky, they had French apple pie for desert . . . basically, pie with icing on top. Yumm.

A few customers still stick in my memory. The most vivid is the Waltzes who actually had a vacation home in Forksville that they came to on a regular basis during the '50s and early '60s. They were really nice people. I remember each time we went into their house midafternoon, "Bandstand" was playing on TV. I always thought they couldn't be Christians if they watched that stuff. How judgmental and weird is that! Then there was this lady who always welcomed Daddy to sit down at the dinning room table while she thought about what she wanted to order that day. It seemed to take forever if I was waiting out in the truck.

Often, an ice cream truck could be heard ringing its way through the neighborhood as children came running from every direction.

Around 4:00 in the afternoon, we'd begin heading north making stops along the way. Daddy always had a tin can hidden under the shelves just in case I had to pee while in route.

My favorite market truck Daddy ever owned was a Dodge stub-nose step van. I think it was a 1951 or '53 van he bought from Alderfer's Garage in Tel-ford, only a mile from our house. That's where he bought all his Chryslers too.

What I remember most about that van was the huge space at the front window. The window had very little slope, being almost vertical. That space was created because the engine was underneath. So it was a nice warm spot to sit in the winter. Daddy often stored a box or two of something there too. But when I was young, on the way home, I would sit there to stay warm.

I said it was a step van. There was a sliding door with a fairly large wide step just inside the door. It was there that Daddy often kept a small wooden barrel of freshly cured sauerkraut. I can still smell the sour cabbage as I pulled off the wooden lid to pick some out with my fingers for a sample taste. Never thought of using rubber gloves or a fork. Fingers work just fine. For many years he sold it that way.

It was that market truck, or one like it, where I got into trouble one day when I was very young. David and I were playing around the truck when it was parked in front of the barn to be washed. I climbed up on the front bumper and was feeling all proud until I lost my balance. To keep from falling on my face, I grabbed onto one of the big windshield wipers and slightly bent it as I fell off the truck. The next thing I remember was a swat on my behind and some "cross" words reminding me not to climb places like that. Can't recall ever doing so again.

For years Joan, David and I all had turns learning the ropes of "huckstering." I can remember learning the route well enough to take it on my own when I was only 17 and 18 while Mom and Daddy went away for a week. I can't recall who went along to help me. But I do remember when Daddy died, it was difficult for Mom and Joan to try following up on the customers until they could sell the business and the truck. I went along a few times during those terribly trying days.

Oh my, were they good ol' days or just good days? Not sure. What I am sure of is that the market route helped Daddy pay off the farm, buy many new pieces of farm equipment, remodel and build new farm buildings and our house and help all of us kids financially. It also was the means which supported his Mission minded Spirit. Because of that income, he could follow up personally the mission work in Mexico, support mission work in Cuba, Estella, Centereach, Long Island, Vermont, Laurelville camp and more. His hard work and long hours and his trust in God made it all possible.

It is notable that he bought the market route when he was only 19 years old. Shortly thereafter, he was diagnosed with rheumatic fever which almost did him in. The doctors actually said that he would likely never work again, he was so seriously ill. His brother Lester helped him with the route those early days. Though Daddy was allotted only 59 years of life on earth, none were wasted.

Today, January 2, 2012, I would be very hard pressed to find just one "huckster" working the streets in the suburbs of Philadelphia. That business is history. And so is "The Market Truck."

CHAPTER 15

Winter Entertainment— a Few Generations Ago

Supper was over and Grammy was humming an old hymn as she washed the dishes in the white porcelin sink.

Grumpop shuffled from the kitchen into the dining room and over to his chair by the northeast window. Grabbing the hand-knit shawl from the back of his rocker, he wrapped it around his shoulder before plopping onto the chair. He sat next to the cast-iron radiator on his right side and the smell of wet socks and gloves drying was obvious.

Grammy's rocker, which I now have in our living room, sat close to the other window on the same side of the house. Between them sat the radio. No television, no computer, no CD player or even a cassette player. No cell phones and no cordless phones. Their entertainment was created if there was to be any. What I do remember was the "AM" radio.

That's right, an AM radio. FM radio was available but not affordable, at least not priced reasonably enough for Grumpop. And TV, even black and white, was very expensive and besides, the church did not approve of such worldly things.

The radio was a piece of furniture about—say 40" high, 30" wide and a foot deep. It was chestnut in color. A nicely crafted piece of furniture actually. Centered near the top front was the dial which looked like a small clock with the numbers 550 up to 1650 AM. The entire bottom portion was covered with a stitched fabric covering the large speaker behind it.

In the evenings when I would come over to play Parcheesi, Grammy would often be sitting in her chair. She would be slowly rocking and humming a tune while darning socks or knitting something.

"John Merrill! You wanna play Parcheesi? I can finish this another time," and up she got trotting over to the built-in cupboard. She was short and stout and always wore the white netting on her head with two white ribbons for a prayer covering.

She rarely was seen around the house without her apron on and was always singing or humming. No different tonight as she reached for the game on the third shelf.

"Here we go. You sit there. If Joan and David come, they can sit over there. Let's start a while."

Fine with me. I liked being with my grandparents. They always made me feel happy and peaceful.

As we got started playing, Grumpop sat listening to one of his favorite radio shows. I can still see him there . . . leaning slightly forward, eyes closed, shoulders covered with that shawl. Sometimes he'd be soaking his feet in a porcelain dishpan filled with warm Epsom saltwater. Who knows why? Maybe it just felt good after a hard day's work.

"Clankity clank. Shhhhuuu." The pipes from the radiator were hot enough and steam had to go somewhere, so the little relief valve opened and out it came . . . chattering as it went. I looked at Grammy then Grumpop but they ignored it. Guess the ancient woodstove monster was still doing its thing. All was normal.

Often "The Amos and Andy" show would be playing which made him smile. A sly grin would appear than a short chuckle and his hand would slap his knee. It made me happy to see him enjoying himself. Somehow, I felt warm and happy inside as we sat at the dinning room table playing games together while Grumpop listened to his shows. On some nights, even before I got into the dining room, I could hear someone preaching. It wasn't long before I heard his name.

"This is the Oral Roberts Broadcast coming to you from Oral Roberts University in Tulsa, Oklahoma." I honestly think Grumpop hoped to be healed from his cancer by listening to that program. Guess it wasn't to be, since he died at the early age of 67.

Anyhow, usually before we finished our game, he'd be heading for the "wooden hill" to bed. Grammy would almost always win the game, but we'd be back another night.

"Sweet dreams Grumpop. Night, Grammy. I hear Mom calling. Time for bed. See you tomorrow," I said. Another day in history and one needing to be recorded for the next generations.

Try it. Lay aside those electronic games, quit texting and twittering, pull those silly buds out of your ears, turn off that colored window that keeps you mesmerized for hours and that thing you lay on your lap or clasp in your palm tapping your fingers on wildly.

Put on your walking shoes, skis or skates and get the blood bubbling. Feel that clear cool breeze on your face. Smell the flowers and pick some. Eat the wild berries. Look for wild game and birds. Pick up a good book and read it. Better yet, write one. Memorize scripture. Sit and listen to a good radio show or a good CD. Play games, any games. Do crafting or woodworking. Yeah, you get the idea. Do it! Laugh, Love, Live. But **live for what matters!**

CHAPTER 16

Uncle Raymond

Raymond was born with special needs and was mentally challenged. He was a brother to my Grumpop, Preston Souder, and an older brother, Mahlon Souder, whom I remember most as a State Farm Insurance agent.

Raymond lived most of his life with Grammy and Grumpop. His room was at the top of the winding wooden stairs leading to Grammy's bedroom. But most of his days were spent either in the basement or the attic except for meals.

Raymond slowly clip-clopped down the cellar steps. His dark brown sweater hanging loosely on his frail frame, he grasped the grey stair railing as he descended to have a smoke by the dusty coal stove. Early in his life, someone taught him to smoke and he never broke the habit. Smoking upstairs or anywhere else in the house was a no-no. He knew that.

It was almost 7:00 p.m. and daylight saving time had ended. Winter was just around the corner and the warmth of the little bucket-a-day coal stove used to heat water felt great as Raymond sat cross-legged on the antique wooden bench.

He kept his pipe and tobacco stashed on the dusty beam above his bench. When he needed more tobacco, he would walk a half mile across the field to Old Frank Keller's store. Frank never took advantage of Raymond. He was always kind and helpful.

I believe Raymond received a small disability check which gave him spending money. I remember he carried a small leather coin purse stuffed with dollars and coins.

When David and I were quite young, we would quietly sneak down the basement steps and spy on him. Since our cousin Jay lived with Grammy during the summertime, likely he joined us sometimes. Not sure what we got out of it but occasionally he would see us and mumble a line in Pa Dutch. *"Da . . . da . . . demmmin,"* he'd say if we scared him. Sometimes he'd just ask, "Yah?" . . . basically asking if we wanted something. As we sat on the steps watching, we could see him sucking on the pipe and then with closed eyes, let the smoke out. It must have given the poor soul some pleasure. I actually feel a bit of shame for bothering him but hey, we were young and full of it. Thank God for His mercy and forgiveness.

At other random times we could hear him shuffling up the stairs to the attic. Curious, we would sneak up behind him and carefully, quietly position ourselves behind clothes hanging over the railing. There we could watch him playing his own version of solitaire. Long boards had been laid over two wobbly saw horses creating a makeshift table. Two little windows helped to light up the room so he could see. Plaster would occasionally fall from the low sloped ceiling making a mess on his table. He would spread small square, flat tin boxes around the table putting pieces of paper in some and under others.

I never could figure out his game nor could I ask him because he only spoke Pa. Dutch. I knew just enough to barely communicate with him. Matter-of-fact, his vocabulary was less than that of a three year old but he comprehended much more.

On rare occasions, Raymond came along to church but not often. As best he could understand, he accepted Jesus as his Saviour.

A true story was recently told about Raymond. Bishop Jonas Minninger was at Rockhill to perform a baptism for a class of applicants. Apparently my great-grandfather was in attendance with his 21-year-old son Raymond. The bishop had asked the congregation to kneel for prayer and the baptism candidates to remain on their knees to be baptized. As the congregation sat down Raymond went forward to kneel with the ones to be baptized and John went after him to have him sit back down. Jonas M. waved the father away and went on to baptize Raymond. This had a profound effect on my great-grandfather, John D. Souder.

Raymond loved babies and little kids but never held them. I remember him asking my mom or Grammy if the child I was holding was mine. When told that it was mine, he would say, *"I yi yi . . . yah?"*

"Yah," Mom would say.

And then he would put his hands on his knees and laugh. Oh Raymond, bless you.

After Grammy and Grumpop passed away, Raymond was under Mom and Daddy's care for a while. I guess he would have been close to 60 years old by then. He still slept on the other side of the house in his room but ate meals with us. I was 16 when my Grammy died. Over the next couple of years, I recall a number of times when Mom and Daddy were away and I was on the farm alone with Raymond. Since he could not cook or prepare his own meals someone had to do it for him. The old standby was canned tomato soup and toasted cheese sandwiches. He'd sit and wait while I prepared it and before we ate, I would say a prayer. I'd try practicing what little Dutch I knew with Raymond during those meals. To show his appreciation and approval of the meal, with raised eyebrows and a nodding head, he would simply say, *"Yah!"* I would respond with, *"Guut, net?"* Meaning "It's good isn't it?" Then he would amble over to the other side of the house to rest in a chair or back down to the basement for a smoke.

Raymond had an older sister, Edna. Her husband, Herb Kulp, was my great uncle. He was quite a character. I remember going to visit them with my parents one day and surprise, surprise, a skunk met us at the door. We backed up as Herb laughed and said not to worry, it was de-scented. It was a lot like a little kitten. He told us he bought it at the Gilbertsville auction.

One hot summer day while baling hay we drove across some holes in the hay field. On the next round, five baby skunks and the mom came out and walked around only to go back in the holes when they saw us. Daddy got an idea. He ran across the road and came back with some feed bags and a couple shovels. He was grinning as he gave one shovel to Ernie, our hired hand. They both began to dig out the family of skunks. The idea was to catch the little ones and hopefully keep the mother in the hole. Then give them to Herb to take to the Gilbertsville auction. Well, you guessed it. We all got sprayed good before it was all over. I don't remember what we did with the skunks but I do remember running home to get a bath.

We stripped to our undies before going in the house and let the clothes outside. Mom suggested we mix tomato juice and water. It helped but did not take the smell completely away. That was a Saturday evening. We bathed again in the morning before going to church. As David and I followed Daddy into the back door at church, someone commented, "Whewww something smells like a skunk." Daddy snickered and turned around pulling us with him. That was one of the few Sunday services we ever missed. When Raymond heard about it, he laughed and kept saying *"Yah? Yah,"* and slapped his knee in delight.

As time went on, Uncle Mahlon was insisting that Daddy put Raymond in a State Home 20 miles west of the farm. Mom and Daddy still thought they could take care of him but eventually agreed to Mahlon's idea. The day came for the big move to the Johnson Home. Mahlon and Daddy had tried hard to explain to Raymond what they thought was best for him. But it was quite obvious by his demeanor and mumbling, that he was not in favor. They convinced him to go for a visit which proved helpful. After some months with a physician's help, they were able to admit him to the home where he spent the rest of his days. I remember when Mom called me one day to tell me Raymond had passed away. It was very bittersweet. Those last years during the transition were very difficult and stressful on Mom and Daddy as well as us children.

Raymond was a dear old soul, poor in spirit, and poor by the world's standard. But we loved him just the same. Certainly God created and loved him equally as any of His children. Only He knows the full purpose for Raymond's life. Jesus said, "We should love the Lord our God with all our hearts, with all our soul, with all our mind and with all our strength. And that we should love our neighbor as ourselves." Who is our neighbor? Remember the story of the Good Samaritan? Anyone in need is our neighbor.

Next time we see Raymond; he will be talking, hearing and understanding clearly and joyfully in the presence of Jesus, family and neighbors, living in a mansion prepared for him by His Saviour.

CHAPTER 17

Famous Fruit Trees
on the Farm

Down by the cellar entrance to the farmhouse, next to the grape arbor, stand four or five young boys. Not just their hands, but their pants and tee shirts are stained purple with grape juice. Daddy had given us a 5-minute break from unloading 3 big wagons of hay before heading back to the hayfield.

"Man are these sweet," Sonny said squeezing grapes from the skin into his mouth and sucking out the juice. It was a favorite treat on a hot summer day on the farm. I'll bet we downed 4 or 5 bunches daily till they were gone. David, Harry, Sonny, Donnie, myself and other neighbor boys enjoyed the treat.

A large fenced-in garden was next to the grape arbor bordered on three sides with luscious black raspberries. When they got ripe, it was first come first eat. Handful after handful was stuffed in our mouths, again staining hands and shirts. Mom used to pick them in the early morning and Dad would sell some on the market route. Mom froze boxes of them for winter treats too. Yum, yum!

That garden was full of goodies; lots of rhubarb, strawberries, carrots, lettuce, mint tea, and herbs. The field below the turkey pens produced hundreds of ears of sweet corn. Weeds flourished resulting in many blisters from hoeing those stupid weeds out.

On the south side of the garden and next to the old wood shed stood the largest walnut tree on the farm. Two wash line pulleys were attached to the tree. One on a pole on the opposite side of the garden and one on the house where Grammy and Mom could hang their wash out to dry. In late fall, large green walnuts littered the ground below the tree. They were so bitter that we never used them. But we had to rake them up and throw them away. The tree was ancient. I asked the people who bought the farm for first option to that tree if it was ever sawed down. I received a verbal agreement that turned out to be worthless. I hoped to use the wood for benches and tables.

Now here's a tree I'll bet most of you cannot claim ownership of—a persimmon tree. It stood tall and shaded the horsey swings next to the driveway across from the barn. Many a hot summer hay day, we boys and Dad sat under its shade eating watermelon to cool down after unloading hay bales into the steamy hay maul. If it was late summer, pale orange persimmons dropped on the ground daring a brave soul to give 'em a try. They'd better be good and ripe, even soft and almost squishy if you wanted to eat one. Unripe persimmons would make you pucker up as if you'd just bit into a sour lemon doused with old vinegar. Actually, it was much worse. Your mouth would turn inside-out drawing your checks so tight they would kiss inside. Take it from me; don't eat hard persimmons. Few boys had nerve enough to try one twice. Since I took a liking to them, I would search for the squishy ones and hesitantly bite into it. Umm-umm-Umm! On occasion, Daddy would buy a small crate of them to sell on the market route. Now those babies were huge! They were about the size of a big orange. When they were soft and ripe, the juice would sneak out of your mouth and make a mess of your face. But it was worth it, let me tell you.

At the base of the persimmon tree and facing the road stood a very old stationary porch swing. At one time it gave restful pleasure to weary souls, but now it was barely safe to sit on, so there it sat reminding people it was once worthy. Daddy painted it John Deere green like so many other wooden pieces on the farm. About six feet above the old bench swing hung a wooden sign about three feet square. It was one of many scattered around the conservative Mennonite community. There must have been some kind of scripture rally going on that produced the signs. Our persimmon-tree-sign boldly announced the words, "PEPARE TO MEET THY GOD."

Out behind the barn on the west side and toward the church on the cow-path road were two pear trees. Not your ordinary pear trees. In 1717, our great, great, great, great-grandfather brought seeds from a Keifer pear tree in Germany and planted them there.

I never quite figured out what was so special and why he ever bothered to bring that seed. The pears never really ripened enough to eat them. They stayed hard long after frost and until they rotted. Maybe someone knew how to preserve them, we never did. We boys gathered them up and fed them to the hogs. All I know is that historian John Ruth from Harleysville spoke about these trees and seemed to think they were special.

Special to me was the ol' gnarley, big branchy mulberry tree that shaded the double story chicken house below the garage. Daddy liked to store old lumber standing up around the trees to shed the water. It was a place for little boys to crawl in behind and hide, while playing hide-n-seek. The lumber also could be arranged in ladder style so we could climb up into the massive tree. Once in the tree you could climb out several limbs and over onto the roof of the chicken house. Now that was a good view . . . until Daddy, Mom, Grumppop or someone yelled at us to get down out of there, and right now! Have you ever tasted mulberries? Good grief! It's about time you try some. If you don't like stained fingers and lips, forget it. They look like big long blackberries until you bite into them. Then you see they are kinda purple and a taste all their own. I remember another big mulberry tree overhanging the road to one of our fields. When the wagons were full of hay, we could sit on the top row and carefully snatch some mulberries off the limbs as Daddy drove under the tree. We'd shake and strip them off onto the hay wagon and eat to our heart's content. Now that made boys with happy bellies!

When that ol' tree got cut down, my cousin Jay (Sonny, we used to call him), cut a hunkin' big piece of the mulberry tree out for me. I have it in my chicken house today. I also got a small log from it and cut some lumber to make things. Hanging on our back porch is a glove holder I made from that childhood gem. The grain is bold and proud and the color is almost yellow. Now there's a treasure.

Across the pond and over the meadow next to the neighbors' ground stood two hickory trees. In the fall when the nuts were ripening, squirrels visited those trees as did I, with Daddy's Winchester 22 pump. Not sure how many I got of those big grey beauties but my mom wasn't fond of fried or cooked squirrel. When I saw them in the pan or pot, I knew why. They must be related to the rat family, although they taste quite good. As for the hickory nuts, my Grammy Souder told us to spread them out on the picnic table or on trays to dry in the sun. On cold winter days, we'd go down in the cellar and bring some up to crack. A hammer on the concrete porch floor did the trick, but you still had to use something sharp like an ice pick (I know . . . dangerous) to get all the nut meat out. Hickory nut cupcakes topped with vanilla icing was a special treat and worth all the effort.

Our farm had a sizeable apple and peach orchard too. Across the road up on the bank where at one time, chicken shelters shaded by the trees, dotted the orchard in summer. I remember hooking up the Ferguson 30 tractor to a homemade trailer loaded with 55-gallon drums. Some had chicken feed in them ground up with home-raised grains by a local portable hammer mill. I'd back up to the barn, and fill several up with water from a hose. Since that would take a while, I'd try to do other things like wash eggs, play basketball, ride bike . . . until I'd hear, "John Merrill, watch the water, it's running over!" Dah . . . getting side-tracked was so easy. When all were filled and lids secured, off David and I went across the road, up the hill into the orchard to feed chickens. By the time we got there, a 1/3rd of the water had spilled out and occasionally, while going too fast, one would slide off. We always hoped Daddy wasn't nearby to see that.

There must have been 20 fruit trees in that orchard. Various kinds of apples, yellow peaches and one tree of my favorite—white peaches. In the fall we picked the apples off the ground, bagged them up in 100# feed sacks and took them to Ziegler's. I loved watching the huge wooden apple press squeeze out fresh cider. Daddy sold some on the market route.

Unfortunately, no one took time to keep the trees trimmed and sprayed and little by little they died or were dug out to make way for more profitable use of the land. By the early '70s, the old orchard became a corn or wheat field. Then in the mid '90s, a housing development took over. A sad transition but so prevalent in urban areas.

I have to wonder who took the precious time and tender loving care to plant and nurse that orchard to life? One of my forefathers did. For all I know, they may have wrapped up special seeds and brought them over on the ship from Germany or Switzerland. But now, none of those precious trees are on that property. They succumbed to something called progress. Really now? I've planted my own fruit trees on the farm in Sullivan County. We get 4-5 bushels of pears every other year but not many apples. Do your generation a big favor—plant fruit trees. Even if you don't see the harvest, someone will surely appreciate it . . . and maybe write about it.

A prayer song we sing sometimes before a meal:

"Oh, the Lord's been good to me,
and so I thank the Lord
For giving me the things I need,
the sun and the moon and the apple seed.
The Lord's been good to me . . .
Johnny Appleseed, Amen!"

CHAPTER 18

Dogs of the '40s and '50s . . .

My earliest and fondest memories of our dogs is "Snowball." Talk about "terrorists," he was one. Don't misunderstand me, he was a small rat terrier, pure white except for a black nose. Daddy liked to have rat terriers around the farm for, you guessed it, rat control. They were everywhere. With all the chickens, turkeys, geese and ducks to feed, there was plenty of wasted food to glean. Snowball was a very sweet loveable little dog, always running by our side sniffing out his prey. As we'd enter the chicken pens, if an unlucky mouse or rat, no matter the size, was sighted, it would soon be history. Can you envision this little dog, smaller than a large cat, lunging at a rat and grabbing it around the neck? He would shake it so ferociously you'd think his head would fall off. Usually, he would break its neck and be looking for the next one. Occasionally, the rat would win the first round by biting Snowball, drawing blood. No matter, he would sling it off and go back for another round till it lay still.

In the meadow near the pond nestled in a semi circle were a dozen or so range shelters for growing chickens. A double strand electric fence kept most of the young leghorns from rooming too far. Feeders attached to the sides of the shelters had to be filled daily. Obviously, feed would be wasted as the birds ate and attracted rats seemingly from the whole town nearby. Uncle Charlie, the town chief of police, would enjoy target practice at least once a week after dark. Daddy would hold the flashlight while Uncle Charlie would take aim. If he was lucky, he may reduce the population.

Clean out days became exciting adventure and sport. Daddy had a large metal frame built which mounted on the tractor's front-end loader. He would get it in place, post me and David and Grumpop and sometimes Mom at four corners of the shelter. One with a shovel, one a fork, one with the 22 rifle and the other with a long stick. It was now a war zone. Snowball was on high alert, the hair on his neck raised and he was growling. As soon as the shelter began to lift, rats of all sizes scurried everywhere. So did we with our weapons but Snowball did most of the damage. Tunnels had been made under the manure where some would stay until we dug them out. He would grab them by the neck and with a vicious twist they would take their last flight as he ran for the next one. If I recall correctly, Daddy said he got about 25 that morning. Yes, he paid the price with some nasty bites but the scars tell the story of Snowball's victories. They named the breed appropriately, "rat terrier."

There were other favorites. Trixy, a toy terrier; Spotty, my mixed black and white spotted terrier; Duke, my first beagle hound; and Porky.

Yes, ol' Porky. He was Uncle Lester's dog. Don't know where he came from but could he howl . . . *wooorrroorrr, woorrroorr,* he'd say whenever he felt like it. What he enjoyed most was howling at the moon which drove us all nuts. He was the scraggiest long-haired mess of a dog you'd ever seen, but more friendly than ugly. He'd shake his long, ratty, knotted-up tail when he saw you coming. Hair drooped over his eyes till he shook it free to see you. I guess Uncle Lester figured he looked like a porcupine. Unfortunately, I remember him being tied to a leash on the wash line down below the house near the garden. Poor Porky, I hate seeing dogs tied. But the road being next to the house was a threat to his existence.

Spotty. What a friend to his end. I have a picture of him sitting on my lap licking my face. I was a dog lover from the time I could walk and I guess they knew it. One day he came up missing. The next day I convinced Mom to let me take my bike and search the neighborhood. I rode all the roads within a mile of the house without any sign of him. Tears were shed. I asked the neighbors but no one saw him. More tears. I guess he's enjoying his heavenly hunting grounds.

Growing up, I always envied hunters. Our next door neighbors, Harry Sr. and little Harry had beagles. Harry Sr. was a gunsmith and did lots of hunting with his beagles. If only I could have a beagle. One day someone offered me a male beagle.

Colored brown, black and white with those long droopy ears, he was regal looking. "I'll name him Duke," I said. Duke he was and he loved to hunt rabbits. When hunting season came around, off we went across the narrow inlet to the pond and into the upper pasture next to the cornfield surrounded by fence rows—a perfect place for rabbits. "*Baarooohh,*" he howled with his nose to the ground running a crisscross pattern through the meadow. "*Baarrooohhh, baarrrooohh.*" A rabbit raced out of the grass many yards ahead of him beginning to circle back around. Duke kept up his pace, nose to the ground, ears a floppin' hoping to catch him any moment. Alas, Mr. Rabbit found a muskrat hole in the bank by the crick (slang for creek). Digging him out was futile so back to the meadow we went.

Duke was buried in Sullivan County the first year we moved here. Don't know where at the moment but he made it this far, that I know.

CHAPTER 19

Strawberry—the Tramp and Other Hobos

His name was Strawberry . . . that's right . . . Strawberry. How great is that? He seemed ancient to me and David as we peeked in the little steamed up window. We watched him scoop the last bit of tuna fish out of the tiny can and throw it on the floor of the warm brooder house. He would come sporadically when the weather turned cold, looking for a warm place to spend the night. He often had a small can of tuna or Spam among the small bag of belongings slung over his back and wore baggy grey pants and worn-out sneakers on his feet. He came looking, hoping for shelter and maybe a warm meal. My Grumpop, which would be my grandchildren's great, great-grandfather, was still living on the farm at that time and knew Strawberry quite well.

There were others like him. I don't remember their names though. One would stay in the hay mall of the barn, but only after Grumpop would ask him to hand over any and all matches he had on him. Barn fires were common and some believed it was because of these tramps who slept in the barns. If they smoked, they were blamed for the fires.

However he got the name, who knows, but Strawberry was our favorite tramp. Sad to call him a "tramp" but that's how they were known. Although others were called "hobos." I only remember being in the room with him actually one time but it engraved a picture on my mind for life.

He was probably my build, with heavy whiskers on his wrinkled face. He wore an old beat-up straw hat, and walked hunched over, but what I liked most about Strawberry was his kind and gentle nature. I never heard him complain about how hard life was or anything. He seemed grateful to be there. He spoke slowly and softly if he spoke at all while sitting on an old wooden bench. It sat close to a small coal stove with a metal pipe extending through the thin wooden wall of the brooder house. The warmth of the stove did double duty keeping Strawberry warm as well as the baby chicks, ducks and geese.

It was common practice for my Grammy Souder, to fix a plate of whatever they had for supper for Strawberry to eat. Someone would take it out to him as he waited patiently in the brooder house. I don't know why he was not asked to come in and eat with them or us, but that's the way we did it in those days.

To give you a feel for his little "motel," the room was the size of Mike's old bedroom or about 10' x 12' with a low 6' ceiling of open beams usually collecting webs of dust.

In the room, there were two large things called batteries, which were like wire racks in layers with a canvass hanging down over three sides. Each layer had an electric heater and small fan to warm the chicks or ducklings until they were big enough to go to another larger pen. So this left just enough room for the stove, a bench, a feed barrel and a small area to walk around the battery. The bench must have been long enough to work as a bed. I don't remember any other bed . . . or maybe he just slept on the floor of wood shavings.

Strawberry would fix old broken umbrellas to make some money to buy what little he needed to survive. I remember him carrying them around as he came and went. Usually by morning when I went outside, he was gone for the day. Don't know where he went, just gone. I think he must have known Jesus though. My Dad and Grandpop would be sure to tell him about God and Jesus. I hope we get to see him in Heaven.

So there you have it, a true story about my friend Strawberry. He had very little, but made a big impression on me. Susan remembers tramps and peddlers coming to their house in Harleysville in the same era. How times have changed. These days, people like Strawberry would be picked up by police. I like to believe God picked Strawberry up and gave him a small mansion along the river of life. Now there's a pretty picture.

GRAIN HARVEST . . .

Barley and Bible school. Yeah, they go together. Didn't you know? Bible school was the last week of June to the first week of July. Almost every year, the barley crop was ripe for harvest the end of June. Mom and Daddy thought it more important that I attend SBS (summer Bible school) than helping with the harvest. For a nine year old to try convincing them otherwise . . . well, forget it. Actually, I appreciate their convictions and learned much from the Bible.

Each day after SBS, it didn't take long to change clothes and gobble up a sandwich before running out the door and across the road to the field. Daddy was driving the tractor pulling the combine while Ernie tied the bags of grain.

The first combine Daddy owned looked like a huge upside-down bathtub painted green with a large open mouth ready to devour anything in its way. It would eat a 6' swath which was cut and elevated into the machine where it separated grain from stalks and chaff. The grain poured out of a double elevator chute into feed bags each capable of holding 100 lbs. Ernie, our hired man, stood on the combine's platform tying and changing the full bags. When tied, he'd throw them onto a slide board where they stayed until they reached the end of the field. Then he'd pull a rope to release the slide latch dumping them on the ground.

I wondered why Ernie always wore a big red farmer's hankie around his face when he rode the combine. A few years later when I was barely old enough to take over that job, I knew why and wore one around my face. The dust was incredible. By the end of the day, the hankie had changed from red to black sparing my lungs some grief.

The combine dust was bad enough but nothing was worse than jumping into the storage bin in the barn to shovel the barley to the rear of the bin. Itch? Let me tell you. If you ever had hives, then you have a feel for the sensation after shoveling barley. Nasty stuff. In spite of the summer heat, we wore long sleeves and long pants during barley harvest.

Daddy's next combine had a large bin to hold the grain instead of a platform with a bagger. That eliminated the dreaded dusty job of riding the combine to tie bags. But we still had to shovel the grain into the storage areas in the barn.

As the farm prospered and grew, so did the size and quality of Daddy's machinery. I. G. Rosenberger was a John Deere farm machinery dealer about 8 miles away. No shopping mall, 5 & 10 cent store, nor any candy store held more attraction for two young farmer boys than I.G's. "Gotta go for parts," Daddy told Mom. "Can we go along?" piped up David and I quickly.

"I guess so. Go get in the truck," he said, and off we ran like happy boys out of school for the summer.

Now and then, Daddy would get looking at new farm equipment and sometimes even sit down in Rolands' sales office to discuss a deal. That was always exciting, fun and even a bit un-nerving listening to them working out a deal. First, figuring out what options to include on the new item, then what was it that Daddy wanted to trade in. Finally, the bottom line, the total cost at the bottom of the proposal.

"Oh, my no," Daddy would say. "You got to do better than that. My old combine is worth more than that."

"Well now, let's see here. Let me look over my figures and see what I can do. How 'bout this?" the salesman proposed.

Eventually, if Daddy was really serious, there'd be a deal before we left and Daddy would walk away with a little smirk on his face which to us meant— Yes! We're getting it. Then we'd follow his big footsteps to the truck whispering to each other.

School was out and we were much happier little farmers. One day we arrived home from Bible school to a great big surprise. Parked in the lawn near the barn was a brand new combine. Not the small, pull behind-the-tractor kind we were accustomed to seeing, but a huge self-propelled model 55 John Deere combine. It had to be the largest one in the area for that time.

There was no enclosed cab but a platform with a pipe railing around it with a comfortable seat, steering wheel and lots of levers and gauges. The tires stood above our heads. A metal set of steps let you climb up over the tires to the driver's platform. Up we scrambled as quickly as possible and fought to be first to sit there and dream. "WOW! This is really big," I said with a big smile. "Can't wait till I am old enough to drive it," I said.

Instead of a 6' cutting bar like the old combine, it had a 13' grain head on it. Wooden paddles on a big reel were made to bat the grain into the head. The driver's platform sat directly above the cutting head where later we would discover plenty of nasty dust. Its height was about 13' making it too high for the garage. Daddy had to cut a hole above the garage door to make room for the new combine to enter.

I remember the sense of pride as we stood looking in the garage. Hard to believe Daddy had enough money to buy something that big. We were so excited.

Lots of farmers within 10 miles called to have Daddy combine their grain. That's when his custom combining business started. It was fun riding the combine when we got older, watching the big machine eat up field after field filling trucks and wagons with grain.

Since Daddy had such a large farm operation plus a two-day market route near Philly, he needed all the help he could find. Two growing boys were going to be a huge benefit. By the time I was 14, Daddy figured it was time to teach me to run the big combine. Of course, I was more than ready and willing to learn. David would have to be content with driving the tractors for another year or so.

Operating a machine of such size and value meant focusing on the task. No daydreaming. Sometimes, that was a problem for me. *But I could do this, just put my mind to it,* I told myself. It wasn't long before Daddy trusted me and stepped off the combine to watch me do a whole round in the field alone. I did it. I was on my own. My boots and straw hat all but popped off with how big I felt.

Let me tell you, keeping your head straight, so to speak, took some concentration. Listening for strange sounds indicating trouble, watching for sticks or stray windblown trash, correct travel speed, checking the grain coming into the bin, operating the cutter bar and reel at correct height, kept you at attention. Then it was important to check the tailings falling on the ground to be sure you weren't wasting grain with too much fan speed or other wrong settings. All part of the responsible challenge I enjoyed.

The summer I was 16, I was doing custom combining for local farmers at Daddy's direction. On a hot July afternoon, about four miles from home, I was combining wheat in a large field. Working in new fields can be hazardous since you may not know about a fresh groundhog mound, an outcropping of rocks, or a small hidden stump. Long dusty, hot days can be hypnotizing as you go back and forth in the field multiple times, especially when you are in love. My mind was consumed with *my* sweet Susan.

Another date was coming up in a few days. I was excited to take her miniature golfing. This was a perfect time to plan and dream. So I did. After all, by now I was pretty good at running the combine. Well, it wasn't long before the reels on the combine began to bend and twist. The combine was still moving but something was wrong. I stopped the machine but not before having plowed over a big groundhog mound. The knives chattered and the reels had already swatted piles of dirt mixed with wheat smashing and splintering half of the wooden reels. Finally, everything stopped including my wonderful daydream.

My first thoughts were about how happy Daddy was going to be when he heard about this. No, he would be very unhappy and tell me so. "What were you doing? Guess that'll take care of the profit this week." Something similar to that were his words to me. I felt like a kid and I guess rightly so. I could have blamed it on Susan but it surely wasn't her fault and I wasn't about to tell him my thoughts.

We patched up the reels with used wood from home, replaced broken knives and guards and pulled the dirt out of the combine head. The next day, it was fixed and ready to go. My daydream had made three people very unhappy—

Daddy, the farmer, and me. A lesson learned; do not operate machinery when under the influence of daydreams. At least stop the vehicle and finish the dream before continuing. It's also a good lesson to "focus on the job at hand."

CHAPTER 20

It Was an Accident

Like most little farm boys growing up, I wanted to be with my dad whenever possible. I wanted to be like him, impress him, and do what he did. It was a hot summer day in the late 1940s. Daddy was trying out his new New Holland baler on the farm. He operated the farm with deep convictions not to waste anything. So it was with making hay. If the hay rake missed any hay it had to be hand raked into a row so the baler could get it or we would hand fork it onto the wagon. Times were tough and waste was wrong.

On the farm growing up there were many buildings surrounding the barnyard. I'll paint the picture so you can better visualize the scene. The house and barn were right next to the road. Below the house was an old outhouse next to a row of turkey pens separated by a little round house used to store feed in 55-gallon wooden barrels. Another row of turkey pens stood below them. To the right of them was the large machinery shed, a corn crib, and corn bins. Below the machinery shed was a double story chicken house with one room for hatching eggs and starting chicks; the one where "Strawberry" slept. Then there was a long chicken house aside of it and two pig pens below that.

Below all the buildings was a large pond which caught all the runoff water from around the buildings. In a semicircle around the upper side of the pond were a dozen or so small outdoor chicken shelters; where "Snowball" terrified rats.

With that many buildings full of poultry, you have a little idea of why my dad had no problem finding chores for me and David to do.

But back to making hay . . . grass grew quickly around all these buildings. Rather than just mow the grass each week and waste it, Daddy waited till it was tall and then cut it. After it was dry, he would bale it. We had to rake the dry hay into rows around the buildings and then Daddy would drive his John Deere B tractor pulling the baler behind to bale up the hay. At five and six years old, I liked to push the bales off of the baler's bale chute, just for fun I guess. Daddy had warned me to stay away from the baler in case he had to back up sometimes.

I can still visualize the scene in front of the double chicken house. There were two trees close by. One was a pear tree closer to the pig pens and that very large mulberry tree right in front and center of the double story chicken house. Old boards were always stacked up against the tree trunk for use around the farm. The hay had been raked by hand in one row weaving between the trees and the buildings ready for the baler. Daddy was trying to follow the row of hay best he could but couldn't quite make the turn. Wanting to be with Daddy and be his little farm hand, I was right there behind the baler pushing bales away from the baler. I'm sure Mom did not know I was there. I didn't know he was going to back up and I was not visible to him behind the big baler.

Before I knew what happened, I was gasping for breath as the bale chute began squeezing me against the chicken house wall. I could not yell or wave or anything. I couldn't breathe from being pinched tight against the wall. I think it was Grumpop who got Daddy's attention . . . or was it God?

Anyhow, fortunately he pulled forward finally relieving the pressure and I slumped to the ground hunched against the building with my knees up against my chest, crying and gasping for air. Daddy stopped the tractor and yelled for Mom who came frantically running to see what was wrong.

"John Merrill, honey, are you ok?" they both said. I was crying between short breaths and couldn't talk. I was holding my stomach and crying and they were holding me and trying to decide what to do. Daddy carried me into the house and laid me down on the couch. My breathing eased after a while but oh, how it hurt. They rushed me to Doctor Souder in Telford who checked me out and decided nothing was broken and that I was only badly bruised. I would be ok.

It was a very scary time for all of us but in the end we were so thankful that I wasn't killed or had to be hospitalized. That was my first accident on the farm but far from the last. Thankfully, I am still here to tell the stories. Who says angels are just fairies? Not me. God sent one when I desperately needed one.

Now ya'll be careful. God needs good farmers.

CHAPTER 21

Schoolteachers

How would you identify the best teacher you ever had? Would she be the one who was easy on you? Maybe good looking? Most creative? Let me guess, young, athletic and energetic? Surely not that teacher who made you work hardest, gave lots of homework and insisted you read every classic novel ever written?

That's the one I would pick—Ms. Schrack, my high school English/Literature teacher. As a high school sophomore who would have rather been out in the field farming, and I think she knew that by the way I daydreamed, I dreaded her assignments at the close of each Literature class.

"Listen up class, your assignment for tomorrow is: Read the next three chapters of *Tale of Two Cities*. (She may as well have assigned the entire novel!) Also, study those vocab words in the current *Reader's Digest*. There will be a comprehensive pop quiz on Friday." And with a friendly smirk, she said, "Have a nice evening" and dismissed the class.

"Yeah, right. I'm supposed to have 'a nice evening' while reading till midnight," I'd complain.

I was a slow reader, probably because my mind was not on reading. It was more likely on Susan or farming but not reading. Vocab words were a bit easier but no fun either. Now, why in thunder would I choose Ms. Schrack as one of the best or *the* best teacher I ever had? I'll tell you why, but let me start with my first grade teacher.

Ms. Betty Clemmer was one of the sweetest, kindest, nicest teachers I remember. She was soft-spoken and never intimidating. I can remember sitting on my little fold down desk seat, sharing the first reader with someone while we took turns reading.

"This is Dick. See Dick run. Oh, here is Jane. See Dick and Jane run."

If someone stuttered or had trouble reading, she would just politely say, thank you and ask the next pupil to begin. She was a great teacher for first grade.

Ms. Detweiler taught second and third grade. Like Betty, she wore a white covering on her head, and a long plain dress as all Mennonite women did. All girls wore dresses. Ms. Detweiler is remembered for being extra kind, gentle and patient. Many years after we moved to Sullivan County, she and a friend stopped by our house to say hello. She looked much like I remember her even 40 years later.

Fourth grade teacher, Ms. Benner seemed very young and pretty. Seems like all my teachers were pretty. Her dark hair was pulled tightly back under her white prayer covering. She was soft-spoken and kind. Clear with directions and helpful when we had problems, I have little recollection of good or bad experiences there. Later in life she married a man who became a bishop in the Franconia Conference. It was *that* man, Isaiah Alderfer, who approached Susan and me at age 20 to consider moving to Sullivan County to help with the church in Estella.

Ms. Kennel was taller and pretty. I did say pretty, not prissy . . . meaning, no one messed with Ms. Kennel. If she found any of us boys clowning around or goofing off during class, she'd simply stroll back to our desk and ask us to lay our hands on the desk. One swift slap across the knuckles with her trusty foot ruler stung *ga-nunk* (Dutch for enough) to make us think twice the next time we thought about causing trouble. (Guess you noticed, I have not yet mentioned what she taught.) For some it took stiffer discipline. Below our classroom was the coal furnace room. There were lots of pipes coming from the large octopus-shaped furnace producing plenty of heat. If the wooden ruler didn't correct our wrong, the heater room usually did.

Now, I think she made certain the janitor accompanied us there for a short visit. I don't recall any visits personally. Lest you credit Ms. Kennel as the big bad wolf teacher, I'll beg your pardon. She was a good math teacher. And no, she wouldn't stand a chance in today's teaching world, and I'm thankful for that. However, I don't recall any problem with smoking, shootings, or drug-related issues.

It was in her grade that I learned about "bullies." It's strange how someone who you thought was your friend can turn on you when under pressure to belong. So, on a dare from one of the more popular boys this unnamed friend grabbed my shoe rubber and threw it up on the roof where it rolled into the rain gutter and stayed. I fought back the tears until I got home. My dad took a ladder and retrieved it and we went on with life.

Sixth grade moved us into the newly-built FMS, Franconia Mennonite School building. It was a brick building just big enough for probably six small classrooms. No cafeteria, so we carried lunch as before. Prior to sixth grade, once a week, our moms brought a hot meal to school for the class you were in. Mom used to bring great meals. Around Thanksgiving, she'd bring a full-course turkey meal. It was so good, and I was so proud. But that stopped after fifth grade.

Ms. Krady was different in many ways. She was short, not thin, older, single and cross-eyed. Poor soul, I think she was a good teacher but had difficulty keeping control of her class. "Dennis the Mennis" kids quickly found their way under her skin. To her surprise and their delight, they devised schemes to get her disoriented and distracted, then angry.

I will admit to adding to her frustrations. May's warm sunshine brought dormant flies back to life in our classroom. A few of us mischievous minded fellows devised a new sport. Pull threads from your shirt, catch a fly sitting on your desk with a swift swipe of your hand, holding the fly under the desk, tie the thread onto the fly's leg and let it fly. The long thin thread will slow it down enabling everyone to be refreshingly distracted. But who was responsible? That was difficult to determine.

She tried the ruler method, extra homework, staying in at recess but only a trip to see her brother in the principal's office proved effective. I got to visit him one time. He was almost as strange as his sister, but somehow we graduated to seventh and eighth grades. Poor gal, she never really had a chance with the rowdy boys.

I'm now twelve years old and in seventh grade. A young male teacher who just returned from serving his 1W alternate military service in Jordan was assigned to seventh grade. Mr. Stayrock. What he taught well that I remember best was Current Events. He was full of life and great stories and knew how to keep our attention. His regular, enjoyable side tracks were about his experiences in Jordan. It was quite interesting. Thanks Millard!

It was around seventh grade where my ping-pong skills began to develop beyond just getting it across the net. In the basement of the new grade school was a storage room barely big enough for a ping-pong table.

At recess, or after school, kids would gather there to play "round table." The next year a table was put in the new bus garage and an eighth grader, Henry Longacre, taught me how to do "spins." I was on my way to winning the championship ping-pong tournament at C.D. in ninth grade. I just had to sneak in that little bit of information.

Mr. Richard Detweiler was a prominent Mennonite pastor and our principal for two years before he accepted the principal position when Christopher Dock School began. He taught us Bible.

We were required to learn whole chapters of the Psalms, and portions of the New Testament. At the time, I was not happy doing so but later in life I was and am ever so grateful.

Fifty years later, I can still quote many of those scriptures or at least refer to them familiarly. I only wish Bible was taught and even required in our churches and homes today. It was Mr. Detweiler who first introduced us to classical music until Hiram Hershey took over the music classes in seventh and eighth class. Mr. Hershey was much more aggressive with classical music awareness and in teaching us to sing four-part harmony. I so appreciate his persistence and insistence in acquainting us with various forms of music beyond our culture of singing hymns, acapella. As a 12 year old, I could care less about classical music, with one exception. One day he introduced us to a piece I was very familiar with, but I had not known the name of it. He opened the lid of the phonograph (that's an electronic invention of the '30s that plays 78, 33, and 45 rpm hard disk shaped records) loaded the record on the machine and announced the name of it. "This is a piece you will be required to learn. You will be tested at the end of this week. This one is entitled 'The William Tell Overture.'"

As soon as it began to play, my buddy Lowell, and I smiled excitedly recognizing it as the theme tune of our favorite radio show, "The Lone Ranger." Of course Mr. Hershey went on to explain the theory behind that classical . . . which I don't remember.

Again, it was Mr. Hershey who gained recognition as one of the most skilled and favored Choir and Chorus directors in the Franconia Mennonite Conference and beyond. It began at FMS when I was in 7th grade. We were required to stand on stage in our respective voice sections and learn our parts. As a young boy, I began as an alto until my voice changed and I learned tenor which I enjoy to this day.

However, the most significant part of my eighth grade experience was not the teachers nor my classes. It was not what I learned or didn't learn. It was that pretty, dark brown-eyed girl with pigtails tied up in a bun and wearing a prayer covering. Those deep dark waves of hair draping over her smooth forehead . . . that one with the sweetest, cutest smile of all the girls. Her name was Susan Landis. Where did she come from? Why had I not seen her before? I began to ask other kids about her and learned enough to know I wanted to get to know her better. Our love had been born.

It was Mr. Hershey who birthed the "touring chorus" for the 11th and 12th grades at Christopher Dock Mennonite High School. Susan and I both had to try out for both the junior and senior chorus and touring choruses to be privileged members.

Susan loved horses.

Hiram convinced the school board to lease Hageys Bus Service of Franconia, to take the chorus as far as Orville, Ohio, to sing in Mennonite churches in the Spring of each year. We would tour for a week singing in many churches and staying in Mennonite homes.

The biggest excitement for me was being close to Susan while we sang and sitting with her on the bus. Oh, the thrill of young love!

I was delighted to stand just one row behind and two away from Susan. I stood next to my good buddy Merrill Landes singing tenor. Not far away stood a skinny boy singing tenor who began to show promise of greatness. Rodney Derstine was an ordinary Mennonite boy from the community. His voice was so clear and sharp that Hiram pushed him to take voice lessons and major in music. He ended up traveling the world as an opera singer. Unfortunately, he died young. But he made his mark in the world. I only hope it was a mark that impressed God.

Speaking of Mr. Hershey, who we often called Hiram, besides being a qualified and skilled choir director, he was a driver ed. teacher. Later in life he spawned his own real estate business selling farmland. He actually was one of the agents we used to try selling the Souder Farm Estate in Telford, but to no avail. Yes, I have fond memories of Hiram. I also recall practicing with a men's octet in his farmhouse in Salfordville, Pa. My sister, Joan, sang in several of his choirs over the years. Thanks Hiram, and bless you.

As I said prior, Mr. Richard Detweiler was called to be the first principal of C.D.M.S., Christopher Dock Mennonite School where my sister Joan, my brother David and I went. Emma and Kass, Susan's older sisters were the first head cooks at C.D. They retired after 25 years as head cooks and were a tough act to follow to say the least. Back to my memories of Mr. Detweiler.

While principal of C.D. and pastor of a Mennonite congregation, he taught accounting and Bible. He was also a fast runner in baseball and a good basketball player. Few administrative people attained to the respect he deserved and the humility he portrayed. Even when required to do "the dirty work" he was respected and appreciated. Let me explain. For whatever reason, and I say that because I do not remember why, he took me home from C.D. late one day. What I do know is that I was detained an hour after school for some offense I caused that ticked off Ms. Schrack. (My favorite teacher . . . remember?) It was likely for talking or cutting up in class. Ms. Schrack didn't take well to that or any other pranks. So I needed a way home. Kind Mr. Detweiler offered to take me home since our place was on his way home. I remember riding in the front, sitting too close to "the principal" in his black Plymouth sedan. Funny thing was, he never asked me about the reason I was detained but made small talk about my farm life and sports. It was a rather positive experience that could otherwise have stained my reputation and my self-respect. But thanks to dear Mr. Detweiler, he actually boosted my self-image. A lesson to be learned for me and you. "Do unto others the way you would have them do unto you." Yes, the golden rule!

My first history teacher, Mr. Alderfer, was big and bald but not bad. What I recall most was how he engaged those who spoke out and seemed to enjoy history. Folks like me, who had no interest in history (back then) got little attention and struggled to earn C's in his class. Nothing against him, just the way it was. "Greaser, Bruce, Miriam and Kooker" were all "A" students and seemed to know the answers to all his questions while I would be looking out the window watching for Susan to walk by or a tractor plowing in the distance. Rinnnnggg . . . end of class, and off we went to another class.

Fresh-out-of-college Mr. Kauffman, along with his charisma and big bass voice, earned him a lot of happy students. He loved teaching P.O.D., history and physical education and was easily sidetracked which made learning fun and interesting for us. When he called your name with that deep booming voice, there was no guessing who he spoke to. He added an awesome bass voice to the men's quartet. As a young man, he sported a dark black crew cut. After more than 25 years of teaching and retirement, his hair turned a silver white and he grew a full face beard. Nice guy, that Mr. Kauffman, and a great Christian influence on his students.

Mr. Ben Hess was our basketball coach as juniors. Merrill and I were point guards but Merrill, being a bit taller, got more time than I. Mr. Hess knew his stuff on the court and in history class. His slightly crossed eyes behind those thick glasses seemed to always be smiling as he sat on the edge of his desk expounding the lesson. I liked him. When the news of his death came, I could hardly believe it. He had a large family and was a great dad, husband and teacher. He was only about 40 years old. Most importantly, he loved the Lord and was a great mentor.

Stanley Shenk was our Bible I & II and senior health teacher. He was well versed in the Bible and liked to tell stories and jokes and then laugh at them. A bit strange. In family life class, his honesty and frankness made me cringe a bit. I never heard frankness on sex anywhere else and was not used to hearing it, let alone with girls sitting next to me. Looking back, I appreciate his openness to discuss relevant issues in a safe and Christian atmosphere.

Mr. Hartzler also came to us fresh out of college as a science, business math and chemistry teacher. He was my science teacher but I think his first love was astronomy. More about Roy in another chapter.

Paul Hackman was our shop teacher. He hailed from Canada and was a minister in Norristown, Pa. He was soft-spoken, a little too easygoing but understood the use of shop tools. At least four of us senior boys decided to build desks. Two of us opted to use walnut wood. It smelled wonderful and had a rich grain.

Back then, it wasn't so expensive. Though it took most of the year to finish, it was well worth the time and determination. I used it for about 50 years until it needed some repair work on the drawer slides. So there it sits, sadly waiting in my shop for me to get at it.

Mr. Reinford, a very conservatively dressed Mennonite, taught German and math. I think he was brilliant by what Susan told me. He spoke German like he'd been raised in Germany. He taught math and algebra like an Einstein. Though small in stature, his speed on the track was unsurpassed as was his quickness on the basketball court. When speaking to him you couldn't help notice his eyelids blinking. I've heard that's one small sign of brilliancy. No, don't try blinking fast, it doesn't help. I tried it. I didn't have him as a teacher, but Susan would tell me about his heavy homework load and would stay up past bedtime studying because of it.

They called him Willy and he came to C.D. from Ohio as a young man. Willis Miller taught biology, general science and boys' physical education. He was a cousin to Susan and my buddy Merrill. Again, he was not one of my teachers but Susan had him for biology. Ironically, he was ordained as minister of Salford Mennonite Church and Susan and I were the first couple he married. He done well, we lasted for a lifetime.

Janet Martin was the business education teacher. She taught me bookkeeping and typing. She knew her stuff and taught it well. She was Susan's homeroom teacher and class sponsor. She and Pearl Schrack, my English teacher, lived together most of their lives. Ms. Martin was also a drama teacher and was involved with all the major plays the school put on. Great job Janet. Thanks for putting up with me. Without your typing class, how could I be typing this book? I'm ever so grateful to you.

Ms. Pearl Schrack, teacher of Literature and English I, II, III, IV, V, VI, and more. Well, that may be exaggerated. Ms. Schrack, as with most of the teachers, came directly from college to C.D. Young, pretty, smart and energetic, she had no trouble handling a large class. Rowdy boys or girls didn't intimidate her. Rather, she could intimidate them if need be.

Discipline involved staying after class or after school to study quietly or write a phrase 1,000 times what you did wrong and why you won't do it again. That had a way of righting wrongs.

For as often as I was discovered daydreaming in her class, I wonder that she didn't expel me. Ms. Schrack had a way of seeing the potential in a student—especially in those who seemingly were not interested in English or Literature. By the end of the year, you found yourself liking her in spite of the discipline you may have encountered. She did a grand job as our class sponsor and motivator. Always smiling, she found a way into my heart. The few times I had to stay after class as an underclassman caused me to think harder. As hard as I struggled to keep up with reading those dreadful novel assignments, they were good for me.

While many complained and struggled when it was time to diagram sentences for reading and literature, I excelled. Go figure. I just found it interesting. By the end of my senior year, Ms. Schrack had become a favorite teacher of mine. She pushed me beyond my comfort zone and thus I learned more. Our yearbook, called the *Schul-Andenken*, was dedicated to her.

In the front cover of my copy she wrote the following statement; **"You deserve much more than thank you for all your hard work and good cooperation, but thank you just the same. Sincerely, Pearl P. Schrack."** Well, Pearl, I don't know what you saw in my work, but you saw deeper than I did. For that and believing in me and so much more, I thank you from the bottom of my heart.

As of today, October 2012, she is still doing some emailing and reading. She still lives with Ms. Janet Martin near Telford, Pa. God has been good to them and they have been good to so many others. Bless you my dear teacher and friend.

These and more have taught and influenced who I have become. The saying goes, "You can lead a horse to water but you can't make him drink." I would add; "You can teach a person something but you can't make him learn." To learn, you have to want to . . . same as a horse led to water. That which I had an appetite for, I learned quickly and deftly.

My only regrets are that my appetite for learning in school was too small. As I aged, my appetite for learning increased dramatically. Why? I think it must be human nature. Encourage your kids to read, to write, to listen, to think, to be quiet and rest, to appreciate the small and simple things in life and to respect their parents, leaders, elders and TEACHERS. Thank you.

CHAPTER 22

Our High School Days

. . . written to my family after Susan's death

L ooking back, it is baffling how 68 years of my life slipped by so quickly. On the other hand, as I rummage through boxes and piles of papers, photo albums, notebooks, files, *Schul-Andenkens* (school yearbooks), journals, love notes and cards, I see how crammed full of *life* those years were.

It's mid January. Snow covers the ground. My dog, Toby, watches wishfully from the bed, softly growling at birds on the feeder just outside my glass door.

I just finished browsing through the '58 to '61 *Schul-Andenkens* from C.D. Looking intently at Mom's pictures revived many poignant memories. Much of the time I was found next to her. From her freshman year, a spark of attraction ignited a fire within us. Mom was a popular girl though a bit shy. On most of the pictures, her head is tipped slightly but always with that famous smile.

Junior-Senior banquets were a big deal at C.D. They were the Mennonite version of the "prom." The juniors had the responsibility of performing a live play for the seniors' entertainment, after serving a grand meal. Each junior class chose a theme for the evening and decorated accordingly.

Mom's class transformed the gym into an old Venetian street scene. The footbridge, which crossed the bright blue canal, approached a fountain decorated with flowers. The tasty, Italian food and music complemented the setting for their theme—"The Merchant of Venice." Lots of square card tables covered with red and white checkered tablecloths were set for guests. Waiters and waitresses dressed in colorful formal Italian attire, stood ready to serve us. When the meal was finished, we turned our chairs toward the stage and the curtains opened on a dimly-lit street in the historic city of Venice.

Whoever directed the play had great taste in choosing characters. Let me attempt to describe Mom's part. The scene which catches my attention portrays two couples obviously in love. Mom and another girl are seated on separate benches as the guys are on one knee holding the girls' hands. Stanley is gazing at Mom like he intends to propose. Mom's long, dark brown hair is pulled back and pinned with barrettes letting half of it drape over her right shoulder accenting her pure smooth smiling face.

Her dark eyebrows and lashes frame those deep dark brown eyes. The full-length pastel dress flows around her slender waist and a large, wide white collar is buttoned tightly around her slim soft neck.

I'm thinking, *Who wouldn't want to propose to her, for cryin' out loud!* I'm tellin' you, she was an angel fresh out of heaven. Now she's one up there.

Susan, probably 16 or 17 years old.

The next scene shows her standing with the other girl while some guy is shaking a paper at them and yelling at them. She has her head slightly tipped with no smile. But her countenance is smiling in spite of the scolding the guy is giving them.

Watching her perform in those scenes provoked mixed feelings in me. I was so proud of her ability to capture the character. She did it so well, looked so great, and was so charming. Everyone complemented her for it. She deserved every bit of praise she got. My problem was dealing with jealousy. As I watched her in plays, cuddle up to the guys or watched them come on to her, I was too immature to separate her performance with actual life. It accentuated my immaturity.

After the play when we had a chance to get together, she could tell I was struggling with something. "So what did you think of it?" she would ask.

"You sure do a great job with acting. I just have a problem with Stan and Rodney coming on to you like that. That's all," I said.

Her reaction was always the same. "You know it's just a play. And you know I have nothing for them. Don't you?" she'd say, feeling a little hurt. "I'm just doing my part and having fun with it. You know I'm committed to you, hon."

"Yeah, I know that, but that's just the way I feel. I'm sorry." I didn't know how else to explain it. It would take some talking through and after a few days, I'd be over it and she could tell I was okay again.

If only I could have had the same insights I have at this age, it would have saved us many prickly discussions. Mom was so friendly, such a looker, and maybe . . . just a little . . . flirty, may I say? And the guys loved it. For sure, I wanted no other girl but her.

Between Mom's freshman and senior years at C.D., she became steadily more involved with student life on campus. As a freshman, she was chosen to represent her class on student council. That same year, she passed tryouts for the junior chorus, played softball and excelled in track, in a skirt. Yes, no jeans, slacks or pants allowed in those days.

Her sophomore year she joined the nurses' club. But in her junior year she didn't have time for that. She was class treasurer and both of us were on student council and the athletic club. That surprised me that she was voted onto the athletic club. Guess I forgot how involved she was with baseball, basketball and track. The next two years she continued to serve on student council and as treasurer in her senior year. Both of us sat together on the religious life committee in her junior year and both of us sang in the acappella and touring chorus.

Each year at C.D., one graduating boy and girl is chosen by faculty to receive the coveted "Christopher Dock Award." It is the most highly-valued award presented in recognition of all-around campus citizenship, leadership and scholarship during the four years of high school.

"And this year's Christopher Dock Award goes to . . . Susan Landis." The applause was long and loud. She was astounded and blushed with amazement as her name was announced. But everyone affirmed that decision and commended her for the reward. So, you can see the kind of character quality person your Mom was. I was always so proud of her.

In comparison, my reward in high school was . . . you guessed it, ping-pong champ. Speaking of ping-pong, let me tell you that story. If you remember, I wrote about practicing ping-pong with an older, more experienced neighbor weekly for some time.

So by the time I got to C.D., I knew how to put some good English, better known as spins, on the ball. It took most competitors quite a while to figure out how to return them. That gave me an edge which rewarded me with winning tournaments already as a freshman.

A sign-up sheet was posted for intramural ping-pong tournaments. Then a schedule was posted pairing classmates first. If you won, you moved up to the winning bracket until only two were left. An afternoon date and time was scheduled for the championship match. Senior Jake Rittenhouse was set to play me, a freshman. I can see it now:

The ping-pong table sat under the overshoot of the renovated barn, just outside the cafeteria and below the gym; Grebel Hall, the place where everyone gathered to get their ride home at the end of the day. Interested people stood around to see if it would be a fair match or a blow out. Best out of three 21-point games wins the championship. Me, a freshman, facing Jake, a senior, was a bit intimidating. He was known for his big slams.

The 55-year-old table I learned on.

Long story short, I won. Most were shocked to see a youngin' like me take on a polished senior and win. I surprised him with spins and an ability to return some slams. The label stuck and after 50 years classmates still ask me, "John Merrrill, ya still playing ping-pong?" To their surprise, I tell them, "Oh yeah. I play a couple times a week when possible."

HIGH SCHOOL SPORTS

At C.D., sports were limited to intramural only. The school was too small to compete with local public schools. I played baseball, basketball, ping-pong and ice hockey. No uniforms or equipment were provided.

Besides ping-pong, all four high school years, my buddy Merrill and I played point guard on our class basketball team. Merrill was a bit taller giving him a slight advantage but we enjoyed playing together. There was only one black student in the whole school. He was two grades ahead of me but we became great friends. His nickname was "Weasel," probably because he was so agile and quick making it a challenge to guard him. After school sometimes we would mess around and he'd show me some awesome moves on the court.

Our class' first-string basketball team consisted of my cousin, Harold "Kooker" (center), Glen "Sonny" Landis (forward), Merrill Landes (point guard), Larry Kulp (forward) and myself (guard). Others who joined us were Sam Kulp, Merv Zook, Ernie "Greaser" and Henry Longacre.

Kooker was a fighter and very competitive. Sonny could run like a deer and jump like a kangaroo. Merrill and I tended to be trickier with our moves and passes.

In baseball, I played either of two positions but usually catcher. I loved playing catcher since it was an active position similar to pitching which I did on occasion. Merrill usually pitched or played left field. He was a natural.

Ice hockey was probably my favorite sport. The school built a new pond on campus in my freshman year. It provided many days of action on the ice during gym class, after school or during scheduled intramural games. In one of Mom's school diaries, she wrote the following: "I watched JM play hockey today and he got 3 of the 5 goals to help beat the other team . . . " I got lots of practice on our farm pond.

The only other sport I excelled in was the high jump on field day. A new technique was being developed in that era. The style was to roll over the high bar on your back and somehow, land on your feet. I think we had a mattress there on top of a sawdust pit. There's a photo of me doing just that in my senior yearbook. The highest I could clear was 5'0". Wonder what I could clear now . . . maybe 3'.

Your Mom was no slacker either in sports. She was a speed runner, occasionally winning the 100-yard dash. She competed in the 440-yard relay.

She was a guard for the girls' basketball team all four years in high school. On the softball field, you'd find Mom with a glove on third base ready to go. She was a good hitter too.

Together, we loved to play Parcheesi, scamper, racko, rook, Uno, and Memory. Some nights we'd get a puzzle out and work at it.

We did some paint-by-number pictures too when we were dating. We especially liked to ice skate together every winter while we dated. After we married, we continued to skate whenever the ice permitted. Sullivan County's ice skating window is very small due to snow.

On rare occasions, we'd get to attend a public school game Friday or Saturday nights. It was usually at Souderton Area High School for football or basketball. Watching those guys play somehow made me feel small and less athletic. They had hundreds of kids to choose from and the biggest and best got to play. The 50 cent ticket was well worth the thrill of watching Souderton beat up on Upper Perk or North Penn.

CHAPTER 23

One Foggy Night in 1960

It was one of those damp dreary Spring days. Susan and I had spent the evening together which meant likely from 6:30 to midnight. When I drove over to her house in Harleysville that evening, the roads were wet from rain but no fog.

After our date at the Salford youth social, we went to her house and as usual, played some board games. Susan made a couple of toasted cheese sandwiches for us and Emma dished out some homemade vanilla ice cream.

Before we knew it, it was getting time for me to go home. Midnight was the standard curfew for me to leave and I wanted to be a worthy future son-in-law.

My shiny black '57 Chevy sat at the end of the walkway ready to go and after a long goodbye, I headed home. The fog began to thicken as I drove past the church and around the corner past Hartley's Garage. I slowed down knowing there was a stop sign coming up soon. Rt. 113 intersected the road I was on and I hoped the fog would soon lift to make driving safer. It did. But at every low spot I encountered thick fog. Fortunately, there was a white line on the edge of the road and I slowed down to keep an eye on it.

Sweet tunes floated in my car from the radio set on 1160 AM—Wheeling, West Virginia. It was where I reset the radio when I left Susan, since she was no fan of country western music. It generally only took 10 minutes to drive the five miles between us. I passed Joe Clemmer's house, at least I think I did, and the fog was beginning to close in tight. "For cryin' out loud, where's the edge of the road?" I said talking to myself in frustration.

By now there was such a thick blanket of fog that no windshield wipers, bad language, fog lights or white lines helped. I'd been driving the last mile with my head out the window trying to follow that line. Finally, I braked to a stop hearing gravel rattling against the car. I couldn't tell where I was except that I was somewhere on Rt. 113 past Clemmer's. I left the car running with the lights on and got out with a flashlight to look around. Those days we had no flashers to turn on. If we wanted flashing lights, we had to buy portable ones and carry them in the trunk or use flares. I had neither. As I was assessing the situation, I heard a car and saw lights slowly approaching. I heard guys' voices and as it pulled alongside of me, I recognized the car as Merrill's '57 Ford Fairlane. He and a buddy were on their way home as well, going the opposite direction.

"John Merrill, *wass dangscht? Bishda alrecth?*" (What do you think? Are you okay?) Merrill said in his Dutch slang laughing. "Man, this is thick soup, I'm just crawling along while Sonny watches the white line." Sonny was one of our close friends.

"Tell me about it," I said. "I had to stop and check if I was still on the road."

We talked awhile and decided it wasn't going to get any better so we may as well turtle on home. The fog must have lifted cause I don't recall any problems after our little encounter that night.

Remember, there were no cell phones, no pay phones nearby and not many houses around. Anyhow, why would we go to a house for help around midnight? We didn't!

I was happy to be home safely and the next day called Susan to tell her our "foggy night episode." She was relieved to hear of no accident and a safe return.

It's one of those nights I didn't forget.

-Written December 20, 2011

CHAPTER 24

Road Trips While Dating

There was no place I'd rather be than with my "sweet Susan" driving some-where in my '57 Chevy. As we got older, her Mom got more relaxed with her curfews and the places we went.

Harry Bristo's Cinema in Philly was an old converted theater where they showed the latest Christian films. Occasionally we'd take another couple with us to see movies like "Ben Hurr" or "The Robe." Ben Hurr had some violent scenes where Mom would squeeze my knee or my hand quite hard and lean into me. I'm not sure if she was that scared or just part of romance. Either way, it was just fine.

"We got time, how 'bout we stop at the Pixy for a milk shake?"

"Sounds great to us," Janet said.

Mom tightened her scarf and pulled her little pink gloves on. It was win-ter and the car wasn't warm yet. Turning her head slightly towards me with her rosy cheek next to mine, she whispered, "My mom won't mind as long as we're home by 11:30. It's been a long day ya know."

"No problem. As soon as we get our order, we're outta here," I said.

It was Saturday evening and she'd already been up since 4 a.m. for market. By the time we drove in the long farm lane, the conversations had stopped.

"We're home honey, wake up." She wearily lifted her head from my shoulder and sat up.

"See ya, Janet. See ya, John. It was a fun night," she said as we got out of the car and headed in the walk.

It was midnight. The porch light and only the little light above the couch was on; a sign that everyone else was in bed.

"I gotta get to bed, hon," she said. We stood quietly between the outer and inner doors of the thick stone walled farmhouse embracing for a moment.

"Thanks honey, it was a fun evening. I love you," I said.

My first car—'57 Chevy BelAir.

With that melt-your-heart smile, she kissed me and just before closing the door softly said, "I love you too, goodnight. Oh, and call me tomorrow after church, okay?"

"Okay," I said and walked out under the crystal clear, starry sky to my car.

"Country Roads - take me home - to the place I belong
PENNSYLVANIA - Mountain mama -
take me home - my country roads

I hear her voice in the morning hours - she calls me -
the radio reminds me of my home
far away - and drivin' down the road I get a feeling -
that I should have been home yesterday, yesterday . . ."
John Denver (exception - Pennsylvania)

Pristine fresh air, forests alive with wildlife, and quaint small farms scattered about mountain plateaus helped draw us to Sullivan County, in northern Pennsylvania. Our first taste of Sullivan County *together* was with the Rockhill Church MYF. Dave Clemens, a very kind, elderly gentleman from Montgomery County owned 500 acres on Bear Mountain. He had built a cozy, rustic cabin four miles back on the mountain.

He allowed church groups to use it. There were two other small cabins nearby. The guys stayed in one and the girls in Dave's cabin. Black and white photos show Mom and I standing next to each other in a group picture.

The 3-hour drive to Northern Pa. was a new experience. Route 80 was not built yet so we took all secondary roads through beautiful countrysides giving us plenty to talk about.

"Nice farm. That would be a neat place to live and farm," I'd say driving along.

"I guess so, if you like living out here in no-man's land," Susan said. Of course we didn't know a soul between home and the mountains. But we did have friends in Estella; the Goshows. Lowell was my best friend.

Spending time on Bear Mountain felt like being on another planet. No other people were seen within miles of the cabin. Deer, bear, turkey and other wildlife were abundant. No traffic nearby and all dirt roads. We learned what it meant to "spot deer" after dark. It came to be a competitive game discovering who could spot the most deer with bright spotlights. Fifty or sixty was not exaggerating.

The Rockhill Mennonite Youth Fellowship (MYF) gave a program at Estella Mennonite Church one Sunday. Our group brought more people than the little congregation ordinarily had on a Sunday morning. In the afternoon, Susan and I found time alone fishing at Camp Maple Lake just up and behind the Estella Church. Only God knew that 50-plus years later, our daughter and husband would purchase and operate that very camp formerly established by Mike's great-grandfather.

Susan & JM at 18 years old fishing at Camp Maple Lake.

CHAPTER 25

Centereach, Long Island, N.Y.

"Therefore, go and make disciples of all nations . . ."
Mt. 28: 19 & 20

When I was about 10 years old, my home church—Rockhill Mennonite—started a mission outreach in Centereach, Long Island, N.Y. One of my friends, Nevin Heebner, and his family moved there to help with the church work. Susan's brother, JR and his wife, Glenda, had moved there to do his 1W alternate military service. Glenda's Dad was ordained as pastor of the church. So about twice a year, our family visited them in Centereach. So both Susan's family and my family had connections to Centereach.

When I was 17, Susan and I drove there ourselves. I think the first trip we took Kass, Emma and her Mom along.

Five o-clock on a very cold Saturday morning in January, we left Susan's house for Centereach. Just three miles down the road, I noticed the temperature gauge rising above normal. The dumb thing kept creeping up until it registered "hot."

"Hey, I'm going to have to stop somewhere and see what's happening. My temperature gauge is on hot," I announced rather alarmed.

Emma, being the "take-control" type person, suggested, "Why don't you pull in here at I.T's and we'll wake Henry?" I liked the idea since he had a garage and we could pull inside out of the bitter cold and check it out.

I knocked sheepishly on his door and waited. After a while, the lights came on in the kitchen and the door opened. "John Merrill? What's going on?" Henry said standing there in his pj's.

"I think my radiator must have frozen up. We're on the way to Centereach and I better check it out. Could we pull it in your garage and check it out?"

"Sure, let me get some clothes on and I'll be out," he said.

I pulled the car inside and he shut the garage door.

"How 'bout we use the rocket heater to blow some hot air on the engine and see if that helps?" Henry said pulling it into place.

"That sounds like a good idea. I thought the antifreeze was set low enough but maybe not," I said hoping for the best.

We left the heater blow hot air on the car for a few minutes while the women waited in the car.

"There, that ought to do it. Try starting it up and run it for a few minutes," he said. We added some antifreeze for good measure.

By 6:00 a.m., we were back on the road and all was well.

Driving through New York City was a new experience for me. There were two tunnels to go through, tolls to pay and bumper-to-bumper traffic to contend with—very different than our country roads. Emma had been there a few times before and knew the way quite well.

"Turn to the right up here, John Merrill. No, not there, the next light," she said. "Now, look for the Long Island Expressway west."

We arrived in good shape, just a bit stiff and tired from driving five hours.

JR worked in a hospital for his 1W alternate service. He was an orderly and a very good one. He was strong, conscientious and compassionate; a good combination for working with hurting people. For seven years, Glenda and JR prayed for children. At last their first child, Kevin, was born. What a cheerful happy child he was. But it wasn't long before they discovered something was not right. Kevin had difficulty standing up and walking. JR was such a kind caring Daddy.

Many doctors checked him out putting him through all kinds of tests and x-rays. By the time he was three, he was in a full body cast. To this day he is still paralyzed from the waist down. But Kevin has a brilliant mind and now plays competition tennis from a wheelchair. JR and Glenda had strong faith and determination to do whatever possible to have him walk again. But it wasn't to be.

We stayed for the weekend, attending the little church and meeting new people. After a wonderful home-cooked meal, we left for home Sunday afternoon. By 11:30 p.m. we were back at the farmhouse in Harleysville, safe and sound. It was a great way to get to know Susan's family better.

CHAPTER 26

Stargazers

My first introduction to astronomy was in Mr. Hartzler's science class. Roy had a fascination with astronomy and wanted to share his enthusiasm. A few of us in the junior class took to his mentoring and learned to enjoy it as well. I was truly fascinated with the galaxies and constellations. He would schedule a night out in the parking lot at C.D. with anyone who wanted to learn about constellations.

"Bring a good flashlight along and dress warm," he said.

He had this astronomy guide which displayed all the visible constellations in the sky. As you revolved the two-piece guide, positioning it to the correct time of year, you could identify the stars. It was a great hands on learning tool. As you know, I can easily and quickly point out the Big Dipper with the tip of the cup pointing to the North Star. The North Star is the tip of the handle for the Little Dipper. If you take a good bright flashlight and point it at a star, it's amazing how you can identify them. Try it away from city lights. The winter sky is particularly bright and extraordinary. But then summer skies can be just as amazing on a clear night. You will be much more comfortable lying on the grass and stargazing.

In our senior year, Mr. Hartzler asked for four people to volunteer for a project. I volunteered with three other buddies of mine. The project was to hone down a 6" lens to be used in a new telescope for the class. It was nothing cheap. We set up shop in the basement of the Administration (AD) building, just below the library. It was an old, damp, dirt floor area with a low open beam ceiling.

We got to spend the next six weeks of class time down in the basement taking turns grinding and polishing that lens. He would come and check on us but we had plenty of liberty to goof off while one of us ground away at the lens. Susan and her friend, Janet, would peak down the stairs occasionally when she had study periods upstairs.

"Oh . . . my . . . gosh!" one of the guys whispered. "Look here."

We gathered around and to our embarrassment and horror, a small hairline crack appeared.

"Holy cow! Wait till Hartzler sees this. He's gonna kill us," Ron said softly but emphatically.

"What on earth happened?" I said nervously. I knew he would have a fit.

Merv just stared in unbelief as we stood looking at each other and the damaged lens.

To this day, I'm not really sure what did happen. But I do remember Hartzler's red, screwed-up face as he looked at the lens and back at us.

"Okay, boys. Tell me what happened."

Silence.

"Well? It didn't happen by itself. How did this happen?" he said still trying to remain in control.

"Uh . . . we were just polishing the lens when we noticed the crack," one of us said.

"Come on guys, who dropped it? A 6" lens does not develop a crack unless it's dropped," he said getting more agitated.

Silence.

"I'll see you guys in my classroom after school, and I expect some answers." He stomped up the steps and out of sight.

"What can we tell him? We're dead ducks now," Ron said.

The ending is still a mystery. We had no answers except that it developed a crack. I don't know if someone dropped it and didn't fess up or what. But the lens was history and Hartzler was not a happy teacher for the rest of that week. Who could blame him? It was the four of us who were irresponsible and to blame.

Mr. Hartzler eventually relaxed and we continued to enjoy stargazing with him. His patience and sacrificial volunteering on starlit nights was appreciated and gave me a new awe for our Great Creator. "Oh Lord, my God, when I in awesome wonder, consider all the worlds thy hand hath made. I see the stars . . . thy power throughout the universe displayed . . . " One of the great hymns of faith made famous at the Billy Graham crusades and sung by George Beverly Shea.

CHAPTER 27

Susan Landis Souder, LPN

THE FLORENCE NIGHTINGALE PLEDGE

I solemnly pledge myself before God and presence of this assembly; to pass my life in purity and to practice my profession faithfully. I will abstain from whatever is deleterious and mischievous and will not take or knowingly administer any harmful drug. I will do all in my power to maintain and elevate the standard of my profession and will hold in confidence all personal matters committed to my keeping and family affairs coming to my knowledge in the practice of my calling. With loyalty will I endeavor to aid the physician in his work, and devote myself to the welfare of those committed to my care.

Susan graduated from Christopher Dock High School (C.D.) the Spring of 1961. She was shocked to be chosen by the faculty to receive the coveted citizenship award,—"The Christopher Dock Award." I wrote about this in the "High School Days" chapter.

Out of seven girls in Susan's family, she alone had a passion to be a nurse. A classmate of hers, Sara Ellen Stoltzfus, better known as Sip had similar aspirations. Sip lived 45 minutes north of Harleysville in Douglasville, Pa. Her dad was a farmer and her mom a nurse.

Reading School of Nursing was only 20 minutes from Sip's house making it a convenient place to live while attending nursing school. It was a one year program instead of three years to get an RN (registered nurse) license. Susan chose to be an LPN.

Sip's family invited Susan to live with them while attending LPN school. Sip's brother, Dwight, was attending C.D. at that time and needed a place to stay during school days. It was the perfect set-up. Dwight could stay at Susan's house and Susan could stay at Sip's house. The only missing link was transportation on weekends. That's where I fit in. I gladly offered to be the taxi. I'd pick Dwight up Friday afternoon at school and we'd drive to his house where Susan was longingly waiting.

Sunday afternoon, she and I would set out for Douglasville and after visiting a bit, I'd take Dwight back to Susan's house.

No one in their wildest dreams would ever have guessed that 30 years later I would be building a house for Dwight on his very own airport strip in Sullivan County. But it happened. That young boy had become a large developer in the Reading area many years later and was too busy to build his own house in the mountains. So he contacted Rod and I—Brotherhood Builders. Oh the surprises of life.

But now, back to our story.

Susan and Sip enrolled in LPN school and both were accepted. She began her studies in late August, 1961. Sip shared her 100-year-old farmhouse bedroom with Susan. Sip's older brother, Marlin, ran the dairy farm since her father was getting up in years. Marlin liked to tease Mom about getting married—making her blush quite often. Nursing school was demanding. Learning body anatomy can be very interesting, intimidating and difficult simultaneously.

The best and most interesting part of her training were the practical classes. She loved working with the patients. Susan loved to serve and help people heal. She possessed a wonderful balance of compassion and tough love. She knew how to motivate sick and hurting people who needed to get up and get moving without pitying them. The drive back home was a good time to talk about her week. After asking me about my week she'd begin telling me her experiences.

"You wouldn't believe all we see in the hospital. Every morning we help patients get their baths. If they can't get to the bathroom, we help them wash up in bed."

Right away my mind was having visions of her bathing men, so I said, "What about the men? Are there male nurses or orderlies assigned to them?"

"Are you kidding? We all are expected to help men and women. You have to see them as patients in need. Some are very private and modest; others couldn't care less what I see. Oh, we get to see it all. Some men love it when they see young girls coming. I think they lay half exposed just so we DO see them. It grosses me out sometimes, but I'm getting pretty used to it," she said

I was beginning to see the makings of a great nurse. Things like that didn't bother her like it did some.

"They come in all shapes and sizes," she said with a grin.

I knew what she meant and pulled her close to me as we drove home in the dark on Friday night—alone, and so happy to be together every weekend.

"I'm so proud of you hon that you can do that stuff," I said, as she sat cuddled close with her head on my shoulder. I could tell she was tired. Studying day and night while working in the hospital takes its toll.

The 45-minute drive home gave time for lots of conversation if both of us were awake enough. Many trips we weren't. Okay, I wasn't. Many times she was tired but still wanted to talk. But getting me to talk when I was tired was like pulling teeth. Sorry, I lied. Being tired wasn't always the reason for not talking. I'm a dreamer and don't always like to say what I'm dreaming about.

You'd think I could learn to converse, at least with the one I loved so much. At least *she* thought so. I could have benefited from a good counselor or mentor in that field. My lack of conversation was the biggest point of contention between us until later in life. I think she finally gave up trying to change me. And I started to talk more. Just wish I'd have learned it much earlier in life.

Take a lesson; learn what you need to, however you can, while you can. Change yourself and stop trying to change your spouse or friend. Someday it will be too late for either.

God only knows how many trips we made back and forth to Douglasville that year. We did spend many hours in the car planning our wedding day. As you kids know, your Mom was always very organized and carried her planner with her. Even before we married she would write out "honey do lists" for me. It was a great way to see that things got accomplished.

Since we had no computers or cell phones, letters were sent by snail-mail. I still have some of our letters from that year. She kept all of them. There was a large box full of them. Talk about interesting reading. Hmmmm. Some I disposed of for obvious personal reasons.

Susan graduated from Reading School of Nursing in August of 1962. She studied hard and passed her State Boards. Just before our wedding day, November 10, 1962, she received her license in the mail. She was officially a Licensed Practical Nurse and was eligible for an LPN salary. Whoohoo! Every year till the year she died, she renewed that license, whether she worked or not.

She was trained to wear official nursing uniforms including the white cap, school of training pin and name pin. She was covered in white from toe to head—a stunningly attractive sight.

Susan practiced her career with dignity, abiding by the "nursing code of ethics" and the Florence Nightingale pledge. Check out this web site; (www.nursingworld.org).

Her first job was at Grand View Hospital, the hospital where I was born and yes, where Renee was born. *In his heart man plans his course, but the Lord determines his steps. Pr.16:9*—a proverb we highly revere.

Her second and last place of employment was at DarWay Nursing Home in Estella, Pa. She worked there for 13 years terminating in 1995 only because of a knee problem which was generated by cancer. She was head nurse on duty whatever shift she worked and held to high standards. Patients loved her. She was so conscientious and responsible. She was selfless and committed to the best care possible for her patients.

Nurse Susan

"Oh, Margie, don't you look sweet today? Yes, Don, I'll be there in a bit. I'm getting your 9:00 meds right now. Joe's bed needs to be stripped Betty, could you get him while I finish up these meds please? Thanks."

I haven't a clue how she kept her head straight with all the demands on her. I could never do it; bathing patients, charting everything, answering the phone and questions from the Aids, feeding, and tucking them in. Whew! It was a very busy place depending on the shift she worked.

"I dee bettie, I dee bettie," mumbled Mabel.

"I hear you, Mabel. I'll be right there." Susan had to interpret that phrase over and over each day, being the only words Mabel could speak after her stroke. Poor soul. She was so pleasant most of the time in spite of her handicap and Susan was so patient and kind with her.

Occasionally, she would ask me to bring a baby chick or baby duck or puppy in to Darway to cheer up the residents. It sure did wonders for their boredom.

How many nights did she spend caring for the elderly while we slept? How many Christmas Days and Easter Sundays did she work? No record to tell for sure. When she worked the 11:00 to 7:00 a.m. shift, she would try snatching a couple hours of sleep after tucking our kids in bed before going to work.

In the morning, there she was in the kitchen getting breakfast ready and writing notes for the teachers. Soon as the kids were on the bus she was on the couch. Lori or Mike would be playing in the playpen next to the couch as I went out to do chores or farm work. When they were old enough I'd take them with me so she could sleep.

If she was lucky they would play quietly or sleep long enough to get a couple hours herself. Oh, yes, *to be a nurse* . . . what does it take? Unless you are one, you and I will never really know.

There was rarely a tragedy or bloody scene that she could not handle. Take the day she got a call from a neighbor in tears crying "Come quickly." He led Susan to an outbuilding in the woods where she discovered his wife's body in a pool of blood—dead from suicide. Oh, dear God, have mercy.

Blood she could handle, mice—NO!

She has many pins, buttons and award certificates from serving at health fairs, blood mobiles, career days and as a hospice volunteer. Yet she never flaunted them.

Don't forget to celebrate nurse's day—May 6 each year . . . and kids, remember your Mom. All of you salute a nurse!

You've seen the bumper sticker; "Love a Nurse." Well, if you want a compassionate, loving, wife, *marry* a nurse. They make great lovers. If you're a single nurse, marry a farmer or a carpenter. You'll have plenty of opportunity to practice your skills.

Hard work, persistence, patience, conscientiousness and compassion define Susan's nursing code of ethics.

Nursing caps were originally a symbol not only of where a nurse went to school but also of the level of nursing training that she had obtained. This tradition stemmed from Florence Nightingale, the mother of all modern nurses. In the mid-1800s the general medical concensus was that it was more hygienic to have your hair covered. Furthermore, it was considered to be more appropriate for a woman in the company of men to wear a cap.

The nursing cap became a symbol of where a nurse schooled having a colored band which reflected the school. Your hat would go with you wherever you worked. Read more: The Significance of a Nursing Cap | eHow.com http://www.ehow.com/about_6595146_significance-nursing-cap.html#ixzz1Dnr1cJ3m

CHAPTER 28

Wedding Bells

NOVEMBER 10, 1962

"Hi honey. I was waiting for your call," she said tenderly. "Can you believe it, 36 hours from now, we will be married," I said. "No more waiting and wishing."

"I know. I'm so excited," the volume of her voice a notch higher. I could see her smile from the other end of the phone line as she sat on the bottom stair step with the door closed. No doubt she was twirling the black phone cord around her finger as she stared at her "to do list."

"Did you have a good day, sweetie? Did you get finished shelling corn? she said softly.

"Yeah, but you know Daddy. There's always more work to be done. Don't worry," I said in a calm voice, "he'll manage." Not that she was worried but she cared what I thought.

It had been a busy summer. Susan had spent the past year in nursing school at Reading School of Nursing. Graduation was in late August and she took her State Boards test in September. The pressure was finally off and fortunately she'd been promised a job at Grand View Hospital in Sellersville, Pa. Aunt Lizzy Etta worked there in cleaning and helped her find the job.

We had chosen November 10, 1962, to get married for a couple reasons. One, it was *after* harvest time, the busiest time of year on the farm. Two, Susan was finished with her nurses' training and with her license in hand as an LPN, she was ready to work. Also, we both loved Fall.

"Do we have everything on the list covered?" I asked. Knowing she was always on top of things when it came to planning ahead.

"I think so. I can hardly wait till you see me in this dress. Mary did the final touches on it last night. It is so neat and fits great," she said.

I wanted to kiss the phone as I said, "Honey, you'd look great in anything or nothing."

"Oh stop it," she whispered changing the subject. "Is everything set for practice tomorrow evening?"

"I think so," I said. "You have the list." If she kept the list, there was no worry about losing it or missing something. That I could count on.

After Friday night practice we went back to her house for our last time being single. We talked things over with Mom a while before closing the door to the living room where we spent many an evening playing games, talking, looking at pictures and just loving each other.

It was six years since we first noticed each other, and knew that we liked each other. We had dated all through high school becoming best friends and passionate lovers. Our diaries are proof of that pudding. Only by God's mercy and grace, His faithfulness to us, and our commitment to each other were we able to keep ourselves pure until marriage. We were humans created with the same passionate desires like anyone else.

Our wedding day dawned slowly under clouds and a light rain. By noon the wind picked up and the sun peaked out promising a nice day after all. Thank you God.

After a few chores, David helped me wash my black '61 Chevy Impala and fill it up with gas at the farm pump. I remember getting dressed up in our little bedroom—new black suits, white shirts, black bow ties and shiny black shoes. Bow ties were more formal than ties. Renting tuxes was not in the mix. Too expensive and by the bishop's standard . . . worldly.

About 1:30 it was time to leave the farmhouse and my parents who had tried their best to raise me to *follow the path of Jesus*. Thanks Mom and Daddy.

"Well," Mom said with a bittersweet, smiling face, "guess the big day is here. We'll be there soon, I love you." And with those loving words, she kissed and hugged me goodbye one last time as her oldest single son. On the way out the walk, Daddy came hurrying into the house to get ready, having just finished gathering the eggs.

Lowell my best man, and my cousin Harold, met David and I in one of the Sunday School rooms at Salford Mennonite Church to go over last-minute details with Pastor Willy Miller. Salford was Susan's home church. I think I hid our car in Merrill's garage.

Susan's best friend, Janet Swartley, was her bridesmaid of honor and two others. It was expected that she would stay out of my sight until I saw her coming down the aisle. Oh how we both anticipated that moment.

Six school friends were prepared to do special singing at the wedding and there would be congregational accapella singing as well. The time was set for 3:00. Why three o'clock? Because Saturdays were always market days and those of her family who had markets in Philly would have to quit early so they could be on time. Royden gave Susan off for this Saturday. She always went to market with him Saturdays, leaving at 4:00 a.m. and getting home around 4:00 p.m. and giving her Mom all her earnings. The week before was her last day to work for him.

At 3:00 the mixed sextet began to sing from the back of the sanctuary. On the second song, I led the guys in from the front "anteroom" as it was called, to stand before the pulpit for my bride. The church was almost full of family, friends and relatives, all staring intently at us.

My pulse rose in anticipation as the sextet began . . . *Jesu Joy of Man's desiring* . . . It was the bridesmaids' cue to begin their slow calculated walk to the front. Her Mom stood and turned prompting the congregation to stand.

At last, *here comes my bride. Can it actually be.* My face flushed and my chest began to pound with excitement. *My God, what a beautiful woman she is!* I thought. This is our day. The one we thought we couldn't wait for. She wore a white satin dress to just below her knees, covered buttons from the waist to the neck in the back, and pearly beads scattered on the front. She carried a small white Bible covered with roses. A picture-perfect bride, almost too much for me to contain myself. Her hair was dark and wavy held up with a net and a white mesh prayer covering placed neatly on top. Her beautiful face shone like an angel as she gave me that "good for our lifetime" sweet Susan smile, steadily getting closer as she carefully timed her steps. The sextet finished the song and she took her place next to me squeezing my hand tightly and still smiling.

"Who gives this woman to this man?" Willy said.

"I do," said her Mom softly but clearly for the last of her six girls. The congregation was seated and Willy began step by step leading up to the big question.

"Do you, John Merrill Souder, take Susan Landis to be your wife?" I wanted to SHOUT YES! but compliantly said, "I do."

Looking at Susan, he said, "Do you, Susan Landis, take John Merrill Souder to be your husband?"

"I do," she said without hesitation.

"You may now say your vows."

"I, John Merrill, take you Susan to be my wedded wife. I will love you and cherish you, care for you and provide for you, in sickness and in health, for richer or poorer, and forsaking all others, I will be faithful to you till death do us part." Susan said her vows and we knelt together as Willy prayed a blessing over us. The sextet softly sang *O Perfect Love, all human thought transcending* . . . and we stood up. The full impact and seriousness of those vows would one day be tested as by fire. Although very young, we meant every word.

Somewhere in there was a short message and some singing but what stands out next in my mind was the statement, "I now pronounce you husband and wife. What God has joined together, let no man put asunder." Looking at me with a smile, Willy said, "You may now kiss the bride." No veil to lift, just an angelic smiling face looking at me—ready and waiting.

"May I present to you, for the first time (and it was Willy's first marriage to perform) Mr. & Mrs. John Merrill Souder." The sextet sang something and off we marched up the aisle to the rear of the sanctuary to greet way too many people.

Pictures were taken on the front porch of the church and then into the car and over to Mosser's Studio in Souderton to the professional photographer for pictures. It wasn't proper or encouraged to take pictures in the sanctuary at that time.

The reception was at C.D. and Susan's sisters, Emma and Kass, planned a full-course dinner of beef, mashed potatoes, home-grown corn and all the trimmings plus pie and ice cream.

We changed clothes in separate rooms near the cafeteria, took a few more pictures and we were off to our new life together having little idea what the future held. We *did* know who held it.

We had reserved the honeymoon suite at Cross Roads Motel about 15 miles south of C.D. It cost us $14.00. We have pictures of the room and wonderful memories of that night. But it doesn't compare to the wonderful memories we were about to create in the 47 years to follow. God is so good. Thank you God.

Now all alone as I tenderly whisper to her every night before falling asleep, "I miss you so much, I loved you so much, and I still love you, honey." Her sweet voice echos back, "I love you too. Good night."

As we shared a bathroom for the first time and preparing to drive to Florida for our honeymoon, the fact that this passionate love life would end some day, seemed impossible.

"I'll take my suitcase out and check the oil in the car, honey. Be right back," I said. She was primping and straightening up the room as I spoke. We said a short prayer and off we went. No GPS, no MapQuest, just paper maps marked out by AAA for us to follow. Susan was the navigator and a good one. She sat close to me on the bench seat of the car with my arm over her shoulder instead of a seat belt, the map on her lap and her left hand on my thigh.

We enjoyed the new countryside, stopping for lunch before arriving at our chosen motel in Northern Tennessee. I remember the little motel room perched on a hill overlooking a scenic valley. The only other detail you will be told is that somehow, for some reason, her cute little nightie which she briefly and proudly wore, came up missing the next day. I remember her looking for it the next night saying, "Hmmm, I wonder where that is?"

"What?" I said.

"My nightie, it's not here. Actually, I don't remember packing it this morning. I must have left it in Tennessee." She smiled and gave me that shy sweet look. We both laughed figuring . . . so what.

I said, "Well, guess you don't need *that*."

We stopped in Southern Georgia overnight and the next night we spent at my great aunt and uncle's house in Florida. They were very hospitable but did not have a honeymoon suite. After visiting a bit, they showed us to our room and said goodnight. We looked at each other, both grinning and thinking the same thing. *Are you kidding? Single beds?*

We were snugglers and had no need for a queen or king-size bed. We started out close and never needed much room in a bed. Close is good. Closer is better. Just don't go to bed angry. Not that we *never* did, but seldom. It was another good night.

Newlyweds . . . almost 20 years old.

CHAPTER 29

Honeymoon—Early Married Life

Written in 2010

We had planned to be away for two weeks spending some of our time around Sarasota, Florida. Susan's Uncle Melvin and his wife Lizzy Etta lived there. Melvin was up in his 80s and still riding bicycle for exercise. He continued to do that until after his 90th birthday. Melvin's son and daughter owned a motel nearby so we stayed there one night.

Disney World did not exist in 1962. We spent two days at Busch Gardens and Cyprus Gardens. We have some gorgeous pictures of orchids growing on tree trunks draped with Spanish moss. We watched the water ski show. Most of the show displayed pretty girls dressed in skimpy bathing suits doing pyramids on water skis, until Susan had enough of that! Then there was the barefoot skier who I thought was an old man but was likely only in his 50s. Oh, and there was the water skier who went up a 100 feet in the air while holding onto the kite being pulled by a speed boat. It was an impressive show.

We toured an orange processing plant and bought oranges to send home. We picked our own oranges and grapefruits at Uncle Melvin's house to bring home. Fresh, juicy and sweet. A few days were spent sunning ourselves on the beach and looking for shells.

Just prior to Thanksgiving, we arrived home and it was poultry "dressing" time on the farm. That means Daddy hired relatives to help with killing and dressing turkeys, geese and ducks. Close to 200 head in the bottom of the barn. One room was set up for this purpose. We pulled around front of the barn, stopped and waved. They all came to the door in their messy attire to welcome us home. Daddy gave us a big smile and a nod as he continued holding a big turkey over the feather picker. That was normally my job. Susan even came out to help with Mom showing her the ropes. What brave women. I think Daddy was glad to have us back. "I'll be out after bit," I said, and parked the car to unload our suitcases.

We had remodeled Grammy and Grumpop's side of the house for our first abode. Our very own place to actually live and sleep together. *Wow, could it be!* I thought. I carried the suitcases up the winding wooden stairs from the kitchen to the bedroom. Daddy had hired a plumber and carpenter to add a bathroom and closet upstairs for us. We had helped to paint and wallpaper. Our large dresser and full-size mattress had to be lifted up on the roof with the tractor loader and brought in through a window weeks before we left for our honeymoon because the stairs were too narrow and steep. Everything was in place ready for housekeeping.

"Which side do you want to sleep on?" Susan asked, giving me first choice. A window and the bedroom door were next to the left side of the bed.

Actually thinking about protecting my sweetheart, I said, "I think I'll sleep on the left side next to the window."

She said, "That's good, I was feeling a bit uneasy about that side anyhow." So there it was. She slept on the right, me on the left. Everywhere we slept, be it in a motel, someone's house, in a camper, a tent, when we changed rooms or beds, that's the way it was. Today, without my honey next to me, I still sleep on the left—my dog Toby, now sleeps on the right side.

HALF OF THE FARMHOUSE . . .

With all that Daddy provided for us, I didn't know how good we had it. The rent plus utilities were part of my salary for working the farm. I could pull up to the gas pump by the garage anytime the car needed gas. Recently, I came across a bill from Young's Gas Company for 23 cents a gallon.

The entrance to our side of the house was through the enclosed porch. A choice of three doors led to our kitchen, living room or my parents' side of the house. The kitchen had an old bay window looking out over the small garden toward the barn. Our washer and dryer were in one corner next to the winding stairs to our bedroom or to the basement with pantry shelves at the top. A carpenter had built new birch cabinets and yellow Formica countertops. The dining room was between the kitchen and the sewing room (or den) and then the living room. It was more than enough space for a young family. My desk was in the den with a door leading to a hall and over to Mom and Daddy's side. I would use that door when going downstairs to the basement where my work clothes and boots were kept.

At the top of that stairs, Daddy had converted a small closet into a bathroom where we washed up after chores. If we needed a shower after a long hard day in the fields, we used the shower in the basement.

Upstairs we had a small bedroom to go through before stepping up through a very short door to our bedroom. I remember banging my head there often until I hung up a ribbon.

Occasionally, Susan had to work the second shift, 3:00 to 11:00 p.m., at Grand View Hospital. More than once, I tried my hand at baking cookies while I waited up for her. I can almost smell and taste those Snickerdoodles now. The house had a nice aroma when she came home.

Left to right: Donnie Shisler holding Renee, Joan, a friend, Susan, David sitting next to the friend's baby and Spotty.

CHAPTER 30

Alternate Service

Before we married, we had planned to sign up for Voluntary Service or 1W Service. These were alternatives to military service for people like us who had conscientious objections to war. I was in touch with an agency from the Mennonite Conference who was helping to find a placement for us. They were suggesting a State Farm in New Hampshire. Mom could work in the hospital and I would work on the farm for two years.

This passed the government's requirements for service to our country. Plans were underway for us to begin this service a year after marriage.

Must be God had some other plans for us which pleased my dad. He didn't like the idea of me leaving the farm. Susan began to feel nauseated in the mornings before work. Around May of 1963, we were surprised to find out she was pregnant. The surprise turned into joyful expectation as time went on.

As the summer heat simmered down and the Fall harvest was in full swing, it was also time to clean out chicken and pig pens before winter. The only front-end loader for this job was a 5-tine fork with a long wooden handle powered by a strong back and two hands.

David and I were cleaning out a pig pen downstairs in the barn on November 22, 1963, when our country music radio station was interrupted by a startling announcement—"President John F. Kennedy has been fatally shot as his motorcade rode along on Pennsylvania Avenue in Dallas. We do not have all the details yet but we will keep you posted," came the stunning news.

Our mouths hung open as we leaned on our forks dumbfounded. "I can't believe that," David said. "Me neither, what in the world happened?" I said wondering. In a short while, Susan pulled in the drive and came running into the stinky barn, dressed in her nice white nurse's uniform. She was big and pregnant. "Did you hear the news, Kennedy was shot," she said almost shaking. "Yes," I said. "We just heard."

We stood there listening as news of the historical event played out. We had no TV, only radio and news print to keep current in world events. Little did we know that this was a horrific historical event.

Fall gave way to winter and our first Christmas. There would be no tree for us since that was the way we grew up. According to the teaching of our church, a Christmas tree was a heathen practice. In simple words, it was "worldly." A scripture to support that claim is found in Jeremiah. Over time we no longer held convictions about that. So in years to come, we decorated a tree as part of our celebration of the coming of Jesus as a Baby in Bethlehem.

During the holidays we invited friends over to play games. December 28, 1963, Susan's best friend Janet, and her husband John, and Gerry and Margie came for the evening. They stayed until 11:00 p.m. As we climbed the wooden stairs to bed, she began to feel sick. She threw up and said, "I think I'm having contractions. Here's my watch, time them." It wasn't long before we were driving the seven miles to the hospital.

I was asked to stay in the waiting room while they took her to the delivery room. I don't remember how long a wait it was but it seemed pretty long. Not until our last child, Mike, was born in 1974 did they allow husbands into the delivery room.

"It's a girl!" the doctor said smiling at me. "Susan and baby are just fine." I was so excited and nervous. When they left me come in, there was my bride, now a Mommy, holding the sweetest little bundle I'd ever seen. Bunches of dark, wavy hair covered her head. And Mommy was wearing that beautiful angelic smile that never went away. We were just 20, almost 21 years old but proud as peacocks and grateful to God for a perfect little girl. We didn't have any idea what sex it would be so we were prepared for either.

Calling from a pay phone, I proudly announced to Grammy Landis and my parents, "It's a girl. Susan Renee . . . 6 lbs. 13 oz. with lots of dark hair," I said, all smiles as I spoke. I could hear my mom and Daddy's excitement over their first grandchild. For Grammy Landis, being a grandmother was nothing new. She must have had 20 or more grandchildren by that time. Nevertheless, they were very happy and would demonstrate it by helping us many times in years to come.

There's a photo somewhere and I can clearly visualize it, of Susan wearing a long black winter coat carrying three-day-old Renee bundled tightly in blankets ready to leave the hospital. A nurse was standing by her until I came with the car. Number one of four was in "the nest."

The bassinette was set up in the dining room next to the big cast-iron radiator—a nice warm spot to change baby Renee. No official parental training or classes were offered us by the medical profession. However, Susan had lots of practical experience with her nieces and nephews. She babysat for her older siblings quite often. So she was my teacher and a good one.

Now you must keep in mind there were no disposable diapers. We bought good cloth diapers and kept a diaper pail nearby. "Honey, how do you get them wrapped so tightly and how do you pin them?" I asked after a few clumsy tries.

"Here, let me show you, it's not that hard," she said grabbing both little chubby feet with one hand separated by two fingers. "First, go wash your hands," she said while folding a diaper the right way. "Now . . . just hold her up like this, put half of it under her bottom and lay her down on it. Then pull it up between her legs snugly. Using the big safety pins, slip the pin through both ends from the inside out without catching her skin. Now, do the same on the other side only pull both ends very snug before pinning it. Don't forget the rubber panties. There," she said, "that's all there's to it."

"Yeah, right," I said. But when I did it, it didn't look like her job. Eventually I improved enough that she could trust me with changing the kids anytime.

When the diapers were washed she would hang them over the cast-iron radiators to dry during wintertime.

At bedtime, Susan would nurse Renee in our bed before putting her in the crib in the bedroom next door.

In the morning, my mom, Daddy or Joan, or all three would sheepishly knock on the door and come in to see how Renee was doing. It became a common occurrence several times a day. In many ways, living in a double farmhouse next to grandparents, was a positive experience. Kinda like having built-in babysitters. When they heard her cry, occasionally they would step in to see why she was crying. "Shall I take her for a little while," my mom would ask.

"Oh no, she's fine. She probably has a burp," Susan would say. At first, she was feeling a little intimidated since it was our first child. But she soon gained plenty of confidence as Renee grew.

She was an absolute Natural at Mothering. Just ask any of our kids.

CHAPTER 31

Our Calling, Commitment and a Little Bridge

"Come, follow me," Jesus said, "and I will make you fishers of men." Mk. 1:17. And . . . "If anyone comes after me, he must deny himself and take up his cross and follow me . . . for what does it profit if a man gains the whole world, yet loses his own soul." Mt. 16: 24 & 26.

The lump in my throat began to swell as we turned from Church Road onto Cowpath Road. All 21 years of my young life commenced to flash through my mind. Susan sat stoically next to me holding our firstborn child, 10-month-old Renee. But I'm getting ahead of the story.

In the Fall of 1963, God was speaking to our hearts about how and where to serve Him. The short of the story is this. The Franconia Mennonite Conference head of missions, approached Susan and I about moving to Sullivan County, Pennsylvania. Estella Mennonite Church was a small mission outreach of Rockhill Mennonite Church where I attended all my life. The mission church was seven years old but in need of help.

Mom and I always wanted to do a short term of service somewhere, sometime but was this the time or place? Now and then while dating, we would talk about signing up with 1W or Voluntary Service, both alternate forms of service to our country as conscientious objectors to war. We talked about going to New Hampshire where there was a large farm unit and hospital where both of us could be used in our skills. We also loved Sullivan County. I'd been hunting there for five years. My best friend Lowell and his family lived there. After some time praying about it and talking with our parents about it, we felt certain this was the right move. It was a difficult time for Daddy, since the farm was growing and prospering and I had been an integral part of that. I too had enjoyed working the farm with David and Daddy, especially with all the updated farm ma-

121

chinery. Our life on the farm in Telford was comfortable, profitable, and secure with a promising future. As a teen, I had grown to love the farm and enjoyed the challenges and variations of poultry and crop farming. But the burning question was always, "Where does God want us?"

Our decision was finalized in the Spring of 1964. After much prayer and seeking advice from parents and a few others, we were at peace. Henry Goshow, pastor of the little mission church in Sullivan County, Pa., was a big help to us. After a number of trips to the mountains to look for farms, we felt a connection to one in particular about five miles from Henry's place. A big factor in choosing this place was the location. It was in the area where many un-churched kids and families lived.

The farm had a neatly kept double story house, with dark green asphalt siding. The barn was a bank 32' x 42' block foundation structure with weather worn hemlock boards unpainted. There was a small but newly-built machinery shed just large enough for one tractor, a rake and a mower, two nice sized chicken houses large enough for 1,000 chickens each, another shed, a very old grainery and a garage, held upright by a maple log.

Several old apple trees grew between the barn and house and a pear tree by the garage. The buildings and house were close to the hard top road and St. Peter's German Reformed Church was within view just across the meadow. About 30 tillable acres and 50 acres of timberland made up the 80 acres and Mr. Bennett was asking $200 per acre. The fields were all in hay some of which had been newly seeded with timothy and birds-foot-treefoil seed; supposedly a very good legume for cattle.

We had looked at a few others. One was on the other side of Shunk and just before entering the woods going up towards Wheelerville. It was about 12 miles from Estella Church, too far and away from the area Henry had wanted us to work in. One place was over Wheelerville Mountain and another was up in Ellenton. All too far away. There was one farm only a mile from Mr. Bennett's farm which had some potential and was offered at $10,000 for the same acreage but the barn was falling down, the house needed lots of work and there were no outbuildings. Another farm over near the Pardoe brothers' farm had more acreage and a three-story barn that, with a lot of hard work, could have been converted for growing chickens, but both the house and barn needed way too much work. One other farm we briefly checked out was the farm which eventually became Berachah Farm Ministry. All these farms seemed to need lots of work to become functioning and profitable. We needed something to step right into and make a living.

As I ponder that first view of Ken and Ruth Bennett's farm, many thoughts and emotions surface. To us it looked like a dream come true. Lots of nicely kept buildings, clean cut hay fields and a barn to convert for growing veal calves, a nice place for a garden and only five miles from Henry and Irene and the church. In our young minds, the location, size and condition were right. It had potential and we were up for the challenge. I now know that it was God's leading.

My guess is that Daddy's thoughts went more like this; *"How will they ever make ends meet on that farm? You can't make a living growing a few acres of hay and raising calves. The winters are cold and the summers short. Every time they need something, town is an hour away. Is it really the right thing for me to help my oldest son buy this farm?"*

But he never verbalized all their thoughts. I know they tearfully pondered them in their hearts. Instead, my mom and dad helped us with the financing. After all, Dad *was* the mission representative for our home church. Since Joan worked for an attorney, she handled the settlement for us. October 10, 1962, would be moving day.

Months prior to the moving date, we drove back and forth to Sullivan County with lots of volunteer help to get the house painted and cleaned inside. I worked on the barn to get ready for raising calves.

To give you an idea of the simplicity of the house, here is a brief overview. It looked large from the outside. It dates back to the turn of the century. An old summer kitchen room was attached to the rear of the house with the main entrance through it. Old feed bins with rat holes were stored inside. A steep winding stairs led to the unfinished cobwebbed attic.

There was a small porch on the back of this addition seemingly never used. Below the porch were steps to the ground floor basement. You had to bend over to walk in.

The kitchen had green and white swirled immitation tiles on the floor, light orange walls with three three kitchen cupboards. There was a hook up for a washer in the kitchen, no dryer and no dishwasher. A one hole kitchen sink and a door to the basement. A small den off the kitchen, a 12' x 14' dining room and a 13' x 14' living room with hardwood flooring. The upstairs had three bedrooms and a bathroom with a tub, no shower. There was but one closet in the whole house. The windows were single pane with wooden storm windows which left the wind whistle through all winter long. No wonder my dad had reservations. An oil fired furnace blew warm air into most of the rooms in the winter. Mr. Bennett proudly informed me how he heated the house for $180.00

a year. I now wonder if he only heated two rooms for that amount? Of course he likely paid only a few cents a gallon and now we pay $4.00 a gallon. The price of progress.

The week before moving, we were busy packing and preparing for the big day. Susan's Mom and sisters rallied around her sorting and packing and watching baby Renee. Grammy Landis kept Renee for the weekend so we could concentrate on the moving process.

Friday, October 9th was loading-up day. My uncle, Abe Kooker, got permission to use his route truck from Kellers Butter. We carried the things out and he loaded them. The large bedroom dresser had to be taken out through the window, onto the porch roof and transferred via the 3020 JD loader—the way it had come in. It was 11:00 that night before we crawled into my mom's spare bed, weary with wonder and full of thought about our future.

Saturday, October 10, 1964, is a day etched in memory and history that changed our lives forever. We left our parents and home land of Montgomery County, Pa., for another in Sullivan County for the sole purpose of serving God. We had no idea, not a clue what the next 46 years held for us. But we knew *who* did.

According to Susan's diary, Kooker left with the loaded truck at 3:00 a.m. Susan and I left with our truck at 4:45 a.m. My mom, daddy and David left at 5:30. Joan and some others left at 6:00. By lunchtime, the whole truck was unloaded and in the house. Emma made soup and Irene brought dinner (lunch) over for us.

I remember food being spread out on the tailgate of Daddy's pick-up truck. We ate lunch out on the front lawn but it was chilly. Snow squalls mixed with tumbling colorful leaves darkened the sun every hour or so.

By 5:30 p.m., everyone left for home. Everything was in place in each room. Not that we had that much but many hands make light work.

Sunday morning we were scheduled to have a commissioning service at Rockhill Church. So at 6:15 a.m. we headed back down home. We arrived in time for the service. Susan's Mom, Kass and Emma met us at the church with Renee. J. C. Wenger, a highly-educated young pastor and prominent historian mentored by my great-grandfather, John D. Souder, and Isaiah Alderfer from Franconia Mennonite Conference preached and commissioned us to serve at Estella Mennonite Church in Sullivan County, Pennsylvania.

After a fellowship meal, we stopped at the farm for a short visit with my mom and dad before saying our final goodbyes. The plan was to pick up Susan's Mom since she was going to spend the first week with us in the mountains. Leaving the farm and saying goodbye to our families was harder than we

The house in Sullivan Co. when we bought it in 1964.

The well-kept farm buildings and apple trees in 1964.

expected and quite emotional. Claiming Jeremiah 29:14 . . . "I know the plans I have for you says the Lord" . . . we were excited, sad, happy, anxious, and ready to go. We drove slowly down Church Road toward Cowpath, soaking in each farm building, the pond where I trapped and swam in, and the load of hay on the wagon on the barn hill seen in the rearview mirror. My hands would no longer help unload wagons of straw or hay in that barn. We stopped at Cowpath Road to turn left, silent . . . pondering . . .

The lump in my throat grew larger and tears wet my cheeks as we slowly crossed the little cement bridge. How many years had I trapped muskrats under that bridge? How many winters had we skated on the pond and down the little stream? From this point on the bridge, the farm could be seen but was slowly disappearing from sight, but not from memory. My high school sweetheart, tears streaming down her face, sat quietly next to me gently rocking our firstborn child, Renee, swaddled tightly in her arms. Breathing a prayer for safety, I reached over and squeezed her soft hand. The first 21 years of our lives flashed through our swimming minds. Here in "The Indian Valley" of Montgomery County is where we had grown up, gone to school together, got our "degrees" in farming and nursing and started housekeeping. Here, Susan had conceived and birthed our first child. In this farmhouse, historian John D. Souder was born and died after creating 500 pieces of "fraktur." Here is where we heard and answered the call to follow Jesus. "If anyone would follow me, he must deny himself and come follow me." So where He leads, we'll follow.

Six years earlier, sitting in the last pew at my home church, I had heard the call during the singing of an old revival hymn. "I'll go where you want me to go, dear Lord, over mountains or plain or sea . . . I'll do what you want me to do, dear Lord." At that moment in time, with teary eyes, I vowed in my heart to serve Jesus wherever he would call me to serve.

This is it, I thought as we crossed that little bridge and headed north. My home, where I first heard about Jesus, learned to work and love farming was fading from view. A wave of memories and emotions surged through my mind and body, and I'm certain through Susan's. We had made our choice. We would follow Jesus at all costs. It will be "For better or worse, for richer or poorer, in sickness and in health, till death do us part." Sullivan County, here we come.

CHAPTER 32

Sullivan County

GEM OF THE ENDLESS MOUNTAINS

Sullivan County, Pennsylvania, is a breathtakingly beautiful, entirely rural community in Northcentral Pennsylvania's Endless Mountains Region. Sullivan County was named for Senator Charles C. Sullivan who took an active role in passing legislation to create the county. Named for John LaPorte, Surveyor General of Pennsylvania from 1843-1851, Laporte, the county seat, is perched atop the Appalachian Plateau at an elevation of 2,060 feet.

Mountains and valleys, forests and farmlands are the terrain in Sullivan County's 478 total square miles including waterways. The county is known for semi-anthracite coal, timber and tourism. The major em-

Forksville Covered Bridge

ployers are the timber industry, agriculture, and state & county governments. Maple syrup, furniture, candles, baskets, jewelry, art and photography are also made in Sullivan County.

Known as the "Gem of the Endless Mountains," Sullivan County is a unique area with beautiful state parks (Ricketts Glen and Worlds End), breathtaking waterfalls, scenic vistas, small villages, natural lakes, quaint shops and a rich heritage that draws people to its region. In addition, the covered bridges located in Forksville, Hillsgrove and Sonestown are entered in the National Register of Historic Places.

Whether graced by spring pastels, summer greens, autumn hues or newly-fallen winter snow, Sullivan County's mountains are profoundly beautiful. Summer temperatures average between mid 70's and low 80's. Winter temperatures average in the low to mid 30's. Annual rainfall averages 35 inches; annual snowfall averages 70 inches.

(The above synopsis was taken from the internet home page of Sullivan County.) Sit back and I'll tell you lots more interesting stuff and stories about "our" county.

I don't know how they arrived at some facts. For instance, in my journals, I've recorded lows of 40 and highs of 102 degrees in *summertime*. But yes, generally, we average in the low 80's. Winters can be bitter. Here at the base of the Cahill Mountain, I've seen 26 below zero and often 10 below. I love to plow snow with my tractor and most winters provide the opportunity with one exception; 2012. I never got the plow out. We had little snow. There was one winter when we got 12" every week for six weeks in a row. That was back in the '70s when I plowed out the long ½ mile lane for Berachah Farm near Estella about 8 times. Now that's what I call a fun winter! My friend MJ will attest to that. ☺

Lopez is a small mountain town at the eastern tip of our county and nestled between mountains along a stream. It's been labeled "The Ice Box of Pa." They commonly record minus records of 20 to 35 below.

Eagles Mere, our county's piece of property famous for its quaint old houses and cottages graced with huge rhododendrons around a big lake, a golf course, antique stores, an old ice cream parlor known as "The Sweet Shop," the town clock across from the park and people from the cities with more money to spend than time to spend it. It sits high on the mountain along Rt. 42 and is the only town which can boast of a locally created "toboggan run." The fire company built the toboggans for an ice slide made of 14" thick ice cut from the lake with an antique ice cutting machine.

Blocks stacked one against the other from the lake to the top of the hill next to the main road are grooved out with another locally made machine specifically for the unique toboggans. You buy tickets from the fire company before mounting the toboggan which can hold up to 6 people. Ready, set, go and with a push and feet secured around the person in front of you, you are rattling down the track up to 60 MPH. If the lake happens to be free of snow, you may finish by touching the far shore giving you lots of time to visit as you walk the ½ mile back to the top. Depending on the crowd, one evening will get you maybe four runs for a total of $20 for 6 people. A great investment in entertainment.

Eagles Mere is also home of some elegant places to dine. There's The Inn, The Crestmont, or The Country Club restaurant for starters. Each offers fine dining and a delightful atmosphere. My granddaughter, Ciara, lived with us the last summer Susan was here and worked as a waitress at the Crestmont. She loved it, her bosses loved her and we all loved the food and environment. The Crestmont is new since the mid '80s when it was rebuilt following a devastating fire which destroyed the charming hotel built over a 100 years prior.

Three in-tact covered bridges still provide you a nostalgic walk or drive across the Loyalsock and Sonestown Creeks. If you turn off the car engine, you may hear the click-clack of horses' feet on the big wooden planks laid down a 100 or more years ago. Forksville decorates theirs with tiny white lights at Christmastime. The old general store across that bridge now offers wonderful meals and a one-of-a-kind dinner theater to the first 25 guests that reserve. Space is limited. Owner and operator, "Big Mike," a former chef from South Philly, plays first sax and his daughters serve and sing with him. Come check it out. Like Uncle Abe always said when he came to Sullivan County to "get away," "It's like stepping back in history 50 years."

"*Ye ol' Forksville Fair.*" Held annually around Labor Day, nestled along the Loyalsock Creek in Forksville and surrounded by mountains on all sides is our fairgrounds. This year 2012, marks the 161st fair to be held there. A wonderful catalyst for bringing "old folks" together just to "sit a spell" on the plank benches and catch up while the kiddos fly high on the rides.

Old time music from the amusement park float on the mountain air and the roar of tractors deafen your ears as they strain to pull the stone boat or the pulling machine a bit farther than the last guy.

If you want more "noise," buy a ticket to the demolition derby and bring your ear plugs and someone to grab on to. It gets a bit crazy . . . especially after rainy weather.

Of course, like all fairs, and the main reason for their existence is the displays and the animal shows organized by 4-H. When our kids were young, the whole family was heavily involved in showing something. Mike, showing his

4-H pigs, Lor, her bunnies, art and crafts, Brenda some pictures and art and even one year showing a steer. Renee showed flowers, art, photos and bunnies. They all helped Susan with canning and showing some of her prize canned goods and of course preparing arrangements of flowers we grew. Occasionally, I would have nice corn and hay to show. Before the rules and regulations got too extensive, I took geese, ducks, and chickens to show. The Fair gave opportunity for families to bond and contest for the best prize. A side benefit was that if you participated in any way, you got free entrance tickets and usually, some nice prize money and ribbons. The free tickets are harder to come by these days as with anything free. But it still is a great community spirit building event.

Way back before tractor pulls became a high-tech sport, I pulled my old John Deere model 50 (my first tractor) against my neighbor's old "Co-op" tractor and other county farmers. I recall tying a string to the governor to get more RPMs out of it. I forget who won. Don't much matter. It was lots of competitive fun. When I acquired Dad's JD 3020, I entered it in the competition. But the most enjoyment was testing our driving skills through obstacle courses and then timing our skill and accuracy at backing up to equipment, jumping off to set the pin, pull it a distance, jump off, pull the pin and drive to our station. I own a blue ribbon for that one. ☺

"Free ice cream for everyone!" The "Dairy Queen" and her maids serve freshly hand-cranked ice cream till it's all gone. Better get in line. It's a hot day and there's a long line already. The fair committee also gets into the ice cream act by offering a contest. I entered last year and took second place with plain ol' vanilla. Part of the deal was to offer a taste to whoever wanted some until it was gone. No problem, I can make more.

"All kids under 12 line up over here. That's right, over by the cow barn," came a voice over the p.a. system. "Now listen; at the sound of the whistle, Bill will release a small pig and whoever catches it and drops it back into this barrel, wins the prize. Any questions?" Our county agent was kind yet precise. One thing he did not say was that the pig was "greased" up. Some kind of slippery salve was rubbed on the poor little fellow before being released. It was a sight to behold watching those kiddos chase and catch the squealing pig only to have it slither out of their grasp. My buddy, Rod caught one when he was 12. Course he was bigger than most kids his age and his large strong paws managed to hang tight. He took the prize.

Every year since 1957, except for 2011 due to flooding from Hurricane Irene and Lee, the Forksville Fairground hosts the *Pennsylvania Bowhunters Festival,* the third weekend of September. It's the oldest such event in the nation and features a locally designed and created "running dear target." Thousands of participants line up to try their skill at it and many other targets.

Evening shows feature world renowned archers demonstrating their skills and latest products. There are plenty of vendors on hand to sell anything remotely related to archery. I remember buying arrows and peephole sights. My first bow was a re-curve but was soon replaced with a "Bear" compound bow. I never shot a deer with it but had fun trying. Mike, my son, showed me up by harvesting a nice doe the first year he ever hunted with a bow. He shot it from a tree stand as we both waited patiently at the edge of the back field.

"There they come. Wait till they get to that tree near the hay and then shoot," I whispered. He did just that hitting his target precisely. We recalled that incident a couple weeks ago while four-wheeling past the spot. Some things you never forget.

The Pennsylvania Bowhunters Festival Committee is a 501-C-4 non-profit organization dedicated to the promotion of archery and bow hunting and the support of charitable and service organizations. The organization consists of a 16 Member Board, a 75+ Member Operations Committee, and more than 500 volunteers who help during the Festival. No one involved in organizing or running the Festival is paid for their services or reimbursed for any personal expenses.

All profits from the Festival are donated directly to Sullivan County charities, youth groups, school teams and clubs, and service organizations. These include Youth Athletic Leagues, School Clubs/Activities/Athletic Teams, Scholarship Funding, Food Pantries, the Library, Scouting Troops, 4-H Groups, Volunteer Fire Companies, Volunteer Ambulance Services, Victim Services, Community Service Organizations, churches, and many more.

Many from our church, including Susan and I have volunteered at the Festival. It is quite a challenge to feed thousands for three meals plus snacks. Farmers grow sweet corn and volunteers husk and prepare the ears. Bushels and bushels of locally grown potatoes are cut for French fries. The task is huge but managed very well. Speaking of fundraisers . . . !

Fall, in Sullivan County, my favorite time of year, has lots of fun festivals. Another one is the *Sullivan County Fall Festival*. This two-day event is held rain or shine at the fairgrounds. The Mid-Atlantic National Chainsaw Carving Competition is featured. Master logs are carved into a variety of sculptures. Each day, 45-minute carvings are auctioned. Lumberjack demonstrations—competitions like . . . Underhand Chopping, Spring Board Chopping . . . Ax Throwing, Logrolling, Chainsaw and Crosscut Saw contests.

It is very entertaining to watch professional carvers and loggers perform in their element. For many years, I rented space in the yellow building to demonstrate the "art of twig carving." I would sell as many as 35 pieces to curious buyers who never saw "such intricate carved roosters" out of twigs. Some came back year after year to add to their collection.

It was lots of fun. Susan was my merry maid folding boxes, packing, pricing and playing banker for me. My grandkids often sat proudly by quietly announcing "that's our Poppie." A few years, I agreed to teach a few kids. Not a good idea for most kids. It takes good coordination and lots of patience. After sending one kid to the Fair nurse for a butterfly band-aid in lieu of stitches, I gave up that idea. Jessie still brags about his own carved rooster and proudly displays the scar from years ago.

Then there are pumpkins for wee ones to paint, apples to dunk and eat, fresh cider from local orchards, and old-fashioned wagon rides pulled by huge Belgium work horses. Did I mention ice cream? Always ice cream at festivals! Oh, how 'bout topping it off with locally made maple syrup? Try those funnel cakes or plain ol' hot dogs and sausages. You can cool off with pure, freshly squeezed lemonade. Now you're ready to sit down and enjoy the bluegrass band playing behind you.

Father's day weekend signals the time for the Pow Wow at the fairgrounds. Native American and non-Native American people meet to dance, sing, socialize, and honor American Indian culture. At Forksville, the Eastern Delaware Nations Annual, traditional Native American Pow-Wow takes place with dancing, drumming, storytelling, native art, and foods. Traders and Craftsmen display for sale, jewelry, beads, art, knives, furs, blankets, food, and more.

An Indian Chief demonstrates his archery accuracy by shooting dimes out of the air before they fall to the ground. Fascinating!

Sullivan County has its own Delaware Nations tribe right here in the mountains. My grandkids and I visited a real teepee where a young woman was dressed in Native American attire. The teepee was fully decorated and furnished in authentic style.

WinterFest is an event staged at the "Camp Brule Boy Scout Camp" just four miles behind our farm. It features sled dog races on 50 miles of forest trail depending on snow levels. There is ice sculpturing, ice fishing, cross-country skiing, games for kids, and now they have added a huge crowd gathering event—"The Great Ice Plunge" contest. First prize for best costume is a fully paid trip for two, somewhere exciting like Disney World. The ice is cut away in a 20' x 20' area for those crazy enough to dive into frigid water while hundreds of spectators cheer them on. No, I have never done it nor will I anytime soon. Would you?

Summertime has another event I almost forgot about. *"The tour-de-Shunk"* bike ride. This is a 100-mile Bike Ride in Shunk, PA. The Bike Ride has a total ascent of 4,255 ft. and has a maximum elevation of 2,342 ft. The ride has 25, 50 and 100 mile options through some of the most beautiful and challenging roads in the Endless Mountains region of northeastern Pennsylvania. Close to 200 entries are now expected.

Then there's the *"Dairy Parade"* in Dushore. Thousands of folks throng the streets for the parade and contests. A favorite contest for many years has been the cow milking contest. Some kind gentleman farmer provides a very calm natured cow for the event. She stands quietly by as contestants try their hand at it. The milk, if any, that is gotten, is weighed and measured to see who can milk the most in a given time. If you never milked a cow by hand, you should not make light of those who try unsuccessfully. It's harder than you may think.

If you think a dairy parade in the middle of a town is strange, you should come to *"Dushore Founder Days."* In the middle of August, when it's about as hot as it can get in our county, more contests are underway. What is it about people and contests? Anyhow, again in the middle of main street, a dozen or so "outhouses" on wheels with four pushers and one "pot-sitter" pose for the gun shot. Get your camera ready. It'll be a keeper. Hang around, you'll get to see which two are the fastest beer barrel rollers. Oh, yeah, we have some weird contests.

Susan and I have participated in several of the *"Walk for Life"* events. It produces not only funds but much comradery. Cancer has touched most every household and this walk is a way to honor those who have lived to tell about it and to remember those who have not.

The "LT" trail courses through Sullivan and Lycoming Counties, offering hikers 53 challenging miles of trail through Worlds End State Park and the Loyalsock forest. More trails are well marked for hiking and cross-country skiing.

Views from Canyon Vista and High Knob take your breath away particularly in Autumn. The "Haystacks," along the LT trail are legendary rocks dotting the creek for picnickers and hikers to climb and cool off during the hike. God only knows how they got there. Ticklish Rock teeters high above one of the hiking trails giving the illusion of instability. They've been that way well over a century.

Lincoln Falls, four miles from our home, is a refreshing water cascade on Kings Creek trout stream. For years it was accessible to the public until ho-

Lori and her girls near headwaters of the Sock, on their own land.

meowners made it a "No Trespassing" zone. If you fish upstream starting below Lincoln Falls, you can legally find it. Be prepared for skinny dippers. ☺

"The Sock," meaning the Loyalsock Creek, large and small branches, are both excellent fishing streams.

If it were not for tourists and vacationers, Sullivan County may be an unknown county. The weekends and summers particularly, find our county buzzing with activity. There are more cabins and second homes than full-time residents. Deer hunting season brings close to a million hunters to Penn's woods. Those first two days make it seem like half of them are right here. Before the local electric company, R.E.C, bolstered its power lines, we had "brown outs" or even "black outs" the night before, and the evening after the first day of the hunt. As hunters cooked super and lights came on in all the camps, power went out. It was expected to happen until the upgrade came. Thanks R.E.C. guys. We appreciate your hard work to accommodate our hunters.

Until a decade ago, many Sullivan County farmers cooperated like the Amish do. At harvest time, in each community, they would get together with their equipment to help fill silos. Sometimes there were as many as six tractors, wagons and choppers cutting the month-long chore down to several days for each farm. There was a sense of comradery and friendship transforming the hard work into fun and fellowship. The wives prepared large lunches encouraging the men to stop long enough and enjoy a meal. In a sense, it was like a church of its own in action. I was a participant in several of those harvest days.

But those days have given way to much larger farms, high-tech equipment and self-supporting farms. Four and six-row self-propelled choppers with over 450 HP have replaced one-row pull behind choppers. Two hundred HP four-wheel drive tractors have replaced tractors like my 90 HP two-wheel drive tractor. I think the new generation of farming has increased the stress level for everyone. Losing the old way of cooperation and fellowship is a sad realization. Makes one wonder . . . is it worth the investment?

"What does it profit a man, if he gain the whole world and lose his own soul?" asked Jesus.

Don't get me wrong . . . I like big equipment. ☺

Did I tell you, we only have one traffic light in our entire county? No joke. Now you know the meaning of the word . . . "Rural."

You want to breathe clear fresh air? Want to get away from bumper-to-bumper traffic? Tired of locking everything up when you go away? Want to see "outhouse races," or beer barrel rolling contests? Oh, and try your hand at milking a real cow right on the square in Dushore while you're at it. Stop by the old railroad car and see their craft displays. That's up by the Agway Store on Headly Ave.

While you're in Sullivan County, here's some great places to eat: The Whistle Stop, The Jolly Trolly, The General Store in Forksville, High Knob Inn plus those I mentioned earlier in Eagles Mere. Take some roses home for your spouse from "The Blooming Florist" or "The Dushore Florist." Better yet, pick some wild daisies.

Yeah, all this good stuff can be found in little ol' Sullivan County, Pa. We'll get the fiddle out and play some bluegrass music, listen to Willy Nelson or . . . hey, just sit back a spell and listen to the birds. Y'all come!

CHAPTER 33

Four Precious Treasures

"How many kids would you like to have (when) we get married?" I asked curiously.

She turned slowly and looked at me deep in thought.

"Not one or just two and definitely, not twelve," she said giving me that beautiful smile.

I stared out the window of my childhood bedroom, looking across the cornfield stubble pondering our future. We were 18.

"Do you ever wonder what they will look like? What they will be, boy . . . girl . . . smart . . . athletic . . . handsome or pretty," she mused softly?

"I think they will be beautiful and all the above. Look at you. How could they not be?" I said slipping my arm around her and planting a kiss on her cheek. She smiled, deep in thought.

One thing was certain. We would endeavor to raise our children, to the best of our ability, to honor the Lord and dedicate their lives to Him.

Two years later, December 29, 1963, in the birthing room at Grand View Hospital in Sellersville, Pa., she gave birth to our first child. Fathers were not yet allowed to assist or observe births.

"Mr. Souder . . . you have daughter," the smiling nurse said.

When they finally let me in to see them both, my eyes feasted on the most beautiful baby girl snuggling into Susan's breast. She had a full head of dark brown wavy hair, big dark eyes and long lashes and was perfect in every way. Susan instinctively and instantly became the proud, and in my eyes, perfect mother. Had I been a peacock, I'd have been strutting the largest, fanciest plume of feathers ever. It was only 17 days till my 21st birthday.

She will be . . . Susan Renee Souder, named after her mother. We'll call her Renee. From the pay phone down the hall, I called to inform my parents of their first grandchild and Susan's Mom of her 27th grandchild. Oh happy day!

With my little Argus camera, I snapped a bunch of photos for Renee's album. After two nights in the hospital, a young nurse swaddled Renee in her "going home" onesy and blanket, carefully covering all but her eyes and the pink bow in her hair. She gave her to Susan now seated in the required wheelchair and wheeled them to the door where I had the '61 Impala waiting and warming in the December chill. With the fragrance of red roses, flower arrangements, and balloons bouncing on the car ceiling, we drove home.

The bassinette stood warming by the cast-iron radiator just inside the dining room door. A cradle which her father, Elias, had slept in sat waiting in the living room with blankets and pillow. Day by day, week by week, year by year, we would pray, read and learn together how to best care for our first treasure, Renee. Proud . . . no words, could capture our joy.

I learned—from Susan—how to change cloth diapers, pin them on each side without pricking skin, pull the plastic panties up and over for waterproofing and close all the snaps correctly on her nightie or onsey. What a pleasure to care for such a God-given treasure as this.

It wasn't long before I helped Renee graduate from Gerber's baby food to crushed strawberries and ice cream. That's right, strawberries AND ice cream. And believe it or not, to this day, Renee loves strawberries and ice cream as much as her father. Oh, and guess what else? She didn't get sick on them, develop allergies and no one reported me to the health authorities or police for doing such a thing. Were they the *good ol' days?*

Before she was even a year old, I introduced her to sleds, tractors, animals close up, wagon rides, snowmen and snowballs. She listened to country, classical, gospel, acapella hymns, bluegrass and folk music. She lay snuggled in the cradle soaking in the laughter of her parents and friends playing cards or board games late into the night. Next to our own bed upstairs she slept soundly in her new crib.

Yes, she was a good baby and guess what? She still is a good and special child, following the path of Jesus and having given much delight to her parents. Renee has held true to the first child "birth order" declaration. She is a leader and organizer. But more importantly, she loves the Lord God and is passionately following and trusting Him with her life.

It's interesting to read what the name, "Renee," actually means. Below is a partial description from the "**Kabalarian Philosophy**":

You have the gift of tact and diplomacy, and possess a charming, easy-going nature which endears you to others. You have a serious desire to understand the heart and mind of everyone, and could be very effective in a career or in volunteer work where you are handling people and serving in a humanitarian way. This name also gives you a love of home and family, and as a parent you would likely be fair and understanding.

Add to that the cell phone ringtone that I use to identify Renee when she calls me—"The Halleluia Chorus." To me, it's a word picture of her personality; Exuberant.

I believe her kindergarten teacher at the Estella Elementary School had a huge influence on her choice to be a teacher. Mrs. Lawer was sweet and wonderful, continuing her friendship with Renee and our family for the rest of her lifetime. I can still picture Renee that first school morning, stepping up onto the yellow bus holding her little lunch box and waving bye to us. Earl Tubach, bus driver later turned mailman for us, smiled and waved to us indicating she was in good hands. And she was . . . on the bus and at school.

Two years was all she spent in Estella. Sullivan County decided the few small county schools should converge into one large elementary and high school in Laporte. From then on, our children traveled one hour and seventeen miles, one way to school.

School for the most part was fun and a good learning experience. In sixth grade she began learning to play the French horn in band. We cheered as she marched all over the northern tier with the band on every hot Memorial Day in May.

She was at basketball games to cheer on their team. She excelled as well on the school track team. Though she was shorter than some, it didn't hinder her pace. Go Renee!

At age 13, she asked to be baptized. She had accepted Jesus at a much earlier age and was now ready for baptism. The Loyalsock Creek was a favorite place and the cool water only enhanced the experience.

As a young teenager, our concern rose when some boys were becoming too friendly.

Maybe our first pastor's decision to send all seven of their kids to Eastern Mennonite High School in Virginia for their last two high school years influenced our choice.

We gave Renee the opportunity to go to C.D.M.S. for her last two high school years. It turned out to be a great blessing. She grew up loving life, and loving kids enough to pursue a degree in early childhood development at Eastern Mennonite College in Virginia; probably because of a seed planted by

Mrs. Lawer. Summers were spent working at the Worlds End Park snack shop dipping ice cream. Now that makes sense given her love for ice cream. ☺ She also helped out baling hay and unloading wagons for Dad and filling hundreds of water jars for the chicks. Of course, Susan appreciated her cheerful help in the house too.

She married a young Christian man from the Shenandoah Valley, Rodney Martin, and was a passionate kindergarten teacher for 15 years. She retired from teaching when her fourth and last daughter was born, but continued the women's Bible study she began while teaching and still is faithful with it today.

God instilled a passion in her heart to see a Young Life Chapter develop in their local public school. For five long years she and other mothers prayed for that to happen. In due time, God brought it all together and in a big way. With-

in two years it grew to over a hundred kids and is now much larger. Every week, large "YL" groups gather in their house for prayer and parties. All of her girls are passionately involved and the older two, Rach and Bekah, are leaders of YL. Yes, God is good, faithful to visit His blessings from one generation to the next as we honor Him. I bless you, my dear Renee . . . and you have so blessed us. I love you much.

Brenda and Renee on the front porch.

February 16, 1966.

Renee was about to have a sister. Susan was 23, I was 24, young but struggling with back trouble. Susan's pain began during the night. By morning she was packed and ready to go. But my back and hips would not cooperate. Our pastor, Henry Goshow, had to drive us to Towanda Hospital, both of us in pain, albeit, Susan's more productive.

She gave birth to another perfect little girl with lots of dark brown hair and a cute pudgy face. Renee was as thrilled as we were to have a sister. Brenda Kay will be her name. I don't think we knew the meaning but it held true to her personality.

According to one description . . . *The name Brenda gives you a responsible, self-sufficient, and dependable nature. Given the opportunity, you could do well in business developing your leadership, administrative, and managing abilities. Appreciating quality in all things, you desire to be prosperous. You have a strong, determined nature.*

Another source says her name means *"little raven."* I like that. There is something regal about a soaring raven. It soon became obvious that our second daughter would capture the hearts of many. Though she was well mothered by Susan and Renee, it wasn't long until she began to nurture any living creatures; cats, dogs, bunnies, chicks, ducks, goslings and of course dolls. Susan taught the girls to make cookies, cakes and meals.

The girls played house in the play house, chicken shelters, tree houses, snow forts, the corn crib and any building with spare space.

A favorite photo shows Brenda sound asleep on the back porch step with a bottle in her hand. Such a darling little girl. That was when my friend, Lowell, stayed here during the week to oversee the building of our big chicken house. Brenda was his little buddy.

We soon noticed that she liked to keep things clean. She needed no prodding to sweep the floors, pick up toys, put away magazines, dust and general housecleaning. Sometimes she'd put stuff away before we were finished with them. Who knows the minds and makeup of any of us? God gifts us all differently and for our own benefit as community and family. That quality never diminished, but became a trait to this day.

School was a place to have fun and find friends to hang out with. And of course the boys soon noticed this pretty little girl in school. Pulling her away from the bathroom where she spent too much time primping was a daily chore. As she got older, make-up and hairdos were of utmost priority. I wonder if that mannequin is still in the attic? No wonder she chose beauty school over college. Bren graduated from Empire Beauty School after a year of commuting. Brenda was our "hair" girl.

Now it may interest you that she was not too prissy to help fill jars with Renee and later Lori and Mike. And in spite of the terrible smell and filth of catching chickens, Bren was there to help. Did I say we paid them to do so? But hey, she did it.

I forget the exact year, but Bren and a couple friends were baptized in a swimming pool owned by a church member. I had the opportunity of baptizing her. She too had accepted Jesus at mid-week meetings for kids at our church as a young child. For a short time, she played the flute. I loved hearing the sound of the flute.

Bren also worked at Jennings Store in Estella after school and between hair jobs. She also worked part time at DarWay as a nurse aid. It was likely at school where she met her first real boyfriend. Very long story short, she announced to us one day with tears streaming down her cheek that she was pregnant. She was 23. We loved her and comforted her, reassuring her of our total support and help before agreeing together that this relationship was best terminated.

Renee and her newly-wedded husband invited Bren to come live with her in Virginia and begin anew. It was a wonderful arrangement and Renee played the perfect big sister role and Rod treated her like a queen.

Our first grandchild was born in Virginia, September 20, 1989. We were ecstatic, Brenda was overwhelmed and overjoyed alike. Ciara LaRae was the epitome of a perfect little doll girl.

Within a year, Brenda met the man of her life in a beauty shop while cuttng his hair. She married him after a year of dating. Eugene loved Ciara as his own and treated Brenda as the queen God intended her to be. They had Tyler a few years later to complete their family.

She and Renee are blessed to have each other, sharing much of life together with their families and friends. We all marvel at God's grace, mercy and redeeming love throughout her life thus far.

Thank you Bren, for who you have become, a woman of God, not unlike your sisters. You are a blessing. I bless you and love you much.

While Renee and Brenda were still quite young, Susan and I agreed to be foster parents to a young boy 12 years old. He came from a broken home in Canton just 25 miles over the mountain. Ricky lived with us for two years. They were challenging years and may have played a role in Susan having a miscarriage.

I remember having a rough time understanding the emotional time Susan had getting over that. I was young and uneducated in such things and no one counseled us about it. It had to be God's grace that brought us though those difficult days. So instead of two years between the next child like we intended, it was four.

December 30, 1970. Dr. Chadwick at Towanda Hospital, the same doctor who delivered Brenda, took Susan in the delivery room and I waited outside. I know, it sounds strange and archaic to you. Well, at least we had a hospital room instead of a stable. Susan was a wonderful Mother and birthed our children courageously and healthily. Dr. Chadwick came out and informed me of a perfect healthy baby girl. Perfect and healthy are key words. Three girls will have fun together. We chose the name, Lori Ann. Again, not sure where we got it but we picked names we really liked.

As for the meaning of Lori . . . here's what I found: *The name **Lori** makes you very idealistic and generous, with the strong desire to uplift humanity leading you into situations where you can express your desire to serve others. You want to assume responsibilities and to look after people; however, you can become too involved in other people's problems and tend to worry. Your name gives you a natural desire to express along artistic and musical lines. You desire a settled home and family life, and are expressive and attentive to your loved ones.*

Wow, sounds like Lori to me.

Her sisters mothered her like the doll she was. But Brenda had trouble finding hair to comb on Lori. Lori was bald . . . except for peach fuzz. No matter, she was still perfect.

This was the '70s . . . the period of time where the Holy Spirit was moving in special ways on the mountain. Many churches were spiritually awakened, people being filled with the Holy Spirit, even speaking in tongues and experiencing miracles. Our church was not left out but was touched by God's miracles and finding new life as well. So with Lori, we began very early on to teach her to raise her hands when we'd say, "Praise the Lord." Psalms 63

Sitting in her high chair, like a jack in the box, her hands would go up with a big smile to boot. We taught the girls scripture choruses as she listened and hid them in her heart. All three girls have clear and beautiful soprano voices. Dolls were plentiful with three girls now and Lori loved them all. But a favorite was a little black doll. God was instilling compassion in her heart at a very early age for those less fortunate in life.

It's interesting to note here that she spent five months serving in Jamaica under a Christian service program called "YES"—Youth Evangelism Service. It was that service that created a love for Jamaicans so that her entire family returned about 15 years later for a month of volunteer service.

Lori attended Sullivan High all four years, doing well academically and caught the eye and heart of a local young man three years her elder. But in spite of that early love life, she followed her sister to Virginia and graduated from EMC with a Bachelors in education. She went on to get her Masters to teach the hearing impaired from Bloomsburg University.

For a very short time, she broke off from her first love and tried another relationship with a nice Christian young man she met at EMC. Her first love was devastated and "jokingly" tells her so to this day. That new relationship was definitely not to be. Mike was determined and wooed her back without much trouble. Lori enthusiastically said yes to his proposal resulting in a hot air balloon ride across Pa.

Mike and Lori enjoying grain harvest.

Lori loved animals of all kinds, like Brenda and Renee, but even more so. She raised chicks, bunnies, puppies, calves and sheep. Both Petunia and Ivy were great pets until they devoured too much of our landscape bushes. The rest of the story Lori would rather forget. She did have a pony for a while too. There are still remnants of the bunny pens in the rear of my wood shop. I think Thumper was a favorite bunny.

Lori and her friends named our blue pick-up truck "the chicken truck." I believe it was due to taking kids home with it after catching those stinky chickens late at night. The truck would stink for days and weeks after. She got to drive it to school on occasion. She was also fond of creating hide-outs and play areas in the most unusual places. Creativity was her specialty. She made picture frames from scraps of wood in the shop, and invented preserving real flowers on candles and in frames to sell at craft shows. She and Susan made memories going to many of those over the years together.

Lori was baptized in her early teens with her friend Amy. The Lord was preparing her for service with kids and little did we know how impressionable those early years were.

Lori and Renee both took piano lessons and did well with it. I remember trying so hard to get Lori, especially, to sing or play at church. She was particularly shy and would cry if I pushed too hard. It took many years for her to get over her shyness. She eventually began playing and now leads worship and kids' church and is a wonderful teacher of kids both hearing impaired and not. Just ask their Mothers and her peers. She and Mike have three wonderful girls and the best part is that she did NOT move to Virginia. So we get to have at least three grandkids living near us. I affectionately call her "Morning Glori." Lor, you are a real blessing to all you meet. I bless you and love you much.

"IT'S A BOY" . . . JOHN MICHAEL. SEPTEMBER 2, 1974

The end of a hot summer had come. It was time to clean the chicken house and get ready for chicks. My dad was up to help and the neighbors as well. The Fair was over and I was in a foot cast due to a tractor accident at the Fair. A tire ran over my heel and fractured it. Since the pear tree was loaded and I couldn't do much in the chicken house, I used the hay elevator as a ladder to pick pears . . . in a cast. Seven bushels of pairs in fact.

Susan had spent the past summer sweating over hundreds of canned vegetables and fruit. She too was ripe and ready to deliver our fourth child. In fact the night after I picked the pears, she began labor. About four in the morning, she was down in the basement sorting jars for canning. As she finished, the labor pains became more intense and she gave orders to get the car packed and ready.

By early afternoon we were in the delivery room. This time, I was there to hold her hand and encourage her on. She was such a trooper and before long she had pushed Mikey out of hiding and into our world. Dr. Chadwick was busy giving orders and moving his hands quickly in a circular motion. As he gently held Mike in his farmer-large hand, I noticed Mike was quiet and bluish. "There," he said confidently, "we got him just in time." Then Mikey began to wail.

I asked, "What do you mean?" . . . as I looked at the long umbilical cord he was holding and requesting a scissors. "Oh," he said, "the cord was wrapped around his neck three times and he was struggling for air. But he's fine now, just a little blue."

When we realized he was okay, we both audibly announced our gratitude with a "Praise the Lord." We were so happy to have our little healthy boy, and a miracle for extra measure.

The name was no problem, 11 years ago, before our first child, we had both girl and boy announcements picked out and ready. John Michael Souder . . . we'll call him Mikey. He weighed just over 7 pounds and about 19" long. His little head had a soft covering of red tinted hair. We were such proud parents. His sisters cared for him like he was a golden child. To this day, that's what they sarcastically call him . . . "the golden child."

Golden must come with a price. Mike struggled with croup until he was almost a teenager. How many times in the middle of the night did we hold him over the sink, tub or shower while running hot water producing steam for him to breath. It alleviated his struggle to breath temporarily. Other times, I would sit on the outside porch in the cold night air, softly singing, praying and hoping to ease his struggle. Medicine rarely helped.

Before Mike was one year old the doctors noticed his bowed legs and ordered him a set of braces. Each night before bed, we would attach the braces to help straighten his legs while he tried to sleep. Along with much prayer, it must have helped. On the soccer field in high school and college, he became a fearless player. He was so aggressive and able to use those legs skillfully. Thank you Jesus.

But before he out-grew the croup, he spent at least a few nights in an oxygen tent in the hospital. Poor little guy. He wanted to get out so bad but we were required to leave him in for a time.

Here's part of what I found with his name meaning:

*Your name, **Michael**, gives you a clever mind, good business judgment, a sense of responsibility, and an appreciation of the finer things of*

Lori, Mike and I on first cycle.

life. Home and family mean a great deal to you and it is natural that you should desire the security of a peaceful, settled home environment where you can enjoy the companionship of family and friends. Whatever you set out to accomplish you do your very best to complete in accordance with what you consider to be right.

Fearless, curious, creative, athletic, bright, and armed with a great sense of humor, Mike pushed all limits with us and those in authority. But he respected us. He had many friends, some of which we questioned but never denied their relationship. He spent much time with me no matter what I was doing be it carpentry, farming, cutting wood, whatever. We tried hard to instill spiritual principals in him as with the girls at every opportunity.

Mike was a good student in high school but never let school work interfere with having fun and studied just enough to get fair grades.

He went to Messiah College for one year, then transferred to Penn College in Williamsport. College changed his tune and he excelled as he worked toward and acquired a Bachelors degree in construction management. He worked for our construction business, Brotherhood Builders, while going to college. One afternoon in 1994, Mike was driving to school after working construction. He fell asleep at the wheel, rolled his little Honda hatchback three times and slammed into a huge pine tree crushing his car to smithereens. A witness saw it and called 911 certain that he was dead.

His guardian angel must have been busy. He crawled out the back hatch and was sitting with his head in his hands shaking when that witness walked up to him. The police said they had never seen anyone walk away from such a bad accident. It was apparent that God had future plans for Mike . . . "plans to give him a future and a hope and not to harm him." He had only minor scratches to deal with . . . and had to find another car. Mike got a second chance at life. Little by little, day by day God spoke to his heart. He married a close friend of the family, Mercy, who is the love of his life and mother of two boys and a precious daughter.

Mike worked for six years for the largest commercial contracting business in Virginia as an estimator. God then miraculously called him to be the "Pastor of outreach" at a big interdenominational church in the Shenandoah Valley. At this writing, he has pastored there for 10 years and is working on his Masters of Divinity.

Go figure. I would never have guessed our Mike would end up a preacher and pastor. As The Lord's Prayer says . . . "Not our will, but thine be done."

Mike loves his work and is passionate in serving God and mankind. Mike, you are a true blessing to us all. I love you and bless you, my son.

Adding the second name we delegated to each name . . . here's what you get:

John Michael

*The name of **John** has made you serious-minded, responsible, and stable. You love the security of a home and family, you are fond of children, and, as a parent you would be fair and understanding. Although you have good business judgment, you are not aggressive in your dealings because you do not like to create issues. You would be successful in any position dealing with the public as you have a diplomatic and tactful manner and possess a charming, easy-going nature which puts people at ease. People are drawn to you because they feel that you are patient, kind, understanding, and responsive.*

Lori **Ann**

*Your name **Ann** gives you the ability to be creative along practical lines of endeavour. Your ideas can be very original and inventive. You enjoy being with people in a social environment. Your personal appearance is important to you, for you desire to make a good impression on others. Your pleasant manner attracts people to you with their problems and you are capable of offering practical advice, though you may not follow such advice yourself.*

Brenda **Kay**

*Your name **Kay**, creates an independent, determined, and persevering nature. You desire to work on your own or at least where you are making your own decisions. You enjoy working with your hands and can be resourceful and inventive along practical lines. Being much focused on your pursuits, at times you overlook the personal considerations and attentions that create understanding and companionship with others. This name causes you to suffer with self-consciousness in new situations and an inability to be diplomatic when situations warrant. You are loyal in friendships and express candidly. You enjoy outdoor activities with a few close friends.*

Susan Renee

*Your name **Susan** has given you a pleasant, easy-going, friendly nature. Personal contacts are important to you. In situations where you are serving others, demonstrating or instructing, you have the patience to go into details that someone else* *may not think to be important. In your association with others, you are often limited to the more mundane happenings and little personal problems that can be so frustrating to those of an active, dynamic nature. You desire to create system and order in your environment but are inclined to become side-tracked and socialize when you should be working. Your ambitions are not large, as you lack confidence in your own abilities and would sooner not take a chance.*

Mike, Renee, Dad, Brenda, and Lori in Renee's kitchen one year after Susan died.

CHAPTER 34

Back Pains

"**A**ccording to the latest x-rays, here's the bottom line. You have what's called . . . "Marie Strumpel Arthritis." This basically means that over time, your spine will stiffen up to the extent that you will not be able to bend over. Additionally, your neck will become too stiff to move resulting from this 'poker spine' problem."

The words of a neurologist from Tioga General Hospital in Waverly, New York, stunned me like sleet on a cold window pane. But he was not finished; "This is why you are experiencing pain and motion limitations. If I were you, I would strongly consider other career options. Farming and construction are among the worst careers for people in this condition. Obviously, it's your call, John. You are still young enough to pursue an alternate career. But this is my professional opinion. I wish you well."

And with that he dismissed Susan and me from his office and was gone. I don't recall our immediate response in the office but I do recall our discussion as we walked, a bit weak-kneed to our car.

"Well, I didn't expect that kind of diagnosis," Susan said softly.

"Me neither. I'm not sure what to make of it all but I know one thing for sure; I will NOT accept that as a death sentence to my lifelong aspirations to farm and enjoy working in construction of any kind! I will NOT let him or any other doctor control or limit my love for farming. I believe God has called us up here to do His work and He has provided the farm, my abilities and plenty of work to make a living. He will somehow, provide the necessary health and healing for me to continue on."

In summary, those were the words I spoke, I believe prophetically, that day, January 29, 1970. (as per my diary) I was only 27 years old, full of vitality and love for life. I was happily married to my high school sweetheart, a young father of two beautiful girls—Renee, five and a half, Brenda, almost four . . . and our third, Lori, yet to be born that year. We had moved only six years prior to Sullivan County, Pa.

Let me explain our quandary:

By 1970, our farm had grown from 60 veal calves to 80, a large number for those days. The growth was only in calf numbers, certainly not in dollars. I had also rented the small double story chicken house at Bedford's corners, raising 6,000 broilers called "squabs." After much prayer and discernment, in 1967, I hired my best friend Lowell Goshow and his dad, Henry, to help build a large double story chicken house of 12,000 square feet. It seemed to be a "God-inspired" project that potentially could provide enough income to alleviate our financial debt. The bank had agreed to loan us the money and thus on April 24, 1967, the first batch of 24,000 chicks filled the new building with that lovely chirping, almost deafening sound. I still miss the smell of fresh wood shavings covered with tiny puffs of yellow down, and those loud chirping chicks scurrying over the entire chicken house looking for food and water.

This is the time line when work was so abundant (self inflicted), that in order to keep up with the demands on us, I literally jogged from one building or one field to another rather than walk. Sixteen-hour days were common around the farm. Neighborhood boys seemed to be drawn to our farm. I don't know if it was that I enjoyed fixing their broken bikes, the delicious meals Susan served them or the few bucks I gave them after helping out around the farm.

Besides the abundance of work, these were the years (in my twenties) when my back gave me so much trouble. Again, only God knows for certain the cause, but I have my own ideas about that. Given the fact that my frame favored my mom's more than my dad's, I was fairly thin growing up. That's not to say I was a weakling. On the contrary, I probably overcompensated by too much heavy lifting. In my 7th grade, I decided I needed bigger biceps and thus created my own set of lifting weights. I salvaged two bent-up feed buckets that "I thought" my dad wouldn't miss, found some old bags of concrete mix and a piece of ¾" galvanized pipe from our scrap iron pile. Now, I had my own 85-lb. weights.

Then of course, there was the daily chore of emptying 100-lb. sacks of feed into 55-gallon drums used to store feed for all the chickens, geese, ducks, and turkeys around the farm and pasture. At 135 lbs. and age 13, I learned by watching Dad, to carry those 100-lb. feed sacks on my shoulder from barn to shed or wherever needed. It was a tricky maneuver to get the heavy sack from the barn floor up onto my shoulder. Not only was that an unwise maneuver for my stature, but the fact that we loaded and unloaded so many of them every week is what took its toll on my developing body. I didn't take into account that Daddy weighed 60 lbs. more than me.

Every spring, hundreds of 80-lb. bags of fertilizer and seed corn had to be unloaded and stacked in the barn by hand, only to be reloaded onto the flat wagon which was taken to the field for another transfer. The corn planter fertilizer hoppers were about shoulder high from the ground and held about 600 lbs. each. That required 15 bags to be dumped into the hoppers countless times over each season. Though too young, David and I eagerly helped with this process.

Daddy went to a chiropractor occasionally and by my late teens, I began to make my own appointments. It seemed to help my aching back but damage had been done.

By the time I was 29, x-rays revealed more changes in my spine. Another doctor called it "Ankylosing spondylitis." That's a long-term disease that causes inflammation of the joints between the spinal bones, and the joints between the spine and pelvis. It eventually causes a fusing of those joints and is common in men between the ages of 20 and 40. Whatever the diagnosis, x-rays have shown that two of my vertebrae have become fused together by "natural" process. For a long period of time during my late twenties and early thirties, I used medicine to relieve the inflammation and pain.

As previously stated, the pain was so severe on the day Brenda was born, that we called Henry to drive Susan to the hospital in Towanda while I stretched out in the rear seat. Susan with "happy pains" (if such exist) and me with plain ol' back pain. Mine subsided with medicine, Susan's with the birth of Brenda Kay . . . February 16, 1966. Eventually my pain subsided as my lower lumbar stiffened, limiting me but not paralyzing me. Thank God.

One significant miracle happened to me during the '70s. It was the season of spiritual renewal in the mountains of Northern Pa. Some labeled it: "The Charismatic Movement." Many miraculous healings were reported, people being saved and spirits renewed as hearts surrendered to Father God. Special speakers abounded, coming from all walks of life and countries. Testimonies of fantastic healings were recorded and heard round the area and beyond. Canton, Pa, was a particular *hot spot*.

Since we too were hungry for a deeper and closer walk with God, we traveled over the mountain many nights to listen to speakers and experience a new, lively form of worship and praise. We always took the kids with us as did others and they learned new scripture choruses and played with new friends. Melvin and Irene Good made room in their large machinery shed, named *The Glory Barn*, for these meetings where we shall never forget meeting God in a more personal way.

Those days, my back was still unsettled and painful at times. Our church at Estella renovated the former parsonage next to the store for prayer and praise meetings and named it *"the prayer house."* It was there during an ordinary mid-week meeting when Mel and Irene came to visit. Mike was about 2 years old and full of energy. So we let him crawl around the floor and chairs till he finally fell asleep. The girls were over at the church Sunday school room with Florence Barndt who had a large class of kids teaching Bible stories from "Child Evangelism." It was there that both Renee and Brenda gave their hearts to Jesus.

I'll never forget getting out of the car that evening and carefully, painfully maneuvering one step at a time as we entered the prayer house. Susan knew I was uncomfortable and she helped me get seated. I sat almost stoically, wondering how I would ever get out of the chair let alone, go on with my busy life.

Mel was a very positive and happy, almost-go-lucky kind of man. One day, he was actually overheard saying "Praise God" at the sight of one of his dead cows. He had learned the value of praising God in every circumstance like admonished in 1 Thessalonians 5:16-18 "Be joyful always; pray continually; give thanks in all circumstances, for this is the will of God in Christ Jesus concerning you." I have yet to learn this discipline. But I am working on it.

Back to Mel; God had also gifted him with the "gift of healing." He had seen many receive diverse forms of healing as he simply laid his hands on them and beseeched God on their behalf. When the time for personal prayer requests came that evening, I was ripe and ready for prayer. What could I lose . . . besides my pride? So when Mel asked if anyone needed special prayer, I was first to respond.

"Yeah . . . a . . . I'd like prayer for my back," I said a bit shyly. It was one thing to pray for others, but asking for people to gather around me, since I couldn't get up, was hard on my pride. Mel's happy reply was quick and simple.

"Great!" he said as he walked over to my chair smiling and looking at me. "How 'bout we check to see if your legs are equal in length. Sometimes people have one shorter than the other. Do you mind?"

"No, of course not," I said. "But I can't stand up by myself. My back is killing me."

"No problem, stay sitting. I'll just lift your legs up here and check," he said as people began gathering around me.

"Look at this," he said to those who could see. "His one leg is a full inch shorter than the other one. So we'll ask Jesus to correct that right here and now." He suggested that we all praise Jesus for who He is and thank Him for his power to work in our lives. I began to do just that and immediately felt my legs shifting. As the people prayed and praised, I could actually feel one leg involuntarily move forward, slide past the other and return to normal position—perfectly even. Without a doubt, Jesus had touched me and I jumped to my feet without pain, stretched and touched the floor exclaiming, "Praise you Jesus, thank you Jesus!" The pain was gone and my back no longer hurt. I could stand, sit, walk and jump without pain. It was a miracle from God and I was healed.

I still have flexibility limitations with my back but the chronic back pain is history. I do not suggest that all you have to do to overcome your pain and suffering is what I did. God cannot be put into a box like we so often try to do. He will always keep His promise to do what He says He will do. But we cannot and should not suggest that He do it our way. His ways are so much higher than ours and we can never understand them. We live in a culture of instantaneous everything. God lives in timelessness and eternity. Americans hate to wait. Sometimes God's plan takes us through much pain and suffering before He heals us. We are told to ask and believe and He will accomplish what is best on our behalf. "Your will be done, as it is in Heaven." (not our will)

Dave Bauman and his wife Miriam were among a few that kept their eyes open to see what might happen. Susan did too. They witnessed the entire process and knew it was supernatural. God had done what is impossible to man but natural to Him. And we all went home fired up about our miracle-working God. To this day, some 40 years later, I have no longer been plagued with a short leg and relentless back pain. My vertebrae still has a couple fused lumbar but I can basically do what I want to in work, play and rest. Thank you Jesus.

As you read my story, you will find that Susan's story, and possibly yours, is much different than mine. However, God has been glorified and many have experienced a much closer and richer spiritual life as a result of her patient testimony through suffering. Some have entered the kingdom because of her life. God will be God no matter our experience or lack of one.

To Him be the glory forever, Amen.

-Written Tuesday, January 17, 2012

CHAPTER 35

Learning to Lead

I started early in life willing and eager to serve where I could. My home church growing up, Rockhill Mennonite in Telford, had a membership of around 225 people. There was a fairly large group of young folks and when I turned 16, I was voted in as President of the MYF (Mennonite Youth Fellowship). It was a conference-wide organization involving many churches nationwide. I was in charge of the youth from our local congregation, a group of about 20.

We met monthly for fun, and Bible study and occasionally a special speaker or event. I helped to plan hayrides, ballgames, volleyball, miniature golf outings, and even special trips to Estella for a weekend at Dave Clemen's cabin back on Bear Mountain. The MYF shared part of the service at the church with special singing groups, readings and short devotionals. One of the trips to Estella was made with my '57 Chevy with Susan at my side. I was 17. It's hard to believe my dad actually trusted me driving that far at that age.

The MYF harvested their plot of corn grown behind the cemetery at Rockhill in October. Don Detweiler and I volunteered to plow, till, plant and cultivate the corn. We'd gather under a full moon picking the corn by hand, throwing the husked ears into a flatbed wagon with short wooden sides. When the three-acre field was picked, Don or I would haul it to Moyer's Feed Mill in Telford for a cash sale. The money was chiefly used for Missions.

Christmas was an opportunity to bless the "shut-ins" as we called them. An evening was planned to gather and pack fruit baskets. During our Christmas caroling, we would drop off the baskets for elderly and people who were bedfast or needy. We began to learn the principal of . . . "It's more blessed to give than to receive." Being president of MYF was good practice for years to come. We had advisors who helped shape our decisions and guide our planning.

When I was 18, I was voted on a committee to represent the youth, which planned a monthly Sunday night church service. I recall thinking I was too young to meet with these elders and the minister. The elders were likely only in their 30s and 40s. About the same time they asked me if I'd be interested in having my name on the Fall ballot as Superintendent of Sunday School. Now that appeared too large a title to bite into. I agreed to be an assistant if needed. I was needed.

There is wisdom in involving our youth in leadership. What did the Apostle Paul tell Timothy about his youth? I Timothy 4:12 "Don't let anyone look down on you because you are young, but set an example for the believers in speech, in life, in love, in faith, and in purity." Apparently Paul thought it wise to encourage young folks to take leadership roles. But the sobering and qualifying part follows quickly; "set an example in those areas of your life." Without a doubt, we all fall short in setting great examples, even at a mature age. But for the grace of God, no one could qualify as a leader. We are to grow up in the knowledge and admonition of the Lord and "strive" to be perfect, Holy like the Lord. Apparently, someone saw leadership experience in us and they asked Susan and I to consider moving to Estella.

Susan was treasurer of her MYF group at Salford Mennonite Church. She also taught a Sunday School class in her late teens. She was a member of the Spiritual Life Committee at C.D.M.S. She took me along (didn't have to bribe me either) Sunday afternoons to sing at the nursing home in Quakertown each month. God was dually preparing us for future ministry in Sullivan County.

In a sense, these were the years of tilling the spiritual soil of our hearts, fertilizing, seeding, watering and nurturing our souls, preparing us to withstand the coming decades of blistering sun and torrential rain and winds of the world . . . and church. This development would produce stamina, patience, and the endurance needed to survive the enemy's ammunition. In time, we would learn that leadership is not for weaklings. It is not to be flaunted or taken lightly. Failure and disappointment could strengthen or destroy us. And it was His grace that sustained and matured us.

In 1964, we were invited by the Franconia Mennonite Conference to accept the call to serve and we moved to Estella. We were eager beavers. A whole lifetime was before us. Whatever we were asked to do, we would do it . . . except preach. I drew the line there. I never felt called to preach or be the senior pastor of a church. God challenged me on that later on.

Susan and I were quickly immersed in leadership roles. Both of us led monthly boys' and girls' clubs. We taught S.S. I led worship, well . . . led singing back then. I had no instrument, but stood up front holding a hymnbook, gave the starting notes by blowing into a pitch pipe and began directing the congregation (15 people) by beating time with my hand in four/four or three/four time. I actually enjoyed it. I have always loved to sing and worship God.

In high school music class we were taught the basics of choir or chorus directing . . . learning the keys, beats, time and notes. It intrigued me and when given the opportunity, I practiced.

My first embarrassing moment with leading congregational singing happened in Sullivan County. We were new arrivals to the monthly county hymn sing circuit. Dave Bauman, our primary song leader at Estella Mennonite Church at that time, invited me to lead the first hymn at a little country church in Nordmont. Young, confident and naïve, I obliged the offer.

Remember now, never in my 22 years of life had I led songs where there was a pianist. And so, with my trusty pitch pipe in pocket, I slipped to the front of the church and called out the hymn number. I can do this. The hymn was written in three flats. Oblivious to the pianist playing an intro, I blew an E flat on my pitch pipe. But people were looking at me with funny grins and I began to sweat. Dave raised an eyebrow and cocked his head toward the pianist as if to indicate something. I was still oblivious and tried to start the song.

The pianist was baffled by what I was doing as were the people. Finally, I got the hint from Dave that I should forget the pitch pipe and follow the pianist's lead. Duh! How was I to know? No one had instructed me about pianists leading congregations. It was not the way I was taught. We had no instruments. Learning to lead will require attention to the styles of different cultures and traditions. (A good reason for schools, courses and seminary.) I was beginning to understand that I had much to learn. It was a very awkward and disconcerting moment, but helped the maturing process in my leading life. Lesson—"When at a crossroad . . . stop, look and listen." I did.

As our little congregation at Estella began to grow, so did

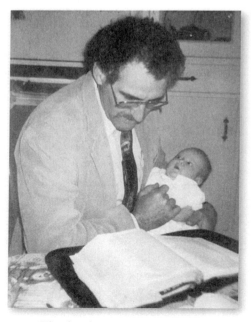

The church was growing in 1975.

my responsibilities. Roles to be filled included S.S. teachers, youth leaders, S.S. superintendent, song leader, Bible school teachers and kids' club leaders. The church lawn needed mowing, buildings needed repairs, people needed rides to church, and neighborhood bicycles needed fixing and on and on the list went. I can do that . . . can't I?

Thanks to my high school buddy Wes Clemmer, who gave me lessons, I was leading worship with my guitar. Henry Goshow, first and only pastor to date, resigned due to his wife's failing health and moved to Arizona to be near family. I stepped up to the plate hoping to find someone to replace him. One of our own former members had recently graduated from Elim Bible Institue. We invited Dan Groff to come. He gave us six months of leadership before moving to Florida.

I was back on the phone to Conference and Elim, asking for any suggestions. The Dean of Students recommended a young graduate, Dan Eby from Lancaster. Dan and Sue accepted our meager offer and spent four years pastoring our congregation. As a result, we experienced much growth and even began a Christian school with Dan and Bruce Boydell's leadership.

Additionally, a huge change for Estella Mennonite during his pastorate was a name change which Dan strongly promoted and we agreed to it. Living Hope Fellowship was born based on I Peter 1:3 . . . "He has given us new birth into a Living Hope . . . " I was lead elder at the time. Although we enjoyed great spiritual growth and added many numbers, Dan left in '83.

Once again, I was overwhelmed with filling the role of pastor. A picture imprinted on my mind, reveals me emotionally exhausted, crashing on the den couch sobbing. After a year of internal conflict with leadership and basic vision differences, I finally released all those pent-up feelings and emotions as Susan sat next to me and just loved me. I'm sure Dan and others had to vent emotions as well. Bruce filled the pulpit for a short season until we established a team of leaders to pastor the church. Up to now, this was one of the most difficult maturing seasons of my life. I accepted the lead role as shepherding pastor. I did very little preaching but much of the pastoral visits.

It was during these two years, 1984 and 1985, as acting pastor that I married two couples. Pennsylvania authorizes leaders who are recognized by the congregation to perform weddings and funerals without being ordained. During this time I performed several burials; local men without a church, Ellery and Leonard Hatch and our own dear Jackie Lund. I had spent many hours by her bedside singing and playing my guitar as she fought cancer. It was a very difficult funeral with grandkids and family saying goodbye.

Church leadership requires much dependence on divine guidance, grace and God's strength. God saw us through those hard times. By now, the team was ready for a lead pastor.

After gratefully working with Eli and Kaiti Beachy 18 months as an interim pastor, God led us to hire a full-time pastor; Randy Brunstetter. Our initial contact with him was through Renee and others who attended Spuce Lake Retreat Camp, a Mennonite-owned camp. Randy was Renee's camp pastor and she loved him. He was humble, yet charismatic in belief and a dynamic speaker. I was lead elder and the elder team interviewed Randy and Julie before committing to them. There was no doubt with any of us that Randy would work for us. Julie on the other hand, gave us pause to consider the cost. She clearly stated that she would not fill the "traditional pastor's wife" role making no bones about it. However, she was willing to commit and support her husband if pastoring was his choice. It was and they came.

Their first Sunday at Living Hope Fellowship was memorable. From the podium, I welcomed their family. Julie made her non-traditional statement wearing a short, snug-fitting pants suit, leading her kids with Randy smiling them on. His enthusiastic style of preaching chock-full of football object lessons captured most everyone. Like in any church, a few were skeptical.

Since this is about "learning to lead," I'll exempt much of Randy's story. However, we all had much to learn about working together and leading with grace and mercy yet strength.

About halfway through his ministry at LHF, Randy began struggling with the oversight of Franconia Mennonite Conference. There were issues he and even the elders had difficulty with. Eventually, he made good his threat to resign his credentials from FMC, leaving LHF without a properly licensed pastor. I believe his motives were pure and honest since he could no longer conscientiously abide by their doctrines. I applaud his convictions but felt the way he went about it was devastating to us.

The next disputed step was to invite a Pentecostal evangelist for a week of meetings at LHF without the consult of all the elders. Very long story short, the results were basically destructive to LHF. We lost half the congregation over two years' time. In his defense, the loss was due to other struggles in the church. To help understand the division caused in our fellowship, another brother and I were invited to attend a meeting at a disconcerted member's house. The purpose of the meeting was to hear "the other side" out. We noted their complaints and later held a congregational meeting with the help of FMC mediators to resolve the differences.

The elders and Randy sat silently listening to the complaints of disgruntled people. I hope you never experience a meeting like this in any church you ever attend. It is anything but Godly. People were sincere with their convictions and expressions of discontent, but they were sincerely wrong in the way it was expressed.

This my dear reader, is not the way we Christians should live. This is not the Jesus way. He asks us to "forgive one another, speak the truth in love, be kind to one another, love one another, live at peace with all men as much as it lies within you." The meeting only caused more division and strife.

Randy eventually resigned and soon gave his wife the divorce she was seeking and moved away. It was very sad. Susan and I really loved Randy and cared for him. His marriage was in jeopardy and we knew it. I bless him and love him. He is a dear man. I hold no animosity or grudge but totally forgive him. Randy is welcomed in our church whenever he comes back, which he does, and is welcome in our home. God used him at LHF but I will always wonder why we needed to experience those incredibly troubling times.

Near the end of that time, I resigned my senior eldership since I could no longer agree with Randy's leadership style. We did what we thought best as well as some others, including the last two elders. Before he left, he helped LHF find another network of oversight, Hopewell Network. I helped to give guidance and fill in the historical pieces of our puzzle as they provided the tools to rebuild our congregation. After another difficult year, I believe God laid it on my heart to recommend a young man who had grown up in our church to be pastor. He had gone to Bible Institute, been a missionary in Kenya for four years and was leading a small home church nearby. Scot Magann accepted the call to pastor LHF in 2002.

Since then, God has slowly but surely transformed him and LHF, our belief in God and each other. God has been merciful and gracious and patient as we began to enjoy our differences and believe that they are actually our strengths. We learned to accept differences in worship leadership styles. We learned to accept each other's shortcomings and mistakes. We learned to forgive, to repent, to confess, to express encouragement instead of exposing each other's weaknesses. We learned to love again.

When Susan got really sick with cancer in 2009, I resigned all responsibilities of leadership and Scot blessed my decision freeing me to care for Susan.

If anyone else could attest to the adversities and challenges of leadership, Scot can. Since graduating from Bible Institute and his four mission years in Kenya, God has continually been transforming his leadership qualities. It's quite miraculous what God can do if we follow His lead. What "marvelous grace of our loving Lord . . . grace that exceeds, our sin and our guilt." He can redeem any circumstance, and make our black sins white as snow. Praise You!

You've heard it said, "Behind any successful man stands a woman." I'd like to say, "Aside of a successful man stands a woman, or . . . a wife." Let me tell you, Susan was my most valuable gentle critic and wrong-way-motion-detector whom I credit with much of my success in leading. God of course, receives the ultimate credit for showing all of humanity the correct path and how to stay on it. "Lead on Oh King Eternal!"

CHAPTER 36

Farming in Sullivan County

Days were getting shorter as Fall colored the Cahill Mountain in 1964. It had been a year of severe drought. In September just before we moved, neighbor Richard (Dick) Brown, had requested to make the field of hay between the barn and the church. I approved and he later told me that he got 24 small square bales from the 8 acres of hay. Mother Nature had not been kind to the mountain that summer. Fortunately, veal calves and poultry don't eat hay. Any hay I could make would be a cash crop and supplement our small income.

I was 21, full of ambition and vision with a passion to farm. Good thing I was young. Plenty of testing was on its way. Sixty veal calves use lots of water. Two months after we moved, the 80-foot drilled well went dry from lack of rain that summer.

Fortunately for house water, there was a hand-dug well in the frontyard which had a small pump tied into it. But for the calves we needed much more. I gathered 50-gallon drums from neighbors and loaded them on my little truck and headed for a stream. Four miles back of North Street and beyond the Boy Scout camp was a small falls. Some years prior I had taken my '57 Chevy there with Lowell to give it a bath. The stream bed was solid flat rock and very shallow water. Someone had made an access for vehicles.

So every day for two months, I backed up to the falls to fill five barrels of water while waiting for a well driller to come and drill a new well. That got old so I called Gochanuer, the Mennonite plumber in Wheelerville. They came and did a test. He tied a weight on a string and dropped it down the well. I was told by the former owner that the well was 60-feet deep and he never ran out of water. So much for that story.

The weight passed 60 feet and finally hit bottom at 82 feet. Halleluia! Apparently there was a slight ledge where the original well pipe got lodged and couldn't get to the bottom. Mr. Gochanuer decided he would try to bypass that ledge with a new pipe and he succeeded. By the end of the day, we had a new pump and plenty of water. The extra 20 feet of water was sufficient until we built the new chicken house. Then we drilled a new well near the house. We hit a great water vein producing over 20 gallons per minute. Thank you Jesus.

The transition from my dad's farm in Montgomery County to Sullivan County was monumental. Here's why.

Dad's farm had a machinery shed full of the newest and up-to-date equipment needed for every crop we wanted to grow from planting to harvest and storage. The feed and seed mills, equipment dealers and service shops, and hardware stores were within five miles. Markets for most any produce or crop was close by and available. Land was fertile and very productive. Aside from weather, all conditions were prime for those of us called "farmers." Growing seasons were long enough to afford three if not four crops of hay. The elevation, type of soil, no rocks or steep hills and proximity of everything was as good as it gets.

Contrasted with our farm in Sullivan County which had a much shorter growing season, very rocky soil, high elevation, and every market, feed mill, equipment dealer and store only within 40 miles, made it incomparable. I knew it would be hard. I knew it would stretch my faith but we moved on God's nudging and guidance.

Before Route 80 was built, we traveled through Berwick where I bought my first tractor, a 1952 Model 50 John Deere. I paid $1200.00 for it. It had 32

My first John Deere tractor, with Renee and Brenda on my lap, mowing and crushing hay.

HP compared to my dad's 3020's 72 HP. I bought a two-bottom pull behind plow compared to dad's mounted four bottoms. My first disk was a small well used one I bought from Herb Eby. It was about 6' wide, best built for gardens. I soon found a used 12' spring tooth harrow and chained a plank on the back. It didn't come close to Dad's 14' transportable disk and cultipacker, but it was cheap and worked. For a corn planter, I had an ancient two-row pull behind that worked well but was slow going compared to Dad's new four-row planter.

My hay equipment consisted of an old John Deere # 9 rear mounted 7' sickle bar mower, an Oliver hay crusher. Dad gave me his old Grimm tetter. The first couple years, I used neighbor Dick Brown's model 66 New Holland baler and his Oliver 60 tractor. The tractor needed a ring job so bad it spit out black rings of smoke in a consistent pattern as it chugged slowly along as if to say, "Please fix me . . . now."

The baler worked most of the time except when the engine refused to start or the knotter failed to knot the twine or a sheer pin broke, usually when a thunder storm was threatening. Oh, it was a challenge.

I bought a 32' bale elevator the third year and used it to get the bales higher up in the hay mow. On my way home, pulling it up Forks Mountain with my pick-up, one of the wheel bearings began to smoke and the wheel almost fell off. I cobbled it up enough to get home. We used Dick's rickety old hay wagons the first couple years until I was able to build some of my own racks on used riggin's.

I found a 13' Ontario grain drill to sow oats and twice, wheat. Wheat refused to grow on our soil so I decided to try buckwheat. A few of the locals had success so I tried it. It grew well but so did the dear by eating it. So oats became the old standby. Corn grew well if you could get it planted early and the weather cooperated. That seemed to happen every fourth year.

The early frosts killed the immature corn shriveling it up resulting in the smell of peanut butter as it heated in the crib. The smell and mold didn't bother the rats. They infested the corn crib along with squirrels from the woods.

I bought a 50-year-old Oliver #5 one-row pull behind corn picker from Laverne McCarty down on the Millview Flats. It was a morning picker. Morning dew moistened the husks and the picker worked well. Dry conditions; dirty corn. Slow and steady was the best pace.

A man from Muncy had a portable grinding mill on a truck who came to our farm, ground up the corn, mixed with oats, some hay and supplement. We fed it to the pigs, geese, ducks and chickens. I'll never forget how mad the guy got one day when, accidently, one of my old hammers went through his mill, hidden in a bale of hay. Some "fat-n-fancy" words flew that day. I couldn't blame him and apologized plenty.

Feeding my 200 geese by the pond.

Since I was well trained in raising poultry of all kinds, why not do it in Sullivan County? So I did—with pullets, layers, ducks, geese and free-range bantams which at night, painted everything below them black and white. We even raised some ring-neck pheasants and a few quail to release for the game commission.

To contain the several hundred ducks and geese after they were big enough to graze, we erected a double wire electric fence just a foot off the ground to keep them in and hopefully, predators out. The charge was so strong that we lost a few young ones each year as they reached over the fence for greener grass a bit too far. The result . . . fried goose but not to eat. A couple hundred geese could graze an acre of grass within a month. If you didn't move the fence to greener acres, they would . . . and did, turn the turf into stinky mud. Geese and ducks can be awfully messy.

In the Fall just before Thanksgiving and Christmas, we would corral them in an old wooden snow fence. The pick-up was loaded with wooden poultry crates and backed up to the fence.

I would catch them and Susan would crate them, holding onto the wings so not to bruise them. We would catch and "dress" most of them for Thanksgiving and the rest for Christmas. I say "dress" when actually it should be "undress." But "dress" is the correct terminology. We would hire several people to help pull pin feathers and "other things" in the process. My dad helped me find some used poultry dressing equipment down country: A rubber fingered automatic feather picker, some large funnels, a large heated water vat to soak them called a scalder, hangars, and some 50-gallon drums to hold cold ice water for cooling. If you want to know more, ask Marliss, Lucy and Rod Goshow about the process. We would dress up to 175 chickens, ducks or geese a day. The geese and ducks took one extra step; there was a large container of melted paraffin wax heating over a double electric hot plate. After the feathers were removed, I'd dip them in the wax, then into the ice water to harden the wax, and then place them back over the picker. This would greatly reduce the manual labor to remove all the pin feathers. No kidding.

The goose and duck down was carefully salvaged in burlap bags and hung to dry in the heater room or on the heat pipes in the chicken house when we were heating the house for baby chicks. After a few months of drying, we would re-bag them and send them to a company in Grand Rapids, Michigan, to be used for down pillows. If I recall correctly, we received around $1.25 per lb. netting us about $100.00 each year. It was worth the awful smell in the chicken house as the feathers dried.

Another entrepreneurial attempt to raise income was an egg route. I know, an egg route in the mountains of Sullivan County? Were you delirious? No, just full of ambition and needing income. So we filled the two small chicken coops Mr. Bennett had built with leghorn layers. There were 500 in each one. When they began laying, we gathered, washed, graded and boxed the eggs for sale. The old milkhouse was our staging area.

This was after the veal project "bit the dust," which you'll read about later. Susan was a huge help in all these projects, offering to do whatever needed done. She gathered, washed and helped me grade all the eggs on an old grader which separated the eggs by weight into divisions of pullet, medium, large and extra large trays. We boxed and marked them accordingly and every Wednesday, I'd load the old Ford station wagon up with eggs and head toward Towanda. I developed the route as I went, stopping to ask if anyone was interested in fresh farm eggs each week.

Knock knock. "Farmer here. Anyone interested in farm fresh eggs?" By the time I reached the borough of Towanda, I was out of eggs.

There were a few who said they had to wait till the next week to pay and being the nice guy, I let them charge. Bad idea. In the end, they stuck me good, albeit not such a great sum of money. Eventually, the chickens quit laying and I decided to drop the route and sell the layers.

In the early 1970s, brother-in-law Abe Landis, bought a farm with the intention of raising beef. We used our barn to start the calves on a milk machine called "The Robot." It was built to automatically feed powdered milk to 50 calves. It never really worked well.

Though an ingenious invention, the calves either drank too much or not enough. That endeavor got chalked up to experience and "The Robot" still sits in the corner of the old milkhouse waiting for a proper burial.

When the calves were large enough, we moved them to Abe's barn across the fields and started another 50 bull calves. As they grew, we developed an automatic feeding system of corn mixed with supplement for the older cattle, dividing them in two pens so we could house almost 100 cattle. I built feed bunks and hay racks for them and a large feed bin up in the barn. We had a trench for silage and a skid steer loader to feed them in the large open feed lot. Abe had a 3,500 bushel Butler corn drying bin erected with a perforated floor to dry the corn with a propane gas dryer.

I was the farmer, maintenance man and caretaker of this operation. To provide enough corn for all these animals took more than my 110 acres of corn. So he bought corn.

Unfortunately, in 1974, the corn prices skyrocketed due to 20% interest rates and other factors. It eventually put Abe out of the cattle business. I can still see him backing a large cattle trailer down to the barn with his Eagle AWD car. He hauled eight 1000-lb. finished cattle down to his butcher shop, GraBrams in Harleysville, every other week or whenever enough were ready for market.

Abe's love for farming and business also enabled me to get more heavily into farming, something I deeply enjoyed in spite of the high investment and long night hours of field work. I needed bigger equipment. The small model 50 John Deere tractor needed help.

I found the tractor of my dream; a 4020 diesel, no cab but lots of power and BIG. Next I bought a new 5-bottom semi-automatic reset plow and a 13' disk and a four-row corn planter. I was set to go and go I did. That's when I needed a hired man and found several to help me. We ran hard and long, sun up to way after sun down. With my mom's help, I bought a new hay baler with a thrower after the first one broke, built 3 rack wagons to catch the bales and bought a used 9' New Holland haybine to replace the old 7' sickle bar mower and Oliver crusher.

I had owned a pull behind 7' combine which I used for custom combining of oats in the area. It was time for a larger more efficient machine. I found a New Idea Uni-System at a John Deere dealer in Allentown. I built my own cab for it which worked well for a couple years. Mike was only two years old and loved crawling up into the cab and pretending to drive it.

Finally, a cab tractor. Loading straw bales.

I switched to round bales to save labor. A great decision.

In 1976, I traded it for a self-propelled #55 John Deere combine with a 13' grain head and a 3-row corn head. It was the one I used to do custom combining and corn shelling for several years even driving clear to the other side of Wyalusing to Camptown for extra income. The late nights caught up with me one day while driving back home after the combine broke down in Camptown. I was driving the only Volvo I ever owned and coming down near Devil's Elbow, I fell asleep and ran over a guard rail stopping short of falling into the creek. Oh the joys of working long days in the fields. Well, yes, it was joy most of the time.

Eventually, by 1985 I believe it was, trying to run the farm, family, church leadership and a new building business got to be too crazy. I had to decide whether to sell the combine and downsize or buy a bigger and better one. I sold the combine, the disk, plow and planter, and was happy to have less headaches and more time for our family.

Farming, however, never got out of my blood. And so, even though I sold all my big equipment, eventually, little by little, I bought other equipment to replace it, only on a smaller scale. I continued to make my own hay except for a few years when I let a neighbor make it on shares. Eventually, we made the transition from small square bales to big round bales. The difference was astounding. No more handling each 35 to 40-lb. bale, all 7000 of them, first stacking them on the wagon in the field, then onto the elevator and into the hay mall, and finally stacking them tightly in the mall only to have to handle them again when loading a truck or feeding them.

I eventually sold my square baler and bought a used Gehl round baler which made large 600-lb. bales. I bought a couple bale spears which mounted on the tractor to carry and load them. Now all that hay could be handled quickly and easily by machinery. It was the best transition in my farming career. To this day, in 2012, I continue to use that baler and the big round bale method. Only, I now have a larger JD 6400 tractor with a cab on it. Yes, a cab. Not that I needed one, but it was a dream I had for many years. Factor in my allergy to dusts, molds and ragweed and you tip the scale of should I or shouldn't I buy a cab tractor? Okay, so I splurged. Nevertheless, I bought one. It's been a pleasure baling too. Oh, don't forget the investment factor. ☺ John Deeres usually increase in value. I rest my case.

CHAPTER 37

Rocks, Rocks and More Rocks

"**Y**ou know . . . without all those rocks, the soil in Sullivan County would never warm up enough to produce crops. So be thankful for the," were the wise words and harsh truth of an elderly Christian gentleman. He had lived in Sullivan County all of his 80 years. I stood there dumbfounded.

"Guess I never thought of it that way," I said thinking about what he'd just said.

Reading back over some entries in my 1965 diary made me laugh and also want to cry with pain as I relive farming those first years in Sullivan County.

Quoting from my diary ". . . Tuesday, May 10 – started plowing back field . . . 1/2 done. Wednesday – plowed more of back field but mold board broke, couldn't finish. Thursday – broke tip off of plow share, Rudy fetched new parts for me . . . . put new one on and finished back field by 10:00 p.m. Friday – plowed side hill . . . plowed up awful and plow trips too often. Started Rudy's fields.

"Week of May 17th; Monday – took 10 calves to T.M. Landis in Harleysville, brought 20 little pigs back. Tuesday – made more geese fence around pond. Cultivated patch. Wednesday – started harrowing . . . terrible shape . . . sod lumps and stony . . . picked lots of rocks and stones up. Harrowed it about 4 or 5 times to get it nice."

Now let me give you some background so you can appreciate the agony. I grew up in Montgomery County, Pennsylvainia. My guess is that the word "rock" isn't even listed in the farmers' almanac for that area. We had no clue what it was like to farm ground that "grew" rocks. No sir. Plowing was a pleasure to enjoy . . . and we did. We used disks and culitpackers, not harrows. That area was not mountainous. It was located only 200 ft. above sea level—not 1700 ft. like Sullivan County—so the soil warmed quickly.

However, looking at the good hay and corn crops growing on those mountain fields when we moved to Sullivan County, you would never know the trouble they'd been through to get those crops to grow. I sure didn't. So as the weather cleared, I hooked up the two-bottom trailer plow to my first and prized tractor, "Johnny" model 50. I was so proud of its whopping 32 HP two-cylinder engine. My very own tractor and plow.

No problem, I thought. *It WILL take me longer than with Daddy's new 3010s but I can do it.* Oh how naive I was. But with youth comes determination. With determination comes accomplishments and bad words. Sometimes. It was a difficult learning process but one I wouldn't part with. It matured me and taught me patience and endurance.

More diary quotes:

"Week of May 24th, 1965; tried to finish planting corn in back field . . . got caught in terrific rain storm . . . field drenched and muddy. Went fishing . . . caught 3 rainbow trout.

Monday, June 7; baled hay for Henry with neighbor's model 66 NH baler . . . baled 186 bales at 6 cents per bale. Friday – mowed side hill, raked church piece – got baler greased but motor wouldn't start . . . hay must wait.

Following week; Tuesday – raked side hill but not fit. Wednesday – raked hay into double rows, looked ready but wasn't. Thursday – rained all day . . . spoiled value of hay.

Monday – baled side hill . . . real dry but poor quality. Baler knotter misses tying so many. Wednesday – sprayed corn . . . raked hay till wheel broke. Fixed rake and finished raking hay . . . baler broke down. Forecast – rain, so borrowed Dale Bennett's baler . . . got rained out after 34 bales – Susan loaded all of them while I baled.

Thursday – Canvassed for Bible school in morning . . . raked hay in afternoon. Got baler fixed. Corn in poor shape in back field. Army worms and ants destroyed 7 of the 9 acres. County agent recommends I harrow it under and sow grass. Too late to replant corn.

Friday – baled hay below church . . . good shape . . . 435 bales."

Dear God! Farming . . . it's a wonderful life . . . if you can keep your sense of humor. Anybody wanna farm?

CHAPTER 38

Real Mountain People
. . . Like Ellery

"Listen, my brothers; Has not God chosen those who are poor in the eyes of the world to be rich in faith and to inherit the kingdom He promised those who love Him? If you show special attention to the man wearing fine clothes and say, 'Here's a good seat for you,' but say to the poor man, 'You stand there' or 'Sit on the floor by my feet,' have you not discriminated among yourselves and become judges with evil thoughts?" James 2: 3-5

ELLERY **HATCH**, 79 of Forksville RD 1 died Tuesday, Aug. 6, 1991 at Leader Nursing home, Williamsport. He was born Aug. 2, 1912 in Elkland Township, Sullivan County, the son of the late Raymond J. and Laura Carter Hatch. Ellery was a life-time resident of Sullivan County. He enjoyed farming and worked for the farmers in the area. He had attended the Living Hope Fellowship while health permitted and was a member of the Sullivan County Senior Citizens. He is survived by three sisters, Goldie Galloway of Alexandria RD, PA, Vera Gunyon of Reston, VA and Anna Hatch Stefano of LaPorte; one brother, Leonard Hatch of Forksville RD and several nieces and nephews. The funeral and committal service will be held Friday, Aug. 9, 1991 at 10 a.m. in the Russell P. McHenry Funeral Home, 119 Carpenter St., Dushore with Pastors Eli Beachy and John Souder from the Living Hope Fellowship officiating. Relatives and friends are invited to call at the Russell P. McHenry Funeral home, Dushore on Thursday from 7 to 9 p.m. Burial will be in St. Peter's Cemetery, Hugo Corners, Elkland Township. —*Towanda Daily Review*

He was 30 years my elder. When I first saw him, he had the appearance of an 80-year-old mountain man, even at the age of 50.

171

"Get me a Snicker bar and two *Grits*," he grunted . . . his baseball cap cocked sideways with one crossed-eye on me as I got out of the car.

Hmmm . . . two papers, why two? I thought, and asked him . . . "Did you say two papers?"

"Yeah, two," he mumbled.

I ran into Jennings Store, got my milk, a paper for me and two for Ellery. I handed him his papers and couldn't resist asking again, "Ellery, why two papers?"

In his younger days, besides working part time picking rocks in farmers' fields, he peddled the *Williamsport Grit* newspaper to local families scattered around Elkland Twp., not by means of car or bicycle, but on foot. It must have taken him all day to peddle a couple dozen papers but it produced pocket change for "taters," tobacco and his Snicker bars. I knew that he could not read or write and was told by other neighbors that he signed his name with an "X." So, why two papers?

His answer was short, "Gotta have 'sompin' to start fire in the morning," he said as though I should have known.

Shocked and a bit humored by his answer, I just said . . . "Oh, okay, just wondered."

Ellery was always dressed in dark tattered clothing, old sneakers and a grungy baseball cap tipped to one side. He seldom shaved. In wintertime, a dark, long heavy overcoat, same baseball cap, brown cotton gloves and black buckle-up galoshes kept him warm and dry. He lived with his sister, Anna, and their aged mother in an old farmhouse on North Street at the time we first moved to Sullivan County.

Ellery Hatch, 1912-1991.

The photo of Ellery with a frost-covered beard was taken by Dr. Shoemaker. Doc gave it to me with the explanation that he saw Ellery walking a pig on a leash on North Street that day. So he stopped and took the picture. It is a classic of Ellery in a natural pose—an impression you can't forget.

We first noticed Ellery pushing an old steel wheeled wheelbarrow loaded with random lengths of barn boards, up North Street. I waved to him as I drove by. He turned his head slightly and kept walking. On another day, I discovered how far he actually went with that wheelbarrow. He wheeled it almost two miles to a fallen down barn on the future property of Sanford Alderfer. Sanford named it, "The Lone Pine Hunting Camp."

I stopped to talk with Ellery one day. He seemed very shy, never lifting his head much but with a slight grin he answered me. I was surprised that he wasn't too shy to ask, "Who are *you*?" We exchanged greetings and became friends.

I found out Ellery worked for farmers now and then so I asked him to help me pick rocks. It was comical and interesting trying to get him to ignore the small ones and just pick up the big ones. Didn't seem to matter much what I said, he picked the ones he felt like picking. Susan would make him lunch and he would relish his food in silence. I learned later on that Annie and he lived mostly on potatoes. They loved potatoes.

Each Christmas eve, we'd be outside Ellery's house singing carols. His sister Annie and their mother lived there too. Henry would take a prepared fruit basket from our church to the door and knock. No one would come so he'd set it on the top step. Year after year, same scenario and no answer. Just some sounds and a window curtain moved indicating that someone was still living there. I found myself staring at an old rusty car parked under the pine tree, flat tires sunken in the ground, weeds and saplings growing up and over it. That car was packed full of junk. I mean "p-a-c-k-e-d." And I wondered . . . *why*? There it sat for decades until the property was sold and someone moved it. The house still stands, but with the roof sagging and caving in, I doubt it will stand much longer.

Eventually, Ellery agreed to accept our invitations to join us at church. By then, his mother had died and Annie and Ellery moved into a relative's house down in the dip beyond our house. That's the house where "Ace" and Helen Ryman lived. I'll get to that later.

We'd pick up Ellery and also go down to Forksville to pick up Edna Boecker. That turned out to be quite entertaining. By the odor in the car, neither one must have bothered to bathe more than once a month, if that. God was stretching us and showing us how to love and be loved. Our kids received a whole new side of education scrunched into the back seat with Ellery and Edna on the way to church.

The part of church life they enjoyed the most was "fellowship meals." They soon became a "three-some" upon finding Gladys Heinze. Gladys was a little old lady who came faithfully to church with Henry and Irene. All three "mountain people" had either coal or wood stoves for heat and to cook with. Consequently, their clothes soaked up the odors and dust produced by the stoves. Mix that with cats and dogs, a goat or two and you have a unique, natural perfume.

I believe God has a sense of humor to mix just the right people to help filter and refine our judgmental attitudes. It worked. We had to change our views of others many times as we lived among these wonderful down-to-earth people.

Ellery and Annie both eventually had to give up their humble abodes and sign into a nursing home. Ellery went to DarWay initially and then moved to Leader Nursing Home in Williamsport where he died at age 79. I'll never understand how he survivied 79 years without the hygiene most of us think mandatory for health. He must have had an incredibly strong immune system. Susan worked at DarWay when he lived there and I would visit him. We'd play checkers. Yes, checkers. He had no clue about the rules or any simple strategy, but we played. He moved whereever he jolly well felt like it and I followed suit until we called it quits and he would win. ☺ It was childlike and good for both of us. We visited him in Leader Nursing Home a few times and played checkers there as well. The day he died, the world lost a simple, humble but great teacher. He taught us a "Jesus kind" of simple living.

Annie continued to live alone for a few years after Ellery left until her health failed desperately. Susan would go into the rat-infested, dungy place she called "home" to wash and care for her about twice a week for some time. We told her how nice it would be at Laporte or DarWay and how kind the nurses were. She insisted she stay there until finally, through the authority of home health nurses one sad dreary day the sheriff escorted her out of her filthy environment to The Laporte Nursing Home. I remember the occasion as though it happened on Holy ground. Lew Hope, with a nurse assisting him, carried a stretcher into the house with Sheriff Adams following behind fully clad in his authoritative attire. What was so impressive was the way in which they approached Annie, sitting sick and frail on a blood-soaked blanketed couch. Never did they chastise or talk down to her. They treated her with dignity and professionalism just like Jesus would have. It was a very sad yet a kind of Holy exit from a near hell hole to the likes of a palace. We visited her there on occasion, until her final days. Annie and Ellery both enjoyed the comforts of real civilization for a time; at least I think so, before finally feasting at the heavenly banquet table.

Ellery's brother was from the same mold. But he was more of an independent loner than the rest. He lived in a little shack back on Minersville Road behind our farm. Being a bit younger and having gone to school a few years, he managed to get a driver's license.

Owning a vehicle was his pride and it got him to the saw mill on time each day. Leonard stacked lumber as it came off the head saw 8 hours every day. He lived with his dog in that shack just large enough for a wood stove, a small bed, a bench and a small table. His dog slept in a little hutch outside. About once a month, Leonard would stop by the farm for a bale of hay . . . for his dog. Opening the back door to his car or truck, he said, "Just put it in there."

He'd pull out a dollar bill to pay me but I didn't want pay. I tried to refuse it but I can still see him shaking his head up and down shyly saying, "Yo-o-u-uu – ta-a-k-e-it." He stuttered; I assured him he didn't need to pay for it but he insisted. Occasionally we'd talk about God. He said he wasn't religious but that someday, he'd come to church. Often he'd say something about Ellery going to church and guessing God liked Ellery better than him. It was funny and yet very sad. He never did come to church, but said that he believed in Jesus and prayed to God.

The last time I spoke with Leonard was down at Jenning's Store, parked by the gas pump on a cold winter day. He opened his window and said he wanted gas. I offered to pump it for him and surprisingly he took the offer. After pumping the gas he handed me some bills and asked me to get him a bottle of Pepsi, some white bread and something else. I did so and handed him the change which he refused to take. We said goodbye and off he went.

The next week I viewed his body at McHenry's Funeral Home in Dushore. A handful of people did likewise. His obituary closed the last chapter of that particular Hatch family living on our mountain, The Cahill.

"The King will reply, 'Truly I tell you, whatever you did for one of the least of these brothers and sisters of mine, you did for me?" Mt. 25:40. To hear those sweet words will be . . . Heaven.

"There goes that little yellow Jeep again Susan," I said looking out the window early one morning soon after we had moved to Sullivan County. "I wonder who it is?" I soon found out. He was Ace Ryman. That's what Rudy called him. Who is Rudy, you ask? He's another mountain man who lived just up the dirt road from us.

Ace was Roscoe's right-hand man. Roscoe Burgess' sawmill was a mile down the road past Whiteley's farm on the left. According to Rudy, Ace was responsible to fire up the big steam boiler which powered the sawmill. At lunchtime and at the end of each day you could hear the boilers loud, high-pitched whistle as he shut the boiler down. Within a mile or two from the mill you could tell it was noon or 5:00 and quitting time. That was Ace's job and he did it well for the few years he lived after we moved here. The whistle blew for the last time in 1970, just before the big auction of Roscoe's Mill and contents.

I missed seeing that little yellow Jeep, with no roof or side panels, come chugging past the house at 15 mph each day. His wife, Helen, was left to raise three little foster children whom she consistently whipped into obedience . . .

well sometimes. They were more than a handful to be sure. Boyd, Bobby and Jimmy. Oh, the memories. I had each of them in boys' club, Sunday School class, Bible school classes and youth group. They all caught chickens for us, stacked hay wagons, picked rocks and stole stuff now and then. It was an experience I wouldn't ask to repeat nor would I want to have missed it. They brought their flimsy bikes to me to be fixed like I owned a bike shop. It was a great way to interact with them and I actually enjoyed it.

Unfortunately, I think they all spent time in jail. I was privileged to help marry Jimmy in the early '90s. The marriage lasted about 11 years until Jim couldn't keep himself out of jail. He harvested the fruit of the "reap what you sow" law. Every now and then, I get a phone call from his brother Bobby asking me to bail him out of some predicament he'd gotten into. It's so sad . . . and difficult to know how to help. God be merciful.

I think God taught us so much through these "mountain people" over the years. I wonder if they learned anything from us? Hopefully, they learned about Jesus.

Now take Rudy, for instance . . . oh my, what a character. Rudy Conrad lived up the dirt road on land adjacent to our property. I rented his land most of the years we lived here. His wife, Ruth, was an angel. She froze and canned lots of produce that Rudy grew in their garden. She picked over a hundred quarts of huckleberries on their property each year to can and to sell for profit. She also loved kids. We soon became good friends with Ruth and Rudy and claimed them as second grandparents to our kids.

When Renee was barely three years old, one summer day she came up missing. Apparently she liked Ruth so much, she decided to visit her. After much distress and not finding Renee, Susan noticed two people walking down the dirt road towards our house. It was Ruth holding Renee's little hand.

Neither of them was distressed. Rather, they were happy and enjoying the walk. I guess our explanation to Renee about why that wasn't a good idea sunk in because it didn't happen again.

Rudy was a rare bird. First of all he was raised through the Depression having to learn what hard work was. He told me many times of his long 8-mile trek over the Cahill Mountain to the booming lumber town of Laquin. That was back in the 1920s and '30s. After graduating from 8th grade, he would stay there all week and walk back and forth weekends to live with his parents in the house which he later inherited. We acquired the property back in 1998 from his daughter, Rose, which I turned into a vacation rental. We call it "Rudy's Place Vacation Rental." Appropriately named, I think. (*www.rudysplacevacationrental.com*)

Rudy told about when he owned one of the only threshing machines in the area and farmers would bring their piles of sheaves to him to thresh for a small fee. The old threshing machine died and rests next to the vacant barn hill on what is presently, "Rudy's Place Vacation Rental."

He told us stories about his ventures as a lumber jockey, buying and selling standing timber for folks for a nice profit. I wonder if that's not the reason why Rudy always had such a "fat" wallet. He did tell me he didn't trust banks and that you couldn't trust politicians. Many times, he'd ask me to "come and sit a spell." During those resting times, which I curiously endured, he would laugh as he replayed the stories of FDR and his shenanigans. I was never sure if he liked FDR or not. He had some crazy stories about those years after the Depression.

He should have run for township supervisor because he was always complaining how the road crews messed up. I remember him helping to put up snow-fence along the roads. Five-foot snow fences were erected each Fall and remained in Spring to keep drifting snow from piling up on roads. A shovel or bar made a good leaning stick as he told stories while the others worked.

Tinkering and gathering stuff pleased Rudy. His outbuildings were full of "junk" he'd purchased at sales, for a "bargin." Most of those bargins created a huge junk heap back in the woods behind his house. A few of them decorate the wall of the garage or some antique dealers' store. One man's junk, is another's treasure. We all experience it in some form.

"Do not store up for yourselves treasures on earth, where moths and rust destroy, and where thieves break in and steal . . . " Mt. 6:19

Rudy often told us that Ruth and he made a promise early in life. They promised to care for each other till death do part them. When Ruth's health began to fail, Rudy set up a bed in their living room next to the window. The old coal stove was cranked up to about 85 degrees in that room. Home Health Care and Meals on Wheels afforded them to live out their promise. The garage which I cleaned out 9 years after Rudy's death was proof of his hoarding and Meals on Wheels. Hundreds of tinfoil plates and platters were stacked high in the garage. Who knows for what?

Finally, the day came when Rudy could no longer care for Ruth and she was taken to the hospital and then transferred to DarWay. We noticed that Rudy visited her every day, driving himself in his pick-up truck. Then came the day when he could no longer drive and he waited for people to take him. Before Ruth died, she no longer knew who was visiting her. Rudy went anyhow, tears wetting his face, feeding her meals with trembling hands. It was as sweet as it gets. Thankfully, they knew Jesus as Savior.

I think Rudy died of a broken heart at the age of 93 in 1993. It was the same year and age as Grammy Landis died. God bless him.

Dyton Simpkins was a man after God's own heart. We called him "Dykie." I don't know where he came from but heard he had married into the Hatch family via Ellery's sister, Naomi. When I first met them, they were living in an old farmhouse on Joe Collins' property above "Lick Crick," at the bottom of Devil's Elbow.

Dykie reminds me of some Old Testament characters the likes of rag-clad Jeremiah, the weeping prophet, Amos, the poor sheep herder, or the prostitute courting Hosea, loving her against all odds.

I remember going to Dykie's house to invite them to church. They were both very shy and what we would refer to as "backward" people. We would see them drive by slowly on occasion in very old cars. Then they moved to another place in Overton and finally we realized that they were homeless and were living and sleeping in their car. He would stop at our house when his car needed water for the radiator or air in the tires. It was the least I could do. Our hearts ached for them and we wondered what God would have us do for them.

One day he ran out of gas nearby and we gave him some gas. Since we really didn't know them very well, I wasn't quite sure if we could trust them. My distrust was confirmed sadly one day as we returned home from town. There sat Dykie's car parked next to our unlocked gasoline tank and he was pumping gas. What I said or how I reacted, thank God, I don't recall. I only remember one statement I made to him; "Dykie, all you have to do is ask me if you need gas and I'll be happy to help out. But please don't take it without asking."

Our relationship cooled for a short time and then we became *real* friends. Chuck in particular, having a heart for kids and special needs people, became his best friend.

Because of his relationship with the Hatch and Ryman families, he was given a place to live after his wife, Naomi died. That's when some of us from Estella Mennonite Church got more involved. His "home" was a small dilapidated shack in the woods above the Ryman's house just off a small dirt road between our road and the road to Whitley's.

Like his brother-in-law, Leonard, the contents of the shack were a bench, card table of sorts, boxes of stuff, an old unreliable coal-oil or kerosene stove for heat and a low Army bed frame with a thin torn mattress. Everything, especially his clothes, reeked of kerosene.

Dykie slept in the same clothes he walked, worked and went to church in. It was difficult to tolerate the smell as we took him to church time and again.

But it was Chuck Berke, Marliss' husband, who did the "Jesus thing" and gave him a bath in their own tub. Marliss tells me Chuck even used a small hack saw to trim his toenails. Leave it to Chuck to not only think of it, but to "do unto others as we would have them do to us."

Many a cold night, Chuck and I took turns checking on Dykie to make certain he wouldn't freeze to death alone in his shack. The wicks in the kerosene stove needed constant cleaning. We helped him buy 5 gallons of kerosene when he ran out of cash. Back then, I think it was only 15 cents a gallon, fortunately. But Dykie's paycheck was small and he was often too sick to walk the 5 miles to work, which made it smaller.

God gifted Dykie with a love for kids. He wrote a few poems about kids, albeit difficult to read. I recall a 3-page letter handwritten on crumpled paper about how God loves the little children and how we should pay attention to them as Jesus told His disciples to do.

Chuck encouraged him to read it in church. He shuffled to the front that Sunday morning in his tattered overcoat and baseball cap, pulled out the tattered papers and began to slowly read his poem. His large stubby hands, scarred and stained by kerosene, and handling rough-sawn lumber, shook slightly as he read how Jesus called the little children to him so he could love them. Talk about touching hearts and spirits . . . he did.

It was a dark sad night when Chuck and I found Dykie lying on his dusty, blackened bed, bundled up in his overcoat, stiff, cold and lifeless. He had traded his shack for a mansion in Heaven. Annie had called us to go check on him. She hadn't seen him for a day and a half and was worried. That was in the early 1980s.

I think it was Chuck who had a small golden plaque made in memory of Dykie. It hung at church for many years in memory of our humble, little mountain man. Who would have guessed that a road would be named after a poor old soul like him. But if you drive past that dirt road today, there's the sign; "Dykes Road". The shack is gone, burned to the ground and replaced by princess pine and brush. But his life and love for God and children remain a treasure, a legacy not to be forgotten by us.

God says . . . "He raises the poor from the dust and lifts the needy from the ash heap; he seats them with princes and has them inherit a throne of honor." I Samuel 2: 8

Thanks God, for people like Dykie, Ruth and Rudy, Ace and Helen, Leonard, Ellery, Annie, Naomi, Edna and Gladys . . . and oh, so many others like them. We saw Jesus walking among us. Sometimes, we just didn't recognize Him.

CHAPTER 39

Dirt Bikes, Snowmobiles and Four-Wheelers

"Hey guys, lean front, hug the gas tank on this one . . . here we go," Danny said with a big grin. The front wheel leaped high as dirt and dust covered those behind him.

Sunday afternoons were our opportunities to visit and have some fun. During the growing-up years of our family and church in Sullivan County, we spent many hours with older couples at church. There were none our age. Dave and Miriam Bauman lived in Lincoln Falls with their four kids. They were exactly 10 years older than us but we enjoyed visiting together. Pastor Henry and Irene Goshow were 21 years older and still had three or four of their seven kids living at home. Henry and Irene were like second parents to us and on occasion, babysat Renee and Brenda.

There were some community families and neighbors we occasionally spent time with too. Another family we enjoyed visiting, was Marvin and Dorothy Groff. They lived over Wheelerville Mountain near Canton on a large farm. They attended our church. Marvin lead singing and Dorothy, an elementary schoolteacher, used her skills teaching Sunday school.

The Groffs had two sons, Danny and Devon. They were smart and adventurous kids. When we met them, they were probably ages 8 and 10. Their love for the dairy farm was displayed by their cheerful attitude with daily chores. I was also amazed at their mechanical skills on the farm.

These two boys helped spark my interest in dirt bikes. We were at the Groff's for Sunday dinner (lunch) one warm summer day. The boys had excused themselves and soon we heard the bikes start up.

All of a sudden Dorothy went to the window and said, "Susan, John Merrill, come here and watch this."

"Are you serious? I can't believe that. He's going to kill himself," I said dumbstruck. From the front window we saw a bike racing up the road from below their house. It was the neighbor boy, Chuck. His bike was almost vertical as he stood on the back pegs balancing his Suzuki 185 like a pro as he roared past the house up the road for about a quarter mile.

"Just wait," Dorothy said, "Danny'll be right behind him."

Sure enough. He was only 14 and could control that bike like a pro. With the front wheel high in the air, standing on the rear pegs, body leaning forward, he raced the bike like a circus monkey on a flying trapeze.

"I know, I know. I told Marvin they're going to hurt themselves," Dorothy said. Marvin continued enjoying his lunch, but added a brief comment, "They're just having fun. At least I know where they are."

"Good grief, now here comes Devon," I said. He didn't make it to the top of the hill doing a "wheelie" like the other two but for a 12 year old, it was way beyond anything I'd want to try.

Up and down that hill they roared with the front wheel in the air for quite a while. Each time trying to avoid any legal vehicles using the road.

That was my first experience with dirt bikes. Henry and Rod Goshow were the first to own dirt bikes on our mountain. Henry thought it was a good way to spend some quality time with his son who was struggling "to find himself." This was a great way for Henry to help find him. Rod rode an orange Suzuki 250, and Henry, a red 185.

Lowell had his Kawasaki 350 parked in the garage and Leon his Suzuki 185, so when they came back home, they could ride together.

That left me without a ride except on occasion when I would borrow Henry's. I began to look for a used bike to buy and found one in great shape in Canton. Canton had a deal-

ership for Suzuki cycles and Artic Cat snowmobiles, serving many happy riders. The one I saw for sale was a red 185 (185 c.c. engine). It was only a couple years old and in great shape. I paid $250. Back then, that was a lot of cash.

I'm really not sure how or why, but Susan approved of it. She even encouraged me to get it, knowing how much I envied the other guys with bikes. Of course this would mean she would be in the house or alone with the kids while I'd be out riding. Nevertheless, I bought it.

I can't express how much fun I had on that dirt bike. Sunday after Sunday we mounted our bikes after a big Sunday dinner at Henry and Irene's house and headed down or up the hill. Often, there would be five or six of us. Danny and Devon would ride over the mountain picking up Ken Gochanuer to meet us at Henry's. On occasion, Leo Heatwole, Carol's husband (then, boyfriend) from Virginia, would be up for a visit or Leon and Lowell would be there for the weekend and there would be seven or eight of us.

"Follow me," Rod said, and before I even had my bike started, he was off. Up through the woods behind the chicken house following old deer or log trails he went. Up over the ledge onto the grassy field with the rest of us not far behind. Back down and across the road into the woods we roared ending up at the bottom of their property where he stopped for a chat.

Leon, always being the big risk taker, suggested we try a new trail up over the hill in front of us. It was really more of a challenge than a suggestion. He cut loose with his bike flinging mud, sticks and dirt everywhere heading up the hill in a mad zigzaging pattern, picking his way over ledges, around boulders and trees, over rotten logs until he reached the top. One by one, we all followed. Some of us having to turn and head to the bottom to start over with a second attempt. Before long we were all on top laughing and joking about those who had to make second or third attempts. Then we'd head back down to try it again, only faster each time. If you didn't lean forward far enough on the steepest trails, the front end would come up and you'd wipe out. Miraculously, no one got seriously hurt.

Then there were those long rides up to the old strip mines on Barclay Mountain and the rides to Laquin and up to Sunfish Pond or over to Wheelerville via game commission roads that were supposed to be closed.

The more memorable ride was on a Sunday when Leo was here from Virginia visiting. He was quite fond of riding, though maybe not as experienced as some. Challenges were always enticing and no one would want to "chicken out." There was a power line over the mountain someone suggested we try out.

To get to it, we had to ride down to Lincoln Falls, down Elk Creek Road about a mile, up through an old pasture to the bottom of the power line. We stopped to survey and evaluate our approach. Of course, Danny chose to go first. He was used to laying on the gas tank, front wheel in mid-air and clearly adept with balance. No wonder this hill didn't intimidate him.

Dirt bikes were built for rough terrain and were quite durable. But this one would test the limits. Most of us made it to the top without wrecking. But a couple didn't. Leo didn't. His bike came up too far, too fast and before he could correct the momentum, the bike came up and over as both crashed to the rocky ground. The bike's wheel kept spinning until someone hit the kill switch. Lifting the bike off Leo, they quickly helped him up to check on the damage to him first. He was bleeding and sore but okay. As with crashes like that, a light gets broken, clutch or brake handles and fenders get bent, but generally we get up and ride.

Surveying the trail from the top of the hill was not the greatest thrill. That came *during* the ascent and maneuvering all the natural obstacles en route. I had my share of spills and thrills during those wonderful hours of trail riding. I'm certain though, if Susan knew or would have happened to observe any of those climbs, she would have been horrified. ☹ No doubt God sent angels to guard us on those rides.

It is worthy of mention that Pastor Henry rode with us many of those times until the age of 56. I was often amazed at his riding skills at that age. Danny went on to graduate from Elim Bible College and did a six-month pastoral interim for us at Estella in 1984. My red Suzuki 185 rests comfortably in the old red shed beside our garage patiently awaiting its resurrection day. I hope it doesn't have to wait much longer. ☺

It was 1970 when I was first introduced to Artic Cat snowmobiles. Susan's brother, Abe, decided it would be fun to snowmobile in the mountains. He already owned some ground and had built a nice cabin a mile behind us called Kahill Lodge. Seems like we had much more snow back then. Abe knew some guys near him around Harleysville who sold Artic Cats. He decided to invest in a couple and bought a trailer to haul them up here. His first was a Puma 440 and the second a 640 c.c. He bought covers for them and outfits for him and his wife, Grace.

I'll never forget the thrill of riding those machines. Even 20 below zero didn't stop us from riding. Never had I experienced such speed on snow as with those snowmobiles. Sanford Alderfer also joined us with his two machines. One day we decided to take a long ride. We gassed them up, and headed up over the Cahill. I led the way since I was more familiar with the mountain. We followed heavily snow-covered township dirt roads until we reached Deep Hollow back on the mountain. Then we rode old log trails and abandoned roads over the mountain down to the Schrader Creek near Monroeton, 20 miles from home. We picked our route by instinct best we could, hoping our gas would last the trip. Back through the mountains we roared, enjoying the clear cold air and scenery, stopping occasionally to chat. Over frozen creeks, across the abandoned lumber town of Laquin and back up the "no winter maintance" road past Minerstown we rode, stopping at the old Quinlintown schoolhouse for a drink from a flowing spring. A stainless steel cup hung on a tree limb for visitors.

After about 6 hours of rough riding and great sightseeing, we arrived back home ready for some hot chocolate. Susan was always happy to serve us, even after tending to the kids while we rode the mountains. I must say, I felt a twinge of self indulgence and guilt.

She never made me feel that way, it was just my sensitivity to her

My latest upgrade. Toby enjoys riding too.

having to stay behind. I did take her out riding now and then but I think she went for my sake more than for her own pleasure.

"Thanks honey for being so tolerant of my frivolous, costly, fun-filled activities." Guess I'll never change. Now I have my own fleet (3) of snowmobiles sitting in the converted chicken house to store machinery, waiting for the next big snow to come. My reasoning . . . it's for the kids and grandkids. Yeah, right.

And now for the past five years, we have evolved into another generation of fun machines . . . four-wheelers. Guess if I want to pass blame for that idea, it would best go to Big Mike. My first and startling introduction to the four-wheeler sport was a green three-wheeler that came racing down the hard top road across the field towards Hugo's Corner. I had huge doubts that whatever it was could stop at the stop sign and wondered who would be riding so fast and crazy.

Whoops . . . it was Big Mike coming to take Lori for a ride . . . or maybe not. It was Big Mike, and we were about to be introduced to our future son-in-law. But first we watched him perform one of those "Danny Groff pull-ups."

About the time he got in front of our house, up came the front wheel as he stood upright, head down, full-bore throttle, roaring up past the church at 90, well, maybe 50 mph.

"Was that . . . Mike?" I asked Lori standing there waving with a huge smile.

"Ahh . . . yeeaaah . . . that was . . . Mike." My mind was spinning trying to determine my response on his return to our house. I needed to explain, clearly to him how I felt about such actions.

"Hey . . . ahhh . . . Mike . . . nice three-wheeler you got there." Not wanting to offend or intimidate him on his first visit to see Lori, but needing to inform him of my disapproval of such actions, I continued washing my car as I spoke.

"Just want you to know that we don't do that around here. It's too dangerous on these roads with all the log trucks going by. Don't mind if ya ride over here, just keep it down a bit more, okay?" I can't remember his reply but he still came around to see Lor. That story gets repeated, I mean expanded, by Mike quite often at family gatherings.

Over time, I backed off and began to enjoy his free, adventurous spirit. In fact, I began to enjoy fast rides myself. It was even okay to pull kids on inner tubes behind his three-wheeler on the snow and on the pond ice. Susan was more cautious requesting everyone wear helmets or at least ride slowly. But even she began to tolerate the speed, pray and hope for the best.

There's this vivid memory of the day when all the kids and grandkids were home, we were skating and Mike was spinning around on the pond with his three-wheeler. He hooked a long rope to a large tube and began pulling kids around. Mikey, who was then about 13, got on the tube and I could soon see that Mike was up for some fun. He spun this way then that, and then made a long arc around the bank of the pond. The tube, with Mikey hanging on for dear life went flying across the ditch and pond bank and went air-borne, spinning Mikey into the air in a tumble of snow. To this day, a couple of the son-in-laws, no names here, claim I jumped up yelling, "He's hurt, he's hurt, come help!"

I know I over-reacted to what I saw as a concerned Dad, but it's always more fun to "enhance" the story. Well, it all ended with everyone still in one piece and laughing a lot. Guess "all is well that ends well."

Some years later, I decided it was time to own a four-wheeler. So I bought one from Rod Martin's brother. He had a Yamaha 250 and wanted to sell it. It was well taken care of so I bought it. One bike, or one of anything for that matter, isn't much fun when there are lots of riders waiting for a turn. So a couple years later,

I bought my second one from, "racing Billy." He sells used and some new ATVs near Shunk. It turned out to be a very good investment. The kids and grandkids have had lots of fun with them too. Well, at least most of the time.

There is . . . this one incident I will relate for fun's sake. It was the day before I married Marliss, September 2, 2011. Kids and grandkids were outside playing and riding four-wheelers. A particular son-in-law of Marliss' was enjoying taking his son, Jack and Bruce's daughter, Natili for a slow ride. All was going well, as far as I knew, until I heard some commotion and people yelling out back of the house. I ran out to look and noticed Mikey helping Damon pull one of the four-wheelers out of the pond. Story has it that Damon was coming around the pond with the kids when he hit a hole. The four-wheeler jumped sideways and began to slide into the pond. Using his good common sense, he quickly put the kids on the bank as he fought with the machine trying desperately to reverse the process. Mikey happened to see or hear him call and ran to the rescue. By the time Mike got there the machine was basically submerged. But Damon shoved and Mike and Bruce pulled until it was back on dry ground.

The kids were a bit shaken and Damon was soaking wet, but no one was hurt. It took a few hours for Mike and Damon to empty the gas tank and try to dry everything out, but it wouldn't start. After a few months' rest, I completely disassembled the carburetor and cleaned everything out and put it all back to-

Poppie and one of the grandkids ready to ride.

gether. On the first attempt to start it, it purred like a kitten and has ever since. Oh the memories we make!

Mike and I enjoyed clearing trails in our woods for our four-wheelers and snowmobiles. We continue to groom the trails and create new ones. They are great for hiking as well.

If only Susan could see the fun we have in our woods these days. On the other hand, I really believe she can see that. But the trails she walks in the forests of Heaven far exceed any experience we could ever imagine. So I anticipate many long walks some day far beyond Sullivan County with her and all our loved ones. Come Lord Jesus, Come!

From dirt bikes to snowmobiles to four-wheelers; what will it be next? I suspect, more of the same with more family enjoying more trails in more places. So y'all come. Get back to nature with one of Poppie's toys. Just stay out of the pond!

-Written January 12, 2012

CHAPTER 40

Holiday Traditions

Since it was important for Susan and I to see our families over holidays, we chose to drive the distance and see both sides of our family.

We agreed to celebrate our own Christmas on Christmas eve. That way we could pack up and travel down country to our parents on Christmas day.

We waited till after the first week of deer season right after Thanksgiving to get our tree. Come to think of it, we didn't even have a tree for the first few years of our marriage. Mennonite tradition and doctrine taught us from the book of Jeremiah, that it was the "heathen" people that cut down trees and brought them into houses to decorate. We both grew up under that doctrine and tradition without a Christmas tree or for that matter, no Santa Claus. Those were "worldly" practices.

Santa Claus . . . now that reminds me of a story.

Since our Christmas tradition was to celebrate the birth of Christ and to disregard the world's hype over Santa, we ignored anything to do with Santa Claus. It happened that a close neighbor enjoyed displaying a large plastic Santa on top of his roof near the chimney. It was lighted well at night. Our young family of two was driving by one day when four-year-old Renee excitedly blurts out, "Daddy, look at that little fat man up on the roof, what's he doing?"

I can't recall my response. It was so funny and yet profound to think that at four years old, our daughter had not yet known about Santa. I guess if you try hard enough, you can shelter them quite a while. Back then, we took some pride in protecting them from all the "worldly" influence of society. But it was time to do some explaining.

I think it was around the time Renee was two years old that we decided we wanted to include a small tree as part of our joyous celebration of Christ's birth. But why buy a tree when you can cut one in your own back woods? That year we had a little 3' white pine "Charlie Brown" tree lightly decorated with little white lights. Just the right size for a little girl and a few presents.

As our quiver of kids grew larger, so did the trees. We took our pick-up with a hand saw, our Flexible Flyer sled and a rope and headed down the road. A neighbor had an acre or so of trees we could cut for $5.00. When all four kids were still home, the whole family went for the tree. Of course each one had a different opinion of which was the best, so the majority ruled, unless Mom was along, then she ruled.

When the kids left for college, Mom and I went for the tree. I left her pick it out 'cause I knew we'd all be happier. My pick always seemed to have a "hole" somewhere or was lopsided, too short or too tall. You know. Anyway, we ended up with great-looking trees at low prices, cutting them ourselves at local tree farms.

It was also tradition to hang a star on the stone chimney and arrange a manger scene in front with a spotlight on them. In later years the manger scene was moved in front of an outbuilding using a spotlight to cast the shadow on the building. Besides the star on the chimney, a large wreath was added. Some bushes were decorated with tiny white lights and set with timers.

Up until Mom's last year with us, she insisted on electric candles at each window. Not just at our house but Rudy's Place as well. Seemed like every other trip to town, we'd buy another pack of little white night lights. I must say, it was soothing and peaceful to look at and especially cozy with the house lights off at night. A few years I went a bit crazy and put lights in the milkhouse. Why not celebrate? It's Jesus' birthday. So we did.

It's now the day before Christmas. All is set. All is well. WFLN, our Christian radio station is warmly saturating our house with "Joy to the world, the Lord is come . . ." Renee is in rare form. It's her "bestest" time of year. ☺ Brenda has the house cleaned up—it's her specialty. Lori reorganizes the little play house I built for her. And Mike, at seven years old, is full of pranks for his big sisters. ☺ Presents have been bought, wrapped and laid neatly under the tree. Mom has planned ahead very well, lots of cookies are in tins, she bought plenty of shrimp, scallops, fish, and has baked and cooked all afternoon. Christmas eve is our traditional Christmas. We always have a large meal featuring seafood and of course some wonderful desserts. Sometimes it was fruit pies, sometimes a triple cheese cake, fruit salad or raspberry Chantilly. Um um um—makes me salivate!

After a wonderful *gut* meal we would clear the table, guys and gals alike, and head for the living room. Most kids from little on, like to perform and "do shows." Ours were no exception. "Hey y'all, come sit down. We have a show we want to do." That phrase was heard over and over whenever our families gathered around. And so we sat . . . and waited . . . til they finally got their thing together. Little kids, little ditties. Grade school kids, bigger ditties. But then they get older and even the parents get involved. That's when it really got to be fun. We laughed so hard at the skits they all drummed up that we were crying . . . it was so hilarious.

For instance, the girls had decided to act out the entire Christmas story described in Luke 2: 8-20. It involved, of course, the angel scene, the shepherds, and the scene at the manger. Now these skits eventually evolved and grew into some fancy random productions precisely to honor Mom and me and in some way tell the Christmas story. So Mom and I sat on the couch, often with my arm around her, waiting and watching with great anticipation.

Many of these skits and moment by moment actions were videotaped from about 1988 until 1999. We have boxes full of those hilarious and crazy times.

In the front door come a couple of guys wrapped in blankets holding large sticks or cattle canes; Shepherds. ☺ From the kitchen and into the living room come two shrouded people carrying a baby; Mary and Joseph and baby Jesus. ☺ Crawling on the floor are several kids covered with wool blankets; Sheep. ☺ A couple of characters hunched over with blankets covering them; Donkeys. ☺ Way before they all get assembled and while someone is narrating, the guys start laughing and so do the kids. Before they can finish, the cast falls apart from laughing so hard. Mom and I are in stitches, soaked with pleasure derived from our creative kids and grandkids.

Oh yes, "A merry heart IS good like a medicine!" Each year, for many years, they all rallied their imaginations to perform some hilarious drama. Often Poppie and MawMaw's little quirks were the inspiration for the props and the skit. Phrases like . . . "what-in-the-world was that" or . . . "that's the limit" or . . . "now John Merrill, stop teasing." Ways they might imitate MawMaw could be . . . "oh, are you wearing that?" . . . or hold a phone to their ear while pretending to cook and set the table simultaneously.

Big Mike was especially clever at miming and imitating us. We loved it 'cause we knew how much they all loved and respected us. Such a treasure!

When we got things put somewhat back to normal, we gathered around the living room and sang some carols. With Susan sitting next to me on the couch, little ones scattered on the floor and the rest surrounding the living room, I read the Christmas story from Luke 2: 8-20 from the King James version of the Bible. While the kids and grandkids were still quite young, I challenged them to memorize that portion of scripture. Each year we attempt to continue saying that portion by memory.

For many years we bought presents for everyone. When the people numbers got higher, we picked names. After a while, the tree couldn't hold the presents and we limited our gifts to one per person. Cryin' out loud, whose birthday is it anyhow? Mom and I always gave money cards with a nice check inside. It was always appreciated, albeit without fail, you know who pipes up with "You got $____, I only got $____." All in good fun of course. Like most mothers, Mom still bought a small gift for the girls and little things for the grandkids.

It was also our tradition to hang stockings from the fireplace mantle and stuff them with little trinkets. No, Santa had nothing to do with it. It was worth the smiles and big bright eyes as they opened gifts. Midnight came too quickly Christmas eve and if the little ones were already sleeping, they were carried up to bed. Silent night, Holy night, all is calm, all is bright . . . and all are tired and happy. We have been blessed beyond measure.

As the family grew and expanded with boyfriends and spouses, we would sing carols for Ruth and Rudy, Annie and Ellery, and Mary Lyons, our elderly neighbors. It blessed us as much as it did them.

If we had snow, we'd snowmobile, sled and build forts; if we had ice on the pond thick enough to skate, many of us would skate. I loved being the pivot person pulling a long line of kids doing "crack the whip." Without fail, most of them would fall down laughing their hearts out or moaning from pain.

If it happened to be a warm fall and winter, we'd take a walk through the woods to the back field. The nostalgia of those walks or sports is unforgettable and cherished memories. My heart aches to want them repeated. But life affords only one go-a-round. We make the most of the opportunities we are afforded and prize and ponder them in our hearts . . . for eternity. Thank you God for such a wonderful store of riches.

THANKSGIVING

Until our kids were older and dating, we made the trip down country to our parents for Thanksgiving. Both my parents and Susan's family made a large turkey. My dad raised his own and always dressed one for their dinner. Both families made a delicious meal of stuffing, which we appropriately called "filling," mashed potatoes, fresh frozen homegrown corn, turkey and gravy, cranberry sauce, candied sweet potatoes, relish trays, rolls, and lots of desserts. They consisted of fresh fruit salad, pumpkin, apple, and my favorite, warm mince-meat pie a la mode.

When our family got too large to traipse down country together, we started our own Thanksgiving tradition at home. Practically all the above items minus a few pies were present on our table.

For many years we read short stories of the Pilgrims' first Thanksgiving and demonstrated the simplicity and meagerness of that celebration. We put three kernels of corn on each plate representing the severe shortage of food they had and yet they celebrated. It helped contrast the extreme difference of circumstances from our gathering. The original Pilgrims were grateful in depravity yet they focused on their freedom and life itself. We in our generation attempt to show our gratitude through abundance. I doubt any of us middle class Americans can really comprehend the full meaning of the word "grateful."

I remember a few celebrations when we invited neighbors without families to join us. One was especially meaningful, and stretching, involved an elderly widow. She lived alone in a large dilapidated trailer packed so full of stuff there was barely room to get in and out. Boxes full of food, clothes galore, new pots and pans, you name it, she likely had it. To enhance the already sour moldy smell, a little yappy dog left its mark everywhere and slept with her on the heavily blanketed and rotting couch.

It was incredibly sad. Mary insisted she needed everything including many multiples of most things. My involvement with Mary developed because of my empathy for her situation. She stopped by initially asking if she could fill water bottles.

That became an every other day chore filling 25-gallon jugs. Her station wagon was her truck and also packed full to the roof with stuff. I tried fixing her water pump and plumbing and some waiting-to-be-a-fire faulty electric, but I eventually decided I was only enabling her.

It was this "dear Mary" whom we invited for Thanksgiving dinner. Surprisingly, she accepted our offer. That year we were eating at Lori and Mike's house in their new large living room. Mary was the guest of honor. Not only did she eat plenty, she ate up all the attention and couldn't stop talking.

It was interesting to say the least. She was happy to accept a large plate of leftovers as we ended our celebration before we took her back to her most humble abode.

A number of people attempted to help her but gave up. She would constantly call, always needing something, if she found out you were willing to help. She would drive slowly into your driveway and lay on the horn till you came out. Shyly and with that toothless grin, she'd let you know what she wanted.

After filling three house trailers with her "stuff," involving government rehab housing, Area agency on ageing, and home healthy nurses, it came down to one more agency to get her to leave that filth—a sewage inspector. Before he left the property there was a sign on the main trailer dated and stamped; an eviction notice.

Dear Mary finally, and with much relief for all involved, went to a home for the ageing 50 miles north. She did return summers to get some stuff but never returned to stay. Dear God, forgive us for judging her. May she know peace and comfort and security as only You can give.

EASTER

As with other holidays, we took turns hosting the extended family. When we gathered at our house, tradition took us to Goshow's Hill for sunrise service. Rain, snow or sun, we stood there remembering and celebrating the Resurrection of our Lord with hymns, scriptures and prayers.

"Christ the Lord is risen today, Ha-a-a-a-le-e-lu-u-ia!"

It's the most joyous Christian celebration of the year. "For the Lord God omnipotent reigneth . . . Halleluia, Halleluia, Hal-le-e-lu-ia!" Renee's anthem and signature song, I could say. When I hear that song, I think of Renee. In fact today, that is her designated ringtone on my cell phone. ☺ She has always been our drama queen, loving to express her enthusiasm in song and praise and of course, she should.

Though we do not promote the world's emphasis of Easter . . . the "bunny," plastic eggs and such, we do enjoy painting and hiding eggs for the kiddos. What fun. But our main emphasis is on the Resurrection of our Lord Jesus Christ. We absolutely believe it, teach it and practice the significant reality of it; Jesus has once and for all conquered death and sin and has made atonement for us on the cross, rising to life again to give us the opportunity to believe and receive His free gift of eternal life. Thank You Jesus!

Grammy Souder in particular, loved the egg coloring and hiding event. Grammy's face always lit up when the kids came and when she could do special things with them. A big ham dinner with all the trimmings and desserts was wonderful. As the kids got older and grandkids came along, we carried on the egg tradition and a big meal. It included ham, candied sweet potatoes, green bean casserole, mashed white potatoes, corn, homemade applesauce, pies and chantilli desserts. We sang choruses before eating.

After Lori and Mike and their girls returned from their mission month in Jamaica, they taught us a wonderful kids' chorus called . . . "It's alri-i-iight, it's alri-i-ight, as long as I have my Lord beside me, it's alright . . . " a happy, clapping-to little chorus we still use today.

An all-time favorite song before eating has always been, "Johnny Apple-seed . . . Ohhhhh the Lord's been good to me, and so I'll thank the Lord . . . for giving me—the things I need . . . the sun and the moon and the appleseed, the Lord's been good to me . . . Johnny Appleseed, Amen." There's a second verse but I'm unsure of it.

We were sure to teach old favorites of the Landis clan as well. Here is one: "For balmy sunshine, for nourishing rain, dear Lord for thy goodness we thank thee. For food and thy care, rich blessings we share, dear Lord for thy goodness we thank thee. We thank thee of God."

And this one: "Jesus has the table spread where the saints of God are fed, He invites His chosen people come and dine. With His manna He doth feed and supplies our every need, oh 'tis sweet to sup with Jesus all the time. Come and dine the master calleth, come and dine. You can feast at Jesus' table all the time. He who fed the multitude, turned the water into wine . . . to the hungry calleth now, come and dine." If you are familiar, you will hear the four-part harmony loud and clear.

The richness of tradition is priceless. When you are growing up, it seems like stuff for old folks and something to endure. Years go by and then, even as soon as college days, the value and treasure of tradition begins to send roots deeper and more securely. Eventually, these songs, scriptures, memories, pictures, videos, silly and good games, little ditty dramas . . . become incredibly valuable investments, cherished forever. They will beg to be shared with new family members for generations to come.

Please continue to value and journal them for your own grandchildren. You wouldn't know about these if someone didn't take time to tell you.

Follow the instructions of Moses; (regarding scripture).

Deuteronomy 6: 6-10 . . . "These commandments that I give to you today are to be upon your hearts. Impress them on your children. Talk about them when you sit at home and when you walk along the road, when you lie down and when you get up. Tie them as symbols on your hands and bind them on your foreheads. Write them on the door frames of your houses and on your gates."

In my words . . . Please take to heart and pass along the good things you were taught when young. Do whatever it takes to pass this on to the next generation. It's okay, you'll figure it out. You can do it. I trust you.

Bless you. Poppie.

CHAPTER 41

Hayfield Surprises

There's an old saying I like, "Make hay while the sun shines." Seems like Sullivan County is only allocated two months of sunshine out of the year so we work hard and long to get the hay made when it shines.

It was a hot day in August and the hay was drying well. I had agreed to make the hay for Berachah Farm five miles from home. Berachah Farm was a non-profit organization created to help troubled teens. After raking the hay and giving it a few hours' dry time, I greased the baler, fueled the 4020 John Deere and hooked up two wagons in tandem behind the baler for the trip to the Farm.

There's something energizing about driving a big diesel tractor without a cab. The fresh air with all the fragrance of summertime in the mountains surrounded by newly-mown hayfields is intoxicating. And then there's the sense of pride and power by piloting a 100-horse-power tractor with three pieces of equipment in tow. Add to that the smell of diesel fumes and black smoke trailing off into the sky is all part of what makes a farmer farm.

If you've never farmed, it's hard to relate.

There's also the challenge and satisfaction of maneuvering the wagon train over the roads, into the fields and down each neatly raked row of hay. It's likely how Susan felt as she deftly pinched the pie crusts before putting them in the oven. Doing it neatly and efficiently and watching her family enjoy the results produces a deep sense of satisfaction.

On this fine sunny day in the late '70s, I was working a field just below the Nisbet's house on the property next to Berachah Farm. My baler was equipped with a bale thrower and I was pulling a rack wagon behind to catch the bales. I usually had one or two older kids riding the wagon and stacking the bales so we could get more bales on the wagon. If no one stacked them, the bales just piled up randomly but only half as many.

I had instructed the young man from Berachah Farm how to stack the bales and particularly, how to avoid getting hit by the flying objects coming out of the thrower. He understood. However, it's difficult to keep them stacked properly if all is going well, meaning the hay is dry, no breakdowns, and bales are pumping out at a rapid rate. All these prime conditions allow you to bale faster.

The boy couldn't keep up. So I would get off and help him stack now and then. The first wagon was almost full but unfortunately, it was leaning more to one side. Not good, especially on hillsides.

I saw it coming but too late. Baling parallel with the side hill field, I avoided an outcropping of ledge rock with the tractor and baler but the back wheel of the wagon crossed it as I was attempting to get all the hay in that row. Like in a slow-motion video, the wagon wheel came off the ground and the bales shifted to the down-hill side.

Over it went sending bales tumbling down the hill. In the middle of them went my hired man, head over heels. I shut down the baler and tractor and quickly jumped off to check on him. He was already scrambling to his feet, shaking his long head of hay-seeded hair. He was dazed and a bit shaken but nothing broken.

Thank you Jesus, was my first thought when I saw he was not badly hurt. We sat there stunned on a bale of hay, my heart pounding as we discussed what just happened and possibly why it happened and thankful to be able to talk about it.

By this time people were on the scene wanting to see who was hurt or how they could help. No one hurt, but lots of help needed. First we had to unload what was left of the hay on the wagon rack as it lay horizontal, wheels in the air. I went for another tractor, carefully hooked a long chain to the wagon and slowly pulled it upright. Some boards were broken and the rack was a bit out of shape but still in tact.

By late afternoon, we had gathered up the bales scattered on the ground, finished baling and headed to the barn. This one would go down in history as either lucky or having had some divine intervention. I choose to believe the latter. There was at least one busy angel that day in the hayfield.

I clearly recall another "incident" on a sunny afternoon on our farm. Each of our kids got the opportunity to drive tractor early in life. Renee was happy to help as a young teenager. Susan could continue her many household chores if I had someone else drive while I stacked.

In the field between our large chicken house and St. Peter's Church were long heavy rows of dry hay ready for baling. It was the early '70s and I had a 4020 John Deere pulling a new New Holland baler with a thrower to toss the bales onto rack wagons. Everything was going fine. Renee had gotten the hang of baling, guiding the rig alongside each row and traveling at just the right speed. I was stacking the bales as they flew out of the thrower. Just as we crested the top of the hill facing the road with a large wagon full of hay, I had a strange sensation. There was a bump as the tractor and baler continued on pulling only the tongue of the wagon attached to the front wheels. The connecting center pipe which held the front and back axles together separated. The loaded wagon of hay dropped to the ground with a thud leaving me behind as I yelled for Renee to stop.

I don't know if she was dreaming, singing, or just paying close attention to the hay going into the baler, but she continued baling for a few hundred feet before noticing the wagon and me separated back in the field. She stopped and by that time I was running to get her attention.

There was no use scolding or reprimanding her. She was as dumbfounded as I was humored. We both burst out laughing and talking about it as we headed to the barn for another wagon.

Since Renee was first to learn about hayfield happenings, there seem to be more memories with her involved. This one happened during her summer break from college. I was raking hay in the back field, the one way back beyond the woods. Round and round the nine-acre field I went on the JD 3020, raking 9' swaths, one row at a time. As with most hay days, the sun was bright and hot.

Renee baling for Dad.

Though I loved the open fields and operating equipment, raking can be as monotonous as cultivating corn. Lest I fall asleep at the wheel and cause a tragedy, I decided to park the tractor and find a cooler place to rest a bit.

Ahh, there in the shade of the big rear tire under the tractor. I shuffled under the tractor behind the large tire and lay on a row of soft hay with my hat next to me. Snoozing wonderfully for I'm not sure how long, I was awakened by someone calling my name.

"Dad . . . Dad . . . DAD?? Dad . . . are you OKAY?" Renee's distressed shaking voice came closer as I sat up to see tears in her eyes, sweat on her forehead and carrying a jug of Susan's peppermint water to refresh me. She had assumed the worst seeing my legs sticking out from under the tractor as she came running across the field toward me. Needless to say, her trembling body and mind were relieved as she hugged me and in a scolding tone said, "Dad, don't ever do that again. How was I supposed to know you were resting? It sure looked like an accident!"

I can't recall ever doing that again and we both have treasured each other more than the day before.

CHAPTER 42

Memories of DarWay

DarWay is always first on our church's caroling list. Lori asked me to lead knowing how I enjoy it. By their smiling responses and seeing them sing along I could tell it sparked pleasant memories for the guests.

This time Marliss was with me. Life is so good with her by my side. I almost can't believe how much better, how much happier life is with her as my wife after so many lonely months.

But tonight at DarWay, someone was missing. Susan was not there. Marliss mentioned the void when we were walking out to the car. You will hear more about Marliss later.

She said, "I kept looking for Susan in there. I can't think of DarWay without her. I thought she had to come down the hall or around a corner or out of a room."

It was sad, but on second thought, a happy thought.

For 13 hardworking years, Susan had labored generously and mercifully at that facility, sometimes working the night shift, often the evening shift. That way, she would be home to get the kids off to school or off to bed. She could sleep while they were in school.

I remember both of us helping to renovate the old Estella school building. Darwin Higley and Wayne Quail bought the building for the sole purpose of turning it into the first community nursing home in our county. We sanded those deathly dark hardwood floors night after night to bring new life and light into the rooms. I remember the partitions being built and helping to paint trim. Susan helped a bit with that too, even with four kids to care for.

The first director of nursing was Ms. Katherine Hess. Dora McCarty was involved somehow and later became the administrator. Ms. Hess was a kind lady and easy to get along with. Soon after the grand opening, Susan was hired as an L.P.N. Susan was well liked as a person and employee. Quite often she would come in to fill a void from someone sick or missing. She was in her element caring for the elderly and did it so well.

"Now don't be afraid to touch them. They won't hurt you and touch is very important for healing and health, especially for older folks," Susan would tell us.

"Oh, Patty, now don't you look cute today. Where did you get that bow in your hair? John Merrill, come here, Charlie wants to show you his puppy."

It was a stuffed toy, but she acted like it was real and called it by its name. She was so natural and confident it was like second nature to her. No matter when we went in to visit her while she was working, she always wanted to show us people and have us talk to them. She could do three or four things simultaneously or so it seemed. No, I really believe she could do that! Lord knows how, I sure didn't.

"Here are you meds, Ida. Yes, it's that time again. Now open wide and here's some juice." All the while making certain she had the correct dosage and patient.

She always wore her uniform when she worked—never in casual clothes and never without her white hat and pin. To me, she was a beauty . . . pure white, clean, smiling and sexy. No wonder some of the men tried to hit on her and invite her into bed with her. No, I'm not making that up. She would tell me about those episodes when she got home.

There was no need for alarm, as there were always other employees nearby and hey, what's an 87-year-old geezer capable of anyhow? Susan always knew just how to distract their feeble attempts or just ignored them. I can remember her telling me how sometimes she had to close a door and let the old guy cool off and then come back later to give him his bath or whatever.

Weird things happen as people age. I've noticed we are all ageing.

Twice a summer, they had campfire evenings. Dora McCarty, the administrator during the time Susan worked there, did some neat things for the benefit of the guests. This was one. Rod and I were invited to play our guitars while the employees helped wheel the guests outside to the campfire. Hotdogs and marshmallows were roasted over the fire. It was a great morale booster.

There was one patient, Don, who played guitar with us. He had been a semi-professional player and liked to still dabble with it. So we'd play old familiar tunes to cheer them up. Some clapped, some sang along, others just sat and stared or ate hotdogs and marshmallows.

I can see Susan in her white-clad glory helping someone drooling and trying to handle a hotdog with shaking hands while sitting in a wheelchair. Many such tender visions are still easily had by a visit at DarWay like we did tonight.

Sunday afternoon service was another special event. For a time, I took LHF's turn to lead the once-a-month church service at DarWay. Often Susan would accompany me with her alto voice. If she was working that day, she would be certain to give as many guests as possible the opportunity to get to church. That meant extra work for nurses and particularly, aids. It was not always appreciated when Susan encouraged this as you may guess. Nevertheless, She would give the orders to invite those able to get to church. The service was just a half hour. Those who were accustomed to church participated in singing and sometimes, with loud applause or comments. It could be very interesting.

Then the guests all needed to be returned to their rooms, by wheelchair or assisted in walking. I always felt like . . . I wonder . . . I hope I never get to be in this place or one like it. God have mercy. At one time, they probably felt the same.

I remember some singalongs in the lunch room area. I remember walking in Sunday afternoons to the sound of a live piano. Sure enough, there sat Mr. Broschart, a short balding guy, playing old gospel hymns and singing along all alone. Whenever I sat down to talk with him, without fail he'd get around to saying . . . "I can't understand why the Lord just don't take me? Here I am week after week, month after month and for what?" Even with questions like that, he would laugh and was typically optimistic and kept playing the piano. He also could be found sitting in his chair by the bedroom window praying his rosary.

DarWay . . . good memories, sad memories, funny ones, irritating ones, pleasant and not so pleasant come to mind. But over the years since its conception, a heap of elderly folks have come and gone and have been cared for by mostly good and gracious people.

Susan's nursing career at DarWay was cut short to 13 years in 1994 only because her knee began to give her trouble. Trouble, it turned out, was the start of cancer which commenced her first major surgery in Philly in January of 1995. She thought she'd be back but God had other plans. The absence of her by-weekly paycheck pinched our budget but God was faithful to provide other creative ways to make ends meet.

It's no surprise to Marliss and me . . . and you, my dear family, that memories and visions like these make us miss her. That's how it should be. Our loved ones, who were really loved, remain close to our hearts. In fact, their spirits are ALIVE and well and in many ways permeate all phases of our lives. She still speaks to us every day to help us make a difference.

Tonight, we could see her touching, smiling, laughing, charting, and cheerfully serving mankind as though it were Jesus himself. Hers was a life well lived. She made a difference and "lived for what mattered."

Today, tomorrow and until God calls us home, Marliss and I will carry on and live for what matters as long as we can. The bar has been set, the example given and we will remember.

-Written December 17, 2011

My Building Career

Daub's Grocery Market in Souderton, Pa., was an especially good source of wood for my projects. Saturday mornings, I'd ride along to the grocery store with my mom, hoping to find orange and cantaloupe crates they had thrown out on the scrap pile. The boxes had long thin boards that were nice to work with.

"Sir, can I have some of those wooden boxes on the scrap pile?" I would sheepishly ask hoping for a . . . "Yes you can" answer. They usually said I could have them but if my neighbor, Russie got there before me, he would have gotten the best ones first. Back home with my free and treasured boxes, I would carry them into the basement or *cellar* like I called it. There I would sit and work on the little wooden bench I had built from heavier boxes. With Daddy's approval, I had nailed shelves up under each cellar step to organize my nails, bolts, small tools, paper and pencils. Underneath I stored my wood supply. I'd found some old used hinges out in the milkhouse where Daddy's *real* shop was. I used them to make a couple doors for the shelves to keep things in place.

Under the shelves I had built a small portable work table out of scrap fruit boxes and junk wood that Daddy was going to burn. There was no extra money to buy new wood. I drilled holes on the top for pencils.

Sitting on the bench, I carefully disassembled the boxes and removed all the nails, separating the thin boards from the thick boards and stored them in stacks under the steps. Daddy had lots of new and used nails in the milkhouse of various sizes. I separated them into baby food jars or fruit cans on my shelves. With a small hammer, saw, ruler, tape measure, square and a little electric jigsaw, I was ready to build. I'm glad now that we had no TV! It allowed time for creativity.

The jigsaw was a Christmas gift that got lots of good use. With the saw came a pattern book for crafts and knick-knacks. Building little corner shelves of various detail were fun. A little wooden duck with holes across its back made a pencil holder. Bookends were a cinch.

When the board supply began to get low, I would ride my bike up to Russie's house to trade and bargin for more wood. Sometimes, I'd have what he wanted and vice versa. I had one advantage. Sometimes, Daddy would have leftover boxes from his market route in the city and I had first choice. This was the beginning of learning how to "wheel and deal" to get the stuff you needed cheap. For supplies that I couldn't find for free, Mom would take me to Shelly and Fenstamacher, a hardware store in Souderton. There she would buy me little quarter pint cans of paint, finish nails, screws and sandpaper. I'd walk out of there with my goodies grateful and anxious to create something new.

As I grew older and my building skills improved, I would try my hand fixing up the poultry buildings on the farm. Sometimes Daddy was impressed and other times, he wondered why I did that. Oh, I had my reasons.

When I was a teenager, I'd read about housing laying hens in cages. It seemed like a great idea to me. You could house multiple times more birds in a smaller space supposedly at a greater profit. My idea was to partition off half of the barn floor and install laying cages. We'd only have to build one wall and a ceiling. Daddy's idea was to leave it as it was and forget it. Guess who's idea won? You're right. Not mine.

After acquiring our own farm in Sullivan County, Pa., I was the handyman who fixed and renovated. Nothing seemed to intimidate me. From a very young age, I had always watched carpenters and construction workers to learn how they built things. I practiced on my own buildings rather than hire someone to do the work. It was much cheaper though not always as professionally done.

Eventually, I got requests to help other farmers or neighbors with a building project. I learned more. I kept watching and asking questions of those I trusted as good craftsmen. Early on, I had figured I could do most anything. It took many years before I decided it was better to hire those who specialized in plumbing, drywall, advanced electrical work, concrete, fireplaces, brick work and more. Yes, I could do a bit of all those things but not efficiently or very well.

In 1977, besides my farm, I began working for a builder in Laporte. I helped build his house one winter. He taught me lots of things about the building trade and spouted off plenty of expletives for free.

Daddy passed away suddenly in April of that year and my work with Bob had to be suspended. I had to take over the farm work for Mom to finish up the crops he started. It was a long hard year for Susan alone at home with the kids and doing chores for me as I went back and forth to keep both farms going.

For some time I'd been toying with the idea of starting my own building business. In 1979, Pastor Henry Goshow gave his resignation due to his wife's deteriorating health. He moved to Phoenix and his son, Rod and his wife Lucy moved back home. Rod and I started a building partnership in August of that year. Brotherhood Builders went well for 15 years. We built most anything in the residential trade as the opportunity arose.

Then our oldest daughter, Renee, and her husband Rod asked me to build their house for them. I was thrilled with the idea. At the advice of our accountant, we dissolved the partnership, divided out the tools and started separate building businesses. Rod kept the trade name, Brotherhood Builders and I became J. M. Souder, Builder. I designed Renee and Rod's house on a simple software program on my first computer. In the spring of 1995, just three months after Susan's first operation in Philly, we moved to Virginia and for six months lived out of a nice camper while I oversaw the building of their house in Virginia. It was a sweet though sweaty summer spending much time with Renee's family and working together.

God was gracious and gave us health and safety as we worked. Our first grandson Tyler was born that summer, on June 5th. It was an extra blessing to be there for the occasion.

In September, we moved back home with mixed emotions and I began my own building business alone. I was 52, still full of vigor and ambition, but also interested in doing more volunteer work. This gave me the flexibility to do that. Four years later, the Lord spoke to our hearts after Hurricane Mitch and we packed up once more for three months and served in Honduras with Project Mamma. It was a tremendous blessing for us and to many Hondurans as we offered our help.

Besides many other projects helping our kids, I agreed to do all the finish work in our son,

My Brotherhood Builders' partner, Rod, and me.

Mike's house. For several months in 2004, I traveled back and forth to Virginia with my truck loaded with tools. I'd go down on Sunday afternoon, work through Friday and return for the weekend until the house was finished. I can't express how rewarding and bonding times like that were for our family. I thank God for the strength and opportunity to do it.

Little by little, I began to slow down until Susan's health dictated my entire attention. I was happy to lay down my building skills helping others and attend to Susan's needs. God continued to supply every need as He promised. "Great is Thy faithfulness, Lord unto me."

CHAPTER 44

Twenty-Four Thousand Tiny Yellow Puffs

V eal calves were intended to be our livelihood when we moved to Sullivan County in 1964. Before the year was done, it was apparent that we needed more income. So I found part-time work skidding logs for Phil Randall who worked for Duane Morris, a neighboring lumberman. I enjoyed the job but $1.20 an hour didn't do much for our budget. I spent most of the first three winters working with Phil, his brother Ritt and his Dad. During that time, we prayed and discussed our situation with Henry and Irene and a few others trying to come up with a better solution to our lack of income.

Henry had built a large two-story chicken house and was contracting through Beacon Feed Company out of New York to raise broilers. It was producing a stable income for his family. It also provided some work for his boys.

I had been raised on a poultry farm and actually enjoyed working with chickens especially when they produced a nice income. We began exploring any options for us to get involved. Just a mile and a half down the road from us set an empty two-story chicken house at Bedford's Corner. Merton Bedford had used it many years and now had abandoned it as he was a PennDOT road supervisor.

Hmmm . . . that just may be God, I thought one day as we drove by the house. Susan seemed okay with the idea of renting it if Merton would. I approached him about the possibility of renting and sure enough, he would be happy to do so . . . on certain grounds. He agreed to let me use his old equipment, what there was of it, and the rent would be based on $60.00 per batch of chickens. The turnover time for each batch was only six weeks and then two weeks in between to get ready for the next batch. I would provide all the litter, fix all broken windows and fans, pay for heating fuel (kerosene) and he would pay the electric. It was a deal based on a handshake, nothing more.

I began renting the double story house from Merton Bedford in 1966. The normal cycle was to put 3,000 chicks on each floor—6,000 total. We would only keep them for six to seven weeks till they were about 3 lbs. and then the trucks would come to get them from New York. Sometimes one sometimes two trucks depending on the dressing plant's needs. I'd hire four or five young kids to catch after dark.

I hauled wood shavings from the local sawmills with my pick-up. The shavings cost me $2.00 a truck load and later up to $5.00 a truck load. I would back up to the chicken house and one scoop at a time, shovel them into the upper windows. It took one load for each floor and I'd level them out by hand. At that point I'd be ready for Susan's help in putting the water jars and feeder flats around. With two little girls to care for we set up the foldable play pen with lots of toys, and blankets for comfort and warmth. Whatever it took to keep them happy and safe while we worked.

While Susan filled 60 jars and 60 feeder flats, I got the kerosene brooder stoves working . . . or at least worked *at* it. They were a real PAIN. Just when you thought they were burning good and left for home, I'd discover one or two of the eight had gone out when I returned to check and needed to be recleaned and restarted.

When the stoves were lit, and the waters and feeders filled and set closely around the brooders, we set up a cardboard ring about 12" high around the brooder to keep the chicks near the heat . . . particularly in winter.

Every winter, we had to cover all 20 windows per floor with plastic to conserve heat. When it warmed up, the plastic had to be peeled down to open windows and stapled back up when it got cold. Within a week the jars and flats were removed as the chicks were big enough to eat out of the regular troughs. They then had to be filled by hand.

Oh . . . the girls left the chicken house long before this . . . as soon as Susan had the 60-gallon jars filled with water and the feeder flats filled with starter crumbles, she would take them home to bake, cook, clean, wash or whatever, while I worked on stoves or windows. Often, this work would only be completed late at night the day before the chicks came from Moyer's, Longenecker's, Martin's, or Beaver Spring's hatchery.

6,000 White Mountain chicks, packed a hundred per box, was literally music to my ears hearing that familiar sound which had been engraved into my brain as a small child. Little yellow puffs of fluff were dumped, a hundred at a time, onto the clean warm wood shavings under each stove until the house was full of that wonderful sound and smell.

Yeah! I was back in the poultry business and lovin' it. Susan and I stood by a stove admiring and enjoying our own little *sight and sound theater*. All was well, we could leave now. Sixty veal calves would be bawling for their powdered milk in the barn at home.

And so, we were officially back in the chicken business however, no chickens on our own property. Okay, not totally true . . . I couldn't be without chickens so I'd found some *bandie* chickens we let loose to nest at random around the farm. At least we had eggs of our own. The *real* chicken contract would happen later.

Feed was delivered in bulk and was blown into a homemade wooden bin on the second floor. It was accessible upstairs by lifting a door on a long box to hand scoop the feed into a wheelbarrow with an old coal bucket. When the chicks were young, I just carried buckets around to feed. When they were older, I used the wheelbarrow. Downstairs, I tapped the feed out of a chute into buckets or the wheelbarrow. It was an hour-long chore each day besides washing and adjusting the 8' long automatic water troughs which sometimes overflowed causing a nightmare most of our children will remember happening in the big chicken house at home.

Eben Wiswell, my service man, would come by once a week. He was like a vet in that he'd bring vaccine and medicine as needed. I had to put the vaccine or medicine in the drinking water after depriving them of water for several hours to make them thirsty. He would check on them to be certain all was well and towards the end of the growing cycle he would weigh them.

When they were about 2¾ lbs. he would schedule a truck to come and take them to the dressing plant. The night of catching was always a *picnic*. Well, no, not the best descriptive word. But the guys . . . and some girls were really gracious and happy to earn a few bucks.

The lights would be turned off except for a 15-watt red bulb to help us see to catch.

"Three and three tonight guys" . . . or "three and four" I'd shout to everyone. This meant they catch six or seven birds, three in one hand and four in the other with only one leg of each bird and carry them to the window, hand them out to the guys on the truck and go back for another six or seven until the floor was empty.

Sometimes the guys would try to break their former time record. Better to make a game of it then complain about the stinky mess! Susan always prepared snacks to serve when we were finished. Kool-aid and cookies. Then, I'd usually have to run the guys home. Most of them were too young to drive.

I'd get home around midnight, get a shower in the basement since at that time we did not have one upstairs, and sit at the desk and record who caught, how many, and how long it took. Then up to bed to join my honey after checking in on the girls.

Now it's time to clean the chicken house . . . one shovel full at a time . . . throw it out the window onto the spreader until each floor was empty. This completes one cycle and we're ready to start all over again . . . six times each year.

And that's what we call "the good ol' days." What do you think?

What I can hardly believe is . . . that Susan was willing and ready to help me do this for 35 years or so! I almost feel guilty . . . but that was part of our life and journey. I know she loved me enough to do whatever it took to help make ends meet. OH MY!!! Feels like another lifetime . . . how quickly life flies by.

So . . . be good to each other, work hard but TAKE TIME FOR EACH OTHER. Do what makes each other happy, follow your dreams and visions as the good Lord gives them to you. Only one life, will soon be past, only what's done for Christ will last. But I *do* believe He wants you to *enjoy* life . . . even though sometimes it requires hard work.

Note: Today as I write, 2/21/2013, all the sawmills are out of business except one in Hillsgrove. Shavings would cost at least $150.00 per batch of chicks at Bedford's chicken house. But then it too is about to collapse.

* * * * *

Merton's chicken house was working out so well, I began to dream of bigger plans. In the Fall of '66, designs of a much larger chicken house began to form in my head. Again, I began talking to Henry about it. His was doing well and he was also selling Shenandoah chicken equipment from the Shenandoah Valley in Harrisonburg, Va. I guess the connection was made when his children began going to E.M.H.S. (high school) and E.M.C. (Eastern Mennonite College). Besides being Pastor, Henry was an entrepreneur and businessman and had contacts in all phases of the chicken business and thus a good source for poultry business information. So we talked, prayed and then planned. I vividly recall our conversation in the car one Sunday afternoon as Susan and I drove with Henry and Irene over Ogdonia Mountain to meetings at the Hughsville Campgrounds.

The result of that conversation confirmed my desire to build a chicken house of our own . . . soon. It was time to contact a bank. I didn't want to ask my dad for the money even though he would have had the funds. Guess I figured he wouldn't encourage the risk and I was rather determined to pursue my dream. So we met with the loan officer of The First National Bank of Dushore.

It was a bit weird answering to a young man like myself who sat behind the big wooden desk asking questions about my finances. Just recently, I had seen him stocking shelves in the A&P grocery store.

Before he would loan the money, he was required to send an appraiser out to inspect our farm. Only one little hitch; the inspector noted that our barn would soon need a new roof. So he made me sign a paper promising I'd get it done soon.

Within that year, Henry and his boys, Lowell and Leon, and a few other volunteers helped install interlocking shingles overtop the deteriorating wooden shingles.

As for the loan, I had done my homework by preparing a simple hand-drawn footprint of the structure, and a detailed list of materials given to me by Miles Little of Little Lumber Company in Benton. The dollar value stamped on the estimate was $23,000.00, the amount I needed to build the house. Mr. Taylor agreed to loan us the money at 6% interest. We were now ready to contact a contractor to break ground. Whoopie!

My best friend Lowell, who was Henry's oldest son, had moved to up-state NY and was working with his father-in-law building houses. Why not ask him to oversee this project? It was a no-brainer for Lowell and his boss agreed to give him time off to come and help. If the weather cooperated, we would start digging the end of March, 1967.

I had begun working another part-time job skidding logs for Carl Pardoe that winter. He agreed to loan me his little John Deere 1010 dozer to level the site and spread gravel. But first there was snow to remove from the site. The weather warmed enough to begin and I hired an excavator (I'll call Mr. X) to dig the 410-foot trench and pour the footer. It was a rough and muddy start.

His truck and trailer promptly got stuck in the driveway as the frost had just come out and the lane was a mess. I called a neighbor with an excavating business, to haul gravel for the driveway and pull him out. Eventually, he began digging the trench only to find solid blue shale ledge rock near the surface. The deepest he could dig in the entire perimeter was 26 inches. Our intent was to go 36" to be below frost level. That wasn't possible but it actually saved us blocks for the foundation and we would be on solid rock. What could be better?

Being a young buck of 23 years, I was inexperienced in dealing with seasoned contractors. I thought that offering my own help and ideas would save me time and money and expected that to be normal. Not so. Mr. X did not want my help or my advice with his work. He could handle it perfectly well alone. And so I ignored his cuss words as he struggled with dumping 80# bags of cement into his mixer by hand, as my tractor and loader sat quietly nearby. The big rocks protruding from the lane past the chicken house reminded me of a difficult confrontation for years to come . . . the kind of which I like to avoid. No, I do not hold grudges and so he has long been forgiven. ☺ But more trials would come.

My dad came up when he could to help. He helped mix mud for laying blocks. It took a while to finish several courses for 412 liner feet. Next step was to get enough *crick* gravel hauled in and leveled for many loads of concrete. Learning from my dad's example how to work efficiently, I had devised a plan to get gravel delivered at a fast pace. I hired two different truckers to haul gravel and I would spread it with the dozer. Good plan, right?

The first contractor (no names here to preserve their identity) came on time and backed onto the site, dumped his load and left. The second guy showed up soon after, dumped his load and left. All well and good so far. The big and varied sizes of crick rocks were quite hard to spread. About an hour later, the first guy comes back with another load, backs in and unloads about a 10-ton load, and pulls out. Before he left the barnyard, the second guy pulls in the drive with his second load. Mr. "A" gets out of his truck and walks toward me looking a bit peeved.

In no uncertain terms he let me know that he intended to haul all the gravel or none. No matter how I tried to explain why I'd hired two different truckers, for him it was gonna be *all or none*.

I saw there was no use arguing, so I paid him and he left, not a happy trucker. The other guy fortunately had no problem with my plan so he finished the hauling alone. It was a lesson learned the hard way. How was I to know you don't hire two contractors to do the same job? I soon discovered the answer to that question. You just *don't*.

Dave Clemens was a plasterer from down country—Franconia actually. He was the man who owned 500 acres and a cabin 4 miles back on Bear Mountain and was responsible for starting the church work at Estella back in the early '50s. He was retired and lived nearby working as a handyman. He also was the man who helped me concrete our basement.

That itself, is another story. Briefly, I dug up to 18" of dirt, by hand, out of the basement and wheeled it to the rear entrance. I dumped it onto the hay elevator positioned at the opening of the basement and elevated the dirt and rocks onto my Fergy's front-end loader. Dents in the hood of the Fergy are still proof of that operation.

Dave agreed to help me with concreting the chicken house floor. It took about nine or ten loads of redi-mix concrete delivered from Montoursville. It took four of us three days to pour, level and finish the floor. I remember Lowell and I going out after dark, and hanging a Coleman lantern up for light to finish power toweling the concrete.

By now it was near the end of April and we had a deadline to meet. I had signed an agreement with Eben Wiswell to have the house complete and ready for chicks by June 27th. He needed a date to order chicks and feed. We needed an income.

Little Lumber Company began delivering truckloads of freshly-cut and sized hemlock framing lumber. The barnyard looked like a lumberyard; stacks of framing lumber, 800 sheets of $5/16$ plywood for sheeting and ceilings, 190 sheets of $3/4$ plywood for the second floor, 115 sheets of aluminum roofing, 50# boxes of nails and hardware. We nailed every nail with hammers. Power nailers were only a dream.

And so the fun work began. People came up from Telford and Franconia and elsewhere to volunteer their labor. It was a huge gift of love for us. Susan always prepared lunches and snacks for everyone. Lowell and Henry ate lunch at our table most every day. On weekends, Lowell went back home to NY and came back Monday morning. The girls, Renee and Brenda, toddled around the yard and building, with Susan keeping them clear of danger.

The end of May brought a surprise snow coating freshly-mown hay next to our building. It didn't last long but was an unusual event. We built all 86 trusses ourselves and when they were up in place and anchored, I sat on the peak looking down the ridge.

"Man Lowell, it's perfectly straight. No humps, no dips no curves. How'd we do that?" I said.

I knew the answer, but he was quick to repeat the fundamentals of building; "Square, level and plumb, that's how." That's the only way he'd do it and I liked it that way. We had a lot of fun working together.

Chore-Time Equipment out of Marietta, Pa., supplied the automatic feeders, the 13-ton bulk feed bin, the fill system, and the ventilation system. They came and set it all up in a few days. Henry sold me the watering system and helped install it. Meanwhile, Gochanours of Wheelerville, were installing the heat pipes and hot water boiler for brooding the 24,000 squabs, better known as broilers. Marvin Groff of Canton and his men installed all of the electric and plumbing. After 12 years of problems with the boiler, we replaced the pipe heating system with Shenandoah gas brooders. Henry sold them to me and helped to install them. It was a huge improvement and less troublesome.

I borrowed an old silage blower from Vernon Reibson to blow many truckloads of shavings up in the attic for insulation. One evening, a group of people from church surprised us. They came to help insulate the walls with fiberglass. The building was complete, the equipment worked like a charm, and the heating system was tuned so the hot water circulated properly. It was time to cover the concrete with shavings for chicks.

Susan spread an old sheet out with some toys for the girls to play with, and began helping me fill 240 gallon jugs with water . . . a daily job for the first five days. We folded about the same amount of feeder flats to put fresh crumbles of feed on and set the jugs and flats along each side of the heat pipes covered with red rosin paper. It was a sweet sight to behold.

June 27, 1967. We were ready for chicks. A big truck backed up to the door and we unloaded 240 boxes of 100 chicks each, half up and half downstairs. The chirping of little yellow puffs drowned out all other sounds for the moment. Our goal had been met. Lowell's job was complete. A job so well done and a memory never to be forgotten. I'm sure his wife, Lois, was happy to have him home again. Our dream had come true.

All the time we were building, we had to feed 60 veal calves and keep up with the field work. Susan had the work of regular housekeeping and tending to children as well as feeding extra hungry mouths during the building time. Our commitment to church responsibilities continued. We had no regrets but just did what needed to be done.

1967 - first batch of 24,000 chicks.

Our neighbor on the hill on North Street, Midge Smith, *originally from way back in West Va.* was a curious old soul. One day while I was building electric fence along the road as the new building was in progress, she stopped her car and waved to me. I went over to greet her and our conversation went like this:

"Well, John . . ." she said, drawing the words out slowly and grinning. "What are *you* building?"

"It's a chicken house to contract broilers, Midge."

"Now why would you want to spend all that money for that? I'll bet you in 20 years or so, you'll be tired of it and the building will need repairs and then you'll wish you'd have never built it. You know?" she said with a pessimistic voice. She generally spoke her mind. She meant what she said and never minced words.

It caught me off guard a bit, but I insisted I knew what I was doing and it was going to be a good source of income for us. So went the talk and rumors of the mountain folk but I was never sorry for building the house.

There were aspects of raising broilers that I was not so fond of though. Catching them was just plain nasty. The community is full of retired chicken catchers with memorable stories tucked away in the dark dusty recesses of their hearts. But they will smile as they retell sorry stories of those chicken pickin' nights.

Here are some incidents which made life interesting. The water fountain valves would randomly stick open creating a wonderful flood of water soaking up

New chicken house

the litter. I had to shovel it out by hand or just leave it. Some were small enough to ignore until clean-out time. That decision created nasty mounds of slick litter to slip and fall on. With two hands full of chickens walking in the dark and stepping on those wet mounds, you either sunk into or fell onto it. Not much fun.

The other nightmares could be tripping over feeder lines, hitting your noggin on a raised feeder or water line and getting doused with stinky water while looking for more birds. Neither action was appreciated and all catchers experienced both. I can understand why you ask, "Why did they keep coming back to catch?"

Mike and Lori not shy with chickens.

Thirty years ago, $7.00 an hour for young kids was great pay. The paycheck lured many of them back for more. I often heard complaints from parents about horrific smells coming from the laundry room in their house the next day. Their clothes and shoes should have been left on the doorstep at midnight when they got home. But some didn't think that far. Oh the joys and rewards of chicken catchers!

When our own kids were old enough to drive, they would take other catchers home while I helped truckers bind down the crates. Lori drove my blue four-wheel drive pick-up truck to keep the smell out of our car. Kids named it *"the chicken truck."* Just open the door and you'd know why.

Midge was wrong. For 30 years, from 1967 to 1998, I contracted broilers, roasters, pullets and squabs for as many as seven different companies. The birds were trucked to dressing plants as far away as Maple Leaf Farms in Hamilton, Canada.

Contracting was changing. If it hadn't been for the large feed companies demanding monstrous buildings holding 200,000 birds to get a contract, I'd likely still be raising birds. Thank goodness I'm not. My lungs would surely be shot, and my sinuses have seen enough.

One of the last years I shipped birds to Canada was early spring in 1996. Those trailers held just over 6,000 birds in 640 crates. A huge load of birds. The trailers were so long it was difficult to get in and out of our driveway. Good drivers generally drove in to load and then backed out all the way to Hugo's corner behind our house. This took some skillful maneuvering and most drivers succeeded. One didn't. I warned him about staying on the road since the berms were soft and the trailer would sink. He was doing fine in the midnight darkness with my truck lights lighting the road and with me trying to guide him . . . until he got onto the berm next to our mailbox. I tried to stop him before going too far off the road.

He stopped . . . and as he did, the wheels began to slowly sink. I ran for my biggest tractor thinking (what *was* I thinking?) that I could somehow chain to the upper side of his tractor and hold it from tipping. When I got back with my tractor, all I could do was stand and watch in horror as the large rig tipped on its side across the ditch and into the field. Binder chains snapped, crates rolled and crashed in mass confusion. White chickens were scattered everywhere in the darkness. Fortunately, only the trailer and not the tractor upset. The driver got out of the truck and we stood on the road flabbergasted. All the catchers had left for home, happy to be done after three hard hours of catching. I had been happy too, until now. Now my heart sank and my mind spun in circles.

The driver called the plant and another trailer was sent out. Meanwhile, what to do next? I needed help desperately. Neighbor Bob came over to help and I decided to roundup the catchers to reload. Big Mike came, and three or four others came back to help. We worked through the night corralling stray birds and restacking 640 crates on the ground until 6:00 that morning. The other truck arrived about noon and we reloaded the crates full of birds by sliding them on planks across the ditch onto the trailer. We were about whooped when the truck was finally loaded. Makes me sigh and groan to re-live that nightmare . . . all part of contracting chickens in Sullivan County.

The house has not seen chickens since 1998. Dry, dusty chicken litter still lies on the top floor. The house is cold and dark but not abandoned. It has since been transformed into a machinery shed and storage for most anything including hay. My lungs are happier without all that dust and ammonia. When I step inside the chicken house in wintertime, my glasses don't steam up from the heat and humidity. And . . . I have no desire to re-establish history. The only part I miss is hearing the loud chirping sounds from those little yellow puffs and the smell of clean wood shavings at the start of each new batch of chicks. Actually, as I sit here quietly writing, I can hear them . . . yes, and there's that fresh woody smell of shavings. Ummm . . . that intoxicating smell. It was a venture well done and an income well appreciated. Thank you God for allowing me those 32 years with chicks.

"ADDENDUM" TO 24,000 TINY YELLOW PUFFS

It's easy to overlook important details of these stories and some came to mind the day after I edited the "Tiny Yellow Puffs" story. So here they are.

As our kids grew older, they were expected to pitch in and help with chores that matched their ages. Girls can be just as strong as boys and in fact sometimes they can outlast them. We needed help to care for 60 veal calves, 6,000 chickens at Bedford's, 200 geese and 100 ducks, 24,000 chicks in the new building, and still find time to make hay, grow a large garden and do church work. So . . . when Renee was old enough and barely able to push a wheelbarrow loaded with feed crumbles, I showed her how it was done.

"Just lift here and move it ahead about two posts (or I would move the wheelbarrow) and then use the coal bucket to scoop out the feed. Put a small pile of feed in each flat until you get around the house. I'll start filling jars. Holler if you need me. Oh . . . and kinda shuffle your feet so you don't step on the chicks. They will follow your movement the whole time," I said, and went to go fill jars.

Each of the kids followed suit at the right age. As soon as I thought they could fill jars, I taught them.

"Okay now, here's what you do. Don't worry if you can't do it as fast as me. Just empty the ones out that are less than half full. Turn 'em over and screw off the lids. When you're done with a whole row, I'll turn on the hose and you can start fillin' 'em. Renee, you fill 'em and Bren can put the lids on and flip them over. Make sure they set even or they'll leak out. Got it?"

"I guess," they said sounding as thrilled as a man about to change a messy diaper. Then they started the hour-and-half long process. When Susan and I did it we could flip the jars over, remove the lid, insert the hose, and let it fill while we did the next one. I had become experienced enough to prepare the one ahead while another was filling and then flip the filled one around, move the hose, and prepare another before the last one filled up. It was tricky and you had to know the techniques. I never expected to have the kids do that although I showed them how. Sometimes the hose flopped out of a jar spraying water all over. All part of learning the process.

They got so good at it, I could count on them to feed and fill jars all by themselves. Avoiding squishing a chick was probably the most difficult part. I can still hear either of them say, "EEWW, Dad, come get this one, I drove over it . . . eeww!" The wheelbarrow was extra difficult to move through a bunch of hungry chicks. Jar filling lasted only five days. By five days, I had trained the chicks to drink out of the automatic drinkers saving several hours of chores each day.

If you could ask any of the girls, "What chore did they like the least?" I suspect their answer would be, "Washing jars!" (Besides catching chickens, of course.) First of all, after five day's use, we moved the 240 jars out of the pens into the heater room at the end of the house. Sometime before the next batch of chickens, all those jars and lids had to be washed and stacked to dry.

Our system was to fill an old bathtub with soapy water and put as many jars as we could fit into it. Warm water was carried in milk cans from the house to the heater room to temper the cold water. I can still see them gathered around that old tub with their grubbies on, slopping in the water with rags and brushes.

If there was ever a woman who supported her husband more than Susan, I'd be surprised.

Besides keeping a clean house, baking and cooking not only for her family of six but always extra for neighbors and people in need. She was very active in church and found time to help me with farming whenever possible. Without her (and the kids') support and encouragement, I'd have never accomplished much. And her German style of cooking got great reviews from anyone who ever tasted it. It was superb.

When Lori was old enough to help, the three girls figured out a system. One would wash, one rinse and one stacked them. A radio kept them in good spirits as they worked. If the girls figured out some way to avoid this chore (and they did), Susan would help. I had plenty of other work to do and they could do this. Susan and I also saw this as a way for them to learn the principal of earning their own spending money. What's that verse in the bible . . . "He who does not work, should not eat." (II Thes. 3:10) Who could argue with that?

Typical Susan, cooking and baking while on the phone.

Besides, teaching children good work ethics is a great asset in life. By what I've observed, I think the baton has been received well and is being passed on from one generation to the next.

As Mike grew older and Renee and Brenda had moved away from home, he was my main man with Lori's help, when and if she was still around. By the time Mikey was older, Lor was already interested in one particular young man; another "Mike." In 1995, Susan and I moved to Virginia to help build Renee and Rod's house. We spent six months down there and between the two Mikes, they kept the chicken business going. I was very proud of them to do that for us. They had to organize catching crews and the whole works.

Some time in the '80s, soon after Rod Goshow and I formed Brotherhood Builders and were busy working, I returned home from work one day to a huge surprise. Now that I mentioned Rod's name, I must tell you that he and I contracted chickens together just as we ran the building business together. We got chicks at the same time using the house his Dad had built and we shipped them out close to the same time. This worked well for the feed company. They could haul trailer loads of feed to us making it more economic for them.

Back to the surprise; Feed had just been delivered to fill my 13-ton bin. It was April and the frost had gone out of the ground leaving the ground soggy around the bin. Apparently, when they filled the feed bin, the weight of the feed caused two of the piers to sink tipping the large full bin on its side. There it lay in the driveway, with a few tons of feed spilling onto the gravel. You can imagine the shock on my face as I got out of my truck staring in disbelief. Now what? The chicks will be without feed in twelve hours or less. I could see that I would be feeding by hand for at least a week.

First, I had to dig out the area around the base of the bin to make a better foundation. Then I ordered a load of stone and some redi-mix concrete for a new pad. I had to let the concrete harden for at least a week before setting the bin upright onto the pad.

Farmers learn to adjust, find remedies and fix what's broken on the spot ASAP if they are going to succeed as a farmer. Fortunately, I had some equipment that helped out.

I got my 4" grain auger, put it in through the open top and into the remaining feed. I augered the feed into two gravity grain wagons (where we would feed from by hand) and my truck till the bin was empty including most of what was on the ground. I raised the bin up just a bit with my front loader and crawled into the empty bin with a sledge hammer. It must have been terribly loud banging on the bent side as I tried to straighten some of the damage. Then

I had to unbolt the fill system from the bin to fix the fill tube before raising the bin and reattaching it.

Mike drove the truck hooked with a cable around the top of the bin as I slowly raised the bin from under the top side with my tractor loader. The coordination was tricky but we got it set back up.

It must have been nerve racking wondering if the bin would land correctly and not keep on going. I just know that it worked and we bolted it onto the concrete pad. It stayed that way until this writing—February 10, 2012. It's now past time to take it back down and sell it for scrap iron. I plan to do so this Spring.

Feed floods inside the chicken house were not uncommon. Occasionally, I'd step in the door to find feed at my feet in the shape of a cone leaving me with 1 to 2 tons to shovel by hand. A pipe or hose worked loose and the feed kept auguring into the house until it somehow reached the spot where the switch eventually shut it off. Automatic fill . . . they call that. And it was. So I used wheelbarrows to feed by hand until the pile was used up.

There's a story about cleaning the chicken house that's been told many times over in our neighborhood. It happened September of 1974. At fair time, I had been helping with the old-time tractor pull in the grandstand building. I was standing next to the fence when a tractor backed alongside me quite close. So close, I couldn't get out of the way and the back wheel ran over my ankle. My foot swelled and a kind gentleman took me to Towanda Hospital and I had to get a walking cast put on it. This was just days before Susan gave birth to Mikey—September 2, 1974. The day before Mike was born, I was hobbling around with the cast while neighbors cleaned the chicken house for me. Pears were hanging heavy from our pear tree. While Dave and Durwood, Rich and my dad were working in the chicken house, I was up on the hay elevator picking pears. Do what you gotta do right?

At lunch they came in to eat and told me the funny story. Seems like Durwood was operating the walk-behind garden tractor and blade to push manure down the holes onto the manure spreader. The others were shoveling and sweeping when someone looked up just in time to see Durwood disappear down through a hole. The garden tractor fortunately caught between the blade and the handles and stayed above. When everyone knew Durwood was not hurt, we all got a big laugh out of it and still do whenever the story is told.

Mikey had his own stories to tell. He and I were working upstairs cleaning out with the same garden tractor Durwood had used. It actually belonged to Rod, but we always used it upstairs to push the manure down the trap doors.

It would be good for you to understand how it functioned. Next to each handle bar was a toggle lever. The one was a two-speed control lever; the other was for reverse or forward motion. You could engage either at anytime without stopping. Once mastered, it worked quite well. I was cleaning out corners by hand, moving chicken equipment out of the way, and moving the tractor and spreader as it filled up.

There were five 2' by 4' trap doors spaced evenly down the center of the building upstairs. So I would drive the tractor and spreader under a trap door to catch the manure being pushed down with the garden tractor. Mikey was doing quite well at his first attempt with the garden tractor until all of a sudden down he went through the hole onto the pile of manure. He'd been backing up and forgot where the hole was I guess. No problem, he wasn't hurt. Back up and at it he went as though nothing had happened. Just a bit of pride damage. Later in the day, as if one fall wasn't enough, down he went again through another hole. He was fortunate to land on soft, dry and dusty litter each time. We had a good laugh when I saw the only thing hurt was his pride.

I think that was the last time he went through a trap door. He continued to help but preferred "spreading" the manure instead of pushing it with that garden tractor. Maybe back-up mirrors would have helped. ☺

There's still some dry dusty manure upstairs in the chicken house if anybody wants to try their luck with that garden tractor . . . or not. It's had its day, done its job and sits forlorn over in Rod's chicken house waiting its final resting place.

Contracting chickens was constantly evolving and changing. We started out with Beacon Feed Company, then Purina, Farm Bureau, Clarks Feeds in Turbotville, Krammers out of Middleburg and finally, Agway. Each company supplied their own service man to keep tabs on the flocks. We were generally paid an amount per pound for our labor and they paid for all other costs.

There were many different dressing plants where we sent the birds, starting with Manor Poultry in NY. Then there was a Kosher plant in New York City, and a Chinese plant there as well. We were glad to switch from the Chinese market because they had us raise blacks and reds simultaneously. When it was time to catch, we had to sort them by color. UGH! After that contract we switched to the Canadian market through Farm Bureau which was a good market. Even Agway used that market until the last contract. Oh my, it makes me weary to think of all those late-night catching parties. Glad it's now history. And now you know . . . "THE REST OF THE STORY!"

Contentment

Family photo on deck, 2011.

Susan and her girls.

Dad and his kids, 2011.

1970 Combine Oats

Geese and cattle

Last sticky bun.

Truck load of wood and kids.

Susan in her realm.

Summertime

MawMaw and Ciara making strawberry jam, 2009.

CHAPTER 45

Introducing . . . the Berkes

E arly in the seventies visitors began pouring into Estella Mennonite Church. The church was experiencing a charismatic spiritual renewal and Estella seemed to be the hub for the Endless Mountains of Pa. Preachers, teachers, choirs, bus-traveling evangelists and you name it found their way to our church door. Change was on its way, mostly for the good but not entirely. With anything good and worthwhile comes the counterfeit. And thus not all who stood at the front of the church nor all who sat and listened could be labeled as *sent from God*.

It was during these exciting and sometimes challenging years that a young couple with two small children showed up at our church in a beige Volkswagon van. Chuck, a handsome blond with long side burns, introduced his pretty wife to us. Marliss, tall and blond, held their one-year-old daughter, Susannah, and three-year-old Bruce toddled next to her. An older couple was with them who were introduced as Chuck's parents, Charlie and Annie Berke.

The Berkes were easy to get to know. They were some of the most likeable, friendly people we had ever met. And we had encountered lots of visitors lately. Almost instantly we felt a kinship and over the next months became bonded with them. We learned that Charlie and Ann were recently retired from the education profes-

Susannah, Bruce, Brian, Marliss and Chuck Berke.

sion and deeply committed to the Christian faith. They owned a cabin on Lake Makoma in Laporte, Pa., where they spent much of their summers. Chuck and Marliss were living in the Millville area where Chuck was a teacher at Jerseytown Elementary School.

Our church's relaxed style together with solid Bible teaching, friendly people and good singing appealed to them. After a few Sundays we invited them to have dinner with us. Dinner to us, meant lunch. Supper was what most people understand as dinner. However, Susan enjoyed cooking every meal as though it were supper. We spent these mealtimes sharing our likes and dislikes, our backgrounds, work and play habits and getting to know each other.

We visited them in Jerseytown where they had recently built a house. Marliss and Chuck were an intricate part of the foundation for the "Friends" Christian school in that area. It is still going strong to this day. But the pull of their hearts was becoming ever stronger with friends in the Estella area.

In the summer of 1979, the Berkes decided to put down roots close to Estella. They searched the area for land to buy and God put it on our hearts to sell them an acre of our own property on North Street. Chuck said they preferred a south-facing property and ours seemed workable. We made settlement in August of 1979. That very month, St. Peters U.C.C, located next to our farm, put an add in the local paper requesting bids to dismantle the old church facility next to the cemetery across from the new church.

Chuck saw an opportunity. Here was good aged lumber of all dimensions appropriate for building their house. We talked it over and I agreed to use my equipment and store the material temporarily in exchange for some of the lumber—IF we were rewarded the bid. The bid required the high bidder to dispose of all lumber and hardware and leave the site clean and neat. We offered a bid of $200.00. We won the bid! Our families rejoiced and began to discuss plans to dismantle the old church.

First order of business for the Berkes would be to find place to live nearby while undertaking the demolition project and beginning the construction of the new house on the acre of land in the woods behind our barn, on North Street.

"Susan and I have an idea," I said one day. "We'll set up our pop-up camper out in the yard under the apple trees. You guys can sleep there as long as you need to and even eat some meals with us. How does that sound?"

I can still see the excitement in their eyes and faces as they gladly accepted our offer. It didn't take long to get set up with the awning out over a small picnic table, lawn chairs scattered around and a small wash line. It was summer, so no need for heat . . . yet. Flexibility describes the Berkes perfectly.

Over the next month Chuck and I along with 5-year-old Bruce and Mikey, were busy beavers ripping and tearing down the building. There were thousands of nails for the boys to pull out as we tore into the dusty 100 or so year old building set on a foundation of huge rocks.

The large green louvered shutters were carefully removed and placed on my hay wagon along with other boards for transportation to one of my chicken houses for storage. The windows and doors were stacked and carefully stored away as well.

The wooden Dutch lap siding was in great shape and would be used somewhere on Chuck's house. The flooring was solid maple and tongue and grooved. The roof was covered with old wooden shingles which made great kindling. There were 2 x 6 rafters, 2 x 4 studs and many large beams for the post and beam house structure, all in great shape. At the rear of the building nestled high on the gable end in between the studding, hid a huge colony of honey bees.

"Honey comb, won't ya be my baby oh honey comb be my home . . ." Anyone remember popular songs of the '50s? Oh, yeah, lots of good honey.

Jim Nisbet, an older Scotsman living at Berachah Farm above Estella, was well accustomed to working with bees. He came over to evaluate the situation. He said he could remove the colony and honey. The next day up the ladder he went without any head protection. Another young man, John Beiler from Berachah Farm, followed him up with headgear on. They tore off siding and removed the honey comb. To capture the bee colony, I think they waited until the bees formed a large swarming ball and he lured them into a portable hive to transport them to his home hive. It was quite an interesting ordeal.

Harry Magan's ancient dumptruck came in handy to dispose of trash wood. All the salvageable wood was stacked on my hay wagon and taken to the chicken house for storage until house building time. Many hours of hard labor woven around sweat, laughter, good discussions, sweetened with "Grammies tea" and many snacks helped us though each day. Susan and Marliss' homecooking always awaited our sweaty and dusty, tired bodies at suppertime. Sleep was sweet those nights, camper or house.

When the siding and roofing were all removed, we cut the structure away from the belfry. The last challenge we faced was to dismantle the belfry. How should we do that? Our dilemma was solved with my 3020 John Deere tractor and a long cable. We tied it around the top section of the belfry and to the tractor waiting at the edge of the cemetery behind the church building.

The *Sullivan Review* editor, Dr. Shoemaker, had been notified and he was nearby ready for the photo. Slowly, ever so slowly, I began to pull. There was a lot of creaking and cable stretching and then . . . it broke loose from the foundation and began to move. With a great crash in a ploom of dust and splinters, it was all over. History was caught on Doc's camera and posted in the Sully the following week with an article covering the story. Photos are attached as proof of the puddin'.

August 1979
-Written December 28, 2011

Our family and the Berkes spent many hours together, working, playing, worshipping and even vacationing. A favorite spot was at World's End State Park only 7 miles away where we snorkeled in "the Sock," ate hamburgers and hotdogs, hiked, and swam. As Elders, Chuck and I helped to baptize some of our kids and others in the cool waters of The Loyalsock. For a couple years, Chuck worked with us at Brotherhood Builders. Marliss taught music at LHF school, was the primary piano player for worship while I led worship with my guitar. We drove to church early many times together to get ready for worship.

Susan and Marliss spent many hours cooking, baking, making yogurt, at ladies' teas and parties, and just plain chatting. Our kids played and enjoyed LHF school and field trips together. Chuck was Mike and Bruce's first soccer coach. He was so patient and adept at coaching.

Our families crammed into our pop-up camper one summer as we visited Washington, D.C., for cherry blossom time. Oh, the challenge of 10 people trying to sleep in a camper meant for 6. I dare you to try it. Flexible . . . is the word.

Cookies and ice tea break. Chuck and JM.

CHAPTER 46

Beaches, Boardwalks, and Sand Castles

Funny how some places keep calling you back. For about six years in a row when the kids were still all in the fold, we packed up our little six-person pop-up camper and headed for "Joysey." After competing with throngs of bodies on the beach at Sea Isle City the first year, we decided to wait till the beginning of September when rates drop and the beaches clear.

We packed that little camper full with all kinds of goodies; Susan's prepared meals, junk food, drinks, lots of clothes, sunscreen, bug juice, beach balls and paddles, buckets and sand castle tools . . . you name it. Then we closed the camper and sat on the lid to latch it. We mounted four bikes on the back, hooked up to the station wagon and hoped we wouldn't drag too much over bumpy roads. These days, many lavish in the luxury of a large RV but we were happy with our little pop-up. When opened up, the two ends slid out to provide

Our pop-up camper from '75–'85.

229

double beds, the table and two seats folded down for another double bed. It was close quarters but just what we needed. Our bedroom had a curtain to pull giving us just enough privacy.

The camping area was just across the bay from the beach in a wooded area. It had a pool, a lake, game room and plenty of kids for Mike to befriend. He especially liked finding a friend to bike and swim with. His sisters were happy to stay to themselves playing games or swimming in the lake after we came back from the beach. Susan would prepare meals and I would help by grilling, setting up and cleaning up. We had the routine down pat after the first year or so.

"Hey, don't forget the sunscreen! Yes, Bren, you have to use it. It won't mess your face up." Susan knew she'd burn if she didn't lather it on and sure enough, the first day was hot. Poor girl, she really got burnt. She suffered the rest of the week. I often got burned on my legs while creating sand castle buildings. Susan would keep reminding me "Do you have enough sunscreen on?" Sometimes, I'd ignore it and suffer later. Dumb!

The first year when the kids were quite small, I sat down with them and their little plastic buckets and shovels building normal kid-castles. We made piles of sand with the buckets and drizzled wet sand on the top watching it grow larger and larger till it reached a tiny tip about waist high to a six year old. They loved it and so did I. Back into the surf we'd go riding the waves or boogie boarding on them.

Susan loved the ocean but could not swim. Not that she didn't try. She even took some lessons at the "Y" but finally gave it up. So I would coax her into the water until it got chest high. That was enough. She hung onto me like it was life or death.

Sorry, Honey. We did enjoy the beach didn't we? In fact it became her favorite place on earth. Go figure. No matter, I got her there at least once a year if at all possible. Even the year before she died, we took a trip to Savannah, GA, and Hilton Head where there was a special rubber walkway for wheelchairs. I pushed her out to the end of the walk, sitting there for a bit soaking up the sun, and drinking in the sounds and smell of the saltwater scene.

It wasn't the same, but it was the beach—her favorite place to vacation. I wonder what heaven's beaches are like? Well, of course there are beaches and lakes in heaven!

God said he would make a new heaven and a new earth at the end of the age. If He created earth as beautiful as it is, how much more wonderful must heaven be? Incomprehensible!

Well . . . as the kids got bigger, so did the kid-type-castle. Oh, it was fun for a while but we could do better. So, armed with a few sea shells, plastic shovels and buckets, we began to make a large pile of sand. Most important, we discovered, was to wet and pack the sand as we piled it. If we didn't wet and pack it, it would dry out very quickly and the detailed edges would break off even as we built.

"Pack it down with your feet girls. Keep the water coming, I'll continue shoveling sand to make a large mound." We'd mound and pack until it was a large enough pile to start carving something out of it. It was good to have something in mind before I began. One of the first buildings we made was a log cabin. Then we tried a house fashioned after our own with chimneys, window and doors even detailing raised glass dividers in the windows. We would carve out overhangs on the roof and put dormers on or additions where possible. Finally we cut in steps leading literally, down toward the water. By this time there was a crowd of 15 or more people watching in amazement and asking to take pictures.

Then the girls decided our buildings needed some landscaping. So they'd take turns making little bushes drizzled with water and sand producing a life-like effect. Then it was time to smooth off the area and sometimes, inscribe a name or verse in the sand nearby. What great memories building in the sand by the beach.

We found it was critical to build high enough on the beach and know how far and when the tide came in. Sooner or later, our creation would get pounded by kids or surf. People would actually protect it from mischievous kids until the tide was threatening.

The ultimate sand castle buildings and the joy of the crowds and our family, were our churches. Yes, a church with a tall steeple. This took some refining and practice. We eventually settled on building our churches four feet high or slightly taller. I learned that sea shells, plastic shovels and plastic buckets needed to be replaced with real hoes, some concrete trowels, a large dirt shovel and five-gallon buckets to carry water. The sand needed to be piled very high, soaked with water, and packed down with our feet.

To accommodate the steeple, we made a large pile of sand at one end of the mound, topping it off by drizzling watery sand. Now we were ready to begin. As in any carving, be it stone, wood, ice, fruit, twigs, clay or sand, the artist visualizes what is already inside the mound or subject. He just needs time and creative skill to release it. So he chips, carves, shaves and molds and in time the finished product appears.

Why does this remind me of someone else? God? Yes, God. He took a little pile of dirt, formed it and breathed life into it and it became a living being. And He put within each one a desire to create and produce. No wonder He said, "In the image of God, He created man. Male and female he created them and said they were to have dominion over the earth, fill it and subdue it." "Fearfully and wonderfully he created us . . . and all for His Glory." Portions quoted from Genesis, Psalms and Revelation. Look it up.

As our family grew and the girls married, their husbands joined in on the fun, actually making my job easier. They helped to shovel the sand into a large mound while others carried many five-gallon buckets of water, drenching the sand mound and helping to stomp it firm. When it was large enough, off they went with their girls into the waves or down the beach for shells. It was then that I stood back, took a long hard look and envisioned the finish masterpiece. Something God certainly did. Scripture says that He knew us before we were even conceived in our mother's womb. He has a plan for us. He also made the ultimate sacrifice to redeem us from our sinful doomed state.

During the shaving and molding process, the warm, dry ocean air would cause parts of the overhang on the sand castle church to fall off. Sometimes we tried to adjust or repair them. Other times, it wasn't possible and you lived with it. A lot like our lives, right? Occasionally, there were sea gulls threatening to land on the tedious steeple. The girls and Mike, or even onlookers, made certain that didn't happen. Photos would be proof of our accomplishment.

Susan and I finally decided, we were tired of packing and unpacking and vacationing in our tiny camper. We finally succumbed to the lure of air conditioned condos and motels and we sold the little camper which had given us so much fun and memories to treasure. Friends of ours were vacationing at the Outer Banks of North Carolina. We joined them once or twice, enjoying the dunes and the less crowded beaches as well as Ocracoke Island.

The last couple years of family beach vacations took us to Bethany Beach in Delaware where we rented a large house two blocks from the beach. There were plenty of hands to carry our beach gear including buckets, shovels and chairs. Susan and I enjoyed pulling the wagon with precious live cargo too tired from the long walk. We made sure to taste the taffy, fries, shakes and Kohr's ice cream on the boardwalks.

Poppie and Mawmaw bought tickets for the kiddy rides for our wee-ones. Got pictures of them on carousels, bumper cars, saucers and what have you. I can feel the *wunder-bar* cool evening breeze as we stand at the rail of the boardwalk, Susan and me, hand around her waist, looking off into the horizon as waves crash on the shore and the last kite dives frantically before being pulled down for the night. I can smell a dead crab or fish on the beach as gulls fly overhead calling to one another.

My shoulders and legs burn from the lack of sunscreen, but I say nothing. Susan told me to cover up and I remember. What is she thinking? My thoughts are cluttered and blurred yet in many ways, the reality and uncertainty of life is clear. Bicycles swerve to miss us and a child's cotton candy nearly swipes Susan's skirt. I tighten my grip on her waist and plant a kiss on her cheek, wondering where all the time has gone.

Standing near us are our kids, mature adults. We have six grandchildren and one on the way. Seems like just yesterday it was only Susan and me strolling the boardwalk, dreaming of the future and kids to be.

Now we're scrunched inside one of those instant photo booths cheek to cheek making a memory. The brown-tone photo smiles at me from my truck dash every time I get behind the steering wheel. They are so young! Is that actually us? I remember. How could I ever forget? I mull over the fact of how we could age so quickly? Oh boy, I'm in dream land again. But that's what writers do. Don't they?

So . . . the last time I counted, our family tallies 24. One plus one equals 24! Not two. And that doesn't count my second family with Marliss. Oops, that's another book.

It is no longer possible to house the whole family in most beach houses, not to mention a camper. But the kids kept the tradition. They love the beach. A few even play with sand castles. I saw pictures. They occasionally share beach houses together.

It's those times of close relationships, even with some rough spots, that make my heart leap. But the biggest joy of all is knowing we will spend eternity together on the shores and beaches of heaven in ways incomprehensible! Thanks be to Almighty God, our Creator.

Helping Kaiti build a sand house in Honduras.

One of our sand churches at Sea Isle City.

CHAPTER 47

Dad, Can We Use . . . ?

Never smother the creativity of your kids. In fact, never stifle anyone's creative juices. I recently learned that Alexander Graham Bell created over a thousand inventions. Some of them were very simple but most of them quite complicated and eccentric. I visited his museum and was blown away by all his ideas. But, hey, he invented the telephone. Look where that went.

"Hey Dad, can we use part of the corn crib to make a house?" Lori and a couple friends stood there looking at me holding their dolls, blankets, and dish pans hoping I'd say yes . . . which of course I did.

"Yeah, go ahead, just keep it toward the one end," I said. And off they ran giggling. I even suggested some things they could use. Before long they had it transformed into a play house. An old ironing board, curtains, old rugs, pots and pans, make-shift cradle in a box, and boards arranged to create rooms. I'm not sure how long it lasted, but while it did, they were enjoying something new and special.

When Renee was barely old enough to walk, I was building kitchen furniture for a play house. A sink, refrigerator, stove and cupboards. They were built to a scale meant for young children. They spent many hours playing with their kitchen, imitating Susan as she cooked and baked nearby.

Behind the farmhouse where Susan hung wash was the perfect spot. Under a craggy, leaning, ancient apple tree and between the monster mock orange bush I would build the play house. The tree was every kid's dream for fun. Near the bottom of the trunk was a gapping hole big enough for small kids to crawl into and wiggle up just far enough to peak through an owl-faced hole. What fun. On the opposite side of the tree, I hung a double hay rope to support a swing. It was large enough to hold two kids.

I went down the road a couple miles to Morris' sawmill and bought a pile of rough sawn hemlock boards and studs. After a week of work in between farm chores, we built a playhouse 6' x 8' x 5' high. The siding was 1 x 6 boards lapped and painted rural red. Since wooden shingles were cheap back then, I decided they would look and last best. It had a small tilt-out window on three sides and a big door in the front. One last thing; how 'bout a loft? Yeah! So we built a loft above the rear window and I anchored part of an old ladder to one side for access. "It's fine, Susan, I'll teach them how to safely climb up and back down," I said, trying to appease her fears. My final touch was a sleeping bag and pillow just in case someone wanted to nap.

Even the neighbor girls were attracted to our new little cabin. They, along with Renee and little Brenda carried boards or nails and helped clean up while we built.

The play house was a huge hit for 40 years and more. Even today, grand-kids and friends take their turns cleaning it out and playing house. They put up a small rope for a clothes line, gathered apples in season for baking, and filled the cupboards with little cereal boxes and whatever Susan gave them.

They made mud pies, apple pies, and washed dishes in Tupperware pans in the sink. You'll have to ask my girls about this if you want to hear more of their creative inventions.

Lori was probably the one more likely to ask Dad for supplies for projects. Besides the corncrib play house, there was the workshop bunny room. In the rear of my shop she set up, with my permission and help, little enclosures and pens for her bunnies. Real bunnies. She crafted a wooden sign to hang on the old entrance door which said, "Lori's bunnies." Each one had to be named starting with the buck, "Thumper." It's what he did whenever you came in the door. Eventually, they did what bunnies do and soon there were more than enough. She sold them, gave them away, played with them and just kept them for fun.

As she got older, sheep replaced the bunnies. Well . . . two sheep. She did a swell job of caring for them but sheep find holes in fences like most animals. Sheep, like goats, enjoy trimming shrubbery . . . short. Daddies don't like the way sheep trim bushes. As they grew larger, so did the problem of containing them. To Lori's dismay and in spite of many tears, the sheep had to go. A sheep farmer nearby seemed to be a good alternative and one sad day, we trucked Ivy and Petunia (you have to name them) to Vough's sheep farm. There they enjoyed the friendship of hundreds of their own kind. I'm not sure, but I think there may still be a small chip riding around on Lori's shoulder because of it. Sorry, Lor, some pets' habits just cannot be tolerated.

Roof picnics . . . What next? When the girls had friends over inevitably, there would be a bunch of girls up on the roof of our layers shelter, sitting on a blanket with a basket of goodies. As I walked by, you could see big smiles and hear giggly conversations. Dangerous? Hey, no adventure comes without some level of danger. So I allowed it.

Now Mike's adventures were a bit more questionable. Take the tree houses or tree forts for instance. I allowed the one by the pond in the huge, but almost dead black cherry tree simply because it was where we could see it and the tree was no longer good for harvesting. Of course, it had to be high enough to incorporate a 25' fireman's pole in the center of the tree fort. It took many pieces of used lumber and lots of nails but also provided great fun and time spent at home.

"How 'bout a zip line Dad? That would be really cool," Mike said. "We could start up here on the hill near the tree and zip across the pond. What-da-ya think, Dad?"

"I'm thinking . . . the electric company left a big cable here we could use. And I remember seeing a couple 'meat track hooks' in the shop from Pop Landis' butcher shop. We could use them to hang from. Let's do it!"

We clamped the cable around a pole at either side of one corner of the pond and Mike and Ben tried it out. It took some adjustments but the fun was worth many good splashes.

While cleaning up the shop, I also found some of Mike, Ben and Mark's treasures used in their video making days . . . a long stick with a circular saw blade bolted to the one end and a small dowel stuck through the other end. Beats me what it was used or meant for.

A couple more tree forts showed up back in the woods intended for hunting and hide outs. Many acres, many ideas, many fun hours of creativity. We were certainly blessed to live in the shadow of the Cahill.

CHAPTER 48

Grand Marais

"Where is Grand Marais and where is Lake Superior?" asked Lori. She was only six years old and heard us talking about these places. Susan's nephew, Steve, had recently married a gal from Michigan. Julie's parents owned a cabin on the southern shores of Lake Superior at Grand Marais. They were clearing a piece of land in a wooded area nearby and invited us up for a visit. It sounded like a great adventure for us but we had some hurdles to cross first.

The seventies were tough years raising a family of four. Farming was hard work producing large bills, small checks and little sleep. Although I would have never traded the experiences on the farm for a higher paying job, it would have afforded us fancier vacations. But who needs fancy. Our farm in Sullivan County was priceless and a great place to raise kids.

Grand Marais—Lake Superior—and all the adventure to be had in between . . . how could we afford an opportunity like this? We had friends who were quite affluent and owned a nice camper.

One day while visiting with them Ron said in passing, "Hey, if you guys ever want to use our camper, you're welcome to it. In fact, you can even use our crew cab truck to pull it."

"Wow, thanks Ron, we may just take you up on that. We're thinking of going to Michigan this summer."

"Well, I'm serious about that. God's been good to us and we'd like to bless others. Let us know when you want it," Ron said as he turned to attend to his grocery store business.

"I certainly will," I said feeling excited just talking about it.

Susan and I talked and prayed about it, but it wasn't long before we had a trip planned for late spring—before planting season. Ron lived three hours south of us near my parents' home. We left our car with my parents and picked up the camper and truck at Ron's house. He explained everything we needed to know about it and said to enjoy our trip. Not to worry 'bout anything, just have a great time.

The camper was fully equipped and we loaded all our paraphernalia into the truck and camper. The kids' bikes fit in the truck cap with a small space for a couple of kids to curl up on a sleeping bag and blankets. Mike and Lori wanted to try riding in the back. Oh, the freedom of traveling without seat belts! And oh, the horrors that might have been for the lack of them! Thank God for traveling mercies and co-piloting angels.

We passed the time on interstates and turnpike by playing road games. Susan was our navigator, using AAA maps since we had no GPS.

The kids played a competitive game of tallying state license plates. Another game was to count how many 18-wheelers compared to cars in a given number of miles.

"I got red cars. I got black ones. I got white ones." Each claiming a car color to count and see who got the most before reaching the next rest stop. Before long, it was time to stop and fill up the gas tank. "Whew . . . this thing is a gas hog!" Thankfully, back then gas was only 35 cents a gallon. Hard to believe.

On the road again, I put out my favorite game challenge. "Starting at the next mile marker, lets play 'Alphabets,'" I said.

The game is played by finding letters from A–Z on signs and vehicles outside of our car or truck. And you cannot save up a letter that passed us by. "O . . . K . . . GO!"

"John Merrill, don't you play. It's too dangerous when you're driving," Susan said rather motherly.

"Don't worry, I'll be careful. I'm not in city traffic right now, I'll be fine," I said.

All was quiet for a bit until someone piped up saying, "I'm ready for 'J.'"

"NAH AH!" another said.

"Yah-ha, got the last three off that trailer that just passed us."

"Just got my J," I said though Susan quickly opposed.

Before we knew it, we were crossing the Michigan line. Snap, "Got a picture of it," Susan said. You have to collect pictures of all the states you enter on trips. It's our law. Besides, she loved making a picture album with little quotes for each trip we took.

From the bottom of Michigan to the top is a long way. So we continued the games between potty and gas stops to pass the time.

It was a beautiful cool June evening as we pulled into Grand Marais. Steve told us to meet them at his in-laws' cabin in town. We were all happy to arrive after 24 hours of truck travel. Steve guided us over to their wooded property not far from the shore of Lake Superior. We parked our camper on their lot near an aspen grove under a fresh green, spring canopy. We opened up the camper, stretched out the awning and set up my homemade snap-together picnic table. Steve and Emily were newlyweds and had grand plans for a small cabin in the woods. A few trimmed logs lay onsite and some posts were already in ground for the foundation.

"Here's what we have in mind JaMerle," Steve said as he began describing his ideas. "But right now let's have a picnic, then we can take the rowboat out on the lake. Maybe we'll have some good fishin' tonight."

Emily unpacked sandwiches and some fruit as we caught up on the latest with our families. The kids entertained themselves with outdoorsy stuff after our picnic while we gathered up our gear; camera, fishin' lines and tackle boxes, a few life jackets for a couple kids, and live bait. I asked Steve how long he planned on being out since it was nearly 9:00 but still light. He said, "Oh, probably till 11:00. That's when it gets dark up here this time of year." And sure enough, by 10:30, we could still easily see our lines and the shoreline. Our catch was a bucket full of treasured memories.

The next days, the kids enjoyed picking up beautiful reddish-colored rocks on the shore, smooth rust-colored rocks much different than we have in Sullivan County, Pa. They boxed some up and brought them home. Over the years, I would find them again and think about those days with Steve and Emily on the shore of Lake Superior. I saw a couple of those red rocks not long ago.

I can see them now . . . Mikey toddling around on the rocky beach as fast as his little chubby legs can travel, picking up treasures and throwing rocks in the lake. Lori . . . mothering Mikey when he strays too far and stashing treasures in her pockets, probably thinking of creating her own little barnyard fence for bunnies.

Brenda and Renee are jumping rope with the tie down rope used for the bikes. Then playing that hand slapping game in rhyme and rhythm . . . all of them running to the shore's edge splashing in the still frigid water, shrieking with glee.

It's all worth the sacrifice no matter the cost. Take vacations even if it seems extravagant. You won't regret it. And do it while you're healthy and able.

We spent a few days by the lake playing and relaxing. We crossed the famous Mackinac Bridge and toured the town one day. They speak some kind of French/Native American dialect over there. It was hard to understand them.

Then we packed up and headed back south. Steve brought to our attention before we left that we may want to stop by the "Kellogg" plant halfway through Michigan. So we did.

Battle Creek is located halfway between Detroit and Chicago. The city of 54,000 is also known as "Cereal City," because it's where brothers Dr. John Harvey Kellogg and William Keith Kellogg invented ready-to-eat cereal. Famous TV commercials were aired for many years about two of Kellogg's cereals. Tony the tiger saying how "Gr-r-reat" Frosted Flakes tastes and how good it is for you. Then the all-time favorite—Rice Krispies—Mawmaw's favorite. The cliché of three little munchkins popping up out of the cereal to prove its freshness by squeaking . . . "SNAP, CRACKLE, and POP" as the milk hits the cereal, you can hear all three. Do you remember that? I sure do.

We took the grand tour of the plant, tasting any of the cereals we wanted. We saw how the process started with grains of corn, oats, wheat, rice and more. They showed us how they stripped off the "shucks" of grain and turned the grain to flakes. Of course we got to see how they sprayed them all with a very sugary coating to make kids crazy about the cereal. It works . . . in more ways than one. At the end of the fascinating tour, we got packages of free mini-size cereal boxes and other souvenirs.

Thanks to God, we arrived home safe and sound with our borrowed camping wheels and returned them to Ron. He accepted only a thank you, no money. His gift of giving was our blessing of pleasure. Another album created.

CHAPTER 49

Honduras Calling

"If anyone has material possessions and sees his brother in need but has no pity on him, how can the love of God be in him? Dear children, let us not love with words or tongue but with actions and in truth." The Bible – I John 3:17

It was a beautiful fall afternoon in 1998. My t-shirt was wet with sweat as I mortared the stones in place on the foundation. Stone work was an enjoyable challenge, a bit like doing a puzzle. My work was satisfying. The owners of the vacation home in the mountains were great people to work for and paid on time. Then why was I feeling restless?

Several times each hour, a radio newsflash caught my attention; "Hurricane Mitch continues to bear down on Honduras leaving tens of thousands homeless, and thousands dead. It's been seven days now with 10 inches of rain each day. Mud slides are everywhere and the infrastructure practically gone. Sugar cane and banana plantations are submerged in muddy water and parts of houses are floating everywhere. The situation is dire."

I packed up my tools and left for home, stunned with empathy and pain for the homeless in Honduras. I could not concentrate on my work. Here I was with all the comforts of home renovating houses for people with two large homes and all of us with more money than 70% of the world.

"Is this what God wants of me or could my skills be better used over there?"

Susan and I talked and prayed about what we could do to help. We contacted MAMA PROJECT, a Mennonite organization well established and recognized in Honduras in humanitarian work.

Since Susan was a nurse and I a contractor/farmer, they invited us to commit to three months of service.

I would be assigned as team leader to work with local carpenters (*maestros*) building very small block houses for the homeless. Susan could work with medical teams doing outdoor clinics.

If you want to speak Spanish, getting immersed into the Spanish culture by living among the people is a sure way to learn. We knew absolutely *no* Spanish. But we were ready to put feet to our faith and action to our words.

"Hammer," I said to Santos and Israel, holding it up. *"Martillo,"* they said back to me.

"Good," I said and they replied, *"Bueno."* "Nail," I said. *"Clavo,"* they said. And so we learned together.

The young interpreter assigned to us knew Spanish but not the construction lingo, forcing us to figure a way to communicate on our own. The second day on the job, I brought a handful of index cards and began writing down the English word for each tool, materials, people, places, things or whatever. Below the English word and its definition I asked Santos and Israel to write it in *Español*. We kept cards with the correct pronunciation and slowly began to understand each other. It was actually a very pleasant experience, albeit not easy.

Upon arriving back at the house the first night, I discovered my index card was wrinkled and dirty from sweat and practically unreadable. We soon had them laminated to preserve them. Who is my brother or neighbor?—Anyone in need that God lays on your heart. Santos and Israel taught us, fed us, and loved us. They are my brothers . . . for certain.

REVISITING HONDURAS 2011—DAY TWO

Julita was only five when we first saw her. She was peeking out from behind her frail mother Julia's long skirt, and standing next to their rusty tin shack. Lillian, her older sister of nine greeted us with a big smile. *"Buenos dias, como està?"* she said shyly next to her Mamà bending over her black make-shift oven.

Remembering the correct response we said, *"Bien,"* meaning good. Julia was flipping tortillas baking on a large steel drum lid teetering on cinder blocks.

"Quatos pancakies a dia?" I stammered.

"Doscientos a la dia," or 200 a day she made to sell to support four kids. Barely enough to buy food let alone clothes.

Her stove was heated by a wood fire between three fragile cinder blocks. The homemade oven was blackened by years of daily use as was the front of her tin house. No wonder their colorful dresses and clothes smelled like smoke.

In 1999, Susan and I had responded to God's gentle whispers to go help our "neighbors" in Honduras after the horrific flooding from Hurricane Mitch's 72" of rain in one week. Julita lived in the village of Colonial San Davol on the edge of San Pedro Sulla, a very poor, struggling-to-survive kind of village.

Proyecto Mama, Spanish for Mama Project was the organization delegating our assignment for the three months we agreed to work. Acronyms for Mama – *Mujers Amigas Miles Aparte.* In English – Women Friends Miles Apart. It was established and operated by a woman doctor from Pennsylvania, Dr. Priscilla Benner. Today, 25 years later, many preschools are thriving and hundreds of houses have been built or improved. Innumerable medical clinics held all over the country have saved many lives.

So it was with much appreciation and apprehension as we sat snugly in the front seat of the pick-up. We plowed our way through *loco*, loud traffic, trying to avoid open storm sewer holes, tree limbs, and desperate vendors pounding on our roof or windows hoping to earn a few "*limpiers.*"

Church Elder—Israel, my brother in Christ.

Finally, the noisy traffic eased to the clip-clop of pony driven carts laden with fresh fruit and vegetables for sale, bicycles built for one carrying two or three people, and many pedestrians lugging bags or backpacks. An occasional energetic *amigo* could be seen balancing a 20-foot tree limb on his shoulder walking along the road. Firewood for a few days, hopefully.

It was mid afternoon that day, probably 90 degrees with equal humidity. Most people carried a small towel over their shoulder to wipe their sweaty brow. Good idea. My hat shaded the sun but also held in the heat.

Linda, the Mama Project coordinator drove slowly past Julia and her children waving and jabbering in Spanish—I had no idea what. Later I learned that they were the neighbors and maids for Aurelia and Sènora Conchita, who would be our hosts in between our work team schedules.

Linda stopped the truck and we happily unfolded ourselves and tumbled out with our backpacks and fanny packs hanging on us. We unlocked the back of the truck cap and pulled out our suitcases as children gathered around, smiling, and jabbering in Spanish. Linda warned us to be certain to lock the truck and bring everything inside the iron gate of the courtyard.

Why? We are now in Honduras among some very desperate people, many of whom are part of gangs or need money for drugs. How they support their need is anybody's guess. By force if necessary and often, it was a way of survival. So . . . lock we did. Always.

Aurelia owned the humble concrete house where she and her Mamà lived. Aurelia was hired as the nurse for Mama Project. She had created a small apartment in the rear of her house for guests. Not yet finished but, hey, it had walls, one window and one door, a tin roof, no ceiling, a concrete floor, a commode with no tank or seat or running water and a mattress on cement blocks. What more did we need? We even had one chair and a small table.

For water to wash, cook and a splash shower, there was a *pila*. Basically, a large concrete vat with a rippled concrete side board to scrub clothes. You open the tap for city water to fill the *pila* once a day when city water is not shut off. A five-gallon bucket is the means to get water from there to the toilet or to take a cold splash bath between the concrete walls where some day there may be a real shower.

Why should we complain when many in the neighborhood had no comforts like us? We tried not to. Thanks God for providing a roof overhead, a place to sleep and food for nourishment.

I remember the mixed feelings of our abundance that first year as we carried our luggage around the concrete house to our new living quarters. Children stared, people turned their heads, Aurelia and *Sènora* Conchita smiled, dogs barked, roosters crowed and static radios blared.

Across the alley sat a young boy under a tree curled up on an old couch with a small radio at his ear. Aurelia said he was stoned on drugs and was wasted. Oh dear God, have mercy.

We settled in and wiped our brows as we pondered our new assignment; Help the needy, clothe the poor, house the homeless, and attend to the malnourished . . . with the help of five teams from the States.

Could we even make a dent in the ocean of need? *Solo Dios Sabe*—only God knows the answer to that. Our job is to be faithful to our calling. We tried. We cried. We prayed and crawled into bed, tired and sweaty. Dogs barked, more roosters crowed and thunder crashed as torrents of rain began pounding the thin tin roof over our heads. Sleep? Not till the storm passed by. Then sweet sound sleep . . . for a couple hours and then we awoke from a nightmare. No, it was not a nightmare. It was *real* life at night in Honduras . . . gunshots close by.

We lay close, hugging each other, whispering . . . "What was that?" "Who'd be shooting and why in the middle of the night?" Aurelia had her ideas about who.

All quiet again, we drifted back to sleep to the droning of the little fan in the corner of the room. Four o'clock in the morning, the kooky roosters were contesting who could be loudest in their attempt to awaken us. So we lay there thinking, resting, until 5:30 when *Sènora* Conchita scuffled past the door with a pitcher of water from the *pila* to make *café* . . . as she called it.

That was then. Today, March 3, 2011, I was retracing those first footsteps of 12 years ago to revisit our once humble abode with Aurelia and her Mamà.

Amy Boydell Zorrilla, now serving a four-year term with MCC in Honduras, is driving the little pick-up truck. Linda Robella is sitting in the front, Lori, Kaiti, Beatrice, Abby and I are crammed in the back seat. The A.C. is struggling to keep us cool in the humid 95 degree heat.

I remember driving through this crazy traffic years ago. Amy seems to be experienced and confident in her ability and direction. We pull off the main highway into Colonial San Devol where Aurelia used to live. She passed away in 2005 after a long ugly battle with a brain tumor. Bless her heart. And now, her Mamà, *Sènora* Conchita is also gone.

I'm expecting to visit Julia and her family at her little rusty tin house. But we're passing by the ragged barbed wire fence surrounding her house and no one is here.

"Linda, *donde esta Julia?*"—where is Julia, I ask.

Amy translates Linda's response to me. "She's living at Aurelia's house. She was given permission to live there since she cared for both Aurelia and her mom when they were sick."

"That is wonderful," I said as we pulled up close to the iron gate topped with three barbed wires.

A young girl opened the gate while we pried ourselves out of the rear seat. Julia stood next to her smiling and chatting with Linda. She motioned for us to come in. *"Venga, benvenidos,"* she said. (Come in, welcome.)

I was last to enter and she reached out to embrace me. My thoughts and emotions were in high gear racing backwards 12 years. *Here's where Susan and I came to stay, sleep, eat, rest, visit, laugh and cry together with two gracious women in 1999. And often, Julia stopped by to visit and wash our clothes. We communicated best we could with a mixture of English and Spanish. Now I and Julia alone are left to reminisce.*

We embrace, strongly and long, sobbing begins and tears flow. Lori and the others stand quietly by as tears wet their faces too. It's so hard to enjoy this

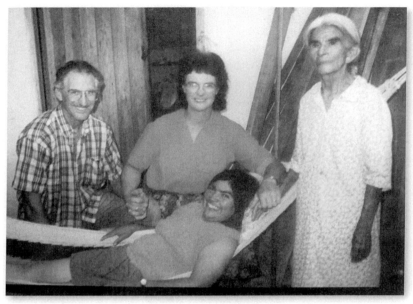

JM, Susan, Aurelia and mother—Señora Conchita, circa 1999.

Honduras 1999—Best Friends

reunion without Susan . . . and they all understand. Words are not necessary. Crying is. It will help heal the hurts, but not erase the memories.

Finally, I gather myself together and notice two small girls sleeping on the couch. Lillian's twins, I'm told.

"Muy bonita ninos," I say. (Very pretty children.)

"Lillian, is working at the *makela.*" (clothing factory) She was only nine when we were there before, helping to clean and doing small chores around the house. Now she is 21 and a working mom with twin girls a year old and no husband.

As we talk Amy interprets and Julia points to shelves on the living room and kitchen wall. Yes, there're still there, shelves I built and installed for Aurelia. The furniture is well worn. The paint is dull and dusty, the curtains light tan from alley dust. But everyone is smiling. Who cares? It's home—a dry and comfortable place to live opposed to her former house.

Thank you God! *Glori-A-Dios.*

When we reached the back door to what was our little apartment and viewed the scene once again, I lost it. Julia came quickly to embrace me as did Lori. We stood holding each other as I sobbed openly. Julia cried quietly as did the others. So many memories. Good, bad and ugly memories. But mostly good. Dear God, this is so difficult, without Susan . . . without Aurelia and *Sènora* Conchita.

Surely God's word is true; "We are like the flowers of the field, here today and gone tomorrow." And they were beautiful fragrant flowers blooming in such a downtrodden place. But though flowers wilt and die, God preserves *us* for eternity. :)

There stands the *pila* (concrete vat for washing clothes and holding water). An old tattered clothesline still hangs above it. I visualize and ponder . . . holding Susan's long brown hair over the *pila* as she colors it while I pour water over her head to rinse. I see us brushing our teeth morning and evening next to the *pila.* I hear the roosters, dogs and loud music coming from neighbors all around us.

Now, it's all but memory to treasure. And I will, forever. God led us to that place, for a precise purpose. A purpose we tried to fulfill as we poured out our lives for those three months in 1999. To you only, God, be the glory.

I left a few gifts with Julia and her children and grandchildren. We took pictures and left them standing in the doorway waving to us.

"Hasta luega, amigas," (see you later friends) we said, wondering if and when we'd ever return.

Solo Dios Sabe, (Only God knows) I thought.

Friday was a more restful, less emotional day. We visited the *Guameleta* (a tourist souvenir shop in SPS). I bought some hammocks for the kids and Lori got some jewelery.

We ate at the Café Sula in Center City. It's an expensive place but a great outdoor veranda, good food and service.

I stayed overnight with Ovidio and Julita. They live in a rather dangerous part of the city but have a very nice house. They've been broken into once in spite of the concrete wall and iron gates. People are desperate. In the evening we went to a local *restaurantè* for *Boleadas*. I love them. It's a tortilla filled with beans and a heavy cream. Yummy!

HONDURAS 2011—DAY THREE

In the morning Ovidio drove us to Buenos Aires, 1½ hours into the country where we had helped build small block houses and a church for people who had lost everything in Hurricane Mitch. Our church, Living Hope Fellowship, in Estella, PA, continues a supportive relationship with that church. The people were so gracious and hospitable, tenderly greeting and welcoming us back. The children gathered around to see our pictures and just love on us. We shared pictures of years ago and took new ones to share later. Our sense of unity centered on our Lord and Savior, Jesus Christ.

The church continues to grow with about 60-70 people—half children. When they sing, they really sing; a bit like the preacher preaches—long, loud and in Spanish. It was a very moving and memorable moment. Though they have little, they dress for church like they have much. "*Glori-A-Dios*" is a well used phrase meaning "Glory to God."

When we arrived at Buenos Aires, we passed the school. It is bigger than before. They enlarged its capacity. *Oh, there's the church on the right. It looks great except for the rusting roof,* I thought.

We drove down the washed-out dirt road to the 12 little houses our teams had helped build, parked the truck and soon kids showed up to greet us.

"Ali, *como esta*," I said. Ali is Israel's oldest son. He is a bit "slow" but "quick" with compassion. He gave me that big happy smile and greeted me with a bear hug and a chuckle. More of Israel's kids come to check us out. Cynthia, the giggling girl who once sat on Susan's lap, now cradles her own daughter, still offering her dimpled smile.

Joshia, pronounced *Hòsway*, last seen running naked on dirt trails stands shyly by, now taller than the barb wire fence. He grins at me from under a cowboy hat and says . . . "*Juan?*"

Israel was getting ready for church. Sure was good to have Amy along to interpret for us.

We visited a bit and then walked down the trail to Victorina's house. She looked just as I remembered her . . . pretty and a good Mamà. A little girl stood next to her. She said proudly, "This is Susanna." I was so happy to meet her. She was a baby the last I saw her and now a pretty 11 year old. I gave her one of Susan's angel pins. I had brought three along hoping to find all three Susannas named after Susan. But Israel's Susanna was not around. I left gifts for her as well.

The next day we toured the city, the outdoor markets, hotels, Central Park with the large cathedral, small typical restaurants, the offices of MCC and MAMA PROJECT—our connection 11 years ago. Many of the same people are still employed by MAMA. They recognized us and warmly greeted us; *"Buenos dias, como esta ustedas?"*

We retraced our steps to Pulhapanzak Falls and later, the beach. The falls is 140 feet high, refreshing and a great tourist attraction. The beach on the northern coast was wonderful. Clear, blue, warm water with palm trees nearby offered us the choice of shade, hot sun or a warm swim. We enjoyed all three plus *pan de coco*—coconut bread freshly made and peddled by native women.

Some people wear t-shirts with the words "Life is a Beach." I did not. While we watch, *and often are* the rich getting richer . . . the poor are get-

The church building we helped build. In English—Living Hope Evangelistic Mennonite Church.

ting poorer. A high rise condo stands at the edge of the mountain surrounding San Pedro Sula, its apartments selling for quarter of a million dollars. Within a stone's throw of it, next to a small almost dry river bed, squat the poorest of Honduras' poor in tin and wooden shacks. Do we ignore them, blame them, despise them or love and help them? How can I love them? What's the *best* way to help them? What can we learn from these wonderful people? Are they really my neighbors? Who *is* my neighbor? So many questions. So many needs that only begin to make any sense when we see each other as family, all created in God's image and for a purpose.

The words of the prophet Isaiah recently caught my eye . . . and my heart; "If you spend yourself on behalf of the hungry and satisfy the needs of the oppressed, then your light will rise in the darkness and your night will become as the noonday." Is. 58:10

So much to ponder. I hope to do more than ponder. Will we put feet to our faith and actions to our words? Like someone said . . . "Life is short, LIVE FOR WHAT MATTERS." I'm trying harder to do that. I hope you are too. *Dios Te Bendiga*—God bless you.

CHAPTER 50

Brothers

D avid Ray Souder was born April 12, 1945. I think he was cut from a mold labeled, "Farmer boy." Not every boy born into a heritage of farming families stays on the farm. Actually, very few do. But David was meant for the farm. Let me explain.

Growing up on a 70-acre poultry farm with many buildings besides the huge house and barn gave plenty of space and reason to explore. It started in the house.

Our house was a two family farmhouse with three stories including a full basement, a wraparound porch and an enclosed porch. We enjoyed many hours of playing hide and seek, roller skating, board games and even playing church on the long stairway. But our favorite thing to play was—"farm." That's right, farm.

David was probably about four years old and I was six. One day Daddy came home with a large piece of thin plywood and an idea. He had noticed how much we liked playing with our toy farm equipment and wooden blocks we called bales. We parked the equipment in a row on the enclosed porch and stacked the blocks, *hay bales* in cardboard boxes we called our barn.

Daddy asked if we'd like to help him build a barn for us to store our equipment and hay in. Of course we did and before long it was time to paint it. There was no question about the color choice because Daddy's barn was green with white trim so ours had to be the same.

It stood nearly as tall as us at the time and held all our machinery, bales and play animals. It also became a favorite place to hide when playing hide and seek. Being the younger brother, David could more easily fit in the upper story of the barn with the hinged roof.

God knows how many hours we spent during our growing-up years playing farm.

Today, December 4, 2011, I was back in the Souderton area. By chance, or rather—providence, we drove past the old barbershop. No sign at all that there was ever one there today, but it *was* there in the '40s, '50s, and '60s.

"Wismer's Barbershop" said the sign on the door next to a bright red and white twirling "barber pole" out front when we were little guys. Mr. Wismer was a short darkhaired man and liked a sharp blade on his *black pearl razor knife* to shave men's necks. I can still see him grab the leather strap, *strop,* as he called it, and switch the blade back and forth quickly over the strop. All the while he and his customers would be in heavy conversation discussing the latest local news.

Maybe it was "the razor knife" that David was apprehensive about on his first trip to the barber. Or possibly it was parting with his curly locks of brown hair. He was blessed with a beautiful curly head of hair and he didn't always appreciate it as he grew older. I can remember him wetting his hair and trying to brush it out straight only to have it go back to curls when it dried all, to his dislike. But that was during adolescence.

On his first haircut day, David couldn't hold back the tears. I'm guessing it was from watching Mr. Wismer using the knife to shave the older men or it was the thought of losing his curls. Whatever the case, Mom and Mr. Wismer agreed to save all the curls and bag them for David. No idea what became of the curls. I doubt Mom ever disposed of them.

Over the years, our *carpet fields* in the house were replaced with fields of grass in the yard. We soon out-grew those fields and rode real John Deere tractors with our dad in real fields of hay and corn. Daddy wasn't slow about training his two sons to drive tractors and help with farm chores. Learning to drive equipment was the fun work which made doing farm chores worth the pain. I started driving tractor at age five and I'm certain David followed suit.

We did most everything together. Since I was the big brother, he learned everything after I did. So many times, I had a big part in showing him "the ropes." Chores for us included gathering hundreds of eggs each day, and feeding thousands of chickens, and hundreds of turkeys, geese, ducks and pigs. No automatic feeding equipment was used in our growing-up days. We fed with buckets, brushed out drinking pans and fountains by hand, washed the eggs daily in a three-minute basket washer and helped grade them weekly. Cleaning out all the many pens Spring and Fall was a huge chore neither of us liked. But he could wield that five-tine fork full of manure as well as any grown man.

My brother grew to be tall, muscular and handsome. Just ask any of his peers. He outgrew me in stature, but still looked up to me as an older brother.

By the time we were teenagers, David was becoming a very skilled farmer. Farming is more than running equipment and feeding animals. To be successful, it takes planning, accounting, risk taking, endurance, self-motivation, a knack for fixing what breaks and so much more. He learned to weld and braze what was broken. He learned carpentry skills so he could build and remodel. He read books on how to be a good herdsman, how to control weeds and insects. David even went so far as to take the "Dale Carnegie" course to learn how to be a better businessman. And he became one.

His meticulous conscientious nature was revealed in his crop journals, bookkeeping, and finances. No tractor was serviced without being recorded in a book with a date, type and weight of oil for each item.

David's animals were well fed and had clean dry bedding. His vehicles and equipment were kept clean and shiny. I don't remember seeing him dressed drably even on the farm. The exception would be in the shop with dirty coveralls after fixing or greasing the equipment. If you had a chance to see that 1964 dark metallic blue, Chevy Impala, you would understand the kind of person who owned it—one who was a good steward of his possessions.

He was fun to be around, was interested in others and was well liked in the community. On occasion, he would tease me about Susan when we were dating. I think it was difficult for him to see me marry and move on with my life. I just sensed that somehow. I really missed my brother when I moved to Sullivan County.

David began to pour himself into the home farm in his late teens and early 20's as Daddy gave him more control of the farm. David began to enlarge everything they did. He built bigger pig pens, cemented the pens, built a large machinery shed, and put up a third steel grain bin for his own shelled corn. He dug a pit for unloading shelled corn and installed an auger to the grain dryer to make unloading faster. He had creative ideas and enough motivation to activate them.

I recall the last year of his life when he told me he was thinking of purchasing a large John Deere tractor. A model 4620 John Deere diesel. Wow, that was really big back then. But he never got to live out that part of his dream. Neither did he get to realize his dream of buying his own farm, likely in upstate New York. I know he was looking at real estate books and had showed me a few he had his eyes on. Daddy was not at all keen on the idea of losing his last son on the home farm. It was a rather intense struggle to determine what to do for both of them. I can't speak for his wife, Ruthie, but I know it was a struggle for David. He would talk to me on occasion about it asking for my counsel and advice.

Lest I forget, David was a committed Christian in all areas of his life. He strove to follow Christ's example. No, he was not perfect. He was human as we all are. But he was humble and intent on following God's plan for his life. Finding exactly what and where that was to take him was more difficult.

At age 28, David and Ruthie were blessed with a child. They had waited a number of years for little Loren to be born. Loren was the pride of his life. Now and then, I come across a picture I treasure and I'm certain Loren will too. The next chapter will tell . . . the rest of the story.

David, in my opinion, you were the best brother earth had to offer.

Fondly,

"Ja-merle"

David and Little Loren, his treasure, unloading corn.

JM and David posing with my tractor split in half for repairs. Circa 1973.

CHAPTER 51

The Hunting Tradgedy

DECEMBER 2, 1974

It was a day in Sullivan County history which many people will not forget. Ten after six, Monday morning, the first day of the Pennsylvania buck season. The sky was dark, six to eight inches of fresh snow on the ground and snowing hard. All of the hunters who had spent the night at our farmhouse in Sullivan County, were trudging through the snow to reach their deer stands before daylight. After careful planning the night before, David would walk with Tim Moyer and his dad, Harold to their stands in the woods behind the barn.

Let me back up a bit and summarize some details to set the stage.

By now you know that David and I grew up on a farm with our sister Joan, on Church Road, Telford, Pa.

Having graduated from high school in 1960, I plunged wholeheartedly into full-time farming, running all of the big farm machinery and helping to care for all of the poultry and hogs.

On November 10, 1962, I married Susan Landis of Harleysville and we had our first home on the other side of the large farmhouse. December 29, 1963, our first beautiful daughter was born. Later that same year we received a request from the Franconia Mission Board to move to Sullivan County, Pa., to help with the work in the church at Estella. In spite of my deep involvement with the farm, we knew the Lord was calling us to move to the mountains to help with this mission work at Estella.

October 10, 1964, we made the move to where we reside to this day, four miles north of Estella on a small farm.

This move put new pressure on David who was already a huge asset to Daddy on the farm. He married Ruthie Fredrick in May of 1966. They made their new home on the other side of the farmhouse where we also had lived. It didn't take David long to begin enlarging the hog operation as well as renting more acreage to produce the necessary crops to feed all the hogs and poultry. A larger corn drying system was installed and by 1974 he was looking at one of the largest John Deere tractors available as his next purchase. Daddy was setting his sights on David taking over the farm. At the same time David was contemplating whether he should do that or move to another area where there was more potential for expansion. It was a difficult period in time for David and Daddy trying to figure out just what would be best and what the Lord actually wanted them to do.

David and sometimes even Daddy would come to the mountains to hunt deer each year for buck season. When possible David would come up with Ruthie to give me a hand at some project. I fondly recall one of those last times he came to help work on my 4020 John Deere. I have pictures of us standing by the tractor which we had literally split in half so we could replace the clutch. It was a challenging but successful project. I remember David and other times Daddy, driving the old International stake body truck to Sullivan County loaded with feed for my geese, ducks and chickens as well as bringing other farm related things.

The date and initials—*J.M.S. & D.S. MAY 5, 1971*—are still visibly etched in the cement today where we mixed and poured concrete by hand for my little machinery shed, though the shed no longer stands. While at work on various projects we would discuss our lives . . . the new miraculous wave of the Holy Spirit during that time and questions we had about it . . . what may lie ahead for each of us . . . but always thankful for any chance to be together. Precious memories . . . how they linger . . . how they ever touch my soul!

SUNDAY MORNING DECEMBER 1, 1974

At Rockhill Mennonite Church in Telford, David stood up to read and comment on the following scripture during the Sunday School period: *"Is. 40:31, But they that wait upon the Lord shall renew their strength; they shall mount up with wings as eagles; they shall run, and not be weary; and they shall walk, and not faint."* Recorded in the margin of Daddy's KJV Bible next to that verse are the words *"last verse David gave S.S."*

David was the Sunday School superintendent at that time. Like anyone else, he never expected that that would be his last scripture reading to the people at Rockhill. As scripture says, "His ways are higher than ours."

David packed his hunting gear after church, said his goodbyes to Ruthie and his only child, Loren, who was just 16 months old and the pride of his life, and headed for the mountains.

The sun was getting low in the west as he arrived. We quickly walked to the woods to check out which deer stand he would prefer. Snow covered the ground and was continuing to come down. Darkness settled in quickly as we unloaded his gear and that of all the other hunters staying with us for the hunt. As Susan and her sister Ruthie were busy preparing supper, David and I checked the baby chicks, fed the calves and stocked the wood stoves before cleaning up for supper.

It was a full but happy house with about eight hunters and our family of six. Supper was a feast as was every evening meal for hunters. The evening was spent playing Rook and other games before spending some time looking at the aerial and topo map of our property. Hunting tales of prior years would be told and laughed about and you could always sense the excitement and anticipation of a successful hunt soon to be. Deer hunting season had become one of my favorite times of the year and stories were part of it.

We strategically planned out our hunting scheme for the first morning, pointing out specifically where each hunter was to sit or stand for the first few hours. Each hunter would check out his gun, ammunition, and hunting gear that evening. Also a "roster" had to be filled out and posted on the camp door to qualify as a legal hunting club if you had more than five hunters. We always filled it out Sunday evening.

All things in order, stories told, phone calls made to home by some, it was soon time to get some sleep. Sleeping quarters were a bit crowded but I don't recall anyone complaining, even with only one bathroom in the house.

A few of the details from here on will be omitted. Some things are better left untold.

We woke up early enough to get the chores done, eat breakfast, and get our hunting clothes on. By 5 a.m. pick-up trucks were going by the house on their way to their hunting spots. Susan and her sister Ruthie cooked up a hearty breakfast of scrapple, eggs, bacon, coffee and hot chocolate and packed lunches. I prayed and read from Psalms chapter 91. That's right, the "protection" chapter. We did not take our safety for granted. Recognizing God's hand on our lives was important. Highlighted in my Bible . . . He shall give his angels charge over thee to keep thee in all thy ways." Thank you Lord, Amen.

Pennsylvania big game hunting hours were from sunrise to sunset and the exact time was given in the hunting regulation booklet and was to be acknowledged and obeyed by each hunter. Our goal was to be settled on our "stand" or "watch" at least 20 minutes before the legal opening time which was about 7:00 a.m.

David was a man who would do things <u>right</u>, if they were worth doing at all. So he was ready to go, dressed in the recommended red hunting coat and hat, rubber boots, and lots of layers underneath to keep warm. His rifle was clean but unloaded until daylight, some snacks in pockets, a small thermos of hot chocolate and a flashlight in hand. We stood just off of the back porch in the heavy snow and I bent down to draw a quick last-minute map in the snow with my finger. He clearly understood where he was to go and take two guys with him. They were Tim Moyer and Tim's dad, Harold. I wished them well and briefly watched him walk toward the barn, the yard light accentuating the snow coming down steadily in the darkness.

No one could have dreamed it would be our last talk and his last walk on this earth.

I got into my 1969 Ford pick-up and took two other guys down the dirt road to the back corner of the back field near Roscoe's pond. As I was waiting for them to get out of the truck, we heard a gun shot. It was still very dark and snowing hard and we commented why anyone would be shooting at this hour in such darkness.

When I returned to the house to park the truck, someone was waving his arms frantically for me to come quickly and I soon was told by Susan and Tim that David had been shot and needed an ambulance.

Panic began to overwhelm me and I said, "No, no, no, where, what happened . . . .?????? Oh God, Oh my God, Oh my God. Please God, NO . . . Please let him live . . . Jesus, Jesus, oh Jesus . . ." and on and on I prayed out loud in frantic and fragmented prayers.

They had already called the ambulance and the police, as I got back into the pick-up and headed for the woods. Since it was not four-wheel drive, getting through the first snowdrift was impossible. I backed up and barely made it around the corncrib spinning wildly and headed toward the woods with a wire fence in the way. I floored it and plowed through the fence praying passionately in English and in tongues and with any words that would come to mind.

It seemed forever to get near to where he sat in the snow supported by Harold, at the base of my side hill field, approximately 500 yards from our barn. He was conscious and saying a few words, like "Oh Jesus" and something about "Ruthie . . . Loren."

Together we carefully got him into the front truck seat and I asked the guys to push as I spun around trying desperately to get enough speed to make the small hill to the barn. I barely made it through the gate at the bottom of the hill when I knew, without four-wheel drive, I would need the tractor to get us back to the house. The rest is a blur except I recall him praying briefly as I was praying the whole while also. My thoughts were a jumbled blurr; *memories, fear, panic, waves of peace . . . heaven, the unknown future . . . who pulled the trigger* and much more. I tried to comfort and encourage him but I was too anxious and upset to think straight, let alone speak peace at the time. With the help of the tractor we got back to the house only to wait for what seemed like another lifetime until the Hillsgrove Ambulance arrived.

During the waiting time I supported him in my arms on the seat of my pick-up parked in the driveway in front of our kitchen window. Susan's brother, Abe, and his boys had heard about it and had come to help out. Abe sat in the pick-up with us. David's last request was for a drink of water. I yelled to Susan or someone to bring him a drink but he wasn't able to drink any. So I just wet his lips.

Finally the ambulance came and we got him into the ambulance. I insisted on riding along for the 38-mile ride to "Divine Providence Hospital" in Williamsport. I remember keeping my hand on his forehead the whole way down telling myself that since his forehead was still warm under my hand, that he was still with us. He was rushed into the emergency room. I had to wait in another room until the doctor came to inform me that he was so sorry, but David had passed away. I now honestly believe that he had actually breathed his last breath while we waited for the ambulance in our driveway.

Rivers of tears coming from way down deep washed my face and those of many others who were part of this experience. Feelings of despair, guilt, anger, love, compassion, helplessness, and finally a calm peace covered me.

Next was the dreaded thought of calling Mom, Daddy and Joan to report such horrific news and to discuss how best to tell Ruthie. This news would be so unexpected and unbelievable that it could send them into shock or worse. It is beyond description and I don't want to recall the emotions of that phone call.

Someone drove Susan down to the hospital with our 3-month-old son Mikey. We drove directly from the hospital to the farm in Telford for the saddest gathering of family in our history. I think Ruthie met us on the walk to the house. What I remember is lots of hugging and much crying and questioning. Answers were few. Three-month-old Mikey was the only physical bright spot among us. Yes, without question, we did experience the loving arms and peace of our Heavenly Father throughout those days. But grief was heavy.

Funeral arrangements were made with the Summers Funeral Home in Telford. A viewing would be held from six to nine on Wednesday evening, knowing that there would be a large crowd involved. The memorial service and funeral would follow the next morning at Rockhill Mennonite Church. As I recall, there were over 1,100 people attending the viewing lasting well over four hours.

I clearly remember driving to the church the morning of the funeral. We were still numb to reality and yet somehow, grasping enough faith to believe that if God willed, He could bring David back to life. I prayed for a sign of three clouds in a row to appear as a sign that this would happen. No such clouds appeared. I resigned my will.

The memorial service included a sharing time. I was one but I don't recall what I said. A recorded song was played of the quartet of which David sang tenor and Joan, soprano. Russ Detweiler gave a short message and tribute and one of the verses read was that of Isaiah 40:31. Most of the remaining moments of that day are erased from my memory except for my desperate attempt to comfort Ruthie and Loren and my Mom, Daddy and Joan. What could be said? What verses would comfort? Only God could ultimately provide the steps ahead. After all, somehow, it had to be in His grand scheme of things, did it not? Yes. We do believe that *He has a plan for our lives.* (Jer. 29:11) *We are not to boast of today nor tomorrow for we know not what the day may bring forth.* (Pr. 27:1) & (James 4:13-15) *His ways are higher than ours* (Is. 55:9) Then there is the verse which a dear old friend gave me sometime after the service: Is. 57:1&2 NIV - *"The righteous perish, and no one ponders it in his heart; devout men are taken away, and no one understands that the righteous are taken away to be spared from evil. Those who walk uprightly enter into peace; they find rest as they lie in death."* That gave me comfort and peace which has stayed with me over the years.

There are those who look at this seemingly untimely death and turn bitter. God's desire is that we *"seek Him while He may be found, call on Him while He may be found; let the wicked forsake his way and turn to the Lord, and He will have mercy on them . . ."* Is. 55:6-9 Tim is a great example of how good came from such a horrible experience. Tim, one of David's hunting companions, turned from his former ways and surrendered to the Lord who gave him a new life. Today, he is a pastor of a church in Spring City, Pa. Praise be to God.

DECEMBER 6, 1974

Upon returning to Sullivan County, some of the missing pieces and questions began coming clear as to what actually happened on that fateful morning of December 2.

The state police and the Sullivan Co. game warden, Barry Hambley, had arrived on the scene within an hour of the accident. Abe was waiting to take the police and the game warden to the scene of the accident with my tractor. The warden wanted to go before the police came but Abe insisted they wait and they soon came. In a short time with the aid of deputies and police, they surrounded the area. After questioning several hunters, they tracked down and arrested the offender.

An empty cartridge was found by the large maple tree at the top corner of the side hill field matching the rifle he was carrying. He was from Williamsport and had arrived early that morning for his first time hunting in Sullivan Co. He had received permission from "someone" at Rudy Conrad's residence, the next door neighbor to our North. He had walked into the woods above our pond to the upper end of our side hill field and took a stand by the maple tree. Claiming to have seen deer running across the side hill field he admitted to firing his rifle at 6:10 a.m. in the morning darkness 40 minutes before legal opening time during heavy snow fall.

Tim and Harold revealed their story to me; David was walking *between* the two of them as they headed up across the side hill field to their stands. I ponder the thought . . . *why the middle one and not one of the others?* Only God can answer that. Being the safe hunter he was, David is reported to have had his flashlight turned ON. I will not report some details here, except to say that Harold stayed with David holding him in the most comfortable position possible while Tim sprinted through deep snow to get help. The rest of the story is reported above except for the following.

Barry Hambley, the game warden, came back later in the week with a metal detector in an attempt to retrieve the bullet in the area we thought it should be. He never uncovered it but had enough evidence to prove the case. A hearing was set two weeks later before the district magistrate in Forksville. I was there and saw the offender. It was an emotional moment yet I held no animosity toward the man. He did not intentionally shoot to kill a human being but a deer. He knew he was guilty and pled guilty. His fines were to pay $1000 of the funeral costs, his hunting privileges were revoked for 10 years and his firearms confiscated. It was the maximum allowed by game laws for that time.

No fine, no penalty could make the wrong right, or bring David back to life. I'll never know what was in the perpetrator's heart or head, but I knew I needed to forgive him. After the hearing I approached him and told him that I knew he had never meant to kill my brother and that I forgave him. Other things were said but I only recall the forgiveness part. He stared silently without responding. God have mercy on his soul. (Ruthie chose not to press charges.)

Sometime in the middle of all this I recall going to the *Sullivan Review* office to put a thank you note in the paper for all the cards, prayers and kindness of so many friends. I'll never forget the sweet compassionate face of the lady behind the desk as she took the information. Some things were said and written about forgiving the offender, and she gently questioned me about that. Tears streamed down her cheeks as she just looked compassionately at me. Maybe God touched her heart deeper than I know.

I also remember sitting at the kitchen table with my good friend Lowell Goshow and other hunters from Henry Goshow's hunting gang. Everyone was in shock and disbelief about the horrific accident and expressed condolences.

Thank you God, for sending so many friends who care deeply when we are going through deep waters knowing words cannot quench our grief. Thank you for the release of tears that wash away some of the sorrow. Thank you for the quiet gentle hugs and kisses of friends we forgot we even had. Thank you for knowing the future and carving out our lives into what best suits you and your plan for us and all of mankind. Thank you that we can count on you and your written word to be true when you say *"Therefore I tell you, do not worry about your life, what you will eat or drink; or about your body, what you will wear . . . But seek first the kingdom of God and his righteousness and all these things will be added unto you. Therefore do not worry about tomorrow, for tomorrow will worry about itself . . . "* Mt. 6: parts of 25 to 34

Forgive us for thinking that we know best when our life should end . . . or not. How foolish to second guess you, the God of our universe and thousands more. Remind me more often that I am here for a purpose, (to glorify you) *"that my life is a vapour . . . here today and gone tomorrow. Like a mist we appear for a moment and then vanish. Help me to say 'If the Lord wills, I will do thus and so. Teach me to number my days, to redeem the time for the days are evil. Search me Oh God, and know my heart, try me and know my thoughts and . . . Create in me a clean heart O God, and renew a right spirit within me . . . restore unto me the joy of thy Salvation and renew a right spirit within me.'"* And lastly . . . *"Let the words of my mouth and the meditation of my heart be acceptable in your sight, Oh Lord, my strength and my redeemer."* Amen.

P.S. I have not said much of David's wife, Ruthie, nor much of Loren, his son. I hesitate to be a spokesman for either while aware that much could be said. Just let me say that about a year after David's passing, Ruthie and Loren moved into a mobile home on a small piece of land next to her sister on the Ridge Road. They lived there for a number of years until Ruthie met a nice young man from the Lancaster area. She married Bob White in October 1979 and they live near Gap, Pa. Bob became a great Daddy to Loren and husband to Ruthie. Loren married Tiffany Hostetter in May of 2001, and they live in the same general area. Bob and Ruthie had a son of their own in April of 1981 named Duane, who still lives at home. If you want more details on their lives, visit them in Lancaster Co.

I have attempted to be as accurate as possible with the sources available and my memory. Given the trauma and confusion of such a time as this, some of the facts may be missing or slightly different than others may recall. Tributes have been given about David's life by others which I have not included. Davids' cousin, Harley Kooker helped to set up an agricultural scholarship in memory of David at CDMHS.

It was a short life by our standards but a full life. The words from one of my favorite hymns speaks loudly:

"When peace like a river attendeth my way, when sorrows like sea billows roll whatever my lot, thou hast taught me to say, it is well, it is well with my soul.

Though Satan should buffet, though trials should come, Let this blest assurance control, That Christ hath regarded my helpless estate, And has shed His own blood for my soul.

My sin, O the bliss of this glorious thought, My sin! Not in part, but the whole Is nailed to the cross and I bear it no more, Praise the Lord, Praise the Lord O my soul!

And Lord, haste the day when the faith shall be sight, The clouds be rolled back as a scroll, The trump shall resound and the Lord shall descend, Even so, it is well with my soul!"

Haymaking on the Telford Farm. Circa 1965

CHAPTER 52

Cars and Trucks

The first licensed vehicle I ever drove was Dad's 1954 Ford pick-up truck. It was a standard cab, green step side pick-up and of course, stick shift. Automatic transmissions for trucks were not available. It had manual roll up windows, A.M. radio, and a heater.

The most recent vehicle I purchased, in 2012, was a 2006, V8, four-door, four-wheel drive, special addition Toyota Tundra. Fully loaded and equipped with more than anyone would ever need. It rides and drives like a car yet can pull a trailer with more than a three-ton load. Cruise control lets you relax your legs traveling down the highway at speeds faster than necessary. But then it cost more than I paid for our whole farm. I know, not fair, that was 50 years ago. Okay, back to the beginning.

At 13, Dad decided my legs were long enough to reach the clutch, brake and accelerator. If I could drive the truck home from the field or take feed from the barn to the chicken shelters, that would save him some valuable time. So he taught me the basics, sitting next to me as the truck bolted and slammed to a stop.

"You'll get it, just takes practice. Let the clutch out slowly as you gently push on the "gas pedal." Shift gears as you pick up speed and brake slowly while putting in the clutch to stop. Try again," he said trying to be patient.

It wasn't long until I was on my own. Before I was 15, I was driving from home to various fields, some on the other side of Telford. Dad's excuse to Uncle Charlie, Telford chief of police, was that he needed me to drive for "farm purposes" and he should pay no attention. That didn't go over so well, but for-tunately, we seldom met on the road.

If we did, and we did, Uncle Charlie put on his rough and tough cop face and informed us that driving without a license is against the law and punishable as such. Daddy smiled and said, "Hey Charlie, we're farming, not joy riding." Somehow, we got by.

Dad traded the '54 in for a 1959 Ford and in 1961 he traded that one for a two-tone cream and turquoise Chevy pick-up with a full 8-foot box. All were stick shift before I moved to Sullivan County. I remember Daddy bringing that pick-up to our farm, loaded with feed he had made for my geese and ducks.

For my first car, Daddy bought me a used 1957 black four-door hardtop, Bel-Air Chevy with red interior and an automatic transmission. It had white wall tires and, for those who care, a 283 V8 185 HP engine. That was a mighty fine vehicle. Actually, in the 21st century, it is a "mighty fine" vehicle. I only wish I still had it. It was the car which Susan and I "catted" around in on dates. It was the car many of my buddies envied. Spring and Fall you could find me under a shade tree in the front yard at home, rubbing Simonize onto it. You had to keep it in the shade lest the wax dried too fast and hardened before you buffed it out. You could see your reflection in that shiny black paint.

"Was I proud, you ask?" You bet I was. But all that glistens is not gold . . . and the desire for bigger and better is human nature. Thus when the transmission began to slip oh so little, I began to think . . . "new car." Yeah, I'll trade in the '57 for a 1961 and I won't have the cost of repairing the transmission of my '57.

And so after only two short years of owning and driving what I categorize now as "one of the best classic cars ever designed," I traded it in on my first brand new car—a 1961 black Impala, two-door hardtop with red interior with an automatic transmission. Against my dad's better judgment, I bought it. If only we young bucks would pay better attention to our parents and elders, we would save ourselves, not only money, but often some unnecessary hardships.

The car was a good car but I gave up $1900.00 and my '57 Chevy . . . which my dad had bought me. I respect my dad. He said few words but I knew where he stood. He voiced his opinion, then let me buy it and learn the lesson of lost savings. I could have chosen to have the transmission repaired but didn't. It was the car we drove to Florida on our honeymoon.

Before we moved to Sullivan County I was looking to buy my very own truck. I found one in Souderton, privately for sale. I test drove it and was thrilled. A dark green 1951

My first truck—1951 Chevy. Circa 1964.

Chevy ½-ton step side pick-up for $350.00. To start the truck, you stepped on the starter button on the floor. It was a three-speed stick shift with no frills and roll up windows. I built sides for the box to haul calves and an extension for the tailgate which made room for 10 small calves. I used that to transport my first finished veal calves to Harleysville, Pa., for a couple years. Again, I only wish I still had it. Why are we never satisfied?

We drove the '51 Chevy truck and the '61 Chevy Impala to Sullivan County when we moved and within several years traded the Impala for our next car. It was a used 1965 Chevy four-door sedan, a good car and served us well until we needed more room with a growing family. This time I went to our local Ford dealer in Dushore, Fitzpatrick and Lambert.

Owner Bob Lambert was not the typical car dealer and owner. He moved around cars, garage and office with his white cane identifying everyone only by their voice. Though handicapped by blindness, all his other senses were incredible.

He typed his own papers and knew prices by memory. He evaluated the trade in cars by feel and asking other trusted employees for what he couldn't see. We bought two vehicles from Bob. The first was a used 1974 Ford Country Squire station wagon, blue with imitation wood side panels. It was the first car with power windows and the first station wagon. What fun for the kids camping out in the rear of the car. Since no seat belts were yet enforced nor thought necessary, they curled up on sleeping bags on long trips.

Somewhere in this timeframe, I got a craving to buy a used VW bug. Henry Goshow was well acquainted with them having owned a VW bus, and several bugs. Besides offering excellent gas mileage, they were easy to work on and fun to drive and not bad in snow.

I found a nice used 1964 model for sale in Waverly, NY, about an hour away. I think I paid $450.00 for it and it was in great shape. Visiting family in the Souderton, Harleysville area now made more sense on a more frequent basis. Problem being, our family was too large. So whenever I needed to make a quick trip without the entire family, it was the car of choice. As long as you kept it "floored" down hills, you may have momentum to top the next hill in second gear while everyone passed you. Likewise, you may even hit 65 mph down hill. Shifting gears with the floor shift lever was fun but the lack of heat in winter was not.

The little pipsqueak engine located in the rear of the car purred along nicely until one day it sputtered to a stop. Peter Caulkins, a friend of ours who moved to Berachah Farm was adept with fixing cars, especially VW bugs.

He helped me "pull" the engine and tear it apart. We found burnt valves and scared pistons. I took it to a garage in Towanda who honed the cylinders and we rebuilt it. This was the *first* time we fixed it. After several engine removals, I gave up and sold it.

The second vehicle I bought from Bob was a brand new pick-up truck in 1969. After three other pick-up trucks and none of them dependable for very long, I was ready for something trustworthy. It is noteworthy that during this season of our lives, we had been spiritually saturated with teaching about the "end times." By all earthly signs, we truly believed Christ may be coming back in our lifetime. I actually thought that this truck may be my last truck I'd ever buy.

Thus with that in mind, I placed my order: Four-speed stick shift on the floor, 6-cylinder engine, an 8-foot box, large 16.5 tires, ¾ ton, and baby blue. Overall, it was quite plain and simple. Four-wheel drive was preferable but un-affordable. It was my pride and joy except for the constant annoying need for four-wheel drive whenever I was on wet grass or snow. Then it was maddening. It was, in fact, the last truck I ever bought and ever will buy without four-wheel drive. That truck got traded soon after 1974 on that fateful morning when this two-wheel drive truck was helpless in the heavy snow attempting to rescue my brother David after being shot by a deer hunter.

I found a nice four-wheel drive Chevy pick-up near Lansdale. It too was baby blue, ¾ ton and stick shift. The traction difference was like night and day. Never again would I sit and spin on level grass or snow and end up pulling my-self out with a tractor. I'll never forget my frustration and lack of patience when that happened.

This truck would eventually get a more gracious nickname, "The Chicken Truck." Appropriately named due to the horrid smell of chickens from transport-ing dirty, stinky chicken catchers home after a night of catching. Due to the poor metal the factory used on the truck, the sides of the bed rotted out and I replaced them with a locust plank flat bed. Maybe I should have renamed it . . . "Mater."

The next three trucks I drove were owned by Brotherhood Builders. One was a small Nissan pick-up which I smashed a deer with and totaled it.

The next one was a very used full-size white Chevy pick-up my brother-in-law John Feldi found for us. We replaced it with a real nice 1989 fully-loaded red four-wheel drive pick-up. It lasted until I dissolved the business with Rod and started my own. I inherited it from the business and ran it for four more years. Then I bought a one year old 2000 GMC green and very fully-loaded four-wheel drive. I still have it at this writing but it sits in the lawn out by the road for sale. It is 12 years old, still runs good but rust has made it somewhat undependable for long trips.

So . . . I replaced it with an incredibly good shape 2006 Toyota Tundra four-door, four-wheel drive, and fully-loaded with a hard cap over the 6-foot box. I have been more than blessed with good wheels under me when I drive.

As for the other cars, during the time of our lives when family was growing older and money was short, Mom Landis, Emma and Kass pitched in to help us buy a new 1979 Chevy station wagon from Bergey's in Telford.

It was the car we pulled a pop-up camper to Sea Isle City for our shore vacations for at least 7 years. What a great car it was. But like all cars, they eventually end up on scrap piles to be recycled.

I bought several cars from Miller Auto in Dushore after Bob Lambert died. We bought a 1984 burgundy four-door four-cylinder Buick, my first Buick. It served us very well and it was the first car Mike drove. He drove it until it blew a cylinder coming up Forks Mountain. Man did it hammer! Oh my!

The next one was a 1991dark blue two-door Buick Regal. It was very sporty and Susan and I really liked that car. After driving it for 7 years, we donated it to someone who couldn't afford a car.

Now we needed yet another car. We found one that matched our wants, more than needs. It was a 1998 burgundy, fully-loaded Buick Regal. We put 165,000 miles on it and traded it in on a 2004 silver Buick Regal in Harrisonburg, Virginia, next to Mike's church. It was the car I used to transport Susan to countless doctor and hospital appointments. I drove it until 2011 then gave it to my grandson, Tyler, for his first car. It still runs great today with over 150,000 miles.

My, my, the cars of my lives. I guess I write about this only to make you realize the many changes life brings and sometimes requires. With all those changes came tough decisions and continual struggle to pay for them. Had it not been for the financial support of our parents through some of those years, the debt would still be mounting. Much thanks to them and to God for getting us through those times. I'm not certain that I would or could have done differently had I a chance to do it over. You pray and discuss decisions with your spouse and make the best choice possible given the circumstances. Life goes on and you grow older and wiser but the cars eventually grow rusty and end up on a recycling heap.

I'm reminded of Jesus' words; "Do not store up treasures on earth where moth and rust destroy . . . but store up for yourselves, treasures in heaven . . ." His promise to us is this; "If we seek first the kingdom of God and his righteousness, then all *these things* (our basic needs) will be added unto us." Mt. 6: 19 & 33. Help us, dear God.

CHAPTER 53

The Applesauce Factory Affair

The credit actually goes to both the Souder and the Landis *Freundschaft* (Pennsylvania Dutch word for families). Both families taught us the art of "making applesauce." So many kinds of good tasting apples were used over the years, it is hard to remember them all. Summer Rambo, the early green apples made wonderful sauce. I remember that as the first applesauce of the season and I used to prefer it until . . . we discovered "Cortland" apples.

CORTLAND: Late season. Almost identical to Macintosh in all respects, but Cortland ripens a little later, is a bit larger, and has a brighter color. (Wikipedia)

When I was growing up on the farm in Telford, we had an orchard across the street with a variety of apples and some peaches. There were probably 20 trees, too many to keep trimmed with all the other farm chores. But we used those apples to make sauce, that is, until Mr. Zeigler came around with his delivery truck stacked with perfect apples without blemishes. Daddy bought from him to sell on the market route. We bought the first of the season, Summer Rambos and Mom made *wunder-bar-goot* light green applesauce.

Back then it was a longer process to make the sauce. After washing them by hand, we cut the seeds and stems out and cut them in quarters. The first method I knew about, we used a heavy weight aluminum cone shaped perforated container. It set on three legs and straddled a pan to catch the sauce. (One like it still sets in the back room today.) After cooking the apples until they were soft, they were poured into the strainer. A large wooden cone shaped stirrer was then used to squeeze all the sauce out of the apples. It was a good way to get your arm muscles in shape. ☺ Then you had to clean out the strainer and start over.

After we moved to the mountains, both Grammys brought apples along to make sauce. They brought not only apples but jars, lids, knives and the strain-

Apple picking at Landon Orchards near Canton. Kaiti, Leah, Bethy and JM.

Lori and Renee making Cortland applesauce in our kitchen.

ers. Over the years, Susan accumulated her own sauce paraphernalia and I built shelves in the basement to accommodate all the canned goods. Grammy Landis, Emma and Kass kept her informed of the latest technology in canning and we invested in new tools. The next step up looked like a hand-cranked meat grinder that worked quite well for a season. The last update we used was a "Sauce Master" juice maker. That's when the fun parties began.

Back in the early '80s, Rod Goshow and I (Brotherhood Builders) were working over the mountain in Canton near apple orchards. Near the end of the day, we stopped by the orchard and brought several bushels back with us. They were Cortland apples. Lucy and Susan and the kids made applesauce. That started the tradition of making our famous "pink applesauce."

Landon Orchards became our favorite choice for apple picking. Initially, back in the '70s, we went there to pick sour cherries, sweet cherries, white peaches and especially apples. Eventually, the cherry trees died off and they increased their apple varieties. Still, Cortland was our favorite.

When the kids, (and income) were small, we'd opt for "drops" which were $2.00 per bushel. We picked only those that had dropped on the ground. As our income advanced and the kids got older, we chose to pick off the trees for $8.00 per bushel. At this writing, it's still only $13.00 per bushel. It became a treasured tradition to travel in our pick-up truck with Lori and the girls to pick apples each year in late September. Within an hour we could pick 10-13 bushels of apples. What a great bonding time and rewarding afternoon topped off with

Susan, Bethy, Kass, Jessica, Lori and Emma. Circa 2005.

an ice cream cone of your choice at Cedar Ledge road side market . . . Poppie's treat. ☺

After 2008, when Susan became more handicapped by cancer, she stayed at home and the girls, Lori and I went. For many years, Grammy Landis and her "crew" came to the mountains in the Fall to do applesauce. They would arrive early in the morning around 8:00 ready for action. The ladies always had a plan for the day bringing pans, knives, aprons, lots of baked goods and the new "Sauce Master." Eventually, they bought one for us out at Lancaster on one of their outings. It speeded up the process immensely. By 4:00 in the afternoon, every dish, pan and jar was washed and dried and put away. The table and countertop usually held nearly a hundred or more containers of beautiful pink applesauce ready for the freezer. It was sweet enough without adding any sugar.

As people aged, Grammy's "crew" evolved and others pitched in. At first it was the two Grammys. Then it was Grammy Landis, Aunt Lizzy Etta, Emma and Kass and occasionally, Ruthie. Sadly, Grammy passed away as did Lizzy Etta. Then it was Emma who kept the "affair" alive by bringing with her Kass, Ruthie and Bob and Mary Jane Bergey. It was a fun mix of people and work. Lots of chatter and laughter enhanced the amount of work. Each seemed to find their position and responsibility in the "Factory." The Sauce Master was hand cranked but it separated the peels from the sauce and there was no need to remove the apple seeds. Grammy's little ode made sense; "Many hands make light work."

An old Amish saying did not apply; "The faster I go, the behinder I get." Their tradition of "steady plodding gets the job done" was well taught and I think, well learned. Thank God for a Godly heritage which taught those principles through daily living.

That pink applesauce has been a big hit down through the generations. God willing, come Fall, I expect to be found in Landon's Orchard picking Cortland apples with grandkids giggling and throwing apples at each other and picking a few. On the way home, we may just stop for ice cream. What treasured memories worth protecting. Y'all come for the next Apple Factory Affair at our farm on the mountain.

CHAPTER 54

Hope Deferred . . . With Grammy Souder

Life is not a beach, as some t-shirts indicate. No, life deals out bad and good to good and bad people. *"The rain will fall on the good and evil."* God never promised us a life of ease without pain or suffering. He never promised that if we follow Him, we will be rich and happy. In fact, what He did say about this life is that, "we **will** have trouble." But He did not leave us to despair but reminded us "not to fear, He has overcome the world."

All of us can relate in some manner to this concept. Susan certainly had more than her share of "the bad." We also had an abundance of good in our life as you can see in this book.

But what I want to share here are some trials that we as Christians, at least in my early days, would rather forget, avoid or ignore. To me, it will show the awesome power of God to sustain us through some deep, dark and dreadful days of our lives. No exceptions.

I was one of the more fortunate souls to grow up in a Christian home with loving, happy parents and siblings. Though there were plenty of stressful moments, a shortage of finances, and a surplus of work to do, I felt blessed.

As time passed, my mom was dealing with more anxiety than we would wish on anyone. The horrific loss to my parents of their youngest son at age 29 was devastating. Of course it altered not only their path in life but more critically, his wife's. Since she, Ruthie, lived on the other side of the farmhouse, now the desire to support her and little Loren weighed on Mom and Dad. They did everything possible to help while dealing with their own grief.

A year and a half elapsed and Ruthie decided it was time to move into her own place. Dad and her parents helped her set up housekeeping in a nice trailer placed on her sister's property on the Ridge Road near Tylersport. The absence of Ruthie and David, and little Loren on the farm, was a huge adjustment for everyone. My sister Joan dearly missed her daily pampering of Loren being only three years old or so and Mom had lost her joy of serving baked goods and treats. But the biggest loss was to Ruthie and Loren—no Husband and no Daddy.

That was between 1974 and 1977. Dad's dream of seeing at least one son take over the farm, had just evaporated with this loss. Dad had found someone to help on the farm. Brian was a pleasant young man whose Mother had grown up just across the fields from the farm. Brian loved machinery and working the farm with Dad and they seemed to have a good relationship. Dad could depend on him and Mom loved pampering him.

All was going fairly well on the farm with his help in spite of the abundance of work. But it all hit a brick wall on April 15, 1977. Without any prior indication of any health problems, Daddy died at the kitchen table that evening. According to Joan and Mom, they were sitting at the supper table. Daddy, as usual, was discussing his plans for the coming days. He was going to plant spring grain in such and such a field tomorrow. Then he made one last comment . . . "Boy, these peaches are really good, we'll have to get these again . . . " And with that his head slumped forward with his body onto the table. Joan jumped up as both Mom and her desperately called and shook him trying to wake him. They called for help but it was too late.

In an instant, Daddy passed away that evening without any pain, without any inkling that he was in trouble. His doctor had predicted this due to a damaged heart valve from Rheumatic fever at age 19; "he would likely die very suddenly from that condition." And so he did. He never suffered.

The funeral director said that his arteries looked like a young man's arteries, clear and healthy. Had it been a few years later, new technology in heart surgery could have saved him.

He passed into eternity enjoying his family, friends, farm life and peaches, having made his peace with God early in life. I'll never forget the distressed call that night. A landslide of memories coupled with a mountain of responsibilities flooded my 33-year-old mind. *What happened? Why? What now?*

"We'll pack up and be down tonight yet," I told Joan and hung up the phone.

I can still see the long line at the funeral home and people shaking their heads in disbelief. Just three short years ago, Mom's youngest son died and now her husband at the young age of 59. Her hopes were shattered.

"How can this be? What will I ever do with the farm . . . the market route . . . all the financial records, taxes, my own health? God, where are you? How could you let this

happen? I can't do this alone!" Mom's thoughts and words were inconsolable. But she had to go on, with my dear sister's help and a bit of my own.

Mom was a petite, attractive woman with a very compassionate heart. She would help anyone in their time of need. Her gift of mercy was well used. She was a consistent and respected prayer warrior whose prayer list you wanted to be on. She never failed to have our favorite food baked or cooked when we came to visit. Strawberry or Raspberry Chantilly was one of her "to-die-for" desserts.

I spent that entire summer of 1977 traveling back and forth from Sullivan County to work Mom's farm. With Brian's help and other kindhearted neighbors, we continued to operate the farm for that season, planting and harvesting crops. We shut down the market route in a couple weeks after Daddy died, however. It was just not possible or sensible to continue it.

The absence of Daddy was taking its toll on Mom. I could see it in her eyes. The remaining responsibilities were insurmountable. Simply put, it was overwhelming and depressing. I took charge of managing the farm to get us through that summer, planting and harvesting, selling and delivering grain to the mill. Joan was adept at bookkeeping and took care of all the legal and financial issues. Without her expertise, availability and many hours of legal work, I don't know what we'd have done. The government only made life more complicated and costly requesting mounds of paperwork. Mom had no clue since Daddy always did the books.

During the Winter and Spring of 1978, Brian and I sorted through piles of tools and farming paraphernalia collected over two centuries. We fixed machinery, shined up tractors and prepared for that dreaded day when we would hire an auctioneer for a huge farm sale. That day in the Spring of 1978, came and went but not without tremendous hard work and more than our share of stress. The Bi-Centennial Souder Farm was now history. A new, but dismal day had come.

With David and Daddy out of the picture on the once super active farm, it sat quietly waiting for something as though taking its cue from the cemetery across the street. It was time to give it up and look for a buyer or developer.

We spent almost ten years working with Glen Garris, a local Christian land developer whom we trusted. After finally clearing hundreds of legal and zoning hurdles, we arrived at a joint-venture agreement to develop the property. He presented us with the final architectural drawings which looked appealing enough for us to sign onto.

In 1992, we broke ground and over the next three years, a new road structure and large double, stone-faced houses replaced corn and hay fields. They actually had the appearance of double farmhouses.

In many ways it was a relief to unload the heavy responsibility of the farm. When I drive past the farm these days, which is rare, many emotions arise from extreme sadness to a sense of peace. I will never forget the sense of pride we felt working those fields with big green tractors and farm equipment. It was hard work with a bundle of good fun mixed in.

The property development produced financial income above anything we ever experienced. Along with that came more decisions, responsibility and a sense of stewardship. Again, many thanks to Joan's excellent bookkeeping and management.

It was always Joan's vision and dream for Mom to have a nice kitchen to work in. All her life she had this pint-sized kitchen to cook and bake for our family and many guests. When Mom wasn't baking, the oven was used for storing bread and cereal due to lack of space.

Finally, an architect was hired to draw up plans. The plan he created was beyond any dreams Mom had but was very pleasing and would be the dream kitchen many gals would envy. It was full of natural light, with a skylight in the cathedral area. Maple cabinets in a U shape were accented by a cathedral window over the sink and her special double oven. A laundry room and bath room stood side by side at the entrance. There was a sit-in breakfast area facing the west with sliding glass doors to the porch. Upstairs, a window was transformed into an archway leading from her bedroom to a master bathroom, complete with two large closets, a long vanity, and a laundry chute.

Mom had never dreamed of such luxury and comforts of home. She was more than worth the cost and certainly deserved to enjoy this "extreme-home-make-over." So in 1995, the exact time Susan and I had planned on building Rod and Renee's house in Virginia, the plans for Mom's kitchen addition were finalized. I wanted to help with the construction but could not because of my former plans in Virginia. While I was busy building in Virginia and Susan was recouping from her first big surgery, Susan's nephew by marriage, Ron Nyce, contracted to build Mom's addition.

My cousin Jay Shisler, who had a heavy equipment contracting business, did the foundation work including all the sidewalk work. Mom thoroughly enjoyed keeping all the workers fed and full of snacks. She cut no corners with her gift of serving.

If you stop to think about it, they were demolishing the only kitchen she ever had to make way for the new one. Where did Mom go meanwhile? She had to move into her sewing room to get away from the dust and dirt. Her bedroom upstairs was even invaded to make access to the new second story master bathroom.

The dining room floor had to be sanded and refinished, the trim work repainted and the window in the living room facing the barn became a knick-knack display case opening to the breakfast area of the new kitchen. None of her former living area was untouched with the dirt of remodeling.

Thank God for having Joan nearby to help Mom cope with it all. Over the years, they had become like conjoined twins, dependent and loving on each other. But the change took its toll by the end of the Summer and the completion of the project. Joan would call me and update me each week and it was apparent that Mom was sinking into deep depression. Mom would call me sometimes and I could tell she wasn't her cheerful old self anymore. Her voice was distant and sad.

She moved in with Joan and John in an attempt to help get stabilized but over time she became despondent and needed professional help. It's difficult to recall the sequence of these events.

I remember sitting in the office with Dr. Kratz at Penn Foundation discussing the options to help her overcome anxiety and depression. She was totally compliant to "whatever" he wanted or we wanted. It seemed like she had no opinion except if a nursing home was ever mentioned. For that, she had a strong negative opinion. She wanted

My mom—Margaret Souder on her 80th birthday.

nothing to do with that. I really couldn't blame her.

It was on a particular visit to the foundation for a treatment, as I recall being told, that a nurse was walking Mom across the lawn from Penn Foundation to Grand View Hospital.

Mom was on medication to help her cope and her body reacted to the meds propelling her into cardiac arrest as they walked. Had it not been for medics nearby who responded quickly and performed CPR, she would not have made it. But God had other plans.

She spent a couple more weeks living with Joan and then we decided she should come live with us for a few weeks. During that time at our house, Susan had been seeing George and Grace Frounfelker in Forksville for some counseling sessions herself. We thought my mom could benefit from their expertise and invited them to sit down in our living room and talk with her. So they came. Mom was very cooperative, apparently saying what she thought they wanted to hear and was very pleasant. After a while Mom went up to her room to lie down and rest.

Susan, Joan and I discussed the problem and determined that Mom needed help beyond their expertise and they suggested a place like Phil-Haven Hospital in Lebanon, Pa. As we discussed the sad situation and were contemplating the options, Mom called from upstairs.

"John Merrill . . . " I went to the stairs and upon opening the stair door, to my horror, there stood my dear mother at the top of the stairs, without any clothes, asking what she should wear. It shook me so badly; I do not remember what transpired afterwards except that we had her get dressed.

It was that episode which sealed our decision to get on the phone with Phil-Haven. Mom agreed with all of us that this was best for her. The details of admitting her are too vague in my memory but a few other incidents are clear. While she was there, she was taken to a hospital for several shock treatments, some of which seemed to help.

I remember Susan making posters with encouraging verses to post on her wall. "You have not received the spirit of fear but of power and of a sound mind!" "God is our refuge and strength, a very present help in time of trouble."

We would read them to her over and over. At times, she would just say, "But I am really trying . . . " It seemed like she was struggling to overcome this by trying too hard. This disease of depression was only going to be healed by God's grace and mercy. It was sad and discouraging but we pressed on and prayed hard.

On one of our visits to Phil-Haven, she seemed to be having a good day. We sat at a table together. I think our oldest children were there and Joan. Mom was in good spirits and we were laughing and sharing good times.

All of a sudden, Mom fell off her chair and promptly hopped back up like nothing had happened. Startled, yet happy that she wasn't hurt after a nurse checked her out, we just laughed together for quite a while. It was a welcome freeing distraction for all of us.

The director gave us regular updates with little news of progress until one day. That day, a very bright and happy day, he called Joan to tell her the good news. Mom had suddenly "snapped out of it" as he said.

"It's the strangest thing," he said. "She just seemed to make an abrupt change for the better and is very coherent and making perfect sense with her answers and questions. This is a miracle."

He determined that it was time for us to take her home. It was an answer to our many prayers. That day was one of our happiest days after journeying through a long dark valley.

Joan had Mom stay with her, bless her heart, and took her to the newly-remodeled farmhouse regularly to help her adjust to the new environment. It took a long time before Mom felt comfortable enough to stay there by herself, but eventually it came to pass.

Mom enjoyed many trips with Joan and John to their beach house in Jersey. One night when they left quite late for Jersey, Mom was helping to carry stuff in from the car to the house as she always insisted on doing. Mind you, she was now 80 years old. Somehow, she slipped or tripped on the sidewalk and fell. The result was . . . a broken kneecap. She bounced back from that fall like a 40 year old, healing up rather quickly.

She lived at the farm alone for five years before cancer was discovered in the Fall of 2000. She opted for no treatments except for the use of many natural and organic products. Nothing seemed to ward off the inevitable. While she was still able to sit up and take nourishment, our children came to visit and exchange a few Christmas gifts. Frail and week, Grammy squeezed out smiles, surrounded by "her dear family." The Grammy they so dearly loved was slipping away as we all wept with that knowledge. Joan poured out her heart and soul desperately trying to turn the tide. Bless her heart. Susan and I spent the last two weeks of Mom's life living at Joan and John's house helping to care for Mom. Hospice came in to help. Jay Shisler brought his family to sing carols for her on Christmas eve. The last three days we kept a candle burning and the moment of her last breath, the candle stopped burning. Mom passed away at Joan and John's house December 29, 2000.

She lived a difficult life but also created many great and happy memories during those 82 years. The memorial service at Rockhill Church was packed out. Many people shared of their love for our angel Mother and Grammy. God graced the end of our sad parting at the graveside by painting the most gorgeous sunset we ever saw. People commented about that for years to come. I am forever grateful and indebted to my dear and mercy gifted Mom. Largely because of your prayers, Mom, "Surely goodness and mercy have followed me all the days of my life, and I shall dwell in the house of the Lord (with you) forever."

I love you, Mom.

Written today—January 12, 2012—three days before she birthed me, 69 years ago. Thanks, Mom.

CHAPTER 55

The Half Pipe

Mike was 14, full of energy and adventure. I was busy with the farm, church leadership and Susan and I were trying to keep all four kids on the straight and narrow path. Our kids were like most kids who stretched beyond the path lured there by any number of things. Thanks to God for His mercy and grace and redemptive power to keep them in the fold.

Friends are such an important element of the path we travel, especially growing up. Most of their friends were a good influence on our kids and I think vice versa. Mike had a few friends whom I viewed as "on the edge," but then, so was he. I'm certain at this stage in Mike's life, studying for his Master of Divinity, he would affirm that assessment.

I liked his buddies, really nice guys, but I didn't appreciate all their choices. Parents like to know where their kids are, who they travel and keep company with and what they are doing. That is, if they really care. We cared. We also had the advantage of living on a farm with much to do and space to move. When our kids were helping on the farm, we knew where they were. But it was more fun going somewhere with friends.

Mike had a really good buddy from church and at school. Ben was a year younger but formed a friendship with Mike at age five when Ben's dad, Bob, initiated the AYSO soccer league in our county. All through elementary school, high school and part of college, they played together. But at age 13 and 14, they got interested in skateboarding and stunt bikes.

The bike phase lasted a couple years. One trick for instance was to stand on the rear pegs of his BMX, front wheel in the air, hopping staccato like in a circle. Try standing up with the brakes held tight so neither wheel moved and jump with the bike up onto a box or platform or set of steps . . . without getting a concussion. You have to be young and fearless for that stuff.

Someone gave them a couple of skateboarding videos. That did it. Ben and Mike had to have skateboards. Okay, a cheap board to start with, wear knee pads and don't kill your self please, was our advice. In time they both saved enough money to buy good boards and some accessories but . . . where to use them? Ben claimed that his Dad was going to build a large ramp behind their house.

A year went by and still no ramp. I had seen some videos of skateboarders. Didn't recognize any names but clearly, incredibly skilled skaters if I must say. Grinding from the top pipe, down and back up the other side getting "big air" in a 360, grind and back into the chute like balls from a cannon. Head bands, tattooed bodies, lean and mean, their attire was more depressive than impressive. Did I really want Mike and Ben hanging around guys like this? What kind of influence is that? Really now?

Mike began dreaming of building a "half pipe" in our barn. A half pipe? I know, I had no clue either before I watched the video. Imagine a large pipe about 12' high lying horizontal. Imagine cutting it in half horizontally. Now you have a half pipe 6 feet high. But you'd have to stretch it out 30 feet so that you could "drop in" from each side with a skateboard.

We began to talk and explore possibilities. Bob and I talked, Ben, Mike and I talked and came up with a plan. We would clean out one entire hay mall up in the cow barn and build it there. I would find another place for hay storage.

The first plan was too grand and extravagant for the room we had to work with. But we decided to use the whole space which was 14' wide x 30' long.

Susan and I agreed that it would be better to invest in building one on our property than to have them drive 30 miles with questionable friends to dubious places. This way Mike would be home more and his friends would definitely want to be here too. I agreed to order materials, and help Mike build it and he would pay for a portion of the materials. We would design it to his liking and put lights up for nighttime jamborees. Any friends who wanted to skate had to sign an agreement and release of liability form which we produced. No problem. So it was in 1988 that we began. We framed it with 2 x 4s and one layer of 3/8" plywood. Then a layer of ¼" tempered hard board for a smooth surface. Each end curved upward to a platform 6 foot high. At the edge of the platform we anchored a 2-foot pipe to "grind" on as they descended or ascended the ramp. One end was a bit higher than the other. When all the nails were safely set and the surface was smooth, the skaters waited no more.

With the radio blaring tunes by Tom Petty and other "none parent" tunes, they were jammin' . . . half of the time on their butts or knees. But with knee pads, no problem. I cannot tell you how many hours, days, or years they used that half pipe. After dark on winter nights, light streamed through the open slits of the barn boards. The droning sounds of skates mixed with the scratchy tunes of the tape player blaring, boys laughing and yelling, reverberate in my ear today. A happy sound. It was one of the best investments for Mike we ever made. He was at home with his buddies during some rough years of his life, and we could influence even his friends.

It was an opportunity for Mike and us to experience another culture in a safe setting. Turned out to be a kind of Jesus and Zacceus or Saul turned Paul story. Twenty years future would find Mike with a much greater understanding and appreciation . . . no, an attraction for friends of another feather.

Once again, the words of Jeremiah 29 ring clear; "For I know the plans I have for you says the Lord . . . and you will seek me and find me when you search for me with all your heart."

Creating the time and spending extra money to do things, sometimes weird things, with our children means sacrifice on our part but if it keeps them close to home, the investment is eternal. Saying no to all their ideas or dreams can produce bitterness and isolation. I prefer happiness and insulation.

Ephesians 6:4, "Fathers, provoke not your children to wrath, but bring them up in the nurture and admonition of the Lord."

We did our sincere best to raise each of our children in this manner. By God's grace and His mercy, their spiritual roots are deep and firm.

CHAPTER 56

A Second Chance

"Now listen, you who say, 'today or tomorrow we will go' . . . Instead, you ought to say, 'If it is the Lord's will, we will live and do this or that.'" James 4: 13a & 15

As I read back over Susan's and my own journals, it makes me weary and amazed reading about our busy lives. I look at our diaries listing all our appointments with doctors, church work, family and friends' interactions and of course our extra busy farm life and I recall to mind the verse above that my dad and grandfather occasionally quoted.

When life is going smooth and everything seems "as it should be," it is quite easy to praise God and say, "Don't worry, be happy." It's normal. It's natural. But do I remember that "the steps of a good man are ordered by the Lord and if he falls, he will not be cast down and that the Lord upholds us with his hand?" To believe that and live like it . . . is "super-natural." I only wish my responses demonstrated God's awareness and a trust in His plans for my life on dark dreary days as they are on sunny days.

I quote from one of Susan's handwritten journals; (Oct. '94) "If it wasn't knowing He's in control many times in the last few months, it would have been hard to go on."

Mid October in 1994 we experienced one of those dark dreary days. Many, many more to come would be "God ordained" for our lives, but when each one happens, it seems, at least temporarily, that God went into hiding. Actually, this day ended with God showing us just a portion of the beautiful tapestry He was weaving in the making of our lives.

Lori and Mike's beautiful outdoor wedding at Camp Maple Lake went off like we had hoped. Almost perfect. We were praising God. Our house, inside and out, had been transformed prior to the wedding and it was paid for. We were praising God. Mikey was in his first year of college at Penn Tech studying for a degree in Construction Management. He was enjoying it and doing well.

So were we. Susan was looking as beautiful as ever having resolutely lost some weight before Lori's wedding. She had been walking every day to keep in shape and it made me hustle to keep up when I walked with her. Marliss and Chuck had set a good example by walking and jogging regularly past our house many years prior. Four days a week working at DarWay as an LPN was a joy for her. Oh, how she loved serving those elderly patients and her nursing care record was proof of that. She had also totally recovered from her hysterectomy in 1991 and was in great shape and loving life.

It was the last year of 15 years with Brotherhood Builders for me. Rod and I were dissolving the partnership that we began in 1979 at the end of that year, 1994. Renee had always said she wanted Dad to build their house if they'd build. 1995 was going to be the year. Rod and Renee asked me if I'd consider it and I thought it would be fun and a great challenge which I felt up to. So I began drawing up plans on my computer for the house. I was enjoying it.

Little subtle hints of something not right were developing in Susan's left knee as she walked up and down the road for exercise between Spring and Fall of 1994. It became painful enough that she made an appointment with Dr. Dr. C. in Williamsport, an orthopedic sports medicine doctor. He prescribed some physical therapy, took some x-rays and prescribed pain meds but nothing seemed to correct the problem. So she endured the pain and kept walking for exercise to keep in shape.

Mike was driving back and forth to Williamsport daily to college those days. He had not yet decided to rent an apartment down there. He was working with Rod and I, Brotherhood Builders, whenever possible to help pay for his college, gas and car maintenance. It made a busy schedule for him working, driving, studying and still finding time to get enough sleep. But then, that's nothing new under the sun for most of us Americans.

It was a beautiful Fall day in October when Susan had another appointment with Dr. C. He had reviewed the latest x-rays and was still trying to determine the cause of her knee pain. So he ordered an MRI and a total body scan. The look on Dr. C.'s face and his body language said it all. With a concerned look, he sat down facing Susan and me and said, "I looked over all the x-rays and I'm not sure how I missed it before but I think I know the reason for your pain." He was dead serious, being the reactionary type anyhow. He stood up, pulled the x-rays out of the folder and clipped them onto the viewing screen.

"You see here, Susan," he went on, "that dark shadow just above your kneecap, that shouldn't be there. Unfortunately, that is a tumor," he said sitting back down and compassionately putting his hand on her leg. "I'm sorry." His eyebrows raised and his brow wrinkled as he continued, "I've ordered more scans and we'll have to get a biopsy ASAP. So I'll set that up as soon as we have the tests back."

We were obviously stunned and had plenty of questions without many answers. But we knew there would be *more* pain ahead before she would experience *less*. With that hanging heavy on our minds and hearts, we left hoping to discover that it was benign.

Our plan for the rest of the day was to eat lunch and go watch Messiah College play Lycoming College in soccer at Lycoming soccer field. Mike had attended Messiah his first year out of high school and had played soccer there but had since transferred to Penn College. Today we planned on meeting him at the soccer game. He had worked with Rod in the morning and then had a class to attend after the game. We were looking forward to watching with him and reacquainting with some of his former soccer athletes.

We got to the school and sat down along the edge of the field to watch. Mike was nowhere to be seen yet. We guessed he'd be along shortly and began looking for some of his former soccer buddies playing with Messiah. Still no Mike.

Someone from across the field came running towards us. It was Mike Hokkanen, his high school soccer coach. No big surprise there. Mr. Hokkanen liked good soccer games and this should be a good one.

He didn't waste any small talk but quickly informed us that our son, Mike, had been in a car accident and was over at Divine Hospital in the emergency room being treated. From what he'd been told, Mike was ok and wanted us to know about it. We asked a few questions but he said he didn't know much, we should just go.

Twice stunned in just a few hours in the same day, we hurried to our car wondering what we might expect at the hospital. We prayed . . . hard . . . all the way to the hospital. Fortunately, it was only a mile away and we were there pronto. I'll never forget the scene when we were allowed into the little curtained-off booth. A nurse was cleaning blood from his earlobe. A doctor was stitching up his arm and hand. He was alive and looked okay. Mike's first statement to us was one of apology. Susan quickly hugged him tight as he said, "I'm so sorry, Mom. It all happened so fast."

"What happened so fast?" we said. Then quickly, "Thank God you're here and it's no worse. We imagined the worst at first when Mr. Hokkanen told us."

"I fell asleep coming down Rt. 87. I'll tell you later," he said.

Susan's journal records that *"It was a near fatal car accident that continues to seem like a nightmare. But God was with him. It is evident that angels surrounded him." She goes on . . . "He felt like God had given him another chance at life, has recovered from his minor injuries . . . a few stitches in his hand and arm, no broken bones, no concussion and no paralysis. Praise God!"*

The state police came to the hospital to get more details of the accident. What burns in my memory is his statement about the wreck; "In my many years on the police force, I have never seen anyone come out alive of a car so demolished as that one, let alone walk away with only scratches!" We were so grateful to have our only son alive and smiling, though humbled.

What actually happened was . . . he was driving his little Honda hatchback (a nice little economical car) and coming down a hill rounding a curve, he fell asleep at the wheel. He told us he woke up hearing stones hitting the right side of the car and tried to keep control but overcompensated and the car went into a roll, smashing a wooden fence and rolled down a small bank and came to a sudden stop by slamming into a huge pine tree near the road. He remembers seeing his life flash before him and thinking "this is it." Both doors were smashed in but the rear hatch was open.

When he realized he was still alive and could move, he managed somehow, to crawl out the back and was sitting with his head cupped in his hands, shaking and crying when someone came running up to him. Carol McElheny, the postmaster from Hillsgrove had been following him in her car. She said, "I could tell he must be drowsy by the way he was driving and I was concerned when all of a sudden his car was flipping over and over." It was a horrible thing to witness. She quickly turned her car around, pulled into a driveway, asked the people to call 911 and ran over to check him out. She said she was certain he'd be dead. Surely no one could escape such a wreck alive. Then she saw him sitting on the bank, head in hands. She was dumbfounded and they were both shaking as she sat down next to him. She told him an ambulance would be on its way. Each time I spoke with her over the next few years, she would just shake her head and marvel at the miracle Mike experienced and she witnessed that beautiful fall day.

Susan and I were ecstatic to have our son alive and in our car as we drove to the garage where the car was taken. I took pictures for proof of the miracle. The car was trash. Crushed and bent like a large building had fallen on it. The roof had caved in, bending the steering wheel and all but touching the seat next to where Mike sat. His seat was laid back giving him just enough room to crawl out the back. The front wheels were flat and bent beyond belief. The car was barely recognizable as the nice little Honda he once drove. We all just stood there in disbelief and simultaneously thanking God over and over again. Never did we think of chastising him for his negligence or carelessness. We knew he'd been burning the candle at both ends too long and things happen.

In retrospect, we all knew that Mike was not in tune with God and was going down a path that held sad consequences. His friends were nice guys but also were not following God's plan for their lives. I recall regularly telling Mike, "Mike, I know you have a heart after God. Someday you will see it. Please guard your heart." He would listen respectfully and I wondered what it would take for him to see that. So we prayed fervently, as we did for all our children. It's almost frightening to think what it takes sometimes to cause us humans to change course in life.

This I know as did Susan. Thanks be to God for giving Mike a second chance. In fact, He gives all of us second, third, fifth, ten and more chances—sometimes. When is the last chance? Only God knows that. We make choices, good and bad which help determine our future. And then there are events which are out of our control which also determine our future. What we must remember is—ultimately, God orders our steps. Our lives are in His hands. Heaven is our home. If I believe that He holds the whole world in His hands . . . He set the moon, sun and stars in the sky and keeps them in perfect harmony, then how could I not trust Him with my life? I can. So can you. "Guard your heart, for it is the wellspring of life." Don't wait for that second chance.

Today, 18 years later, and by God's loving grace, Mike followed God's plan for his life and finds himself happily serving Him as outreach pastor of a large church in Virginia. He married a dear friend of our family and is raising two active precious little boys and a beautiful little girl. He is teaching them to "guard their hearts" and "follow the path of Jesus."

-Written in 2012

CHAPTER 57

Piccalilli Parties

J oan, David and I jumped off the bus and went running up the steps, into the kitchen.

The sweet and sour smell of vinegar and mustard was especially strong. I recognized the smell and knew what was happening. But first, we had to quench our young appetites. We grabbed the graham cracker box from the shelf and the jar of marshmallow spread.

"Hey, that's mine, you make your own," I said to David reaching for my snack.

Out on the back porch (which later became the enclosed porch), stood Grammy Souder bent over a steel round wash tub that was setting on an old wooden bench. My mom sat nearby with a large bowl tucked between her dress clad knees cutting fresh sweet corn off the cob. Daddy was out by the truck under a tree husking corn.

We knew what was expected of us and I'd soon do it but what was Grammy doing? She was short and stout, wearing a long plain dress with a cape (Mennonite attire), and of course an apron whenever around food. Bending over the wash tub, her white prayer covering strings almost touching the tub, she was literally up to her elbows in a medley of cut-up vegetables sloshing around in them, happily humming "blessed assurance."

"Grammy, what are you doing?" I asked. She chuckled as she reached to the bottom of the tub, bringing hands full of vegetables to the top, mixing and sloshing like she was a young child playing at the beach.

"We're making Piccalilli, John Merrill. We have to mix all these veggies together until they are blended just right. You wanna taste it?" she said reaching towards me with a hand full of yellowish wet mixture.

"No, not now," I said and ran out towards Daddy with the last bite of my graham cracker and marshmallow snack. The thought never entered my mind then. But it would only be a matter of ten or eleven years until my mom would be passing on this tradition to the pretty brown-eyed, pigtailed girl that was catching my attention at school lately.

It was a beautiful warm September day on the farm and it was time to use up all the vegetables left from the huge garden. We grew, what seemed to me as the biggest garden in Telford. Daddy sold lots of the vegetables on the market truck or at the farm produce stand by the road next to the house. What was left, Mom and Daddy, Grammy and us kids canned and froze till we were sick and tired of it. By then, the cellar shelves were packed with canned goods and the freezer in the barn was full.

Making Piccalilli always happened at the end of our growing season when we used up leftover veggies. It took several baskets of green beans, limas, red beans, green and red peppers, onions, celery and lots of corn. Daddy didn't throw much away unless it was totally spoiled. So he would glean the last of the sweet corn patch picking every little ear of corn left on the stalk. We would husk them, brush off the silk and cook the ears in a big vat over the gas stove in the barn. Then into a tub of ice they'd go to cool. A few adults sat in a circle on lawn chairs under the persimmon tree next to the barn cutting corn off the cobs while we kids finished husking and brushing.

My mom, known as Grammy Souder to our children, would be working on the beans and other ingredients preparing for the mixture. It was a big event.

The result was over 100 jars or more of the yellowish, sweet and sour mixture of corn beans and what-have-you . . . we called "Piccalilli." And guess how I learned to like it best? You'd never guess unless you grew up with our family. I watched Mom and Daddy put it on eggs, fried or scrambled but best of all, scattered over soft-boiled eggs on bread.

Umm-umm-good! To this day, I look for piccalilli when I'm having eggs, but often have to go without. It's time to make another batch.

Susan's Aunt Lizzy Heckler used to make Piccalilli in mass production to sell. She was quite famous for it in her day way back when.

Today, February 20, 2012, one lonely pint jar of the treasured mixture, dated '08 on the lid sets waiting on the shelf. Will I use it? Can I bring myself to eat it? Not sure yet, so there it sits proudly. I remember helping Susan make it back then. We made about 35 jars that day from canned veggies and some fresh corn. But the tradition is likely to be lost as our kids never really learned to enjoy it like I do.

Catsup; now there's something most kids would never remember watching their parents make. A trip to an antique store would be most educational for everyone. Ask to see a catsup bottle capper and you'll know what I mean. Down in the cellar below my Grammy's side of the farmhouse, up on a shelf set that old apparatus. It looked a bit like a small bumper jack for an old car. It was pretty basic with a vertical ribbed shank, a handle and a plunger. Set a bottle full of tomato catsup on the base, put a new cap on top, push down on the handle and the plunger would seal the cap. Simple, cheap and efficient.

When I was quite young, this was the only catsup I knew existed. We grew lots of tomatoes and it cost practically nothing to make. It was generally runny and coarse but tasted good. Grammy and Mom's canning shelves were overrun with canned tomatoes; sliced, chunky, whole, diced, juiced and who knows how else.

Susan's Mom and sisters were also big on freezing and canning produce from their huge garden. Grammy Landis spent many, many years pushing her one-wheeled, two-handled cultivator up and down the patch of vegetables. Their shelves were a work of art to behold down in the basement or out in the ground cellar under Kass' rock garden. But hey, with a family of 12 kids, it took lots of food.

I'll always have fond memories of the two Grammies, Kass, Emma and others helping us put up corn for the winter. It was a big deal. We'd pick, husk and cut off, up to a thousand ears in a day with plenty of family help. Back on the farm at home, it was common to pick a thousand ears a day several times a week. Daddy would have orders for hundreds of ears some weeks. We'd back the old '54 green Ford pick-up into the corn patch early in the morning while the dew was still heavy. Sometimes we'd have to wear rain coats it was so wet. We'd walk ahead of Daddy with egg baskets while he picked and filled them. It made us hustle to keep ahead of him, emptying and getting back to him in time. Then we'd pull the truck down to the pond where hundreds of ducks and geese hung out. There we husked the corn as the geese and ducks devoured it sometimes before the husks hit the ground. It was a party for everyone, enjoyed more by the geese than us boys.

Guess it's no surprise that when Susan and I moved to Sullivan County, I raised lots of corn and vegetables for canning. At one point in time, we had three gardens going. I even tried strawberries. That lasted about three years till the weeds took over without my constant attention.

Seasons and generations come and go. They all have lots to teach us if we are willing to learn. Some traditions are lost and forgotten, unless we write it down.

I'm writing it down. I'm hoping someone remembers how to make Pica-lilli when I'm gone. The recipe is written down for posterity. But first, plant a garden. ☺

Picalilli ready for the shelves.

Lori and Suan cooking a batch.

CHAPTER 58

Twig Art

"Does the clay say to the potter, what are you making?" (Is. 45:9)
"Dad, where are you? You have to come up to the top floor in section B." It was Lori on the cell phone asking me to come see something. She and Susan had been watching a man carve roosters at the Pa. farm show. Within minutes I found them and knew instantly why she had called.

How intriguing is this, I thought kneeling down in front of his chair where he sat with a small pocket knife and a twig.

It was 1997 and we were at the farm show to see all the newest machinery, the animals, poultry, household items, produce, you name it. But someone carving a twig? Now there's a new twist.

His huge display of mostly chickens and herons caught my attention especially when I realized he had simply carved them all from twigs. Before I knew it, a half hour had gone by as I watched him carve and talk. I bought one and on the way home, I bought a new knife.

This was definitely something I had to try for myself. Creating something from a branch looked like great fun to me. If wasn't long before roosters, hens, pheasants, herons and trees were lining my shelves at home. Each one has its own personality.

They vary in size from less than an inch high to five inches. After years of practice, I've even carved baby chicks for the hens and baby herons standing next to their mom with a fish in her mouth. It was so rewarding and amazing to realize this was actually possible. I was doing it.

After one year, I began to sell them at the local fall festival. As I thought about the process, the Lord put an analogy in my heart. So a short write-up is now given with each carving.

"For You created my inmost being; You knit me together in my Mother's womb. I praise You for I am fearfully and wonderfully made." Ps. 139:13-14

Also I included verses on each carving like the one above or like Jeremiah 29: 11, "For I know the plans I have for you says the Lord . . . "

Thank You God that You created us all differently and for a special purpose.

All this coming from a simple twig whose only value is generally tagged as firewood. Hmmmm??

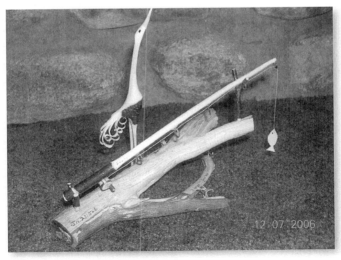

Some of my prize carvings.

CHAPTER 59

Rudy's Place

He was quite a character. To Susan and me, he was like a step-grandfather. He loved our kids as his own grandkids. Always had plenty of time to talk—which he did lots of. I wrote about Rudy and Ruth in the story about "Mountain People." This story picks up in time seven years after he moved out of his house. Hold on, let me explain:

Ruth, his wife, spent her last years at DarWay nursing home in Estella. When she died, Rudy lasted a few more years living alone at home with the aid of home health nurses and Meals on Wheels. But he ended up moving to Dar-Way where he died in 1993. His homestead stood abandoned for about seven years. In the winter of 1998, his daughter came to me with a first right of refusal to buy the property. I had asked her to give me that opportunity and, lo and behold, there she stood in our doorway telling me she was keeping her word to do just that.

Rudy's property bordered ours from front to back giving us the advantage of gaining 64 acres with no one in between us. I had farmed his land probably for the past 35 years. Over the years, I often dreamed of finding and buying an old farmhouse to fix up and either rent or resell. Here was one right next door. Now I must admit, this house was small and in very poor shape but at least the roof was not leaking. If you were a tourist traveling by, you may have never known it existed. Ten to twelve feet high Japanese knot weed grew so thick and tall around the house and outbuildings that one could easily miss noticing the little house in the forest of bamboo-like weeds.

Rudy's rust-colored pick-up truck sat in front of the old garage, wheels half buried in sod right where he last parked it. An old yellow school bus packed full of car and bike parts, oil and grease, and junk he'd gathered over the years sat behind the garage with trees beginning to grow from under it. The garage, actually a transported boat house from Eagles Mere, stood leaning hard to the south. The rear wall bulged out 24" from top to bottom. It had a truckload or two of dirt piled inside, thousands of little tin cans and boxes, car parts, random stacks of old used lumber and other junk provided a safe home for critters. Behind the garage and closer to the house was a small wooden shed. It would have fallen over from neglect had it not been for so much junk in it. Piles of tires surrounded by all kinds of motors, scrap iron, broken glass and plain old junk littered the area behind the house and shed.

Are you ready to buy this place? Come on, lots of treasures here. Well, ok, maybe if I show you the house, you'll be more optimistic. Let's go inside. No, on second thought, come back after I clear a path to the front door. I'll need to bulldoze these bamboo trees out of here and clean the junk off the front porch first. I'll call you when I'm ready. Deal?

It took a few weeks, to clear the Japanese knot weed and junk away from the buildings. My little backhoe tractor got some unusually heavy use. I saved the scrap metal to recycle but found very little else of value.

Now you can come in. Oh, you should know that the family had an antique dealer come in and go through everything, removing anything of much value. They apparently just dumped boxes of stuff on the tables, floor, and beds to sort through leaving what they did not want behind. Careful now, you could trip and hurt yourself.

The refrigerator still had food in it. Close your nose or wear a mask. Cereal and food boxes are still in cupboards. An old Sears freezer half full of rotten meat . . . likely venison. Whew! That was the worst. I ended up hooking a chain to it and pulled it out of the house with my tractor and into the woods where the critters took care of it. There it rests in the woods upside down, maybe a home for skunks.

So this is what you would have seen. Chairs, tables, beds couches, anything capable of holding junk was full of it. Like a tornado had touched down inside the house without blowing out windows or doors. Yes, a true disaster discovery. Now . . . do you want to buy? Do you think it's worth fixing up? Oh, I forgot to tell you about the treasures in the cellar (basement). Nice. A dilapidated wooden steps led to the basement. That old Japanese knot weed grew right through the old stone wall and up through the stairs into the kitchen. At the bottom of the steps was a pond. That's right, a basement full of water with "stuff" floating around. Ruth was an avid canner. Shelves that had been full of canned goods had either fallen off from rotting wood and if not broken, were floating. The sump pump had died many years ago.

That should do it. I'll bet you backed out of the deal now. Can't say I'd blame you. But . . . not me. I still wanted to buy this mess and fix it up. I know,

I hear you. It's insane to even consider such a project. You're wasting your time and money. Are you crazy or what?

But now you just poured fuel on my fire of passion. So buy it I did, at a price you would be proud of. Remember, 64 acres besides buildings and treasures. The junk is free. Sorry, too late, you turned it down. Whether the house had any value or not, the property did. Given some hard work, time and tender loving care, transformation will come. You'll see. Hang with me for three years.

I guess Susan knew how much I wanted the property. She apparently saw the value in making it part of ours. What she wondered about was the wisdom of fixing up such a rat hole. The creative and adventurous carpenter in me really wanted to do this. The timing was right. There was money available from the imminent sale of my mom's farmland, I had ambition and vision and so we sealed the deal.

In the Fall of 1998 I began the project without setting a completion deadline. My son-in-law, Mike, had a large track loader. He brought it over and dug an approach to the basement from the south end and moved the dirt behind the old barn foundation. I used my backhoe/loader tractor to punch a hole in the stone wall and bucket by bucket removed 18" of wet dirt, and everything that had fallen into it. We must have thrown out 500 jars of canned goods. I tore the old chimney out of the center of the house, poured concrete retaining walls around the inside perimeter of the basement, spread 10 ton of stone and installed a drain out to the road. The opposite end of the basement at one time had an entrance but it had fallen in. So we rebuilt that entrance and closed it with a bilco door and new steps.

My two Mikes helped me on that while Jinny Magann and her two youngest daughters cleaned out the upstairs. The girls were trying to earn money for school. They tore out all the lath and plaster ceiling and walls and shoveled it onto my trailer. We had several gigantic trash fires, one of which ignited some old barn beams underground and refused to quit burning.

So I pecked away at the house evenings and weekends and whenever possible. I was still working at my building business while trying to remodel Rudy's. An elderly fellow, Don, helped me when he could and we ripped and tore at the old beast for weeks. It came down to a decision of leaving the roof system or tearing the entire top wall structure and roof off. Pastor Randy convinced me it would be worth starting fresh from the second floor level. So down it came. At that point in time with the house completely gutted, and the second story gone, it certainly appeared like we were tearing the entire structure down.

Much later, during our open house when we welcomed the public to come and see our new vacation rental, a neighbor told me this funny story:

She was driving by the day we had completely torn off the top story and she noticed I was sweeping the upstairs floor. She thought to herself, "What's his deal? If he's tearing the house down, this guy is either a clean freak or he has totally lost it." We laughed and I explained that I didn't like working on top of a mess.

At this point, with everything stripped bare inside and out, the basement concreted and new end walls laid up, I was almost ready to rebuild. But I didn't want to build on a floor system that was 4" off level. So I jacked one corner up as much as possible, but only gained an inch and a half. Better than nothing.

Daniel, my hired hand, pulled thousands of nails and ripped up three layers of flooring exposing the original maple floor which I intended to keep. But we discovered too many big holes burned by hot coals. So I ordered ¾" hickory from Lauchle's sawmill down near Farragut. They made T&G flooring for us and I even kept the #3 boards for character.

Big Mike, what we call my son-in-law, heard about a guy who had 6000 board feet of rough cut pine, random width and lengths and he wanted to sell it cheap because it was not "stickered" (spacers put between each boards). It needed to be used or stickered so I bought all of it for 16 cents a board foot.

About a fourth of it was "wormy" which just gave it more character. There were stacks of lumber everywhere as I sorted, planned, and restacked it until little by little, I used it up. The kitchen and living area was full of stacked lumber until I planed all of it and later painted some for trim.

The exterior and interior walls were originally one layer of solid 1½" hemlock planks nailed to a beam at the bottom and top. Before removing any partitions, I welded two ½" re-bar together and a bolt on each end. Then I drilled a hole in either side of the house, stuck the rod through and with nuts and washers, drew the walls together as tight as possible. Thus the house was more stable while I worked on it.

According to a friend of Rudy's, the 14' addition was added to the rear of the house in 1940. He, Denny Paragini, said he helped Rudy build it. Over the years, Denny bought three acres of ground from Rudy and built a small cabin on it as a reprieve from his busy Italian restaurant in Wilkes Barre. Occasionally, he would show up on our doorstep holding a large tray of his homemade lasagna to express his gratitude for hunting on our property and caring for Ruth and Rudy. A nice tasty perk.

Rudy's Place before renovation.

Rudy's Place complete as a vacation rental.

Big Mike had his own sawmill at the time. He sawed a large hemlock beam out for us to support the second floor. We wanted an open span in the whole first floor room. An old barn beam post supported it in the center and ends.

I spent at least a week cutting and piling rough cut 2 x 10s to length for rafters, 2 x 8s for ceiling joists, 2 x 6s for exterior wall studs and 2 x 4s for interior partition studs. When all these were cut, sorted and piled, I was ready for my construction crew. My former partner, Rod Goshow, of Brotherhood Builders and his hired men had agreed to help frame up the entire shell and get it under roof.

Without any accidents, thank God, we had the shell up, all shingled and sheathed in three days. This was a huge help and morale builder. I was ready to see "new" after all the dust, trash, and destruction of the first year of work. I had left the old porch intact to work off of until the second story was finished. We tore it off and Rod helped me frame up the wraparound porch I had envisioned from the beginning. This was built with lumber cut from big pine trees on Rudy's woods. We exposed the rafters for old time sake. Even the railing was made with that lumber. Windows and doors were bought from a surplus outlet. We framed the openings to fit windows they had in stock. The front door was replaced with double French doors recycled from one of my jobs. The old steep stairs was removed and replaced with a *"winder."* My Grammy Souder's old farmhouse had a *winder* and I liked the unique space saving feature. It was the kind of challenge I enjoy and turned out fine. A straight maple stick in Rudy's woods was transformed into a grab handle for safety.

During the winter months, I heated the house with an old coal stove in the basement. It is still there today, hooked in-line with the new oil fired furnace. A hot water base board system was installed.

Our whole family got involved. Besides Mike and Mike working in the basement, the other son-in-laws helped finish framing the interior walls, running wires, and insulating. The women and even young girls kept us well nourished. They cleaned, dusted, painted, sanded, and worked on the photo album.

There are pictures of the grandkids running around, pounding nails, chasing each other, and having plain old fun. It was encouraging to have the family rally around our project. After all, it was the only house transformation project I had ever done like it. And I had helped each of them whenever possible on their houses. So it was nice to have them pitch in with mine.

Even our dogs, Massie and Sasha, made it their duty to be with me whenever I worked there. If they saw my truck head up the dirt road, they would race through the field and often beat me there.

Drywall is not my forte, so I hired a drywall man and I helped. We left all the ceilings and a few walls for me to panel with T&G unpainted pine.

A temporary shop was set up in the house where I cut, and planed piles of pine. It produced a nice pile of wonderful shavings which work great for litter.

It was time to install that hickory flooring. I could have started square to any wall like normal, but then this was not a normal house project. So I put one wide board down the center of the large room. Then I started on a 45 degree angle in one corner alternating three-, four- and five-inch wide boards and the opposite on the other side giving a diamond effect.

From the same surplus outlet, I bought the kitchen cabinets, countertops and sink. It was an excellent buy. Sad to say and I hate to admit it, they were made in China. I couldn't resist the $1500 savings.

Susan was a real trooper, painting each and every piece of trim with two coats of colonial cupboard blue and pewter colors. We had boards spread out all over the house to dry. When the trim was finally painted and installed, it looked like a very, cozy, livable house. But there was still unfinished work. Toilets, bathroom sinks, shelving, interior doors, oh yes, the doors. We used all Rudy's authentic plank doors and the four-panel doors for rooms and closets. But we came up short because we added closets.

My mom's farmhouse had also been remodeled and she had saved several four-panel doors. I was able to use them and they matched perfectly. I did a small amount of wall papering, Susan bought curtains and I installed shades, and trimmed the upstairs large windows with old barn beams cut in half. For the stairwell railing, I reused the original rafters, sanding and polyurethaning them about four times until there were no splinters.

The grandchildren helped their Moms clean the entire house until it actually smelled like a lived in clean house. It was time to furnish. Again, fortunately, my mom had lots of furniture stored in her attic. Plus, by the time I finished the project, Mom had passed away and my sister didn't need most of her furniture. So, I trucked it home and used it for the rental. Susan had fun going to used furniture stores and garage sales to complete the furnishings. It was rewarding to see how it was all coming together. Susan purchased bed spreads, and all the linens, wall hangings, pictures, and a phone. We even refinished and caned a couple rockers. We found five used rockers from a garage sale in Eagles Mere for the porch.

One of the last projects was putting veneer stone on the front of the house and installing rain gutters.

All the kids and grandkids came home the week before the open house to get everything in place, make beds, put lamps and shades in place, bulbs, oh, so much to think of. Everyone helping, laughing, eating, joking and being what a family should be. The time had come to sit up to the table in "Rudys Place" for our first meal together in this house.

It was a moment of gratitude, a time of remembrance from whence we had come, a time to thank God for what He allowed us to accomplish. The grandkids lined up on the winding stairs for a photo, then out to the porch for another of the whole gang. Rod and Lucy came over to join us for dessert. We sat around and enjoyed stories from the past . . . stories of our work . . . stories of what may be to come. We played some board games and tried out the beds.

Mike, our son, helped me design and create two signs to hang outside which we later wired for lights.

May 25, 2002, the day advertised in the Sully as "open house for Rudy's Place Vacation Rental" was here. Susan and the girls had prepared lots of goodies for the visitors and classical music was softly playing as folks came. The girls made sure the food was fresh and I gave tours. Doc, from the Sully, *(Sullivan Review)* was there taking pictures for his column "Spotlight on business." A few relatives of Rudy's came and admired the house. Many neighbors came, some sat rocking on the porch, and congratulated us on the wonderful transformation and our vision for a vacation rental.

Before we officially took in any renters, Susan and I walked through each room of the house praying God's blessing, peace and protection over it. We wanted this house to be a place of peace and rest. Thus, the verse we chose to use on our advertising; "This is the resting place, let the weary rest." Isaiah 28:12

We advertised in the Sully, the tourist guide and the Endless Mountains Visitors' Guide. We had business cards made and handed them out. Today, after 10 years of business, we have guests year around, many months all weekends are full. In the Summer, most all days are reserved. There are still a few families who reserve a week or ten days since 2002. People have come from many walks of life; as close as a few miles down the road, from England, Canada, Vancouver, Alaska, Maine, Florida, and lots from Jersey, Philly and NYC. Two couples got married there, some have celebrated 50th anniversaries, but many come just to "get away" from the "rat race." They have filled two guest books with their gratitude for such a peaceful, restful respite. Many express their sense of blessing and divine presence. God has been so good to us. Susan graduated to her eternal home. I continue to run Rudy's Place with the aid of a business manager. Until God shows me otherwise, I will keep the doors open to guests.

Now, how many offers do I have? Remember? You weren't impressed and thought I was nuts or crazy. Ok, maybe I was. But then, what fun is there without a challenge? Would I do it again? I'm not sure, but I must say, it was worth the effort!

Go to rudysplacevacationrental.com and check it out. You'll be amazed. And hey, we'd love to have you as a guest!

South view of Rudy's Place.

CHAPTER 60

Westward Bound for Six Weeks

"John Merrill! Don't get out, he could attack you!"

"I just want a few good pictures. I'll stay close to the van, don't worry," I said pulling our small RV onto the berm. It was early September in 2000. We were in Yellowstone National Park enjoying all the beauty and especially, the wildlife. This time it was a huge bull elk at the edge of the woods next to the park road. Cars were pulling off the road and people were getting out with cameras in hand. *This could get ugly*, I thought as I gingerly got out of the car.

It was "rut" season and bull elk were bugling and sparring for the biggest harem in the park. This was nothing to mess with. But I had to get a picture of this trophy elk in the wild. I was fortunate to get a short video and jump back in the van. Good idea! As we pulled slowly away still observing the power of the beast, he bugled loudly and charged the car in front of us. It appeared like he made contact but fortunately they spun away. "Whew," we said, "that was WILD!"

Just around the bend was a huge meadow next to our campsite for the night. It was a beautiful cool evening as the sun was setting. A man stood on the edge of the road with tripod and spotting scope focused on the meadow. Several hundred yards out, proudly posing with 15 elk cows, was another massive bull. He lowered his head, stretched his mighty neck forward and bugled loud and long. It was a rare and amazing sight for us. He then proudly trotted around his harem and possessively watched for any challengers. He seemed oblivious to the tourists as he circled his girls.

That night as we settled into our cozy nest in the van, we could here bugling and footsteps very close by for most of the night. I swear elk were sniffing our camper for fresh hay. Morning dawned bright and cool after a fitful night's sleep and we were back on the road again.

This had been our dream for many years. Travel West! But with the farm, church, growing family and a building business, we had put it off as "only a dream." But now, here we were, living our dream.

In the summer of 2000, we began looking for a reasonably priced small RV to "do our trip." After much searching, we noticed a small flyer on the bulletin board at Jennings Store in Estella, advertising *for sale* a small RV with a photo of it. *Boy that looks familiar*, I thought, *and just what we're looking for*. I yanked off a slip with the phone number and "'ta-dah" it was our neighbor's. Well, actually, it first belonged to Marcella and Maynard Reibson, a retired farmer two miles from us. They sold it to another neighbor, Angie and Jeff Higley, two miles back on North Street. All excited, we jumped in the car and went to their house. It was perfect, a class B, 1986 Dodge van camper with about 84K miles on it in great shape. It had two swivel captain chairs up front, and a bed just big enough for us in the back, enough cupboards and just everything we needed. "Sold," we said, "we'll buy it."

We must have resembled two little kids at Christmastime as we showed it to friends who graciously celebrated our new purchase but secretly, I think, were not envying us as they observed the cramped space we'd be occupying for six weeks. But for us, it was a God thing and we knew it. After acquainting ourselves with the details of the van, we began packing. We were like our grandkids with a new playhouse. Lori had fun helping us pack too. Our plan was to leave September 5th after Labor Day and the Fair. We would spend five weeks traveling the western states and finish up the last five days with our kids in Virginia.

We mapped out our journey heading west through Ohio, Indiana, Illinois, Wisconsin, Minnesota, North and South Dakota, Wyoming, and Montana. After Glacier National Park, we'd enter Alberta, Canada, crossing a portion of British Columbia and down into Washington State. Then follow the Oregon coastline into California through the Redwoods, down into San Francisco, Los Angeles and Palm Springs. From there travel to Phoenix to visit our good friends, Lowell and Lois Goshow and Leon and Gloria Goshow, up to Flagstaff and the Grand Canyon and eventually stand on the "Four Corners"; Arizona, New Mexico, Utah and Colorado. Then travel back through Kanasas, Missouri, Kentucky, and into Virginia to rest with our kids and grandkids. There would be many stops and visits along the way, often spontaneous stops. All calculated, we gave ourselves six weeks so as not to be rushed. At trip's end, the little van would have driven 9,000 fun-filled miles.

Psalm 91 from the Upper Room devotional with a prayer together for God's presence and protection gave us a great send-off that first day. Never take for granted the safety, health and enjoyment of each new day. Thanks to some new cell phones, we could stay in touch with family. Susan called her sisters occasionally and was particularly interested in following news of her older brother, JR, who was in Texas for treatments for a rare bone marrow disease. He would spend three more weeks there before being released to go home.

Our first night was spent in Archbald, Ohio, at Sauder Village Campground. There was a huge post and beam structure there where we ate supper and I was enthralled with the masterpiece workmanship. The next day landed us in Goshen, Indiana, to visit Susan's nephews and their families; Steve and Emily Landis (Steve just recently, at this writing, had a heart transplant and is doing great. Thank God) and Mike and Jan Landis who owned four Dairy Queens. ☺ My favorite ice cream.

Our next goal was the Badlands of South Dakota. We drove 567 miles that day stopping in Wisconsin for some famous cheese and then camping somewhere deep in the corn country of Minnesota. Minnesota has more than 10,000 lakes, and has some fabulous fields to farm. The corn was over 10 feet tall with golden ears nearly ripe for harvest. We stopped in Mitchell, S.D, where we toured the Corn Palace. Huge walls covered with mosaics, meticulously constructed of only grain grown in S.D.

"Hey hon, go sit over there next to that guy on the bench. I'll take your picture." So I did as she said (this time) and shyly slid over next to the colorfully clad cowboy on the bench and grinned. He was a Native American . . . statue, set there for that specific purpose. ☺

Of course, we couldn't pass up a visit to Cabelas. WOW. What a place for hunters and outdoors people!

From there, we set our sites on the Badlands of South Dakota. The further west we went the bigger the sky seemed to grow. The scenic drive through the Badlands reminded us of a "sand castle heaven" combined with the Grand Canyon. Incredible topography.

"What's with those signs for Wall Drug?" I said to Susan. "Seems like there's a sign every 50 miles or so." "Beats me," she said.

Pushing a bit further that day with the gas tank nearing "E," we arrived at Mount Rushmore in the Black Hills just in time for the evening light show. Hard to imagine the enormous 14-year task carving five presidents' faces, each 60' tall in granite, hundreds of feet up on a cliff. Talk about perseverance and determination! We camped near the site that night, tired from another long day of sightseeing, 538 miles. Time to chill out a bit tomorrow, we decided.

Next day we drove through Rapid City and Custer State Park learning more history lessons and trying to avoid collisions with wild buffalo, big horn sheep and antelope. The journal says, "Susan's starting to get the hang of making coffee with a percolator in our camper. Kinda fun. Had the last of Rudy's peaches this morning with cereal." This day, we drove the "Needles Highway." It wove through boulders and forests like a needle pulling thread on a quilt. Stopping by a little café for a snack, we stepped inside to the familiar sound of an old hymn played on a dulcimer. "Susan, listen to that . . . He leadeth me, He leadeth me, by His own hand He leadeth me . . . " We sat down with rootbeer floats, humming and soaking in the soothing sounds truly believing that our God was leading us, even to this very café.

"Awesome," I said, "now let's ride." From the little café at Cheyene crossing in the Black Hills through Spear Fish to Devils Tower we rode marveling at the magnificent sights God had created. As we rode, higher and further west, I noticed the little van was losing power on hills. Gas was $1.60 now, up from $1.39 in Wisconsin and also only 85 octane. We "putted" our way up those long mountain roads at 40 mph max.

Wyoming, here we come. For some 600 miles we'd been seeing signs for "Wall Drug," don't miss it. "Yeah, yeah, we're coming. When we got to the turn off for it, we said, "What the heck, may as well see what's so great about it." Twenty miles of curvy narrow roads, brought us to a very touristy place. Kinda like a hamburger joint inside a wild west pharmacy. It did have a long history to brag about and so they did. Oh well, at least we could say, "Yes, we were at Wall Drug." I have a bumper sticker inside my truck to prove it.

The scenery in Wyoming is just as you see on postcards . . . straight roads with views up to a 100 miles, big sky, wide open prairie and tumble weed.

Now and then you would see a café or cattle ranch, barb wire fences, large stacks of hay bales and not much else. It's the prairie! What did we expect? Stopping in an old west town called Hulett for a look around and to take pictures, we strolled into a little artsy antique shop with a sign "Old Stuff" just for fun. I tried on some cowboy hats and Susan looked at western wear as the young owner approached me. He asked me where I was from. Then he said, "Oh, I'm from Jersey . . . came out here to get away, paint old west scenes to sell and collect antiques and stuff I find on the prairie." We chatted and looked around till I spied an old buck saw on the wall tagged $26.00. He said, "Yeah, I found that one day while roaming the hills out back. I'll take $18.00 for it."

"I'll take it," I said. I wedged it under our bed and hauled that ol' saw all the way home and it now hangs on the wall at Rudy's Place.

We headed out of there with lots to talk and write about, listening to audio books too some of the time. Our next goal was The Tetons, Jackson Hole and Yellowstone, but first some sleep. We pulled into a Wal-Mart, free campsites you know, ☺ and joined about seven or eight other campers for the night at the far end of the lot. We played a game, wrote in the journal, pulled the shades and settled in under the covers for the night. Just about the time we got to sleep, the van began to jump up and down and shake violently as voices screamed profanity and a kid pounded on our rear window. Then all calmed down except our blood pressure. We sat up shaking and wondering. *What in the world? . . .* KIDS!! Guess they gotta get their thrills somehow. Sleep came late that night.

But it was memorable. Guess we should have copied other RVs sporting bumper stickers saying, "When the van's a rockin' . . ." well, you know the rest.

Happy to leave that parking lot behind, we followed scenic Routes 16 and 20 and stopped at the quaint little, western town of Ten Sleep at the base of Big Horn Mountain. That's right, "ten sleep." I had not heard of it either but when I told Renee about it, "Oh, Dad," she said,

Susan in rare form and me lovin' her.

"that is so interesting. I used to tell my girls when they were little and asked 'how far yet' when traveling for days on vacation . . . I would say 'only one more sleep and we'll be there.'"

The town of Ten Sleep actually got its name by being "ten sleeps" (nights) from the Great Sioux Camps to the south and a northern camp to the north in Montana. We shyly checked out "Dirty Sallys," got some ice cream, browsed some western stores and then left with more photos for our album.

The sky seemed to grow ever larger as we cruised the rolling hills, steadily gaining altitude. The van rebelled but I kept the pedal down with our eye to the horizon.

"There they are! Awesome too," she said. Like a movie on slow play, the Grand Tetons seemed to rise out of nowhere. Huge rugged, snow-capped ridges spanned the entire storm threatening horizon, painting a picture like only God could create. And yes, He did a fine job of it.

The famous hymn sung best by our beloved baritone, George Beverly Shea . . . "Oh Lord my God . . . when I in AWESOME wonder . . . consider all, the worlds thy hand has made . . . then sings my soul, my Saviour God to me . . . How GREAT Thou art, how great thou art!" And also, a chorus comes to mind . . . "Oh Lord our Lord how majestic is thy name in all the earth!" And our trip has just begun.

We camped that night at Coulter Bay, in perfect view of the Tetons peaking from behind puffy white clouds and azure blue sky, appearing after the rain as dusk drew near. A mother moose and her calf entertained us in a little swamp nearby as Susan was fixin' tomato soup and toasted cheese sandwiches. Thanks hon! Thanks God!

Morning found us headed for Jackson Hole and hopefully meeting Bill Krise. Bill was the Boy Scout ranger for Camp Brule near us years ago. He and Terry attended LHF. Now he is in charge of fish hatcheries in a four-state area based in Montana. That very day around noon, he was scheduled to be at a hatchery near Jackson Hole. Sure enough, we met up with him and he took us on a tour of the trout hatchery. Jackson Hole was pristine and as western as you'd imagine. Great place. Bought some souvenirs, ate lunch, toured the museum and headed northwest for Yellowstone.

There is so much to see in Yellowstone. We got pictures of wolves, elk, deer, buffalo, moose and fox. Every turn you make, there are stunning sights. Old Faithful was still faithful, spouting 105' into the air after an hour wait. Between 45 minutes to an hour and a half it spouts off day and night. Driving along a stream heading out of the park, we encountered another herd of elk with two large bulls courting them very close to the road. Susan was a bit nervous about me taking pictures, so I did so only from an open window.

Nights were beginning to cool down enough to engage the heater by early morning. It felt good to have heat.

Autumn; warm days, cool nights, flannel shirts and brilliant colors. I've always loved Fall. The aspen were changing to a soft gentle yellow and the white birch groves glowed with beauty in Yellowstone Park as we headed north. On to Helena, Montana, now, to visit Bill and Terry Krise.

Bill was on a tour of his hatcheries but Terry was ready for us when we got there. If you know Terry, you are familiar with her gift of hosting and you won't have to talk much—that's because she has lots to tell you. She loves the Lord and is involved in many ministries which we soon were kindly updated about. The supper table was laden with our favorite foods. Somehow, she knew what we liked and prepared plenty.

We left there heading north along Flathead Lake toward Glacier National Park. The lake is a glittering greenish-blue color likely from the snowmelt from the surrounding mountains.

Evening fell slowly as we pulled into the south end of the park and set up camp. It was September 14th and we had been on the road just 9 days and lovin' each one! Thank you Jesus.

Year 2000 was recorded as one of the warmest in history for the park. Arriving at the summit was a bit anti-climatic with tremendous snowmelt changing the landscape to green. No problem crossing Logan Pass. Even with the snowmelt, creeks and rivers were very low.

Our journal says "Around every bend in the road were new and majestic views to behold." It was so. Some of our most awesome photos come from Glacier National Park. Two black bear revealed only their hind quarters as they climbed the ridge. Exiting the park, we headed on toward Alberta and Calgary, stopping at a KOA campground. They always had nice bathrooms and that pleased Mom. So of course, we looked for them. We traveled 271 miles today.

In Calgary, we visited the site of the 1988 Olympics and did a self tour. Back on the road again till near dark before finding a nice campsite. Nice sites equal nice showers.

"Jesus, Jesus, Jesus . . . there's just something about that name . . . " Someone in the ladies' shower was singing sweetly and confidently. When she came out, Susan found out she was from Tennessee and on their way to Alaska. Sometimes God brings people into your path just to cheer you up and confirm His presence. Thanks God. Before bed, we walked downtown and got some good donuts and a few groceries.

The next day we headed across Rt. 1, the Canadian Highway, through the Rockies, toward Banff. Now . . . if you want "majestic," Canadian Rockies shout . . . MAJESTIC! Banff is very quaint and touristy but beautiful. We ate lunch and headed out stopping at Johnson's Canyon. Susan's hip was hurting some and she wasn't up to walking far, so I went alone with the camcorder. That way she got to see what I saw minus the walking. Next stop . . . Lake Louise. The photos hardly do justice to any scenery. We took our shoes off and tested the lake water. The source being glacier explained the temperature. COLD! Brrr!

The Lodge at the Lake was an incredible structure with many rooms for sleeping. A little store lured us in and low and behold . . . I found a childhood book, *Paddle to the Sea*. I bought one, and later read it to some of the grandkids. A gondola took us to the top of the ski slope where we intended to have a nice quiet time in the restaurant. A big sign greeted us at the top . . . "Wedding in progress." So we got to see a wedding instead. The ride down was spectacular.

Along Rt. 1 we stopped at a campground that had hot springs. We sat in them, soothing our bodies until the 105 degree waters began turning us into red lobsters . . . or close. The next morning, my flannel shirt felt great in the 40 degree British Columbian air.

Some day I'd like to return to British Columbia and take time to digest the beauty. Dwarfed and humbled between its Rockies, I had to concentrate on driving as the wind from big trucks and buses shook our little van. We saw helicopters logging the tall cedars on steep mountains, tasted gouda cheese from a goat farm, ate plate size pancakes smothered with strawberries and whipped cream, and listened to our audio books until we arrived at the border of Washington State. There the border guards made us peel and eat our tangerines or throw them out. ☹

Washington State is big and green, with thousands of acres of Weyerhauser tree farms. They do a superb job of managing their forests by restoration after clear-cutting the forests. Mt. Rainer posed proud and tall in the distance even though it appeared to be very close. As we drove closer, it disappeared under clouds and fog only to be seen in the rearview mirror several hours later. We tallied about 300 miles per day in Canada. A salmon hatchery was en route to Oregon so we stopped.

What an interesting tour, learning of their journey to the ocean and eight years later returning to their birthplace. The hatchery harvested many of the salmon, collecting their eggs before they die and become fertilizer.

Mount St. Helens was next. A film at the observatory showed the total devastation within 100 miles of the volcanic eruption back in 1980. When it blew, scientists said the plume went 80,000 feet high sending volcanic ash hundreds of miles wide. Many scary stories are written and told surrounding that event. Up at the rim the day we went, thick fog blanketed the area creating zero visibility.

Driving down the coastline of Oregon is an incredible experience. Words can't describe the beauty of the rugged coastline. We'd stop at little coast towns, have some chowder, crab cakes, crepes, good local fruit, ice cream and whatever looked good to try. Tasty, yummy fun. It's also interesting to talk with people. We found some really neat folks as we stopped along the way.

"What? Don't chew so loud."

"I can't stand to hear you *chew* so loud," Susan said, "it makes me cringe."

"So how do I *chew* quietly? I have my mouth closed. How am I supposed to chew?"

That conversation was going nowhere. So I just chewed the chips v-e-r-y s-l-o-w-l-y. It's always been a bone of contention between us. Whenever I ate pretzels, chips, celery, or anything that crunched, if I was in close proximity to Susan, she'd close her ears or let me know. All of our kids know about her powerfully keen hearing. Whispering didn't get by her. There wasn't much she missed, that's for sure. All couples learn to deal with differences somehow if they want to enjoy married life. It's just part of learning to accept each other and deal with it. So I dealt with it, best I knew how.

We were driving Route 101 down the coastline of Oregon on September 20, Ciara's birthday. Florence, Oregon is famous for its sand dunes. We checked it out and sure enough, according to the book, there were dunes as high as 300 feet! It was too foggy and dangerous to try climbing them, so on we drove. Oops, almost missed that DQ. Can't do that. My favorite ice cream. Usually we ate breakfast in the van and one meal a day we ate at a restaurant . . . trying to stay on budget. The gas kept creeping higher. The last station in Oregon, we paid $1.83 a gal. Remember, at home it was $1.30. But when we hit California, like everything else there, the price was big too. $2.15 a gal. in Calfornia! As you can guess, I reacted. Susan was always like, "Well, at least we can get it." Wha-da-ya say to that? Ya just drive.

At last! REDWOODS! Jeddidiah Redwood Forest was the first we saw them. Oh, my, my, did you ever! They were totally incredible, enormous trees. As we drove slowly through, getting out now and then just to stand and look and take pictures, we felt like we were in a heavenly cathedral. They dwarf you like ants at the feet of Goliath. It was like something out of another world. Someone said, "They are the gateway to heaven." All we could do was look in astonishment and worship our creator. Some were 3,000 years old and big enough to drive a car though. Our van was too high or we could have done so at one place.

There comes that song again . . . "Then sings my soul, my Saviour God to thee, how great Thou art . . . !!" "What is man, that thou are mindful of him . . . ?" Psalms 8:4

We ate supper at a place called Cattleman's Restaurant. The steaks were great but the smell outside as we entered almost turned us around. Just behind the restaurant was a huge field of cattle and it smelled like a barnyard. Yuck! Inside, it was fine. Just getting that out of our head was a problem.

Before long we were entering vineyard country—miles and miles of them and then orchards of fruit and nuts of all kinds. Then farmland and huge dairies and next . . . dry grass hillsides almost like, waiting for a match to ignite them. The geography changed so often. It was very different than any place we had been yet.

Susan's niece, Kim, Jim and Bev's daughter, was living in Livermore. Her husband moved there starting his business in the Silicone Valley. Our goal was to visit San Francisco and then head to her house for a night. She warned us about the crazy traffic and said to be very careful. Just what Susan did NOT need to hear. Coming down the Oregon coastline, driving around sharp turns on narrow roads was nerve-racking enough for her. Fortunately, Kim gave us a great suggestion—park outside the city and take the ferry in. Not even a parking fee. We knew this was going to be a one-day whirlwind of a tour but so what. We arrived at Pier 39 in time to see the famous seals croaking their funny language to the crowds. Browsing the pier we saw wonderful displays of fresh fruits and veggies. I grabbed up a box of strawberries thinking I'd take them to Kim's until I saw the price; $16.95 a pound. No thank you.

If you know anything about cities, especially San Francisco, you'd know about human statues. Well, I didn't until that day. He stood perched along the sidewalk, dressed in solid silver clothes, and every inch of exposed skin painted silver. We must have looked like the Beverly Hillbillies staring at the guy. How anyone could stay so still, so long for so many people to see, was beyond me. Of course a donation can sat nearby. Cities . . . what you don't see!

We sat down at "Scomas" on the water for supper. Seafood platter and mahi-mahi was delicious. In order to meet the ferry schedule and get to Kim's on time that evening we had to rush a bit. Then we drove an hour and a half to go 40 miles to get there. Kim had a spare room ready for us, almost big enough to park our camper in. Nice. Their house was located on what was a cattle ranch just three years prior. In no time the city gobbled it up. At the time of this writing, the high-tech electronics boom is gone and Shawn laid off most of his 60 employees. As we left Livermore, we soon came upon windmill city. Hundreds if not thousands of windmills standing still across the horizon. Kim said it was California's windmill graveyard. For several reasons, radioactivity and cost of demolition, they abandoned them for cheaper power sources. Go figure. ☹ On our way to Yosemite, now, through more vineyards and nut farms. No, not "nutty" farms.

Sample the fresh-picked fruit if you ever get out there. So yummy. As we got closer to Yosemite, we stopped for gas. Nope! Not spending $2.09 for gas. That's crazy. It's $1.30 at home. So I drove on, closer to Yosemite Park with the gas gauge nearing empty. The next gas station had a big sign up, "Last stop before the park." I stopped to fill up and saw the price; $2.75 a gallon! I questioned the attendant and she said, "Suit yourself, in the park it will be over $3.00 a gallon." I got just enough to get to the other side. I know, I know . . . what's the big deal? I just passed up $2.09 for $2.75. That's the deal! You gotta know me. For whatever reason, I react to high and inflated prices of anything. I think

Lunch in our camper.

it's the way my dad programmed me and I still seem to react that way.

To make a true confession, I silently fumed and fretted, nurturing a bad mood for half an hour or so. Susan could just brush stuff like that off, but not me. Forgive me God. I need a change of heart in these matters.

Driving into the park and looking up at the shear cliffs and waterfalls dwarfed my silly attitude and helped me forget the gas prices.

Our camper dwarfed by El Capitan rock formation.

Over a thousand feet up on a ledge of the granite wall, we were told, were two climbers. With the naked eyesight, you could make out a couple specks. With our binoculars, we could plainly see two people supposedly taking a break or maybe camping out for the coming night on a very small ledge. All kinds of stories are told of climbers, some falling to their death, others miraculously cresting the summit in victory. I don't know the fate of those two. But it sure was interesting to watch and ponder such a venture. No thanks!

Bridalveil Falls, one of the most prominent falls in Yosemite Valley pours its water from 617 feet above. When planning our trip, we were told to stay far back since the wind blows the water strongly and far. On arrival, we wondered where the falls was. It had been such a dry year that the falls was barely a trickle. The Ahwahneechee tribe believed that the falls was home to a vengeful spirit named Pohono which guarded the entrance to the valley, and those leaving the valley must not look directly into the falls lest they be cursed. Thank God we don't believe such things. I feel sorry for those who do and are bound by those beliefs.

Time to head south and as we do, huge Sequoia trees loom like jolly green giants many times over along the road. We drove till dark and camped just south of Fresno, Ca.

It's Sept. 24 . . . Kaiti's second birthday. ☺ Susan calls Lori and talks to Kaiti making her miss her even more. Our journal says, "Susan made eggs for JM instead of the normal—cereal. Seems like it takes a while to break camp mornings, especially when he has to empty the 'poop' tank."

It's already 8:30 and we are heading toward L.A. Susan drives to relieve JM since the roads are not as busy and he can take movies and see the scenery better. Vineyards, large farms, fruit and nut orchards are just part of the beauty. Driving through Bakersfield, JM gets the idea he wants to stop by Hollywood. Oh boy, do we really want to do that? Well, we did . . . or we tried! With the transit strike in its ninth day, traffic is horrendous. I HATE CITY TRAFFIC! We followed bumper-to-bumper traffic until . . . ta-dah . . . the Universal Studios' entrance. We made it . . . or did we? Accidently, I was in the parking garage line and our van would not clear. Horns blew, people waved and shouted and our blood pressure rose. I found a policeman who directed me out of line and back on the highway, only to get caught in more traffic, partially due to a church service ending.

I don't handle city traffic well! "Oh, watch out, there's a man standing right on the edge of the road waving at us," Susan said. "He wants us to stop."

We were in a stop and go traffic lane. Susan rolled down her window to see what he wanted.

"Can you give me a ride?" he said.

"We're lost in traffic. We're from Pennsylvania on our way to Phoenix. We really don't have room for riders and don't know who to trust either."

"I'm a Christian, look," he said holding up his Bible.

We briefly looked at each other and then at him and said, "Okay, get in."

"I'm Ceaser, originally from Guatamela. My wife left me 3 years ago and I came here to start fresh and turned my life over to Jesus. I just need a ride home, please."

He sure seemed honest and sincere and hey, he could be an angel and we, the good Samaritan.

"Do you know how to get out of the city, like find Route 101 and then Route 10?" I said.

He talked quickly and Susan wrote fast until we were back downtown where he wanted to go and he got off. Back on track, (the race track), we carefully maneuvered traffic with his directions which got us onto the 65 mph freeway. I think freeway means "free to go your own way and speed," which they did.

Finally, out of L.A, the spillway dumped us into the San Bernadino Valley which is just as populated and virtually all Spanish. We stopped at a Burger King for lunch and thought we had entered Honduras. *"Bueno, Querdo dos hamburgeso y coka, por favor."* Everything was in Spanish and they spoke very poor English. A little like my poor Spanish. Whoa! A flashback. This is where Jenny Jondrow, Lori's high school friend, moved to . . . I think. But we had some goals in mind and didn't want to take time looking her up. Tomorrow we hoped to make Arizona and see Lowell and Lois.

Driving through the desert can be monotonous. Our audio books helped with those times. Often we'd find Christian radio stations to listen to. Missing church most Sundays made us want to find spiritual nourishment in other forms. Each morning we had devotions and prayed together for God's presence and direction. By the end of that day we arrived at Buckeye, Arizona, a small town surrounded by very lush green alfalfa fields in the desert, thanks to irrigation. We leveled up the camper by a quiet clear stream in the willows and cuddled up. "Night, love you."

On the outskirts of Phoenix, I had to stop at the John Deere dealer and browse. The huge tractors were all equipped with rubber tracks instead of rubber tires. Better traction I guess. I came away with two green caps advertising the dealer's name . . . which I forget.

We had supper with the Goshows, caught up on family news and played a game of croquet, an old fun game of competition we enjoyed on Henry's lawn many years ago. They introduced us to a new ice cream café called Cold Stone.

Oh, boy . . . ya gotta try it sometime. Now they are scattered around the country, not just in the west.

You pick the kind of cream you want, add your choice of 50 different toppings, they slap it onto this sub zero counter, mix it together with paddles and serve it in waffle cones or cups. Whew! Good stuff. After a few days of games, reminiscing, and good eating, we headed toward Sedona stopping in the old copper town of Jerome on the way to check out the history and charming shops. The view from there was fantastic.

The closer we got to Sedona, the redder the hills and canyon got. It was a little like the Badlands in South Dakota with brilliant hews of colorful rock and red dirt. We visited the chapel on the hill. New Age and Native American influence is widespread worshiping creation rather than the Creator. It's sad, seeing the beauty of creation all around there, but not giving God all the Glory. Found some small Indian-style blankets we bought for the kids and headed north.

Flagstaff is just three hours north and on the way to the Grand Canyon, so we stopped for a short visit. The elevation is around 7500 feet piling up plenty of snow in winter. Our goal was to reach the Canyon before dark and camp there. We made it but were very tired and upon opening the little refrigerator, discovered spoiled food. It had quit. No bottled gas.

Susan heated up a can of beef and barley soup and by 8:30 was ready for bed. Bless her heart, she never complained, just continued to serve me.

Our ambitious Mennonite upbringing encouraged us to rise at 5:20 to be on the "rim" for sunrise. About 100 other people decided that would be fun too. Cameras in hand or on tripods, we waited for the show. Show it did, peaking over the horizon in Grand form, majestically lighting the Canyon. A three-hour shuttle bus tour gave us awesome views and information of the Canyon. We left "the rim" mid afternoon with Flo and Larry Shetler on our minds.

Desert roads can be long and lonesome but we found the Native American roadside shops interesting breaks. So we'd stop and browse, buying handmade jewelry for family and friends.

Late in the day the desert heat boiled up a huge thunderstorm ahead of us. Flashes of lightning flashing through dark ominous clouds in the distance contrasted by a beautiful sunset on the desert wall in our mirrors behind us was astounding. I had to stop, get out and take some pictures of another great display of God's creativity. But our camera did not yet have the panoramic capability.

Just before dark, we pulled into a campground on the edge of town. Tuba City is nearly 100% Hopi tribe Native Americans. A small restaurant drew our attention and we walked in, only to find it full and natives staring at us. We left and walked across the street to another one. We were served huge platters of fried flatbread covered with chili beans, lettuce, tomatoes and cheese. Yummy, but way too much. We straightened up the camper, journaled, played a game and hit the hay.

We had debated going to Durango and taking the scenic train ride but opted out after discovering the cost. Instead we did one of our occasional impromptu side trips. Mesa Verde National Park was highly rated and it was on our way. Ten miles back off the highway and down into a deep ravine we saw it; totally in tact and preserved for over a thousand years, rising from the canyon floor hung the cliff dwellers' homes.

Ausushi Indians, a superior ingenious tribe had carved homes into the mountainside. They were more than just caves. We were given a tour by an authentic descendant who explained what their lives may have been like. Room by room, level by level, one story at a time she took us. Our grandkids would have loved playing house there but we couldn't imagine it as our home. By the end Susan's knee was hurting but she said it was worth it. The late afternoon sun was beginning to display colorful shadows on the cliff walls and we knew it was time to get going.

Arriving at Flo and Larry's house after dark, directed in by cell phone, we found them nestled way back in the hills behind Pagosa Springs, Colorado. Morning light gave us a beautiful view of their surroundings. Twelve thousand foot snowcapped mountains towered behind their house with yellow aspens dotting the foothills. To the south were meadows and fields of grazing cattle. Larry designed and built the adobe brick house with huge ponderosa pines for beams, posts, joists and rafters, tucked into the hillside. Tanned hides draped the loft railing and huge elk and mule deer heads peered at us from the cathedral gables. The open meadows were framed in the picture windows.

They were back home taking a break from their many voluntary service stints with WYAM. Larry and I saddled up his horses and rode into the mountains where he hunts elk and mule deer while Susan and Flo caught up on the latest family news. What a treat and memory that was. They took us into town. We sat in the hot springs, ate some ice cream, checked out an old western store and bought a cowboy hat. Susan found a store with locally-made pottery and bought some gifts.

Like Sedona, Pagosa Springs is well known for its New Age flavor. Hollywood influence is prevalent flaunting wealth with fat and fancy houses. No thanks, I'll take "simply country."

Sunday morning we went to their home church small group of 30-40 people. Larry and Flo are great leaders but were experiencing some strange enemy influence. Anywhere God is moving you can expect the enemy to cause trouble. They explained the situation later and we prayed for them and they for us. LHF was not exactly without satanic attacks at times either.

What do Christians do when under stress? Pray? Yeah, we did that. Some eat. So we went out that evening and had a tasty meal at the "Hogs Breath Saloon." Yes, we stayed sober and yes, it was memorable. On the way home, Larry took us back through the mountains to Box Canyon. One more Wow sight. Two coyotes shot across the dirt road and Larry stopped. He had his pistol along and popped a couple shots at them. No luck, but fun. That night we stepped out on the veranda before bed, breathed in the fresh air saturating ourselves with God's Glory in the Heavens.

Next goal was eventually, Colorado Springs and the home of "Focus on the Family." Larry's directions took us up over Wolf Creek Pass. The aspens were at peak and gorgeously yellow. The air was chilly and a light snow on the ground at the pass. On our way was Royal Gorge. A 1000-foot bridge spanned the Arkansas river far below. We took a cog rail tram to the bottom and saw some abandoned shacks along the river.

Back on the road through Canyon City where Susan bought a new watch and on to Colorado Springs. "The Focus on the Family" guard allowed us to park in the parking lot with another large camper. The tour was impressive with the quality, size of the buildings and integrity of the organization.

I've heard some of our family accuse Susan of Jim Dobson being her second husband. She did like his teaching.

We drove through "The Garden of the Gods," a national park full of huge boulders. Then on to the base of Pikes Peak where we bought tickets for the cog rail tram which took us up the 14,100 feet elevation to the summit where I had to sit down after getting out of the tram. Oxygen was readily available for those who needed it. I came close. That height didn't agree with my sinuses. We both had headaches. We made snowballs, drank hot chocolate and ate some donuts before making the hour and three-quarter trip back down.

It was early October and the Presidential debates were raging and we were interested. A motel would give us a good night's rest and we could watch the debate. Thirty-four bucks and a large pizza put us up for the night.

Bush or Gore, who will it be? We cheered for the Republican, Bush. "Lord help us!" Susan wrote in the journal. She got into it almost more than I did. We thought Bush had it in the bag . . . at least hoped so.

Heading north toward Denver, we checked out small western towns, buying lunch and gifts. We toured the Museum of Natural History before arriving at Chris Magann's house. Some 18 years prior, I had married her and her first husband. But she had since divorced and married Tom. He's a nice guy and now they have a stable marriage with God at the center. Rita and Bridget came for supper and we reminisced as we ate.

October 5th; the weather is noticeably cooler and a strong gusty wind made it a challenge to drive on those extremely flat long highways of eastern Colorado and into Kansas. Audio books kept us alert as did the huge farm machinery and fields. My farming instincts fanned fantasies of what it might be like farming out west. Guess I'll never know. But wouldn't it be great to just drive one of those mammoth machines?

I told Susan, "I'm gonna stop and ask that guy if I could ride around with him?" She didn't oppose so I stopped. We were in Kansas on our way to Sterling College to visit Paola Flores. She had a scholarship, coming all the way from Honduras. She is Ovideo Flores' daughter who was a translator for us when we took teams to Honduras in 1999 and 2000. So we wanted to see her, which we did. But first things first.

I pulled off the road into the field and parked the van, then waited for the huge 9610 John Deere combine with an 8-row corn head to come closer. He stopped and asked if he could help me. I said, "Any chance I can ride around with you? We're traveling from Pa. I'm a small farmer and would love to ride a machine like this."

"Jump in," he said, and off we went around the 135-acre circle field. Circular because of the irrigation rigs. He explained that the crop was poor that year due to drought. Nevertheless, the grain was pouring out of the auger as 8 rows of corn were gobbled up and shelled. Soon a large John Deere tractor and self-unloading wagon pulled alongside. They kept moving in syncopated speed as he unloaded the grain on the go. Now, this is serious fun farming! "Thanks man, I really appreciate it," I said descending the six steps to the ground. "No problem, have a great trip," he said.

Paola was happy to see us. Pretty and sweet as always. We went for lunch, talked about our time in Honduras and left her with some goodies and cash to spend. We drove for several hours then stopped at a KOA campground. Susan writes in the journal; "JM doesn't like KOA's that much cause they're more expensive. But there wasn't much choice tonight."

Yeah, I'm a cheapskate sometimes . . . depending what it is. ☺ We went to the laundromat in the campground with Scrabble squares in hand. Played a few hands till the wash was finished, looked at the map, our normal nightly routine and called it another "good" day.

The heater is running most of the nights now. Feels good actually, Fall being my favorite season. Drove all the way to St. Louis and rode to the top of "The Arch." Impressive view and story about it. That evening, Susan called home, talked to Lori who had a great show at Canton apple and cheese festival with her handmade flower candles. Mike and Mercy were at our house, which was full of people getting ready for Amelia's wedding.

October 8; beginning to feel heart strings pulling us toward home. We'd been missing Sunday morning worship services and thought it was time to join one. Given the fact of strained relationships at LHF over the past few years, we were not ready for a charismatic service. Seeing signs for a Mennonite church, we went nine miles out into the country to check it out. I cautiously stepped inside as services were in progress. Bearded men in white shirts and women on the other side in drab colors filled the pews. "Nah . . . don't think this is it," Susan thought like I did, so off we went stopping next at "Community Christian." I went in, got a bulletin and showed Susan. "Do we really want to be puppets . . . stand, sit, sing, stand, sit type of liturgical service?" Nah . . . and back on the road we went listening to Christian radio and audio books. I know . . . we sure are fussy! Guess that's why so many denominations exist.

After experiencing many years of church growth, dealing with relationships and many variables of service styles, we shied away from anything appearing as conflict or uncomfortable. God continued to work in us and our church making it into something that gave Him glory and was a testimony to our community. Admittedly, we were . . . particular!

With Susan now at the wheel, I was resting and enjoying the countryside, especially as we entered Kentucky. Browsing the dial, I found what I liked. The bluegrass state was named appropriately with miles of wooden fences bluegreen grass and Arabian horses. West Virginia welcomed us with great country music featuring banjos, fiddles and guitars as nasal voices joined in the mix.

"Country roads, take me home, to the place . . . where I belong, West Virginia, mountain mama, take me home country roads . . . I hear the voice of my . . . " John Denver is interrupted as Susan says, "Please . . . turn that down, I can't stand her singing." Susan was quick to let me know how she felt about country music. I soon switched the station. With the heater on, we played a couple of "fast Scrabble" games, tidied up the camper and by 9:30 were stretched out close together in our nest. One more day and we'll be in Virginia with our kids. Whoohoo!

Just 30 miles from the kids we smelled gasoline. I told Susan I'd need to stop and get that checked out. The mechanic said it was the fuel pump but said he tightened it up so we could make it to Stuart's Draft where our kids live.

God had been faithful. He had been good to us once more. No flats, no accidents, never ran out of gas. Six years had passed without surgery and only God knew what was ahead for us. For now, we savored sweet memories of five weeks on the road as we shared stories with the kids and grandkids the next few days. A full-sized bed was nice too.

Five fun-packed weeks, and a 9,000-mile journey of joy. It took a sizeable bite out of our savings but the reward was immeasurable. Thank you Jesus. We are SO blessed. Now sit a spell and rest. :)

CHAPTER 61

2003

We visited our good friend, Marliss Berke, in Elizabethtown to help with the wedding preparation for her daughter and son-in-law.

Marliss had just recently lost her sweet hubby, Chuck, in a car accident. He was pronounced brain dead and went to be with his Lord two days after the accident. The cause was never determined for certain, but the doctors and police officers calculated that he must have experienced some form of stroke while driving and never knew what happened. His car hit a utility pole without any other vehicle involved. It was a tremendous shock to the family and many friends.

Marliss called to tell Susan and me and Rod and Lucy shortly after arriving at the hospital. We quickly made the three-hour trip to Hershey and were there to pray and sing over Chuck before he passed away.

Back to our visit a few months later; I worked at her landscaping and Susan visited and helped make wedding favors out of sea shells.

I found a note Susan wrote to Marliss just the other day written on note paper full of sea shells:

"Dear Marliss, We thought you'd like these memories of our day with you. Praying you were encouraged by the love many have for you as you had your B-day without Chuck. Many bitter-sweet times you are going through and though you are not close by, we are with you in Spirit . . . always. Love Susan, dated 7/12/03"

CHAPTER 62

Signs of a Tsunami

Between 2006 and 2009, concerns with Susan's health began to consume us. Now and then, with the onslaught of steadily worsening test results, it's recorded in her journals . . .

"I don't know if I can go on."

No sooner than she would write those words, she would state "But God is so good and faithful. I want to begin days with praise rather than petitions. Seems like I'm consumed with myself these days and I hate it. JM is so good to me and my kids are continually supporting me in prayer and with encouraging verses."

Reading through the journals confirms her close relationship with the Lord. She quotes scriptures she can relate to, expresses gratitude for God, family, friends and church. For instance; penned in her journal, March 6, 2008; "Psalm for today, Psalm 6 – Be merciful to me Lord, for I am faint. Oh Lord, heal me, for my bones are in agony. My soul is in anguish. How long, oh Lord, how long . . . ? . . . and now this song is on family life radio; 'Blessed be the name of the Lord . . . with the road marked with suffering, though there's praise in the offering, still I will say – Blessed be the name of the Lord!' written and sung by Laura Story." *Remember that name.*

Simultaneously, she is making appointments, changing them, going to one, in surgery or recovering from one. At the beginning of 2007, a reversal of health concerns finds me, JM undergoing a prostate biopsy in Williamsport. While I'm lying on a cold sterile table, the doctor extracts 13 specimens from my most sensitive area and Susan is journaling. I quote:

"Lord, we know you are in control. We want what you want for us, but please be merciful to my hubby. We trust you for what's ahead but desire to know that the lump is benign. Nothing is too hard for you. Speak peace to him now, and to our kids."

In a short while, I was back out telling her that the doctor said "Nothing looked suspicious but we'd have to wait a week for the report." Thankfully, it was benign. ☺

Meanwhile, in a hospital in Harrisonburg, Virginia, our son, Mike, was having his own health challenges. Mercy called one day, distraught and crying as she relayed the doctors words; "Mike has Crones disease!"

"My God! NO! NO! Not Crones. Are you sure?" I was almost as frantic as she. I began to pray with her, for Mike and imploring the name of Jesus for healing. She said Mike was in severe pain the night before and finally went to the ER. After being down-played as IBS (Irritable Bowel Syndrome), they treated it as such and wanted to send him home. He was bent over with pain and could barely walk so they agreed to keep him. Put mildly, it was less than acceptable hospital care. Over the next few months, Mike endured some unbelievable bouts of intestinal pain. Doctors seemed a bit baffled with it. Finally, he decided to go for a second opinion to UVA. They announced that his appendix had leaked into his abdomen and he should have an appendectomy. That was the determining healing factor for Mike. Finally after several years of random intestinal pain, relief and healing prevailed. Thank you Jesus!

On a much brighter note, far removed from pain and suffering on the Beinlich ranch comes other news. Bethy, age 4, has made an announcement to Lori; "Mom, I just swallowed a nickel!" "Oh you did? And why did you do that, Bethy?" "I don't know, I found it on the floor and before I realized what happened, I swallowed it."

Well, now what? So Lori called Susan, of course, to see what the nurse would suggest. You guessed it; "Just wait, it will come out in a couple days. Keep checking her stool to be sure it clears."

"Yeah, right!" Lori was not about to enter that field. So Susan did the honors, finding the treasure in a couple days.

But wait, Mike was not going to waste this opportunity.

"Girls, come here. Get up on the hearth. You Kaiti, on the end, Leah in the middle and Bethy on the end."

"Why Dad?"

"Just do it."

In comes Mike with his metal detector. ☺ "Is it in Kaiti?" . . . as he moves the wand from top to bottom. "No. Is it in Leah? No. Is it?" . . . BEEP, BEEP, BEEP . . . "Yes - it's - in - Bethy!"

Now *this* would make a great entry for "Funniest Home Videos," Mike and Lori said. So just for fun they submitted it, sending it to California and waited. Two weeks passed and nothing.

Then a phone call from a private number. "Hello, is this the *Beanlicks?*"

"Yes, this is the Beinlichs."

"I'm calling from America's Funniest Home Videos. Your video has been selected as one of the top three to be drawn from for the $10,000.00 grand prize. If you agree, we'd like to fly you out for a taping in Hollywood, all expenses paid on such and such a date."

Mid January of 2007 found the whole Beinlich tribe in a luxurious hotel in San Diego, enjoying the beach, Sea World and shops all paid for because Bethy swallowed a nickel. Now that was a worthwhile trick, Bethy! But, don't try it again. ☺ They didn't get first place but they did have a great all-expenses-paid-vacation, thanks to AFHV . . . and Bethy. We have the taping of the show if you're interested. :)

Susan continues to journal . . . *"So glad for Lor and Mike and family but I miss them. Our times and lives are in your hands, Lord. Teach me to trust you more completely. So many ups and downs recently—extremes! We know you're in control but it's so easy to take our eyes off you and see only our circumstances. Thank you for being my loving caring heavenly Father. Thank you for your peace that passes understanding and thank you that lately, I'm feeling better."*

The next few days we are in Virginia staying with Mike and Mercy as I help to construct an addition to Mike's barn to make room for chickens, goats and maybe some beef cattle. Mike has the same farming bug as I do, I guess.

Between soccer, baseball and gymnastics, the grandkids keep us hopping from place to place. If we'd live there, I wonder how we could ever keep up with everything. Probably, we couldn't. Susan writes, *"Being here, I know better how to pray for them and all that they have going on."*

On April 3rd, we met with Dr. L. once again. Thank God for Dr. L. What an upbeat, positive doctor and friend he was to us. He is one of the best, renowned orthopedic oncologists on the whole East coast. The waiting room was never large enough nor the visiting hours long enough to do justice to his clientele. Once we waited 2½ hours to see him. That was the last time we did that. Susan could not endure that kind of wait in a wheelchair so the nurse would take her in ahead of others due to our long trip and her level of pain.

He reviewed the Cat scans, MRIs and x-rays. The lump on her left arm is still there but he doesn't suggest surgery. An embolization, surgery which interrupts the blood flow to the tumor may be scheduled later. But for now, let it be. We were surprised (not sure why, with all that's been turning up lately) to hear him say, "There's a new area of sarcoma in your left hip. I want to zap it before it gets any bigger." So she contacts Dr. N. in Williamsport immediately to schedule radiation.

Susan journals; *"Lord help us once again as we face yet another episode. I feel worse for JM than me!! Elaine and Lucy are having a hard time with it and of course, our kids. I know God, you don't allow anything to come into our path unless you allow it. I'd sure like to know the purpose of this new detour—but maybe I'll never know. Psalm 121—I lift up mine eyes to the hills, where does my help come from? My help comes from the Lord, maker of heaven and earth!"*

Mercy is waiting to deliver her baby, but no contractions yet. We go back down to VA to wait and help. Games, unending games with the grandkids it seems.

It's a boy! Jude Landis Souder born April 27th on Bethy's birthday. What joy newborns always brought to Susan . . . and me. With her arm bothering her and permitting only limited use, she never complained to anyone except me. And that was mildly and seldom.

The end of May brought more joy. Our first grandchild was graduating from high school. Oh happy day . . . Ciara looking so radiant and Bren and Eugene as proud as peacocks. Bren, Eugene, Tyler and Ciara were planning a cruise and discovered Tyler's passport had not yet come in the mail.

The Martin clan was planning and packing for their 8-week RV trip west. All told, stress was building and we felt it. Fortunately, Mike and Mercy had finished the apartment in their basement which was a nice place for us to regenerate when needed.

Early June 2007, we head back to Philly Hospital. Dr. L. will remove the lump and clean up the area on her arm. She came through the surgery well with little repercussion. She looked quite alert and chipper when I saw her in recovery.

Doctor L. assured her he had gotten all that he could of the tumor and praised her for being such "an Amazing Woman!" I agreed. A young 19 year old had the bed next to her and was troubled. Susan talked to her and prayed with her calming her down as only nurse Susan could do, always putting others ahead of her own needs. I walked six blocks to stay with Steve K., a Methodist minister from the Quakertown area who was living in the city.

"Hosts for Hospitals" an agency solely for families of hospital patients, put me up there for free. A donation was appreciated. She was discharged in a few days and we stopped to see Kass and Emma on the way home. Once again, thinking of others and knowing they would appreciate her visit.

Arm pain continued to harass her. Pain also increased in her hip making walking troublesome and creating back pain. A chiropractor helped some with that pain.

School was back in session and we always prayed for each of the kids. Susan records her prayers and concerns in the journals. This time; *"There's so much I'd like to do and can't but need to remember to be grateful for what I'm able to do. Froze 400 ears of corn, some beans and now ready for peaches."*

I came down with pneumonia after returning from "SWAP" in KY with a group of volunteers. I nursed it along while visiting Bob Stroble who was in the hospital with much worse symptoms from his MS. They put him on a ventilator and he never really recovered after contacting Mersa, a staff infection. While he was in Williamsport Hospital, his wife Julie, was in Gesinger Hospital being treated for mini-strokes. Bob died while she was still hospitalized. Susan and I went to the funeral feeling very sad for Julie and family. My, my!!

"Jesus draw me ever nearer, as I labour through the storm. You have called me to this passage, and I'll follow though I'm worn. May this journey bring a blessing, may I rise on wings of faith; And at the end of my heart's testing, with Your likeness let me wake. Jesus guide me through the tempest; Keep my spirit staid and sure. When the midnight meets the morning, let me love You even more. Let the treasures of the trial, from within me as I go—And at the end of this long passage, let me leave them at Your throne." Words by Margaret Becker.

The above clipping, neatly filed in a journal, are sentiments soaked in and pondered deeply by Susan.

* * * * *

"Now this is like Heaven, sitting on the rocky coastline near York Harbor, Maine. No one in sight 'cept my hubby, ☺*"* wrote Susan early October 2007. We had always wanted to visit the Maine coastline and finally, we made it. Fall trips were always special. The beauty of the foliage, the pristine fresh air and off-season prices helped make it that way. We had searched travel books and talked with AAA folks and decided to just visit the lower portion of Maine. We booked an old New England style motel which advertised an ocean view. Perfect . . . or so we thought until we arrived. The ocean was across the busy street hidden from view behind pine trees. Nah . . . not staying here.

They refunded our money and we traveled a bit further north where we found a nice quiet ocean view. Just what Susan always dreamed of; resting by the ocean, inhaling the salty, fishy air, a steady breeze sweeping into our room and the sounds of crashing waves on the rocks below. Oh, how sweet it is! Back on the lawn overlooking the ocean we went, windbreakers pulled tight, sitting on lawn chairs at dusk.

Susan with a large lobster in a quaint seafood restaurant in Maine.

The sun was setting and it was just us. I put the camera on a bench, set the timer and cuddled close. There, a picture for our grand and great-grandchildren to salivate on. I can hear one of them say . . . "Really, that was our grandparents? Wow! Looks like they really liked each other even though they're old." And yes, they would be right!

Being old comes at a cost. Some pay more dearly than others. But hey, what's old. I just read in Joshua this morning that Caleb said he was 84 and had the "vigor" of a 40 year old. I'm not nearly that old but still feel full of "vigor" . . . most of the time.

On the other hand, cancer comes to people of all ages. It's so sad to see little kids with bald heads and pale complexions. In 2007, Susan was 64 years old. Getting away on vacations, however short or long was so important to our well-being. Dr. L. and the other doctors all said, "Absolutely, go while you can. Don't wait." So we did. No matter where you go though, no distance is far enough to erase the pain and suffering of cancer. Upcoming appointments and treatments needed to be kept.

The broken and bent screws intended to secure the metal plate in Susan's left arm from an earlier surgery was concerning. Dr. L. was planning another surgery to correct that problem. Must have been divine intervention that changed his mind in early October when he called off the surgery. He decided it wasn't necessary. Rare news like that was so refreshing and welcome. Radiation was presently more important for two spots on her spine. Dr. N. continued to marvel at Susan. He had never seen her form of cancer move from bone to bone rather than settling in on her organs and lungs.

Normally, Leiomyo Sarcoma would have taken her within a couple years as it had many of his patients. "You are a real trooper!" he often said. "In the 25 years of my practice, I have never seen a case like yours. You are one in a million." Well, yes, I would agree she was special.

Being somewhat traditional in nature, we often went to Perkins or Ruby Tuesdays to enjoy a meal out together after appointments in Williamsport. Coming back from Philly, we'd likely stop at Ruby Tuesdays near Norristown. Traditions like that were comforting and enjoyable.

Christmas '07, was spent in Virginia and enjoyed as always. Nonetheless, we were happy to be back home to rest and keep current with appointments. The 19 radiation treatments on Susan's lower back are finished but two holes remain unhealed; an ongoing concern. Side effects of the pain medication make her hungry and hyper, creating unwanted weight gain. ☹

It was tradition for the Landis family to gather at Christopher Dock School annually on New Year's Day. Generally around 140 people come. Each year one of the twelve siblings took responsibility for organizing the day.

This year was Susan's turn. Given her limitations, our kids and many others helped out making it another memorable day. Mike's skit was particularly appreciated. As always, we made the 3-hour trip twice in one day, getting home close to midnight, and very tired.

2008 birthed more pain in different places. Getting in and out of the car, chairs and even walking became more difficult. I did everything in my power to ease the pain and help out. We bought a new power lift lounge chair for her. Though somewhat humbling, it greatly relieved the back and hip pain when getting in or out of her chair. All of us want to be independent as long as possible especially as we age. Thank God for technology and tools to aid the process.

The newest problem and challenge is a result of taking a product called Zometa. Dr. N. advised her to receive it intravenously monthly to help build bone strength and counteract the side effects of all the radiation. Many people, he said, are benefiting from this product. There is just a 10% chance of experiencing one of the many side effects and 90% chance of benefiting. So why not use it? Yeah, that's what we thought. Well, two years after receiving Zometa, Susan began having lower back tooth pain. Nothing unusual given her bad history of teeth and dentists. Oh, how she dreaded dentist appointments.

After several unsuccessful attempts by her regular dentist to fix the decaying tooth, he sent her to Dr. B. in Williamsport, a well-known and respected orthodontist. Not a good sign. Waiting and wondering and trying not to worry is easier said or written than done.

"Oh God, you know I surely can NOT handle yet another problem . . . or do you?" Susan wrote in her journal—January 23rd.

Dr. B. removed a small piece of bone sticking out of the gum as a result of her prior dental work. He sent it away for biopsy and now we wait once more.

"Dear God, please let it be benign and not 'Nuerocrotic jaw,' a side effect of Zometa as Dr. 'B' suspects. Friends and family continue to pray and beseech God for mercy. We submit to His will and plans, knowing that He has our best interest in mind regardless of the outcome. Amen."

Nuerocrotic jaw is "a deadening of the lower jaw," that 10% chance side effect of Zometa.

With Susan still recovering from bronchitis and coughing a lot, we try to rest as much as possible while we wait and she consumes huge doses of strong antibiotics to counteract the jaw infection. Dear God! But her smile remained constant for friends and family.

To help give diversion, our dear friends intervene by taking Susan out for lunch or stopping by to visit, pray and laugh. Bless them.

And now, news from down south; Mercy had an accident on the way to work while rounding a corner and crossing an ice covered bridge. She was alone, driving Mikes' pick-up truck. It did a 360 ending upside down. She managed to free herself fairly unscathed except for her emotions. Thank God she was not hurt badly. The truck was totaled.

Next came a report from Renee. Rod is having severe leg pains. Seems like a pinched nerve but unsure. It ended up lasting six months before PT finally helped correct the problem.

Dear God! We get so entwined and consumed with our problems, we forget to praise You for being a good, great and Sovereign God. There is so much to be grateful for. If only we could remember what You told us; *"In this world, you will have trouble, but be of good cheer ☺ I have overcome the world,"* Jesus.

On a bright note, our kids all came home to surprise me for my 65th B-day. What wonderful kids and grandkids we have! Thank you God.

CHAPTER 63

Five-Star Kindness

It was Susan's 65th birthday and she had an appointment with her orthopedic oncologist. We had driven 200 miles from northern PA to Philadelphia and decided to stay the night and hopefully visit some interesting places in the city the next day. We prayed before we left asking God for safety and to direct our path and that Susan would not need surgery. The results showed that she would not need surgery but needed radiation and another procedure to deal with the tumor. We were happy for that answer to prayer.

After a good night's rest at a nice hotel we again committed our day to the Lord asking for safety and guidance as we drove around the city looking for our destinations.

Over the past 14 years, Susan had had seven surgeries in Philadelphia due to a very rare form of cancer. During each surgery, I had the opportunity to walk the streets looking and listening to new sights and sounds unfamiliar in the mountains where we live. I also had time to contemplate and pray about the new challenges we were facing.

Someday when she was feeling better, I wanted to take Susan to visit some of these places so we could experience them together. Since we had the entire day to do as we pleased, we decided to have a cup of coffee at the hotel and eat breakfast later in the city. We leisurely started out looking for the Reading Terminal. When Susan was a teenager, she worked at a similar market in Philly and I wanted to take her there just for fun.

City and country driving have nothing in common. Although we have driven in the city often, it is still stressful for me. To explain the contrast for us, we live in a county with only one traffic light and know nothing about traffic jams.

We drove right up to the terminal but could find no parking spaces. Yes, we could have parked in the parking garages at a very high rate for a short stay but chose not to. After driving around the city for an hour, getting lost in traffic, and no place to park we decided to give up on that venture.

The next place we wanted to check out was Trader Joe's about six blocks north of the terminal. That shouldn't be difficult. On the first attempt, we weren't able to make a left turn and had to go right instead which got us lost again in traffic. After asking twice we thought we had it made only to find ourselves heading north onto the expressway. That was all the frustration of the city I could take. We agreed we would have to come back another day and another way.

Since there was a Trader Joe's further north and out of the city we set out to find that one. By now it was noon, had not eaten breakfast, and needed gas. So I randomly pulled into a gas station and mini-mart to get gas and directions.

The first two guys didn't have a clue where that store was but the apparent owner overhead our conversation and motioned that I step behind the counter. He seemed like a very kind gentleman and asked where I wanted to go. I said to Trader Joe's somewhere north of here.

He said, "Oh, that's near where I live, here, I'll give you directions." As I was writing them down I mentioned that we should probably eat first since we had come from the hospital in center city and were lost for an hour trying to find that store.

"What are you hungry for? I can direct you to any number of places," he said smiling.

"We'd be happy for a nice little lunch place, nothing fancy," I said.

"I know just the place for you," and began writing directions. "Just a minute," he said and dialed a number.

I overheard him say, "Bill, this is Allan, I'm sending a couple over for lunch and I want you to hold the bill for me, got it?" He hung up and said that the lunch at "Chops" was on him and we should enjoy the meal.

I was stunned. I thanked him and asked him why he would do such a thing for someone he never met.

He said, "This is the city of brotherly love and I want to do this for you." I said I believed that God directs our path and must have directed us to him today for whatever reason. He agreed.

The five-star restaurant was only two miles away on City Avenue. We were not dressed for this. Waiters were in suits and had white cloths draped over their arms. Hostesses held doors open and asked for our coats inviting us in. I asked for the manager and he assured me that yes, he had received a call from Allan and he would take good care of us. We were led to a large plush booth in the corner of a richly-decorated room with well-dressed folks. Our table was covered with a pretty white table cloth with an elegant fresh flower centerpiece.

A lovely waitress gave us way too many choices of the best of anything we wanted. Susan had a delightful fresh seafood salad and I had a blackened steak salad and a bowl of soup. Of course, the coffee was great too. The staff could not have been more pleasant and helpful and we left never having sight of the bill.

I called Allan back on the cell phone number he gave me and tried to express our gratitude for his abundant kindness. I said that we pray God bless him greatly for his extra kindness especially considering the events of the morning. I also said I believe God must have led us to him for a purpose. He agreed that God does that.

When I pressed for what motivated this, he said, "I've been in your country for 30 years now and I can do this for you. Oh, and one more thing . . . the next time you come to the city, you call me on this number and you stay with us."

By now, tears were running down my face. I thanked him and blessed him and with much gratitude said, "Allan, I hope to see you again."

We had never seen nor heard of this man prior to this experience. I don't know if he was Indian, Muslim or what nationality. It doesn't matter. We believe God divinely set up this appointment to encourage and strengthen our faith in him and in America.

It's incredible how one man's act of kindness and generosity can cause a ripple effect to bless and inspire so many people. We will surely pass it on.

CHAPTER 64

Angel in the Crowd

I saw her today . . . walking in a crowded hallway of country folk. Her appearance was somehow familiar. *No, it couldn't be her. But was it?* my mind was churning.

Where did I see her before? I kept walking, thinking it probably wasn't her.

Then, a soft tap on the shoulder. I turned to look. Such kind compassionate eyes looked deeply into mine. Her face was pale but pure. Her hair short, straight and smooth—almost perfectly styled and she was neatly dressed.

"How are you, my dear?" she spoke softly and tenderly as though she could see into my soul. It *was* her. We moved away from the crowd along the hallway to talk.

"I've been thinking of you a lot lately," she said. "I can only imagine your sadness during this season of the year."

My memory caught up with my bewildered mind.

Now I remember. It came to me. Over a year ago, we had met at the Williamsport Cancer Center.

But this day, I was with Lori and Mike at school to watch Bethy recite her lines in the Christmas program. Only a half hour before the program, Bethy got sick. When we got there, she was lying on a bed in the nurse's station with a fever. She had practiced hard and so looked forward to doing her part. She even had new slippers and a cute velvety dress on. Mike swept her up in his strong arms taking her with us. She sat peacefully between Mike and Lori watching her classmates do their thing.

As we walked down the hallway after the program, there "she" was . . . *the angel.* At least I'll call her an angel. I recognized her when she tapped my shoulder and began to speak.

But first let's backtrack a bit.

Toward the end of August of 2009, Susan was given an ultimatum. The Philadelphia oncologist, Dr. H., spoke for Dr. S. and himself.

"Basically," he said, "you have two choices now that the cancer has spread. It's chemo or hospice. Surgery is no longer an option."

I pulled her close to me. We were both stunned beyond comprehension and sat silently staring out the hospital window before responding.

A few days later, I pushed her wheelchair into the Cancer Center in Williamsport and carefully positioned her at the end of a row of seats in a waiting room full of people. There were people of all ages and race. Cancer has no respect for anyone. It is totally evil and ruthless and devours healthy cells mercilessly. We sat quietly for a moment pondering our lives, staring vacantly at the coffee maker in front of us.

Two women walked slowly by us. One looked at us with compassion and hesitated before continuing on for a seat nearby. She looked familiar.

"Where have we seen that woman?" I asked Susan who was looking through a magazine with no interest.

Before she could answer, I whispered, "Oh, I know, I think she was at church meetings years ago when Randy was there. I can't think of her name." Almost before I got the words out of my mouth, she was kneeling next to Susan's wheelchair.

"I thought that was you," she said. "I think I remember seeing you at Living Hope Fellowship years ago. I'm Tina. Are you . . . ?"

While she was trying to come up with a name, Susan said, "Susan Souder."

"Yes, of course, what brings you here, my dear?" she spoke tenderly.

"It's a long story," Susan said, not wanting to go into details. "I start chemo today."

"Oh, honey, I'm so sorry. Let me tell you sweetheart, you are *not* going through this alone. I'm not talking about your husband or others. I mean that Jesus will be holding you in His arms everyday.

"Honey, I know what I'm talking about. By the way, this hair is only a wig. I lost mine a long time ago. I've been battling cancer for two years and this is my third round of treatments. But I'm not giving up. Neither will you." She talked softly and confidently. "Honey, scripture tells us that He will never give us more than we can handle. Nothing is impossible with God. He will be with us even through 'the valley of the shadow of death.'" She went on quoting encouraging scriptures like she was reading from the Bible.

Tears were streaming down Susan's face onto her pretty, red sweater as we sat listening to this "angel" sent from Heaven to encourage us. My cheeks were no longer dry. This was Susan's first day of chemo and we were very apprehensive before this "Tina angel" appeared.

After about five minutes of her kind, compassionate words, encouraging scriptures, kisses and hugs, she assured us . . . "I am going to walk with you through this valley. You can count on that. I will be in touch with you. May I please have your phone number so I can call you when Jesus nudges me to call or write? I'd really like to do this."

Wiping her eyes and wet face, Susan found paper and wrote down the number.

"Thank you so much, Tina. You have no idea how much this means to me. This was God ordained," Susan said softly.

"It's my pleasure, honey," she said and went to her seat to await her own appointment.

We sat silently pondering all that Tina had said. Then the double doors from the chemo room opened.

A petite nurse wearing a beautiful smile called her name. "Susan Souder?"

"That's me," Susan said returning a smile. I immediately got up and began wheeling her toward the open doors.

"Hi honey, I'm Barb, I'll be checking you in and taking good care of you," she said, her smile and gentleness beginning to erase some anxiety.

We entered the room filled with patients. Large leather recliners were spaced neatly apart in a semi-circle. Big glass windows offered a beautiful view of a well-planned garden contained by stone walls and water fountains. A wall painting scene of Lancaster County Amish soothed our troubled minds momentarily.

"We'll go over here to the corner room. It will give us more privacy and you'll have your own window," Barb said. "We'll get you comfortable in a reclining chair and you can order anything you want from the cafeteria. Here's cold water. Would you like some coffee, coke, ginger ale or juice, sweetie?"

She was particularly kind and sensitive. It was obvious that this was "her calling" and not just a job. She was there to serve her patients with class. The love of Jesus oozed from her.

"Water will be fine and . . . guess I'll have some coffee too, please," Susan said feeling a bit more relaxed.

I too began to feel tension fade. Barb offered to help get Susan from the wheelchair to the recliner, but I said, "That's no problem, I'm very comfortable getting her over to the recliner myself. We have our little routine. Thanks anyhow."

With that, she began preparing medical supplies, tubes and monitors for the procedure. She sat next to Susan explaining everything in detail. "Read each sheet and sign where indicated, honey. I'll be right back."

She left the room and we sat there reading all the depressing reactions and potential side effects of the form of chemo Susan was about to get. Being a nurse herself and having had multiple surgeries, she was accustomed to seeing the long negative list of side effects from medicine. She scanned the papers quickly and signed them.

Once every other week for four months, we drove the 40 miles to the hospital to get her chemo. Each time doing blood work, meeting with doctors, asking and answering questions and hoping for good results. Always sitting with many others for an hour and a half to receive the treatment. The nurses, doctors, technicians, and even the valet guy were very compassionate. Even so, the whole ordeal took its toll on our lives.

Christmastime was a bittersweet experience with the entire family home. Her last day of treatment was two days before Christmas. Susan looked as good as any cancer patient could with her head scarf and maneuvering around the house with her new scooter. At least she could be at the table and in her own kitchen giving suggestions for the meal as usual . . . well not *quite* usual. It seemed like her spirits and general health were improved compared to pre-chemo. We always looked for any small improvement to encourage us.

Celebrating Christmas together as a family was always special to us but this one, bittersweet as it was, would be treasured. The kids had to leave sooner than later to resume their own lives. Hugs, kisses, tears and kind words etched another memory for eternity.

The New Year came and went as did more doctor appointments. January dragged into February with more and more complications.

By mid-February her body became so weak, we had to make an emergency trip to the hospital one last time. She never returned home again. All four children and eleven grandchildren made it to the hospital to say final goodbyes to MawMaw.

The room was packed with all 21 of us. The nurses and doctors just looked on from the nurses' station with tear-stained eyes knowing they had done everything humanly possible to help. This was now "our" time, Susan's time.

Susan spent the last five days at "The Gatehouse" at the Divine Providence Cancer Center. The nurses were superb and the doctor was, in my words, "like Jesus himself." My four wonderful children spent every hour of those days with me as we prayed, sang, read scripture, laughed and cried together with Susan. We committed her spirit to Jesus on February 22, 2010. Chemo helped a wee bit for a very short time. God chose to give her a body that will last for eternity. She is once and for all without pain and suffering, rejoicing in Heaven.

The wheelchair and chemo are no longer needed. Tina's calls and letters were a sweet encouragement but also, no longer needed.

Without my sweetheart to care for, and without her to look after me, life can get lonely and at times depressing. I miss her so much. God is truly aware of our needs and the gaping hole in our hearts left by missing loved ones. So he commissions *angels* unaware at appropriate times to do His bidding.

I don't know why she was at school that day. I believe God sent Tina, not just for my encouragement but for her own as well. Tina is in her fourth round of chemo, the reason for her pale face. She is still living life. Still wearing a wig. Still attending school programs, and still noticing people who are lonely and hurting like me. When she asked me how I was doing. I answered sadly, "The best I can, up and down."

"I can only imagine," she said with an understanding smile on her pale face. I could tell she was weak and hurting by the way she bent slightly forward. We stood for a brief moment sharing our hearts.

Then she hugged me and with a kiss reminded me by saying, "We are in the 'Master's' hands, John, and under His control. All will be well."

I nodded in agreement. I hugged her and kissed her, thanking her for taking time to talk. She was soon hidden by the crowd.

May I encourage you to listen for those soft wisps of Angel wings when you are discouraged. No matter the circumstance, those wings of love are ready to hold you close and secure.

An old hymn writer penned these words of comfort: "Be not dismayed what-e're betide, God will take care of you. Beneath his wings of love abide, God will take care of you. God will take care of you—through every day, o'er all the way. He will take care of you . . . God will take care of you."

David the Psalmist wrote . . . "Though I walk through the valley of the shadow of death, I will fear no evil, for thou art with me."

Jesus promised . . . a peace that passes understanding and . . . "Surely, I will be with you always, even unto the end of the age."

Our Hope is in Him alone.

My friend, you never know when you may encounter an angel . . . alone . . . or in a crowd. But be assured, God sends them to us when and where we need them. He may even use you!

-Written October 29, 2011

CHAPTER 65

Epilogue

During those dark days through the valley of the shadow of death, Marliss was praying and calling us to let us know she cared. Susan spoke with her at least weekly and they cried together on the phone. She had lost her husband Chuck after 34 years of marriage, to a tragic accident only 6 years prior. When Susan passed away, Marliss kept in touch. In fact, she began to call just to listen and let me know that my feelings were normal and ok. She encouraged me to take time to grieve and talk about Susan with her. So I did.

We became close enough to establish more than a friendship. Today we are happily married. Close friends for 35 years, both having lost our long-time spouses, we are now enjoying our sunset years together.

Neither of us ever expected this but God must have planned it all from the beginning.

Yes, God is good all the time . . . even when everything around us is not.

CHAPTER 66

Other Places We've Explored

DISNEY WORLD – 1976

Refreshment of body, soul and spirit are so important for healthy living. As I write the painful past of our lives together, I realize I have left out some wonderful experiences we encountered before Susan was too sick to travel. But even during painful times, she still was able to travel. Let me touch on some significant trips we took.

1976, two years after David died, my sister arranged and paid for a trip to Disney World for David's widow, Ruthie, his son, Loren, Susan and our first two daughters, Renee and Brenda. It was a good reprieve from responsibilities on the farm and the tragedy of losing David.

We visited our dear Aunt Dorothy Miller and her dog, Lolla. What a pair they were. Thanks Joan, for sacrificing on our behalf.

OREGON COAST – 1979

It was close to our 17th anniversary and Susan had been diagnosed with *Mono*. Her niece and husband, Flo and Larry Shetler, lived in Oregon and invited us out. We decided it would be a good place for her to rest while I go elk hunting with the Shetler brothers in the Unimatila National Park. So we flew out and she rested with Flo for a week while I hunted.

The Shetlers camped out in a large tent at the base of a big mountain and hunted up top. It was an invigorating week for me and a relaxing time for Susan with Flo. No bull elk were found but we got two cow elk. The meat was as tender and tasty as any good beef I'd had.

The last two days there, they gave us their car to see the coast and stay overnight in a motel. The coast and our stay were fabulous.

I'm on the far right. Larry is next to me. Circa 1979.

OUR TWENTY-FIFTH ANNIVERSARY TRIP
TO EUROPE – 1987

Our kids were old enough by now to fend for themselves. We had some relatives living in France but near Basil, Switzerland. After a big celebration at church, we flew via Luftansa Airlines to Frankfurt, Germany. From there we used our rail tickets to travel around visiting four countries; Germany, France, Switzerland and Austria.

We visited places like the Black Forest, Heidelberg, Strausburg, Basel, Konigsberg Castle in France, and vineyards galore.

Susan's cousins, the Goldschmidts, lived in France, just across the border from Basel, Switzerland. Pierre said not to worry about not having passports for France. He could sweet-talk the border guard which he did. Their farm was like 400 years old and very quaint. They raised a crop called *rape*. It looked like millet. He took us to visit a castle high on a hill surrounded by vineyards.

From there we had arrangements to stay with the Burkhalters who were connected with "Mennonite Your Way" across countries. They also had a small farm, milking a few cows, making cheese, raising herbs and honey bees. A small sawmill sat on the edge of a 1,000-foot precipice. Mrs Burkhal-

JM at the cave.

A kiss on Jungfrau Mountain, Switzerland.

ter took us high up into the Alps where we picnicked and then hiked into the foothills. There she showed us a place where our forefathers worshiped in secret during the persecution of Anabaptists. We prayed and sang in memory of them.

From there we took a train to lots of picturesque towns. Just to mention a few; Lake Luzerne, Interlachen, Wengen, and Zermatt to see the Matterhorn where we stayed overnight.

In Grundelwald, for supper we had liver pattè . . . yuck. But great desserts.

We took the cog rail up the steep incline to the top of the Jungfrau and sealed our 25th with a kiss in the snow. We took the scenic Glacier Express from there to Landeck, Austria, where we visited Salzburg, the home of the film, "The Sound of Music."

We stood in the church where they married, sat in the gazebo where Rafael and Lisal danced, and walked the streets where the children sang, "Doe a deer, a female deer . . . Ray, a drop of golden sun . . . "

Our train went through the tiny country of Lithuania and Innsbruck where we stayed the night, sleeping under big, puffy down comforters. We changed money about five times, struggled to understand languages, ate good, laughed a lot and took lots of pictures. It was time and money well spent.

HAWAII – 1996

My best friend Lowell and his wife Lois, lived in Kawai for three years. Towards the end of their stay, they invited us over for a two-week visit. We stayed in their house, playing card games and eating too much. The ocean water was fantastic and the fish we saw while snorkeling were just as amazing. Fresh fruit and fish were abundant and ice cream a close second. We toured the island with them as our guides visiting places like *the Land of Hon-a-le,* beaches, and even the Big Island of Hilo.

ALASKA – 2006

We joined a tour group of 36 people with "Mennonite Your Way" from Lancaster. Most were of Mennonite background. The guides were very personal beginning each day with devotions and an old hymn.

This was the ultimate trip of a lifetime. Seventeen days traveling by plane, bus, paddle steam boat, train and a cruise the last four days. We even did a five-hour white-water rafting trip. Susan agreed to go since they promised no rapids classified over number two. I almost cannot believe she did it.

We saw Anchorage, Seward, the glaciers, the oil pipe line, lots of eagles, bear, dull sheep and caribou. Lots of these were seen in Denali National Park. We stopped in Fairbanks, Tok, Eagle and the little town of Chicken.

From there we boated to Dawson City and took in a Wild West show and listened to readings by famous Alaskan authors.

We went through Whitehorse and then took the cog rail which followed the forty-niners famous trail for gold, down the mountain to Skagway where we boarded our cruise ship *Holland America*.

A glacier tour.

Carved a rooster on the train in AK.

We took a few day excursions. One was in Ketchikan where we saw plenty of salmon and eagles.

Our cruise terminated in Vancouver but we had no time to visit there. Susan filled three big photo books of memories to enjoy.

CARIBBEAN CRUISE – 2006

This was an enjoyable cruise with Rod and Lucy Goshow. Every other year, Rod earns enough points to get a free trip from his business with YBC, a building supply company. We decided to pay our own way and join them.

The only way Susan could do this trip was in a wheelchair. But she did amazingly well in spite of it. Whenever there was much walking, I wheeled her.

The trip began in a big snowstorm as we tried to board a plane in Harrisburg only to be bumped because the plane was overloaded. No problem, we received $250.00 free rebate tickets and in two hours we were on our way.

Our Carnival cruise ship commenced in Puerto Rico and sailed to St. Thomas first, then Aruba, Barbados, Dominica and back. We rented a car on two islands and toured around. In Aruba, Rod and I snorkeled and actually saw a large octopus—kinda scary but beautiful.

The beaches and sights were some of the most breathtaking we've seen. Susan's photo albums confirm the beauty and joy of this trip and every trip.

THE LAST TWO TRIPS;
MAINE & SAVANNAH – 2008

I wrote about our trip to Maine earlier. This one was in late Summer and was the second-to-last trip we made. What great memories I have standing on the rocky ledge of York Harbor lighthouse. Only four years later, I would be standing at the identical spot with Marliss.

York Harbor, Maine

Life has strange twists and turns. With God, we can know it is all for a purpose.

SAVANNAH, GEORGIA

The events of getting us to Savannah are worth telling. To keep the story concise, I will copy notes directly from my journal. Sentences will be incomplete at times.

Susan's sister, Mary Jane, lives near the Lehigh Valley-Allentown-Bethlehem airport. [LAB]

" . . . 3:45 a.m. December 2, 2008 . . . rise and shine. 4:30 . . . Bob and Mary drive us to LAB airport arriving at 4:50. Security checked bags, threw out hair spray, tooth paste and lotion and checked Susan out like she was some sort of terrorist.

"5:50 . . . boarded Delta flight 4356 . . . 6:15 – liftoff right on schedule . . . BUT a loud noise developed immediately. 6:20 – pilot announces there's a problem and we'll be turning around to head back to airport. Pilot comes back on to tell us the noise is from emergency generators deploying unexpectedly. 6:25 – we're back on the ground safely. Whew!

"We're told to wait for further instructions inside airport. Flight is canceled. No mechanic on duty. Get in line to reschedule flight, but no flight available. Since Susan is on wheelchair we are given priority. 7:30 – After ticket hassle, van service will drive us to Philly.

"7:40 – I ride in front, Susan in back. All is well until 15 minutes from Philly airport. Traffic slows down, my bladder fills up. Driver obliges, stops and I head for bushes. 9:00 – arrive at airport, try curbside check-in but checker says it's a special ticket, go inside. Susan needs to use restroom. I take her.

"They look at our tickets and call for help. Ok . . . it's 9:30, plane departs at 10:15 . . . Courtesy boy pushes Susan and chair to security. Again she is wanded and x-rayed like she swallowed an assault rifle. They ignore our letter from her doctor regarding all the metal in her body. Ugh! Finally, they escort us directly to boarding and onto first-class seating. Whoa. Now that is unexpected but very much appreciated. Thank you Jesus. We never flew in such luxurious class! If anyone deserves it, Susan sure does.

"Our male steward apologizes up and down for the inconvenience and we buckle up for take-off. In a little over an hour we are in Savannah, safe, sound and shaking our heads."

Susan loved to watch Paula Dean's TV show. Not that she cooked as Paula did, but it was entertaining when Susan could no longer spend much time in the kitchen. We had entered a contest hoping to be chosen for free tickets to one of her shows. No luck. So the next best option was to visit her town and restaurant.

The kids gave us money towards our trip so we booked flights to Savannah in early December of 2008 and rented a car upon arrival. We ended up staying in a very nice hotel on the beach in Hilton Head since it had an ocean view. As you know by now, the beach was always a favorite of hers. Only this time we had to use a wheelchair to get around. No problem, I pushed her across a rubber mat placed on the sand for handicapped people to access the beach.

Someone was looking out for us. The fresh seafood

Susan posing with a cardboard figure of Paula.

was as good as it gets and the meal at Paula's restaurant . . . ? Well, we waited in line for a half hour while browsing her store. That's where I snapped a photo of Susan standing next to a cardboard model of Paula. Looks quite real.

The meal was served upstairs in a huge historic building. It was buffet style and the food was down home southern-style cooking with plenty of butter, gravy and biscuits added to the main courses. The desserts were extravagant and sweet of course. Paula knows nothing of gluten-free, low salt or sugar. So we indulged.

The next day we saw the moss-laden-tree-city on a guided trolley tour. It's a wonderful city to visit. We crossed the bridge to see the ocean again and stopped for boiled peanuts along the roadside. Yummy. You should try some.

Next to our hotel was a good seafood restaurant called the Aqua Grille. Superb seafood.

That evening, the full moon peeked crisply through the palm trees, casting a memorable glow on the surf nearby. The sound of that surf and the moonbeams shining through our hotel window that night nestled peacefully into our hearts.

Little did we know it would be our last trip to a southern beach and a fancy hotel. But the hotel she now has is likely built of pure gold on a dazzling endless beach. I can't wait to see her in that setting. :)

CHAPTER 67

Ebenezer, Our Rock of Hope

July 2008; Dr. R., a renown neurosurgeon who was on President Reagan's short list of doctors, performed yet another surgery on Susan. It was to relieve her back pain caused from collapsed vertebrae. Although it was a minimal invasive surgery, Susan says . . . surgery is surgery with all the precautions, needles, tubes, anesthesia and recovery. For a few days she dealt with surgical pain from four different needle insertions and a few staples where he performed the *Kyphoplasty*.

Basically, he inserted a balloon to fill the cavity where the tumor caused a void in her vertebrae and then inserted bone cement into the balloon. The cement hardens in 10 minutes and he has a very small window of time to remove the balloon. She braved yet another round and healed well after more therapy.

Fall, 2008; Susan was still able to go up stairs, albeit, one step at a time and very slowly. Because of her determination and good attitude, she did it twice a day. She didn't want to give up the privilege of sleeping in her own bed, the one we purchased at age 19 just before we married. It was our refuge, our nest, our holy and intimate place to rest our weary bodies. A place we were ourselves, holding hands and curled close before sleep. We didn't want to give that up.

But the time was close and we knew she would no longer be able to go up the stairs. The pain in her left hip was bad and getting worse. Something would soon have to be done. I suggested getting a bed, maybe even a hospital bed, to put in the living room and curtain off half the room.

That would work . . . until she gets back on her feet . . . I dreamed. She really didn't want that and I knew it. She'd rather sleep on the sofa for now.

We weren't questioning *if* God was with us or *if* He was still in control of our lives. The questions were more like, "What are You doing?" "Why are things getting worse instead of better?" "What now?" There were many questions, few answers. That's when we had to really trust that God was still in control of our lives even though everything within us cried, **enough**!

By the end of 2008, Dr. L. was suggesting surgery. Here is a portion of a Dad's Weekly I wrote to our kids in late November of 2008:

Thanks so much for your ongoing prayers on Mom's behalf. You'll likely never know the total results and rewards of those prayers. But Dr. L. made a statement three times today during her 1/2 hour visit which confirms that your prayers are being heard. He said to Mom, **"You are a miracle . . . . a walking miracle."**

I'll take that statement any day over "She **was** *a miracle!"*
After 14 years and a 5"-thick file folder of her history with Dr. L., she is still walking into the office, looking and smiling like a queen. He always asks what's happening and says how good she looks. After going over her list, looking at x-rays and MRIs and reading over the reports he said he saw no **new** *trouble spots.*

When we asked about her leg and hip pains he said she could expect to live with some pain from all that she has had going on. He looked at the hip area he worked on and said, "Basically that hip is 'el-crapo'". . . the bone cement is what's holding it in place. (You'd have to know Dr. L.—some of you do—it made us smile.) He said he saw no reason for it to let her down. It seems stable in spite of all the damage from the tumor.

As for her arm . . . he said, "Yeah, it's falling apart" . . . but there's no need to talk about bone surgery there until she has too much pain. As long as she can live with it, he doesn't want to disturb it. The bone has broken apart since the surgery which initially stabilized it. The plate shifted as the bone continued to soften from the tumor and the screws bent. But he said it seems to have scared back in giving her some minimal use.

Now the tumor which has swollen up on her arm, even after being radiated, should be dealt with. As we discussed options he felt like for now the best option would be an "Embolization." If you google it you will find all kinds of info on it. They do it for lots of tumors all over the body which are basically like hers . . . vascular . . . meaning lots of blood vessels involved. The procedure is done basically to stop the blood flow into the tumor which causes the tumor to die or atrophy. There is no guarantee that it will not grow back but it would stop it at least temporarily. We cannot just ignore it.

He hugged Mom as usual before we left saying, "See ya later babe, take care." We said, "God bless you and don't retire yet." He said, "Well, I'm 57 and not quite ready yet to retire."

The Embolization was performed the end of 2008 causing the most intense pain to date. Basically, it stalled the tumor growth temporarily.

Another big surgery, the most difficult thus far, would be scheduled for early 2009. First, he had to have the part designed and custom made for her.

That would take a few months. I believe the Lord gave me some divine insights as I walked around the house inside and out . . . dreaming of what would be best for Susan. *That's it,* I thought one day as I looked out the dining room window toward the old playhouse I had built 43 years ago. *We can build out the back and make that window a door to a master bedroom with a bathroom and walk-in closet.* I went outside and began measuring and envisioning the new room. It could work. I discussed it with Susan. She was interested but a bit overwhelmed, knowing it would mean another big project, expensive and a lot of hard work. And how would I have time to do it. We wouldn't want to hire someone to do it all? And of course she never liked being the reason for extra costs or attention.

I began drawing up plans on my computer and with the help and consult of our two Mikes and Charlie, our neighboring architect, we came up with a plan. It would be 22' x 24' set on a full poured concrete basement with an exterior entrance toward the pond. My first plan was for 18' x 20' but thanks to Mike, I enlarged it. There would be a full-length covered porch, neatly attached to the existing deck for us to sit on, where the kids and grandkids could gather. There would be a 5' shower stall and a bath large enough for handicap access, a sizeable closet and a big bedroom with plenty of room to maneuver a wheelchair. We would use 36" pocket doors for easy access.

Mike Beinlich offered to do the excavating. He had forms to set and would pour the concrete wall. I would hire Rod Goshow and his crew (Brotherhood Builders) to help "rough in" the structure. Herb Eby could do the plumbing, heating and electric. I'd have a new septic tank installed during the excavation and I would finish the project.

All these plans were being made during the early winter of 2009 as we awaited the huge surgery she desperately needed to fix her collapsed hip socket due to cancer. The surgeon was waiting for the part to be designed and custom built hoping it would be available in March but we kept waiting.

Mike found a good deal on a nice Cat excavator and bought it. It was perfect for the job.

I had begun digging with my little John Deere backhoe and was making slow progress. I was tearing out the old basement entrance when I hit something really hard. It would not move. I kept digging and discovered it was a huge boulder smack in the center of where the new basement entry would be. It had to be moved, but not by my backhoe. Mike had his big Cat excavator hauled in. The comparison was like that of David and Goliath. The area to be excavated was practically all rock. He worked his way down to the boulder. After some tedious maneuvering, he had it in the grasp of the big bucket. I asked him to set it over to the side and we would do something with it later. It was huge.

With the basement dug, Mike and I set up footer forms, and with Eugene and Tyler's help, we leveled the stone for the floor and footer drain. The day prior to leaving for the hospital in Philadelphia, we poured the footer.

At last, April 1st was determined as the big day of surgery. We went down the night before and stayed at the Comfort Inn, my main place to stay during surgeries. Long story short, Susan spent the entire month of April in the hospital (another story) fighting one infection after another. All the while, Mike was forming walls and pouring concrete in preparation for us to build when we got home.

April 27, 2009, Susan was discharged and transported to Willimsport Hospital Rehab Center. She spent 10 days in rehab while I was working on the addition. I spent a number of days staying overnight in the hospitality room provided free by the hospital. I drove back and forth daily to work on the addition.

May 6th they discharged her and allowed me to drive her home. What an emotional reentry to our home it was. Brenda came to stay for a week to serve us. A tremendous support. I continued to work on the addition with some volunteer help. I helped Herb Eby do plumbing and electric. During Renee's helpful week, she wrote in our journal that we were two silent busy beavers working away. She didn't hear much talking but a lot of hammering, sawing and other building noises.

The journal records the significant events surrounding the "Ebenezer Rock." Sunday, May 17th, family radio aired the old hymn, "Come thou fount of every blessing." Our daily devotional, "The Upper Room," for that day was about listing our blessings and quoted the same old hymn as the theme. It also pointed out the phrase, "Here I raise my Ebenezer, hither to, my help has come," and the value of making or setting up remembrances of our blessings.

It should be noted that Susan was always encountering one trial after another almost every day. It often seemed like we'd take one step forward only to fall back two the next day.

Sunday morning, May 17th, Renee, Lori, Mom and I decided to have our own little service at home. Brenda had gone home and Renee had come for her week of "maid work." Some would call it "coincidence" that Lori chose to play piano and sing the song, "Come thou fount," for one of our worship songs. I call it providence. As we sang the verse about raising our Ebenezer, I decided it was time to look up and read the reference about that phrase.

I Samuel 7:12 – "Then Samuel took a stone and set it up between Mizpah and Shen. He named it Ebenezer, saying, 'Thus far has the Lord helped us.' The context records the story of Israel writhing in fear as the enemy was preparing to attack them. They cried to the Lord and Samuel offered up a lamb and petitioned the Lord on their behalf. God heard their cries and routed the enemy without

Israel having to even fight. And so Samuel set up a stone between the two cities of battle as a "remembrance" of what God had done for them—thus far.

The idea came clearly to me that morning as we talked about this story and how it related to Susan's past and present pain and suffering realizing that, yes, she is still here with us. God has not forgotten our state of affairs. Somehow, He is using it "all for His glory." And so, we will set that big rock out in front of the house between the old living room bay window and the new bay window. Thus everyone who passes by can see it. And if they ask about "that rock," we will say, "That is our Ebenezer rock," and we can testify to God's hand on our lives.

And so it is, the rock of remembrance sets proudly amid Susan's memorial flower garden in front of the addition facing the road where all can see. Her favorite flower, "black-eyed-Susans," surround the rock as do lots of "Jonnie-jump-ups." Three "female" Holly bushes and one "male" Holly bush stand close behind representing our three daughters and our son. A rose bush, with thorns (my representation) grows off to the side. Daffodils, tulips and larkspur (the grand-kids' representation), cheer the bare concrete wall under the bay window. Two different "bleeding heart" plants shed bright pink tears along the wall. One bleeding heart is a split from Susan's dear friend, Josie Henning. Other perennials (representing a myriad of friends and family), of various colors grace the garden. Birds come to drink and sing at the bird bath and thank her. Even Toby made his trail through the tulips wagging his friendly tail.

Susan got to see "the rock" planted firmly in its place but without the blooming flowers. That came only months after she moved to her heavenly home where only she and those present can appreciate the indescribable beauty of heavenly rock gardens.

"Here I raise MY Ebenezer, it's only by Thy help that I've come!"

Written today, March 31, 2012 – Susan's earthly birthday . . . in her memory. JM

CHAPTER 68

LHF's Centennial Celebration

2 006 was an event-filled year. In July, Living Hope Fellowhip's 50th anniversary was celebrated as was the 100th anniversary of the church building. All those whoever pastored at LHF or Estella Mennonite Church were invited and I believe, actually came. There was lots of camaraderie as friends from as far back as the '50s came to reminisce. The old hymns and stories were refreshing and inspiring.

I hosted a round table discussion with Pastor Henry to relive the history of the church. A tent was erected in the lawn for fellowship around snacks.

The massive attempt to contact all whoever came to LHF was well worth the effort as we renewed old friendships. The goal of honoring Christ, the rock on which the church is built, was achieved.

CHAPTER 69

40th Wedding Anniversary

November 10th weekend of 2006. Our kids planned a wonderful celebration of our 40th wedding anniversary. The event was staged at the Camp Brule Boy Scout camp just four miles behind our farm on North Street.

Many of our friends and extended family attended filling the dining hall to joyful capacity. Funny stories were told, our favorite hymns and songs sung, and a photo album created and a powerpoint presentation greatly enjoyed. The kids told some entertaining stories about growing up. The girls recalled how they tried to sneak onto the bus wearing clothes they knew were questionable at least with Dad. Each of the children affirmed us for their strong Christian upbringing and the sincere love they experienced growing up.

I recall one amusing incident with Chuck and Marliss. Marliss began reading an inspirational and somewhat nostalgic writing which was quite touching. Well, she got only a short way into the reading when her emotions got the best of her. So, handing her glasses to Chuck, she said, "Here, you read, I can't."

The writing went something like this; *there are some people who come into your life for a while and then leave. Some come and go and you never remember. Others come into your life and never leave your heart. Susan and John were friends like that,"* she said.

As you know, Chuck and Susan graduated to Heaven. Marliss and I live on to remember and treasure our lives.

Our next milestone, our 50th, never came to pass. Our last anniversary, 47 years, was celebrated in our own dining room as our Pastor Scot and Phenny, and Rod and Lucy came to cook and serve us gourmet style just three months before Susan's death. What wonderful, loyal friends.

CHAPTER 70

A Treasure in Jars of Clay

S he was number 11 in a family of 12. Sweet as a dewdrop on honey-
suckle, and more interested in you than herself. She wore a smile that
could melt an icy heart. Overall, on the pain tolerance chart of 1-10, she
should claim a 12 but didn't. After 15 surgeries in 16 years with cancer, her
body was ready to retire. But her mind and smile were not. Four pillows,
two towel rolls and an ice pack provided some comfort to her aching body
in bed. Sleep came in two-hour spurts interrupted by whispers of, "Sorry,
honey, I need to use the commode," or "My knee hurts, would you mind
changing the ice pack?"

"Of course not honey, I'll do it right now," I'd whisper.

To give you an idea of one routine, here's how it goes: Put her slipper-
socks on for traction and warmth, remove all pillows and towel rolls and lower
the adjustable bed, set up the walker next to the bed, carefully (always gently
and carefully) slide and lift her legs out of the bed with one hand and the other
under her shoulder. Now, while bending correctly, help her stand. The walker
is there for support as she slowly moves her feet around to position herself. Put
a prayer shawl around her back for comfort. Move the walker and help her sit.
Go sit on the love seat next to her and wait. A few minutes later, "Okay honey,"
she'd whisper, and though sleepy, I'd gladly reverse the routine to get her back in
bed.

"There, do I have that pillow right? Is the towel roll okay?"

"Maybe just up a little more under this leg," she'd say and I'd crawl back
in to snuggle for a couple hours hopefully.

Being a nurse, she was adamant and accurate about her medicine schedule. With Susan's help, Lori had created a detailed daily schedule which we
printed for each week. The medicine, dose, and time were checked off when
taken and any notations or reminders recorded. These became our journal and
reference for doctor appointments.

Over the years, the medicine regimen evolved and increased depending on the surgery and pain level. Balancing pain medicine the last nine months of her life was challenging.

Five times daily we made certain she got her medicine. Other incidental meds were added as needed. As the nurse in her dictated, she counted out each prescribed amount and put them in small dishes for the next time.

Following the last two major surgeries on her hip and left leg in April of 2009, the pain level continued to elevate until it was unbearable. I mention this because it was so different than prior surgeries. Before, they were able to control pain quicker with much less medicine.

Many patients get relief and do well on a 20-40 mg. level of morphine after surgery. Sometimes even lower doses will do it. With the horrific trauma to her body from one major and five minor surgeries in the Spring of 2009, the pain continued to increase.

The pain management nurse kept raising the morphine level while assuring us that it was okay. She would always say, "There is no reason to be in pain. There are many different options and prescriptions for us to control it. So don't worry about the dosage or getting addicted. You, Susan, are not one of our patients whom we worry about addiction. We want you comfortable."

And so the dosage was increased until it reached 800 mg. a day. Something had to change. Dr. L. suggested she see Dr. H., another oncology specialist in Philly. After reviewing her history and current condition, he recommended switching from morphine to methadone. Upon hearing the word methadone, we were a bit stunned. "Meth . . . say what . . . methadone?" He quickly assured us that it was very different than "crack meth."

"Many cancer patients do very well on this," he said, "and I believe it will make a difference in Susan's pain quickly." Well that was certainly good to hear!

The transition was not as smooth as we had hoped, giving her some ugly side effects. But within a week, the pain began to subside and be tolerable. Finally, after one month on the new medicine . . . some relief.

THOUGH I WALK THROUGH THE VALLEY OF THE SHADOW OF DEATH, YOU ARE WITH ME

"I'm making an appointment for you to see Dr. F. this afternoon. After looking at the C-scan of your lungs and with that cough, I'll feel better getting his opinion before you go home for the weekend," Dr. A., the oncology doctor said in his Kenyan accent.

"He is a pulmonologist within our system and can see you in an hour. Barb will give you the paperwork and directions to his office. Hope things work out for you."

Questions of all sorts and sizes swirled around in our dizzy minds. I released the brakes and wheeled her down the hall to the elevator and waited. "Wonder if it's bronchial or something worse?" Susan said softly.

"Guess we'll soon find out." What else could I say?

We found the office and the secretary gave us three more forms to fill out before the doctor could see us.

Finding a spot to park the wheelchair, we sat as she checked off the questions. Of course there was the usual question of, "Did you ever have surgery and if so what?" Susan carried an index card listing every surgery, doctor and phone number.

After quite a while, the doctor opened the door, smiled and introduced himself. "I'm Doctor F., you can come into my office over here," he said.

During our wait he had reviewed her history just a bit and looked at the C-scans of her lungs.

"How are you feeling?" he said with a slight smile. "You look pretty good actually."

Susan said, "I'm having trouble breathing and I wonder what you think about the C-scan?"

"Well . . . ," he spoke with some hesitation. "There is no question about the cancer in your lungs, but I would expect you to be having much more difficulty breathing than you are. Besides, someone with such invasive cancer generally does not look as good as you look," he said sitting on his stool looking from Susan to the pictures on the screen.

"My inclination is that your cough is due to your bronchial rather than from your lungs. So I'm going to give you a prescription for two kinds of puffers which should relieve the symptoms in a couple days," he said confidently.

She asked him to call the prescription into Wal-Mart to save us some time. Susan was always thinking ahead regardless of her pain or discomfort.

We were still stunned and having difficulty comprehending all that was said. So many terms and scenarios were thrown at us recently that it was nearly impossible to think clearly. He answered her few questions . . . however vague and then left us to check out at the desk.

Just before we opened the door to leave, he came back to tell us he was going to order oxygen for Susan since we lived so far from the hospital and it was late Friday afternoon. He said that the company would deliver to our door that night yet. They would explain in detail how to use it. He was also ordering a portable tank just in case we needed it in the car at anytime. Again, we were a bit dumbfounded wondering if he was expecting the worse to develop. But we figured the doctor knows best.

Since getting in and out of the car was such a struggle, Susan waited patiently in the car with the seat reclined while I ran into Wal-Mart. "I'll be as quick as possible, honey," I said.

Her reply was almost always the same. "I'll be fine, just leave your phone on in case I need to call you," and she reclined slightly in her seat.

Fortunately the prescription was filled and ready and we were soon on our way home. Dusk was falling quickly as we headed north on Route 87. Before we passed the Gateway Restaurant, we caught up to a van with the word *Oxygen* printed on the rear doors. I blinked my lights a few times and pulled around him, then slowly pulled to the side of the road indicating that he should do the same. He pulled over.

I told him who we were and suggested he follow me. He liked the idea and off we drove. The 45-minute drive was a quiet one, both deep in thought.

Even with my hearing handicap, I could hear Susan softly wheezing, her head back and eyes closed. I reached over to hold her hand. Good, it was nice and warm. She squeezed mine ever so softly as if to say, "I'm glad you're here, honey." After 47 years it's not hard to know what each other is thinking. We held hands till we got to our driveway. Then she put down her window and I knew she wanted to get the mail. That was the routine each time we arrived home.

We pulled in the drive and up to the ramp at the back door. The van pulled in behind me. It took a while to get Susan out of the car and into the house. I could tell breathing was difficult but her hip and arm were aching badly too. She never said so, but I could tell.

As quickly as possible, I took her to the bathroom and helped her from the chair to the commode, closed the door and got her nightgown. "I'm coming!" I yelled, hoping the guy could hear me. I let him in the house with the oxygen tanks, tubing and gauges and showed him where to put them. He hooked them up while I helped Susan get her nightie on.

That took some doing since there was still a small area on her left hip which needed the dressing changed twice daily. We had our routine—each knowing what to do—when and how. After getting her back into the wheelchair, I washed her partial plate and sprinkled some Fixodent on it. Meanwhile she brushed her teeth and washed her face with the warm washcloth I had ready for her. Then I carefully maneuvered her back to the bedroom and into bed. Thank God for our new master bedroom.

By this time the guy was finished and waiting to explain it all to us. He gently put the tubing around her neck and positioned the ends into her nose. "I'm setting the gauge at *number two*," he said. "That's pretty normal and should be adequate for you tonight." He showed us how to adjust it but we said we were sure it would be fine and thanked him.

She said it actually did give her some relief but not all that much. Thank God once more for the adjustable bed. Now she could position herself with her legs above her heart (to reduce leg swelling) without propping so many pillows and towel rolls under her. It was still something of an art to get her settled and comfortable but when she was settled, she could usually sleep. Strong meds helped.

I asked her if she wanted some fruit or something to drink but she declined. "Who Loves Raymond," one of the shows we often watched at night, didn't seem funny that night. She took her 9:00 meds and I sorted out her 10:00 meds putting them in the little custard dishes three times a day like she had instructed me.

At 10:00 she wanted to use the bedside commode so I helped her over, then I sat in her recliner and prayed quietly. *Dear God, what is happening? What more do you want from her? How much more will you allow her to endure? Would you please relieve her breathing tonight? You know how she is hurting and suffering. Why, God? Why?* I prayed, too often to remember.

. . . PERPLEXED BUT NOT IN DESPAIR

Back in bed with labored breathing, she settled in for a few hours, hopefully more with the help of the puffers and oxygen. "Night honey, I love you," I said tenderly unfolding the fingers in her left hand so I could hold her hand. We always held hands to fall asleep.

"Night, love you too," she said with a weak whisper. In sickness or in health . . . bedtime was our favorite time of day. But now it was so much more difficult with all the sensitive and painful areas of her hurting body.

"I love you too." . . . How I loved those four sweetly spoken words. How I treasured those words . . . and always will . . . "love you too . . . love you too . . . love you . . . love . . . "

It seemed like only a few minutes passed and she needed to have her leg readjusted and wanted a drink of water.

"Sorry, honey," she said over and again day and night. Oh, how bad my heart ached for her.

"It's okay, honey. Whatever it takes, I'm here for you. You know that. I'm sorry too honey, that you hurt so much," I said and jumped out of bed to get whatever she needed. Several times through the night she asked for things and tried the puffers as prescribed but without any relief. The wheezing was worrisome and we wondered what was happening. "I will do whatever possible to make you more comfortable," I said. It was a long, sleepless night.

Early Saturday morning, before the sun was up, she was wide awake telling me she could not go through another night like that. We decided to call the on-call oncology doctor and ask what to do. The answer was clear—"Go to the ER." Susan heard me talking and said that's what she wanted to do. She never was quick to say, "Let's go to the ER," so it was obvious, she was in distress.

I called Lori and told her the situation and she was over in a short while. Lori packed some clothes and makeup, her meds, and a nightie while I helped Susan dress and wash up. We talked together as we packed and dressed. I ran out to do the few chores and told Toby he'd have to stay home. His ears drooped extra and he looked bewildered. So did we.

Lori was so kind and gentle but quieter than usual. I knew what she was thinking. I think we all knew what each other was thinking. "Is this it?" But the words were not worth the breath it took to express them.

Grabbing the oxygen tanks and tubing at the last minute before wheeling Susan out, I loaded them first. She just may need them on the way down. By 9:00 she was ready and *I had* to be ready. She looked around the bedroom, then the bathroom, then the dining room as we passed.

"Wait . . . put those cards in the box over there," she said being sure to have the house clean and tidy. *Tradition you know.* Then out through the kitchen, her special domain, she barely took time to look at it and out through the back porch I wheeled her . . . all of us deep in thought. Only God knew what was ahead, but He wasn't saying . . . or was He?

We both knew the routine to get in the car. Breathe a prayer. With the car door open exactly square with the ramp, pull the wheelchair as closely as possible. Be certain car seat is all the way back and reclined halfway. Remove both leg supports from the wheelchair and lock the breaks. With just enough room for me to stand between Susan and the car seat, help her out of the chair while she pulls herself up with her good arm . . . quickly move the chair back as I gently let her down onto the seat using one foot to hold her's from slipping. Kneel down to help lift her bad leg ever so carefully into the car with just an inch to spare. Do not twist her leg or the hip prosthesis could dislocate. *We had that experience.* As she pulls herself back with one good arm and pushes with the one good leg, move her leg over and onto a cushion. Help shuffle her over into the center of the seat making sure she is as comfortable as possible and belt her in. Take a deep breath and thank God.

If that doesn't make you grateful for a healthy body, nothing will.

Always . . . before we backed out of the driveway, we prayed, "Dear God, please watch over us as we drive. Protect us; give wisdom to the doctors and patience for us. Please, dear God, be merciful to Susan. She needs your healing touch. Amen."

This time though, I was already going down the road as I prayed. Time was running out. Susan's breathing was not good.

When we got to the state shed three miles down the road, I said, "I think we should call the kids."

She said, "You'll just worry them, just keep going." But Lori and I both thought they should know so I stopped briefly while I had a signal, to call Brenda.

I could tell by her breathing that I needed to keep moving. If it hadn't been for the portable oxygen tank we got just the night before, I doubt she'd have survived the 40-mile trip.

I had called ahead to tell the ER that we were on our way and they were waiting with a wheelchair when we pulled up to the hospital. Hospital personnel wheeled her directly to a small curtain booth as two nurses attended to her. They asked the normal questions, took her vitals and made some notes. It took a while for the doctor to come in. He was an older doctor who seemed way too laid-back.

His slow, quiet, and drawn-out mellow speech made him impossible to understand. When he decided to admit her and send her up to a fourth floor room, we felt better. She was ready to get some relief and hopefully breathe more freely.

As they wheeled her on the portable bed, several nurses and technicians scurried around us setting up monitors and machines. There was a window facing the helicopter pad and even before she got settled, medics were rapidly transferring the young child we had seen downstairs in the ER and his parents stood sadly nearby. Who knows what trauma or problems they were experiencing. Life is NOT fair.

In and around a hospital you see so much pain and sadness. And Susan was always thinking about that other person who was in pain. I'm sure it helped diffuse the seriousness of her own problems temporarily. But then, that was Susan . . . always cheering for the less fortunate. What a wonderful attitude. Bless her.

"I wonder what's going on there? It's so sad," she said softly through the oxygen mask. By now they had her hooked up to various monitors and were paying special attention to the amount of oxygen she was requiring.

Our family doctor, Dr. P., *happened* to be doing rounds on our floor when they were working on her and he found out she was there. He stopped by and immediately sensed the seriousness of the moment. He began to question us about her living will. Did we have it with us and do the kids know that she was here? He very strongly encouraged us to call the whole family and let them know.

I can still hear him say, "Susan, I think it's time." When she questioned him if in fact we should call all the kids, he again said, "Yes, I really think you need to."

No one knows when his last day on earth will be. But this was like receiving a death notice. Looking into Dr. P.'s kind, sad eyes as he spoke told a story we were not hoping to hear. And it must have hurt him deeply to have to express it. He is such a compassionate kind man and had cared for Susan many years. But there it was. The time to call the family and tell them their Mom and MawMaw was very ill and to come as soon as possible.

While Dr. P. was talking with us, the nurses and techs were working diligently to make her comfortable without much success. In our hearts, we knew it was very serious.

When the oxygen monitor reached its maximum limit of delivering *15* units and her breathing was still in duress, the head RN called the ICU and announced they were sending Susan up immediately. Remember, the night before the oxygen technician had set the machine on number *two* and said that should be fine.

Oh dear God, dear God . . . our hearts cried. I immediately got on the phone as did Lori. She was with us this whole time, experiencing the whole trauma. With tear-filled eyes and trembling voices we told the rest of our kids to come as quickly and safely as possible.

At times like this when you love someone so much, nothing else matters and you do what it takes to get to the bedside of your loved one.

So they did, coming at all hours of the dark night, ignoring the speed limits and praying hard. It felt like a bad dream . . . no . . . in fact, as I write about it, it was more like a nightmare almost as though I'm writing a fiction novel.

I want to assure you without a doubt, God was with us! We eventually felt His peace that passes understanding.

"The Lord is near . . . do not be anxious, but by prayer and petition with thanksgiving, let your requests be known to God and the peace which passes all understanding will guard your hearts and minds in Christ Jesus." Phillipians 4:5-6 (my paraphrasing)

Peace seemed to come and rest on us when we needed it most. Just like God. He is there when we need Him most. And He was . . . and continues to be! Our souls are anchored on the only true Rock, the Rock, Christ Jesus.

"I lift up my eyes to the hills . . . where does my help come from? My help comes from the Lord who made Heaven and earth." Psalm 121

Peace, was most evident on Susan's face. Yes, in spite of all she'd been through and still had to endure, that sweet, angelic smile was glowing.

"Blessed assurance, Jesus is mine, oh what a foretaste of glory divine . . . "

STOP, TAKE A BREATH . . .

Reading these details is painful. Writing them is even more difficult. Living them day by day, month by month is exhausting. Maybe you've experienced something similar. So you know. If not yet, you probably will. But as a child of God, you can be assured of His presence and peace to carry you through.

It's time to breathe fresh air from outside the hospital. I had to do that often; many times on long walks to South Street for a milkshake or Whole Foods Store for fresh shrimp. Sometimes exploring the old St. Peter's Church or a park to just sit and think.

So for now let's talk about some fun stuff. Moms need their children; Children need their Moms. Girls especially need one-on-one with Mom.

For many years, Susan and her girls scheduled time together for a weekend get-a-way. They planned it halfway between our house and Virginia where Renee and Brenda lived. A Hampton or some real nice motel would be reserved as a base for their shopping, and dining experiences. They slept in double beds in the same room. They modeled the mottos in our house . . . *Live, Love and Laugh* and another *Live For What Matters.*

There was plenty of laughter as they relived stories about each other growing up. They shopped for little prizes for the kids, ate great food and came

Renee, Susan, Lori, and Brenda.

back refreshed and happy fulfilling the scripture which says . . . *A merry heart does good like a medicine.*

Up until the last year, they were able to keep this special weekend get-a-way. I'd encourage any parent to consider such a venture if you value bonding family relationships.

Mike and I did of few of our own father and son outings though somewhat different. One year before Mike had kids, we set up camp in a tent along the Appalachian Trail as it crossed the Sky Line Drive near Waynesboro, Virginia. We hiked a few days and ate our fill of hotdogs and junk food. Another year we just did day hikes on the trail. A small stream near Mike's house worked great for a day trip in kayaks. The picture on the next page was taken in our own woods.

Now we have two four-wheelers for the family to use on our wooded trails when they come home. When there's enough snow, we get out the snow-mobiles.

Ice skating on our pond has always been fun with all our grandkids if the timing is right with snow and cold weather. "Let's see who can catch Poppie?" My skates are over 50 years old . . . the same ones I used as a teenager.

Soccer is the springtime sport that most of my grandkids excel in. Seems every year they are traveling far and wide to tournaments. And now as they get

Poppie, Emmett, Mike and Jude.

older, it's baseball and basketball tournaments. What fun watching your kids and grandkids play sports . . . except for that nasty baseball imprint on Tyler's elbow . . . and soccer shin splints for others. Oh . . . how 'bout that soccer game six-year-old Jude played? Sixteen to nothing? And Jude had 14 of the goals. Go Jude!

The heap of videotapes locked in our safe are proof of hundreds of Mike's soccer games, indoor and outdoor that Susan and I attended. Whew, makes me weary thinking of all that running. Now our own children are driving all over the country doing the same thing with their kids. It's all a matter of choice and what your feel *matters*.

There, do you feel refreshed? I do. But before we settle into *The Gatehouse* for Susan's final transition, let's breathe a bit more of that fresh air. Turn the page.

CHAPTER 71

Short-Term Missions

O ur Mennonite roots sprouted many servanthood shoots drawing nourishment from the Holy Scriptures: I quote Matthew 25:35-40 New International Version (NIV)

> *35 For I was hungry and you gave me something to eat, I was thirsty and you gave me something to drink, I was a stranger and you invited me in, 36 I needed clothes and you clothed me, I was sick and you looked after me, I was in prison and you came to visit me.'*
>
> *37 "Then the righteous will answer him, 'Lord, when did we see you hungry and feed you, or thirsty and give you something to drink? 38 When did we see you a stranger and invite you in, or needing clothes and clothe you? 39 When did we see you sick or in prison and go to visit you?'*
>
> *40 "The King will reply, 'Truly I tell you, whatever you did for one of the least of these brothers and sisters of mine, you did for me.'*
>
> Isaiah 58:10, 11 . . . *if you spend yourselves in behalf of the hungry and satisfy the needs of the oppressed, then your light will rise in the darkness, and your night will become like the noonday. 11 The LORD will guide you always;*

These scriptures and many others inspired our hearts throughout our lifetime. When we were aware of neighbors or people in need, God had instilled compassion in us to help.

Year after year when we were able, we responded to the appeals for help from several non-profit agencies. Mennonite Disaster Service (MDS) is a national organization which responds to natural disasters.

SWAP is another, the acronyms meaning Serving With Appalachian People. Its base was mainly in Kentucky and West Virginia.

A SWAP project in West Virginia.

MAMA Project, an organization established to help malnutrition problems in Honduras. MAMA means, *Mujeres-Amigos-Miles-Aparte* or Women Friends Miles Apart.

SAMARATINS PURSE, a global organization established by Franklin Graham to aid disaster-stricken countries is still very effective in reaching needy people.

As the mission coordinator for our local church, I organized many teams over the years for short-term missions. Generally, we spent a week or two helping destitute people. Besides the extended trips to Honduras in 1999 and 2000, we have been on service projects as faraway as Colorado, S. Carolina, Louisiana, Kentucky, West Virginia, Michigan, New York, Chicago, and Long Island, N.Y. We have been to many in our own state, our county and nearby towns.

Every time we sacrificed time and money to help others, God has blessed us beyond our imagination. Living life with a mind for missions, be it near or far, long or short-term, God's promise to make His light shine on us and guide us held true.

You *cannot* spend yourself on behalf of the hungry helping destitute people and go broke. God always brings an abundant blessing on both the needy and the giver. This we found true over and over.

And then I think . . . why am I surprised that my children and now, our grandchildren, have such a heart for the needy in our world—as faraway as Africa? It's God's promise to uphold His Word and the principles He ordained.

It's very heartening to see many young people in the Christian church grasping the baton of *meeting the needs of real people* . . . the mission of LHF.

CHAPTER 72

Renee's Tribute

The night that Mom was admitted to ICU, I took my Bible into the waiting room and asked God to please speak to my heart. When I opened the Word, I opened to the parable Jesus told of the Wise and Foolish Builders in Matthew 7. This is what I read:

"Therefore everyone who hears these words of mine and puts them into practice is like a wise man who builds his house on the rock. The rain came down, the streams rose, and the winds blew, and beat against the house; yet it did not fall, because it had its foundation on the rock."

I knew instantly what He was telling me. The next morning, I went into Mom's room in the ICU. As I entered, I saw that they had put a BY PAP machine on her mouth and nose to help her to breathe.

She smiled at me through the mask and said, "Do I look like a fighter pilot?"

Typical Mom . . . able to find the humor in the pain. This is when I told her what I am about to tell you.

I said, "Mom, do you remember when I was a little girl, you taught me the song 'The Wise Man Built His House Upon the Rock.'

We used to sing that song almost joyfully.

We made motions of the rains coming down and floods going up and smiling all the while.

I was reading the Bible last night and God gave me new eyes for something I had never recognized until then.

You are that wise man, Mom.

You listened to His words.

You put them into practice.

You spent your entire 66 years doing that very thing.

And when those rains came down . . . and they did . . . it was not light, whispy rain and bubbling streams.

It was torrential downpours and raging floods . . . it was cancer.

And when those streams rose . . . and they did . . . it was radiation, surgeries and, chemotherapy.

And when those winds blew and beat against the house . . . and they did . . . it was pain like few of us have ever known.

But in spite of it all,

Your house was saved, Mom!"

At that point, I was holding my Bible in one hand and rubbing her arm with the other, all the while listening to the machine help her to breathe and keeping an eye on her monitor on the wall.

Now, I looked deep into her eyes and said,

"You did it, Mom!

You heard Jesus' words and you put them into practice your entire life!

Your house was beaten. Your house was battered.

But you did not fall!

You stood on that Rock and you could not be shaken!

You did it, Mom!"

She smiled at me through the mask.

I put my Bible down and said,

"And THAT is the end of today's sermon."

Then she giggled out loud.

And those of us who knew Mom, know exactly what that sounds like. ☺

I cannot be more thankful for the example that she not only taught me as a little girl, but more importantly, lived out right in front of my eyes until I saw her take her last breath.

Through her example, I know and believe, that it is possible to experience horrific pain, incredible disappointment, endless struggle, and deep suffering and still trust that God loves us and cares for us in the midst of it all.

Thank you, Mom. I love you.

-Renee

CHAPTER 73

Williamsport ICU

. . . But we have this treasure in jars of clay
to show that this all-surpassing power is from God
and not from us. [8] We are hard pressed on every side,
but not crushed; perplexed, but not in despair; [9] persecuted,
but not abandoned; struck down, but not destroyed.

[16]Therefore we do not lose heart. Though outwardly we are wasting away,
yet inwardly we are being renewed day by day.

II Corinthians 4:7-9, 16

W e were able to converse and she seemed much more relaxed in spite of all the tubes and the BY PAP to aid her breathing. She could actually talk through the mask, albeit a struggle.

Cat-scans, x-rays, and a cardiogram were taken. BP, heart, respiration and temperature were constantly and digitally monitored. The beeping of the monitors was unsettling as I watched the numbers and lines fluctuating rapidly and irregularly.

Nurses charted and did regular monitor readings. Her nourishment was clear soup and water sipped through a straw.

Mike came to give support to Lori and I. The rest were on their way a.s.a.p. Tension was building. By late evening most of the children and grandkids had arrived. The college girls showed up about midnight. Lori and I kept contact with everyone by cell phone checking to see how far they were. Tears fell freely that evening for fear of losing Susan before all the family arrived. Speed limits were ignored, hoping, and praying desperately to get to the ICU before it was too late.

Thank God they all arrived safely while Susan could still clearly converse with each of them. Since it was a weekend, there was a large empty room available for all of them to spread out . . . on chairs, couches, or the floor. Sleep did not come. They took turns standing by her bedside in small groups, visiting. By Sunday afternoon, I decided we should all be together in the room. All of us had time to hold her hands, pray, cry and talk with her that day.

For brief moments, we removed the breathing apparatus so she could kiss each one and whisper a final "I love you," eyes full of tears. And if you knew Susan, you know a smile would accompany her love words, even through the pain of the inevitability. It broke her heart to see her precious little ones heartbroken. What could she say? What was she pondering? What could she do? Nothing but smile through the tears and squeeze their tender little hands.

I cast all my cares upon you . . . I lay all my burdens, down at your feet . . . anytime I don't know what to do; I will cast all my cares upon you. A little familiar chorus from the past that we sang, prayed, and attempted to practice.

Prior to everyone getting there, Dr. K. decided it was worth tapping the fluid from her right lung, a procedure called *thoracentesis*. First he asked if I and Mike and Big Mike wished to see the c-scans. I hesitated first but then agreed we probably should take a look. At the sight of a large blackened area, my heart sank. Yes, there indeed was lots of fluid. This tap would alleviate her labored breathing, at least for a time.

The order was given and preparations made. He had her sit on the edge of the bed facing me as I stood. Then he explained that he would be inserting this long needle (about 8"), into her lung from her back. Oh, how it hurts me to recall procedures like this. She had so many different ones over the years. Her body had become a pin cushion and a battle ground between cancer and hope. (By the way . . . hope won, the cancer died!)

He then instructed me to stand on the opposite side of him as he pushed and I supported Susan. He numbed the area and soon began drawing the fluid. I am continually amazed at her pain threshold, how gracefully she withstood the onslaught of tests, treatments, needle after needle until there was no good vein left to draw from.

When Dr. K. finished, he had drawn almost two liters. The procedure helped for a day or two but he concluded not to repeat the procedure. The high risk of infection and the severity of the tumors nullified its success.

Have mercy on me, my God, have mercy on me,
for in you I take refuge. I will take refuge in the shadow of your wings
until the disaster has passed.
Psalm 57:1

Hear my cry, O God listen to my prayer.
From the ends of the earth I call to you,
I call as my heart grows faint;
Ps. 61

By the next day, Sunday, another scan revealed more fluid build-up. It signified the rapid spread of cancer and her body's inability to cope.

Dear God! How do we pray? What is your plan? We submit to You, we surrender her body to You, I prayed, but please be merciful and gracious with my dear, sweet, Susan.

I insisted someone always be there holding her hand, ready to respond for whatever she may need. She slept some, but tried to converse with whomever was there when awake.

The older grandchildren had to drive back to Virginia for school Monday. One by one, hesitantly and emotionally spent, they went back in the room to say goodbye. It was one of the most heartbreaking and agonizing experiences our family encountered. The girls trembled with grief, knowing it was their last visit with MawMaw on earth.

For we know that if the earthly tent we live in is destroyed,
we have a building from God, an eternal house in heaven,
not built by human hands.
II Corinthians 5:1

If it was not for the assurance of eternal life and seeing her again, it would be hell on earth and hopeless. And so after kisses and hugs from us, they left . . . slowly and sobbing. Not only my heart, but my whole being ached! I can only imagine what Susan felt.

Now Renee's husband, Rod, and the two youngest girls . . . Brenda's husband, Eugene and their son Tyler . . . Mike's wife, Mercy and the boys, all began their painful process of last goodbyes. They too had to get home for work and school. The bonding experienced in those final moments with Susan sprayed a sweet fragrance of love and compassion that I shall re-

The Gateway

member to my dying day. It was a priceless treasured gift poured out on Susan and me. I cannot express the gratitude in my heart for the love of a caring family. Thank you!

By Monday noon, Dr. K., the nurses and our family doctor, Dr. P., agreed that we should consider moving Susan over to *"The Gatehouse"* at Divine Providence. He kindly and briefly explained to us that it was a hospice unit where Susan and our family, would be much more comfortable. Exactly what is . . . . *The Gatehouse?*

CHAPTER 74

The Gatehouse (Inpatient Hospice)

The Gatehouse is a seven-bed short-term in-patient Hospice unit for the management of pain and other symptoms relating to a life-threatening illness. In addition, patients who are struggling with discomfort may come to the unit for treatment, then return home or other living arrangements.

By providing a peaceful, home-like environment, The Gatehouse makes a difficult time easier for both the patient and his or her loved ones. Families can spend quality time with patients in private bedroom suites, a comfortable family room, a kitchen and a meditation room—all while patients receive around-the-clock, skilled nursing care to manage their difficult symptoms.

Alexander Nesbitt, M.D., Hospice medical director, brings a great deal of compassion, training and expertise to the Hospice Program. He has been with Hospice since 2000 and is the only physician in the area who is Board Certified in Hospice and Palliative Medicine. Dr. Nesbitt works full-time overseeing Hospice care in patients' homes and in the inpatient Hospice unit, The Gatehouse. He has dedicated his life to providing much needed care to patients at the end of their lives.

The air was brisk but the sun peeked out as Susan was being positioned into the ambulance for the short transport to The Gatehouse. As I touched her arm and blew a kiss, I thought . . . *This is probably her last earthly ride before Heaven.*

The Gatehouse was cheerfully decorated, spacious and comfortably arranged. Susan's bed faced the bathroom which she instantly noticed and asked to see. So we wheeled the bed closer as she affirmed the accommodations. At first she expressed hope of getting a shower until we encouraged her to just rest for now.

While she was being checked, she said she was hungry. *Whoa . . . that's good* we thought, and asked her, "For what?"

"Soup," she said, "do they have any tomato soup?"

Mike quickly ran to the kitchen scrounging for any soup and came back with a can. She asked him if they didn't have any chunky style? Back he ran to check soon returning with a larger bowl of some soup. It was one of those strange, unexplained spurts of energy and alertness that we reveled in for a few minutes. Laughter mixed with tears can be a welcome respite.

It was so like Susan. She knew what she wanted and how much. We embraced the moment. At The Gatehouse, their goal is to make the patient comfortable without all the monitors, tubes, needles, beeps and buzzing. Even the BY PAK mask was exchanged for a more comfortable one.

"The Lord is my shepherd, I lack nothing. He makes me lie down in green pastures, he leads me beside quiet waters, he refreshes my soul . . . even though I walk through the darkest valley, I will fear no evil, for you are with me . . . ." Ps. 23 NIV

All my children, Mike, Lori, Brenda and Renee insisted on staying until the end . . . or whatever. The Gatehouse provides separate rooms for family to sleep in. So the girls had one and Mike and I another. We took turns doing care vigils and sleep shifts for the next four days. We'd sleep for three to four hours and then sit together with Susan as she rested. Many hours we all just sat close together, reminisced, prayed and read scripture, some to Mom, and some to ourselves. It was a tender time of divinely anointed bonding. Nurses came in every 20 minutes to check on her, change dressings, dispense medicine and do charting.

Susan occasionally opened her eyes but rarely spoke. When she did, we all were instantly alert and listening. We stroked her smooth unwrinkled arms, rubbed her feet and back, kissed her sweet body, cried and laughed. The closest thing to an earthly miracle of healing, of seeing angels over her bed, or having Jesus enter to heal her, came in the form of the director of The Gatehouse—Dear Doctor Nisbett.

If ever we saw Jesus in action on earth, it was through Doctor Nisbett. Humbly and quietly he sat down with us. With compassionate tear-filled eyes, he asked what he could do for us. He wondered if we thought Susan was comfortable from our perspective. He explained to us how they would care for her without all the distressing complexity of the ICU.

He sat, listening, watching and pondering before he carefully spoke a word. He assured us that Susan was now more comfortable and not experiencing pain. Thank you Jesus! They were words of comfort and encouragement . . . words from experience having dealt with death, pain and suffering.

He was a faithful husband, caring father, educated physician, but most importantly, he spoke words from the heart of God himself. Thank you Doctor Nisbett.

The nurses also deserve much praise. It was evident they were there to fulfill a calling and not a paycheck. One nurse was nearly due to deliver a baby. She delivered a few days after Susan's death.

The girls sat facing the window and noticed something strange happening. It was a cold snowy day with about 8" piling up in the parking lot.

"Look," they said, "the snow is going up." Sure enough, next to the window of Susan's room, snow was not descending, it was ascending. It was at this moment, four days after she entered The Gatehouse that Susan drew her last breath.

> Precious in the sight of the Lord
> is the death of his faithful servants.
> Ps. 116: 15 NIV

We felt the snow was significant and indicative of what Susan was now experiencing. Her spirit was ascending. Death came softly and peacefully without any indication of pain. We stood at the bedside, hands on her body, sobbing as Susan and a host of angels danced with joy. It was her Heavenly birthday! She had made it Home. She had fought a good fight, run the race, kept the faith. She had FINISHED WELL and was welcomed home by a huge cloud of witnesses unseen to us, but embraced by her.

> I have fought the good fight, I have finished the race,
> I have kept the faith. [8] Now there is in store for me
> the crown of righteousness, which the Lord, the righteous Judge,
> will award to me on that day—and not only to me,
> but also to all who have longed for his appearing.
> II Timothy 4: 7-8

It was over. The battle was finally won, although not by our design. But we surrendered our lives and Susan's into God's hands. A strange and subtle relief settled over us. Through the tears, we began making phone calls, signing papers and gathering our belongings.

Now to face the inevitable—prepare for the graveside service, memorial service and greet a multitude of friends, family and acquaintances.

Celebrating 45 years of marriage—the photo on the cover of Susan's Memorial Service and this book.

Surely your goodness and mercy shall follow me
all the days of my life,
and I will dwell in the house of the Lord forever.
Ps. 23: 6 KJV

IN CELEBRATION OF THE LIFE OF SUSAN LANDIS SOUDER
March 31, 1943 ~ February 26, 2010

The above picture was taken at a friend's wedding. We rarely danced due to our conservative roots. This photo reflects the prize for the couple married the longest on the dance floor at Jonica's wedding.

Strangely enough, I'm writing these memories of exactly three years ago today, March 6. It was an unusually warm day as our entire family walked slowly up the road to St. Peter's Cemetery. It's nestled between woods and a field along our road. The burial lot faces our farm across the road.

The words of an old gospel hymn remind me that . . . *this world is not my home, I'm just passing through.*

Toby walks next to me on a leash. My family is all around me. Many friends and extended family stand waiting at the gravesite. It's a surreal scene as we gather around. From the far side, a trumpet plays "It Is Well With My Soul." Yes, my soul is secure. It's my emotions that are shaky.

Someone reads from Psalms 57 and 61. "In God is our refuge and hope. We find rest in Him alone."

Our tear-stained roses are gently placed on the casket. *Can this be real?* Nothing is heard but the soft sobbing of grieving loved ones. Words cannot explain the throbbing in our hearts as we embrace each other. It's over, the battle is done. But for us as Christians, it's been won!

By noon, a host of friends join us 35 miles away at CBC—Community Baptist Church. LHF is way too small to accommodate this crowd.

Only two weeks ago Pastor Wheeler introduced himself when he stopped by The Gatehouse to visit. I had never met this meek, humble, and compassionate man. He offered his help even so far as to offer their facilities if we needed them. We did.

About 300 people gathered to celebrate Susan's life. We sang favorite hymns and a few choruses and shared our broken hearts with our friends. Pastor Scot, whom we've known from a child, shared scriptures she loved. He spoke kindly of her patient battle with cancer. Scot often reminded Susan of seeing the smiling face of Jesus on and through her.

Our kids and grandkids shared tributes which I've recorded in the next chapters.

School friends, neighbors, nurses, doctors, many church acquaintances, some of her aging family and some we didn't know greeted us in line.

LHF catered the meal with such style and abundance that her sisters would have proudly affirmed.

A family photo finished the memorable day of celebration. The angels, Susan, and the huge cloud of heavenly witnesses rejoiced . . . including Pastor Wheeler. Now he too has joined the heavenly hosts. I wonder . . . *Did they have an angel food cake?*

One last note regarding her memorial, the funeral director posted an online guestbook for folks to sign. Within a few days, the book recorded 16 pages, way more than he had ever seen in over 25 years.

CHAPTER 75

Brenda's Tribute

When I think of Mom, words like humble, forgiving, loving, funny, patient, compassionate heart, and generous come to my mind.

Mom had a gift of encouraging others. It was always important to her that we learn to send thank you notes and birthday cards to people.

She continued to do that even when she was not well. Reaching beyond herself was only part of what made her so special. Hopefully, I have instilled this in my kids by reminding them to be thoughtful.

Mom's unconditional love and forgiveness helped me get through some rebellious teen years. I knew she was praying and covering my life like a blanket—taking me safely through those times. She always had notes on the table when I'd come home late at night, not scolding or critical, just: "We love you, Bren. See you in the morning."

It was the grace she dumped on me that brought me back to my deep roots in Jesus.

Mom let me practice on her continuously, when I went through Cosmetology School. She was always so gracious and willing to be of help, encouraging my career.

Now, as I do hair for ladies in the Retirement Community, I often think of Mom and how she helped me to be comfortable and loving with the elderly. She always took us to visit the residents where she worked as a nurse when I was growing up. They loved her so much.

Mom was so nurturing. I like to think I got that from her when I became a Mom, but my kids would probably use the words: smothering or suffocating. Mom just had a way of making us feel loved and cared for every day, even when I moved away, she always brought each of our favorite foods when she came to Virginia. Bean salad for Eugene, *funny cake* for Ciara and *hard cakes* for Tyler, etc. Dad would come in with huge coolers and boxes of food for our pantries and freezers giving us this look like: "You know Mom!"

I find myself doing this for our daughter now that she has her own apartment at school . . . and MawMaw lives on!

One of Mom's favorite quotes that we've talked about often was: "Be kind . . . for everyone you meet is facing a battle of their own."

I love this and will be forever changed, keeping my eyes open to others . . . because that's what Mom did even in her last days here on earth.

In honor of Mom . . . Be kind.

Bren

CHAPTER 76

Lori's Tribute

I'M LORI, DAUGHTER #3

Most of my life I took my mom for granted. She washed my clothes, sang songs to me at bedtime, drove me to piano lessons, and made my favorite meals for birthdays. She later kept my children overnight and always encouraged Mike and me to have dates as often as possible . . . but honestly—sometimes my mom could drive me crazy.

During the teen years, she'd insist that we eat a good breakfast before school and when my friends spent the night she'd call up the stairs, "What do you want for breakfast girls?" I'd yell back down, "Nothing"—just wanting to spend time in front of the mirror and get on the bus . . . but my girlfriends would whisper, "Tell her French toast or eggs and bacon and blueberry pancakes." They knew she'd make anything we wanted. My friends loved mom.

During wedding planning time I decided I wanted the guys to wear shorts and go barefoot. It was an outside wedding. I didn't want a big meal—just cake and fruit. Well, the guys being barefoot didn't really make her even raise her eyebrows but the "just cake and fruit" part—THIS was a problem. You know mom, she could NOT have people driving from a distance and not feed them properly. End of story . . . there was appetizers and chicken and pasta and salads and fruit and cake—enough for two weddings!

You know mom loved the phone. So many times, in the past 15 years, I'd hear the phone ring then run through the hall, down the stairs, find the portable phone somewhere on the other side of the house and it would be mom saying, "Hi Lor, I'm thinking about Easter dinner. Do you think we should have French cut green beans or the regular cut kind?" Oh mom, she loved the details.

Well, in the past year, she had to give up tending to the details. Her body became more and more broken. But she became more and more valuable to me. I treasured her more, when she couldn't physically do anything for me, than I had during my whole life. I cared for mom in ways I never imagined I would, helping her dress, fixing the wig on her head, trimming her toenails, fixing her lunch on a little tray. She handled it with such grace and humility and gratefulness to me.

This scarf I'm wearing is mom's. I remember when she saw it at Talbot's and loved it. She said she would never pay that amount for a scarf. Dad bought it for her of course. I think she only wore it once. In the last few months, I'd push her, in her wheelchair, into her closet and she'd look at that scarf and say, "I wish I had an opportunity to wear that scarf again." She never did. Well, there's no better opportunity than today mom—here, in celebration of your life. I'm sure you're wearing way more beautiful silk scarves in Heaven—a new color for each day. I can barely wait to share them with you one day in our forever Home.

CHAPTER 77

Mike's Tribute

March 6, 2010
Dear Mom,

Hi mom. I wonder if you saw all the people who came to church last night to visit. It was incredible seeing all those wonderful people who knew you. Some you met once and some you've known your whole life. You left a profound impact on many. No one loved us quite like you did.

You were always generous with your "I love you's"—telling us several times a day. Writing "I love you's" on post-it notes attached to everything. I have a couple voice mails of yours saved on my cell phone just so I could hear you say it again and again and again . . . It's one of those phrases that never gets diluted. And now we tell our children the same thing—all throughout the day.

It brings me peace to know that you were able to love us like this not because you were superhuman, but because you knew (and now KNOW better) the God who calls himself Love. You always had a fresh well of love and patience and grace for us, for me especially.

Or do you show contempt for the riches of his kindness,
tolerance and patience, not realizing that
God's kindness leads you toward repentance?
Romans 2:4 NIV

There were times in my life where I took for granted all the kindness, tolerance, and patience you POURED over me. Even when I was getting home at 5 a.m (and I know I must have worried you sick), there would always be a note—*"Mike: Glad you're home safe, see you in the morning, I love you."*

You didn't judge me or lecture me or try and DEBATE my way into Heaven. You saw through my attitude and my self-centered, reckless behavior and believed in something far better for me. In the same way the sun slowly and steadily melts the snow, God's kindness, through you, changed me. You showed

385

me the qualities of Jesus that I couldn't deny. Who could reject a love like this? Thank you, thank you, thank you.

The often-quoted love chapter (1 Cor. 13) really starts with the last verse of Chapter 12: *"And now I will show you the most excellent way"* . . .

You knew the most excellent way of raising us as kids, loving your husband, serving this community.

It was a life of RELENTLESS . . .

Love

Joy

Peace

Patience

Kindness

Goodness

Gentleness

Faithfulness

Self-control.

Thank you for caring for us like this.

You are the best mom a son could ask for and with God's help, I will be faithful to carry on your most excellent way.

I love you.

Mike

Mike and Dad kayaking the sock.

CHAPTER 78

Grandkids' Tributes — Three Oldest

CIARA:

Summers in Pennsylvania were always special for Rach, Bekah, and I because we got to have our Poppie and Mawmaw all to ourselves. Mawmaw loved teaching us how to make our favorites: strawberry jam, pasta salad, Grammy's tea, and blueberry buckle.

I will always treasure my special summer in the mountains. Last summer I had the privilege of living with Mawmaw and Poppie. The memories we shared will stay with me forever. Every morning I looked forward to taking coffee and morning cake into Mawmaw's room and talking with her. Whether I was having boy issues or just wanted to chat, she gave me wise and encouraging words perfect for the situation. It was always a fun afternoon when I got to work on my latest art project with her. We would drink tea and watch cooking shows and she would ask me questions about my art. She showed faith in my creativity and constantly affirmed whatever I worked on. At dinnertime, Mawmaw patiently and joyfully taught me family recipes that I now use in my own kitchen. And every night when I would come home from waitressing, she would ask, "Well, did you make good tips?" Always showing her concern for others; always encouraging; always being a blessing and an inspiration to everyone around her . . . I love her so much and am so proud to call this friend of mine, Mawmaw.

RACHEL:

We were always excited to play Chickenfoot and Dutch Blitz with Mawmaw and Poppie, and watch "Family Feud" and cooking shows with Mawmaw. We loved taking day trips with Mawmaw; shopping, followed by a treat at the Jolly Trolley. Mawmaw always ordered one vanilla shake, one chocolate shake, one basket of onion rings, and one basket of fries to share.

Many of you may not know what a sense of humor my Mawmaw had, but she never failed to make me laugh. I remember finding it hilarious when she knocked over a rack of clothes at the Jolly Trolley and then said, "That was a riot!" when I teased her about it later. Even just a few weeks ago in her room in the ICU, she gave us a little comic relief by saying, "I never did like attention, but I guess this is a sure way to get it!" ☺ Just recently I've had a chance to share my passion for nursing with Mawmaw. She was always interested to hear how my anatomy class was going, and how my nursing meetings went. I can't wait to follow in her footsteps and serve the Lord and other people through my career. I am so grateful for the time I got to spend with, and get to know this amazing, gracious, courageous woman of Jesus. I am so thankful she fought for us as long as she did. Mawmaw, you're my hero. ☺

BEKAH:

We remember working in the garden with Mawmaw, French-cutting and canning green beans, picking huckleberries with coffee cans tied around our necks, and gathering fresh flowers to put all around the house.

Almond Joys and French fries were favorites of ours
Along with cooking in the kitchen and picking
bouquets of flowers.
She lived far away, but never missed a beat
Arriving at my soccer games and plays, cheering from her seat.
My family made many trips from Virginia to PA
She made her house a home, my favorite place to stay.
Open arms at the door, and welcome signs on the table
Everything in its perfect place, with her famous post-it label.
She smelled of lavender and had beautiful soft skin
Along with a sense of humor and a sunshiny grin.
She held her head high when life wasn't fair
And faithfully she lived, with love and through prayer.
My Mawmaw loved Jesus with every beat of her heart
And decided to trust him completely from the very start.
I so admire the way she joyfully lived her life
No one could ask for a better Mawmaw, Mother,
Best friend, or Wife.
I will love you Mawmaw, all of my days
But you deserve to be with Jesus now, forever and always.

CHAPTER 79

My Grateful Tribute

Written and read by me at the memorial service. March 6, 2010.

TO MY LIFELONG FRIEND,
SWEETHEART, LOVER, COMPANION, & SOULMATE

Almost 47 years we have loved and cared for each other as we promised we would. My most precious and sacred memories are those where I had the privilege to care for her 24/7 when she could no longer care for me or herself. When we said our vows, we meant it . . . "for better or for worse, in sickness and in health, till death do us part" . . . though we were very naive.

Thank you honey . . . for choosing me for your husband and best friend . . . for all the love notes stashed away in our nightstand from our teen years till just a week ago . . . for saving all the cards we gave each other so we could read them over again. . . . .

For being willing to leave family and friends to move to Sullivan Co. to help with the church.

For birthing our four wonderful children.

For loving each of them through every phase of life unconditionally.

For loving each of their spouses just as much as our kids.

For consistently showing your love to each of the 11 grandkids.

For sacrificing your wants to make time to provide fresh canned and frozen food for us.

For taking the time to make beef roast, gravy and smooth mashed potatoes, and corn.

For baking the special pies you know I liked . . . ground cherry, strawberry rhubarb and apple.

For driving the tractor to rake hay before the thunderstorm came so I could bale hay.

For driving clear to Wyalusing to pick me up late at night when I was doing custom combining, and bringing my lunch out in the field.

For your wonderful one in a million SMILE that greeted me every time I came in the house.

For feeding the calves, chickens and whatever else we had when I had to be away down country while at the same time caring for the kids.

Making time to teach Bible school, Sunday School classes, Girls' clubs and Youth group.

For caring so deeply and tenderly for the DarWay residents those 13 years before cancer.

For always looking out for the needs of others rather than complaining about your own limitations.

For being a hospice volunteer and caring so much for those dear souls.

For your devotion to Jesus and your concern that others know Him too.

For your deep unwavering love for me through all our years together.

So many people are going to miss you honey—people you probably never thought of—like:

The Frontier phone company . . . I don't like the phone like you did.

Wal-Mart Pharmacy . . . they won't see me as much, thank God, but they'll get over it.

The home health nurses, P.T, the chemo and radiation staff . . . but I'm glad you don't need their help anymore.

Drs. L., H., S., P., N., K., A., and others will miss your sweet smile and gentle spirit. They will be happy you are finally free from cancer—forever!

Your sisters will miss hearing your voice on the phone when they call you, and you ask them how they are doing before they get to ask you.

Toby already is disoriented not finding your warm lap to sleep in.

And of course I will miss doing the BEST SERVICE PROJECT I was ever called to do . . . caring for you.

We will never know how far and wide your light has reached. It was much brighter than you ever imagined.

Over the last few years, our love for each other has blossomed so much deeper and purer in spite of this horrendous 15-year journey with cancer. I would rather God could have chosen a smoother path or a different tool to accomplish the same results. But I'm not God and I choose to believe that His ways are best and much higher and beyond comprehension.

As surely as cancer is evil and bad . . . God is good and faithful and we chose to trust His plan.

I've not shared details of Susan's battle with cancer, particularly the past year. It was one she fought with grace and dignity. That will take a book that I hope to write some day.

I cannot tell you how blessed I am to have been her husband and care-giver. I don't regret one minute of serving my sweetheart.

In closing, I want to read the words to a song written by Robin Mark:

"WHEN IT'S ALL SAID AND DONE"

When it's all been said and done
There is just one thing that matters
Did I do my best to live for truth?
Did I live my life for you?
When it's all been said and done
All my treasures will mean nothing
Only what I have done
For love's rewards
Will stand the test of time
Lord, your mercy is so great
That you look beyond our weakness
That you found purest gold in miry clay
Turning sinners into saints
I will always sing your praise
Here on earth and in heaven after
For you've joined me at my true home
When it's all been said and done
You're my life when life is gone.

Someone wrote this about Susan; I quote "If our glory is to reflect Jesus as the moon reflects the sun, Susan was a FULL MOON."

Thanks Honey, for letting Jesus' love shine so brightly through your life and loving me so deeply.

CHAPTER 80

Bowery Mission Trips

Written February 1, 2011

Haggy's Bus was waiting at Rockhill Church Sunday afternoon. People of all ages were filling the big bus scheduled to leave at 2:00 for the Bowery Mission in New York City. The MYF was also represented by at least a dozen teens including Susan and myself. This was our first trip to the Bowery but not the last. It would leave an imprint on our lives in more ways than one. It was a chance for us to be together—close together. Four hours up, three at the Bowery and four hours back.

Here . . . I'll let you read Susan's intimate words directly from one of her diaries:

November 29, 1961 – "<u>We</u>" left at twenty of two for the Bowery. A group from Rockhill went. We played alphabets a lot of the way and jacks. We ate our lunch when the bus stopped. Clint Landis, their minister, had a terrific sermon for the men, but it also challenged me!! During the invitation, at least seven came up to the altar. It was really touching. Afterward, they treated us to coffee and buns. We left for home around quarter after nine. We had such a neat time on the way home. After a night like tonight with my Honey, it makes me wish we had trips like this every week!!"

"I got my 'wish' tonight." It was indescribable!!

November 30, 1961 - A few lines;

"I wish it was last night this time!! Then we'd have the whole ride home from the Bowery in front of us yet!! I had that study with 'Him' again today. Got nothing done – like usual. The seniors played the faculty today in activities period. The seniors were terrific – especially "my lover boy!" I'm so glad for my honey's picture!! When I got in my room tonight, I just sat and looked at it for a long time! (I even kissed it!) but it wasn't like the real him!"

This was written about one year before our wedding. Can you tell she liked/loved me? Duh!

The ironic thing is . . . I now sit in my bedroom and look at her pictures for a REAL long time, and think; *She's so beautiful, so full of life, so pure, so . . . well . . . look at that smile, I just want to grab her and squeeze her tightly. She looks so happy, so cute, so HER, so healthy. Now she* **really** *IS* . . . and then . . . I kiss her picture.

But she's right; it's not like the real her! Thank God for pictures though. At least it is *still* life.

So you see my children, there's a glimpse of why I say . . . . your Mom was one, hot Mamma . . . a great lover. A great communicator—even when she was silent.

I could tell when she was upset, what she was feeling, thinking, wishing, praying, lamenting, hoping, or planning. I could just tell. After dating her four years and living with her for 47 more, we had *better* know each other that good.

There were other trips to the Bowery and each was memorable. The experience of seeing humanity at such a low state and then to witness God's love breaking through was inspiring.

"I am come that they may have life, and have it to the fullest," Jesus. Jn. 10:10

Obviously, sharing a bus seat with my teenage honey was romantic; a good day and a night to remember.

CHAPTER 81

Pink Knit Gloves

Written six months after Susan's death for a writing class.

. . . Preserved in a plastic bag resting in a drawer for over 50 years were these dainty, hand-knit pink gloves. I can see and hear my sister and me talking about this being a perfect Christmas gift for my fifteen-year-old sweetheart. She had totally captured my attention and love and I wanted to impress her with something special. A little knit flower on the ruffle with a small shiny stone in the middle . . . gloves way too small for male hands . . . the smell of many days gone by, but the memory of her opening the thin white box and her special sweet smile said it all. She liked them. She loves me. They warmed the hands that caressed my cheeks . . . that held me tight . . . that calmed my fears and worries. It may have been puppy love but it grew into an ocean deep love that matured through a lifetime. Here they lay on my chair . . . still and unused . . . her one hand no longer able to use a glove . . . crippled from cancer . . . and now totally whole and healed in Heaven. But they ooze happiness, joy, peace and a deep compassionate love . . . those little pink gloves.

* * * * *

The song below ministered to us so often throughout Susan's final days and the years after. In fact, we played it during Marliss' and my wedding which you will learn more about. Please ponder carefully the inspired words written by Laura Story:

"BLESSINGS"

We pray for blessings
We pray for peace
Comfort for family, protection while we sleep
We pray for healing, for prosperity
We pray for Your mighty hand to ease our suffering

All the while, You hear each spoken need
Yet love us way too much to give us lesser things

'Cause what if your blessings come through raindrops
What if Your healing comes through tears
What if a thousand sleepless nights
Are what it takes to know You're near
What if trials of this life are Your mercies in disguise

We pray for wisdom
Your voice to hear
And we cry in anger when we cannot feel You near
We doubt Your goodness, we doubt Your love
As if every promise from Your Word is not enough
All the while, You hear each desperate plea
But long that we'd have the faith to believe

'Cause what if your blessings come through raindrops
What if Your healing comes through tears
What if a thousand sleepless nights
Are what it takes to know You're near
And what if trials of this life are Your mercies in disguise

When friends betray us
When darkness seems to win
We know the pain reminds this heart
That this is not, this is not our home,

'Cause what if your blessings come through raindrops
What if Your healing comes through tears
And what if a thousand sleepless nights
Are what it takes to know You're near
What if my greatest disappointments
Or the aching of this life
Is the revealing of a greater thirst this world can't satisfy
And what if trials of this life
The rain, the storms, the hardest nights
Are your mercies in disguise

CHAPTER 82

"Mom's Clothes"

Written June 22, 2010

We began sorting out Mom's clothes today. The girls asked me before they started if I was really ready for this and I assured them I was. I'd been in and out of the closet for almost four months since she died, without too many tears. The closet has been way too full with not only clothes but lots of things we needed to help keep her comfortable. So, why not take out her clothes and decide who gets what. They wanted me nearby and I wanted to be a part of it.

What I wasn't ready for was watching clothes go into bags that I loved seeing her wear. Even though I knew the girls and grandkids would get some and maybe her sisters too, that wasn't the issue. When I saw the red sweaters come down and the dresses I ordered from the "Coldwater" catalogue for her for Christmas and birthdays go into bags, I lost it. The knot in my stomach had already moved up to my throat and was about to unravel me as I cried . . . "I can't handle this."

Renee and Lori both softly commented that they knew it would be very difficult and they were concerned for me. So I went to the den and sat in my desk chair and let it out . . . quietly as I could. It felt like we were erasing her from my life little by little, bag by bag and I didn't want to let go or give up the good memories of the clothes that covered my sweet Susan. I know they were just clothes . . . material possessions we all need to part with sometime but . . . how . . . when?

The thought crossed my mind later this evening of what the Mother of Jesus felt as she sat near the cross watching the soldiers crucify her son and cast lots for His clothes. I know . . . there is NO comparison . . . but I wondered.

I sat and cried as I noticed the memorial card of her beautiful face and well-dressed body staring back at me from my desk. I tried to distract myself by going out to get the mail, but found only three pieces of junk mail. More tears. I turned from the computer to my desk and saw another picture of her. They are everywhere and I want it that way. She was so beautiful.

I gathered my composure and walked into our bedroom where piles of clothes were strewn down the hallway. The girls were folding clothes on the bed and Toby was curled up in the middle of them. I said I had no idea it would hit me this way. They were very caring and compassionate and said they prayed before starting and agreed to see it as only clothes, knowing Mom would have wanted them to "just get on with it." I totally agree . . . but unless you've lost a spouse or Mother who was very dear to you, the impact is different.

I suggested that we keep a few items which were my gifts to her . . . two sweaters and they chose an outfit which I'd been thinking about as well. We also decided to keep outfits, shirts and skirts which they really liked on her and ask her sister Mary Jane to make something with some of them—scarves, hankies, pillow covers—to be creative. I liked that idea better than boxing or bagging them all up for Goodwill.

I decided to call Nancy Mueller. She and her husband Rick are physical therapists who live just up the road. They were an incredible help over the past year. Every day for a solid month last year they came teaching me techniques to help Susan. They brought us transfer boards, belts, ankle supports, wrist braces, drop arm bedside commode—you name it. All free of any charge. They would come at the drop of a hat whenever we needed help. They showed me how to help get her into and out of the car. They showed me how to get her from the lift chair to the wheelchair, from the bed to the commode, the car to the wheelchair, and how to sit her up and lie her down without hurting my own back.

I needed to return all these "handicap tools." Nancy came and with much compassion, remarked how Susan was such a special person and had worked so hard and gracefully, it was truly amazing.

There were many items we needed to decide how to disperse of them.

Today we had planned to go to Knoebel's but then it started raining. So we decided to sort clothes. I'm glad that part is over. There is more to go through but not for right now. The dresser has things in it that I can't give up yet.

Night is hard enough without her and I will keep her nighties and other things for now. I know God understands and certainly all the kids understand. They are so good to me and so patient and offer wise counsel. We sure do need each other.

Dear God, we need your mercy and grace to get us through this difficult transition from what was normal to what seems so foggy and strange. Thank You for the strength You gave the girls today. Thanks for all my children, seeing them follow after You . . . for the grandchildren, each one so beautiful and special.

Why have we been so blessed? Thanks for the wonderful 47 years You gave me with such a special Godly woman as my Sweet Susan. Oh how blessed I am. And oh, how I miss her. If it weren't for the fact her pain and suffering is over, I would want her back until the day I die. But knowing she is with You dancing for joy and forever free of pain, I can live with hope eternal.

I love you honey! I love you Renee, Bren, Lor, and Mike! I love all "twelve," yes twelve grandchildren. I love you all BIG MUCH!

I love you Lord,

Goodnight.

CHAPTER 83

I hugged her last night . . .

Written November 3, 2010

I saw her walking toward me outside in a park. I ran up to her and hugging her I said, "I'm so glad to see you, honey. Let's go over here and lay down on this bench."

We lay there facing each other for a short while. She was beautiful, youthful, perfectly healthy and yes, it was my real Sweet Susan. As dreams go . . . the next scene was me wondering where she went, looking for her. I found her inside a house with other people in pj's helping to clean house. Weird. Then we were soon outside again walking and talking together. She was young and even more beautiful than I always saw her.

I woke up hugging a blanket realizing it was not her and remember saying, "Oh honey, honey." Instantly she was very close smiling at me. I remember waking, sitting up with eyes wide open and looking intently as she slowly faded and disappeared. I blinked and she was gone.

I was now awake with scrambled and fragile emotions to ponder. To hug her, have her alive and close if only for a moment, was worth the hurt of seeing her fading away again.

I *know* where she is.

I'm going to keep a journal by the bed from now on.

CHAPTER 84

What's It Like, Honey?

Written February 19, 2011

Dreams and my imagination cannot grasp what it's like for you. You've been gone for a year now. It seems like an eternity sometimes and other days, seems like yesterday that you left. You said good riddance to that battered and pain racked body in exchange for one beyond comprehension. My dreams confirm you as young and beautiful, full of vitality. Is that how you feel? Does it seem long since you last saw us? What did you do this past year? Oh, that's right, time is non-existent there. So how does that work?

It's cozy and warm as I sit writing in my chair. The temperature plummeted from 60 to 25 in twelve hours. Yes, I'm still into weather watching. You know me. There's a gusty wind whipping and twisting the trees wildly. Small tornado-like snow squalls dance in contorted style on the side hill behind the barn. The cattle stand at the hay rack bracing themselves against the wind and snow. The bird feeder is empty as seed is scattered by the wind.

Are there snow squalls in heaven? Really? You mean the wind isn't cold and stinging? That's so hard to comprehend—warm, fluffy snow—like colored feathers floating gently across the pearly mansions piling up transparently on the golden streets. Hmmm.

What happens to it?

Hey, where'd you go?

The fire glimmers in the corner of "our" bedroom while Toby sleeps curled up on the edge of the bed. Your pillow has been replaced by his brown doggy bed. *(Sigh, a tear . . .)* A Frisbee, bones and a ball, squeaky chicken, and his bunny toy litter the floor instead of your slippers and socks. Your wheelchair, walker and bedside commode are not here, thank God. *Sigh . . .*

Books and papers, camera, and printer litter the card table next to my chair as I write. The radio is silent and the TV screen is blank instead of gourmet cooking shows. When you were here, I loved watching and learning to cook with you. But no longer.

There they go—the wild tom turkeys heading for the hemlocks at the edge of the side hill field. My binoculars expose their beards. Thanks God. You feed the birds of the air and the beasts of the field. How much more do You care for me? I lift up my eyes to the hills. Where does my help come from? My help comes from You, the creator of heaven and earth . . .

Hey, you're back. No temperature? I don't understand. No degrees of heat or cold in Heaven?

Good grief, now that's a mystery.

Do you miss us, honey? We sure miss you. I mean, we *really* miss you. Yesterday, coming back with the tractor from burying Donna's dog, I got to thinking about last year this time. You could hardly breathe even with oxygen. Cursed cancer! Do you remember that? You don't? Well, it all came rushing back to me—how horrible that must have been for you, and I started to cry. No, I mean bawl. I started pitying myself for not having you near me anymore. I wanted you here so bad. I cried all the way home.

A big log truck passed by and the driver looked at me but had no clue what I was feeling. I parked the tractor in the shed, closed the doors and stumbled into the house still bawling.

Toby jumped up to lick the tears running down my cheeks. I couldn't stop. I grabbed the laundry basket full of clean clothes and walked back to "our" room, set the basket on the bed and walked into "our" closet. Your pretty pink dress suit still hangs next to my suit coat. I buried my face in it and cried hard. When I finally stopped, part of the coat was a darker pink. Sorry, honey. Did you say, you have much brighter silk ones? I should have known.

I hope it's not as hard for you as it is for us. I know, we can't compare, how could we? Only you and the heavenly hosts could understand. I'll try to trust Him with all the unknowns and questions. There's so many.

Are you watching all that's happening down here? No, not the world—our family. Did you know Rod and Renee are on their 25th anniversary cruise now? How 'bout little Eva? Isn't she sweet? Did you know Rach got a 96 on her last test? She's following your footsteps. She'll make a great nurse just like you. Kaiti . . . she's as tall as me now and so athletic. You should check out her *gooie chalk blog*. ☺ Leah, the "always smiling" reader has lots to talk about too. I call Bethy "my little MawMaw." She looks just like you, honey, really.

Did you watch any of Tyler's games? He's as tall as me too and finally filling out. Ciara, she's deeply in love with Joseph. It's tender and sweet, as it should be. Like we were. :)

Emmett and Jude, did you see that cute picture Mikey sent me yesterday? What great little men of God they're turning into. Full of it though.

Rissa calls me once in a while. I love hearing her little girly voice. She's such a trip . . . a little Rach, if you ask me. You probably knew before me that Rayah cut her hair. She's so sweet, even no hair would become her. And Bek-bek, our little Bekah has grown into a model . . . the Godly kind. Are you watching them all grow up? Really? I hope so. Somehow, I thought you were, but only God knows how.

Gettin' hungry. It's 10:30 and time for eggs and bacon. You're kidding. You don't get hungry, but still eat all you want without gaining weight? And nobody ever gets sick? Incredible.

Is it fun preparing all that heavenly food for millions of people? Do you like making giant angel food cakes? I bet you do.

Emma and Mom help too? That's wild.

I'm helping Lor' with worship tomorrow at church. I'm actually enjoying singing again on the worship team. It took a while to get back into that after you left.

What's that sound? I always enjoy harmony you know, but that . . . ? It's the most perfect harmony or . . . how can I explain it . . . music from Heaven. What's that like, honey?

I know . . . I'll just have to wait.

Do you remember this song, honey? Lucy referred to it at your memorial service:

"Save a place for me, I'll be there soon. But don't be sad if I cry, it just hurts so bad sometimes. 'Cause everyday reality is sinking in, and I have to say goodbye all over again.

You know, I bet it feels good to have the weight of this world off your shoulders now. I'm dreaming of the day when I'm finally there with you.

I've asked the question why, but I guess the answer's for another time. So instead, I'll pray with every tear, and be thankful for the time I had you here.

I wanna live my life just like you did—make the most of my time, just like you did.

I wanna make my home in the sky—just like you did.

Oh, but until I get there, until I get there—save a place for me, save some grace for me, I'll be there soon, I'll be there soon." I love you honey!

Words by Matthew West.

MY PRAYER TODAY

"Lord of Eternity, blessed is the man who walks in your favor.
Who loves all your words and hides them like treasure
In the darkest place of my desperate heart
They are a light, a strong, sure light.

Sometimes I call out your name, but I cannot find you.
I look for your face, but you are not there.
By my sorrows, Lord, lift me to you; lift me to your side.

If you are my defender, who is against me?
No one can trouble or harm me if you are my strength.
All I ask, all I desire—is to live in your house all my days.

Lord of Eternity, Father of mercy, look on my fainting soul.
Keeper of all the stars, Friend of the poorest heart,
Touch me and make me whole."

Words by Fernando Ortega

Be assured Hon, with the help of "our" friends, neighbors and of course, "our" family, I'll be okay. Come see me as much as you can while I sleep. Please. That's when I miss you the most. Toby says hi.

I STILL LOVE YOU, HONEY. *Love you too.* Hey, I heard that. :)
So . . . no time zone there? Hmmm, give me a few seconds, see ya soon.
Hugs and kisses . . . your eternal one.
JM

CHAPTER 85

Now That You're Gone

Written November 28, 2010

S ometimes I just sit in my chair in silence staring across my empty bed as I watch the side hill field through the naked winter trees. Toby's sleeping at my feet while I search for movement of deer or turkey. There's a jumble of thoughts crawling through my mind at times like this. Things I miss, things I don't. Things I wish and things I hope. Stuff I regret and stuff I treasure; all a tangle of emotions begging for answers and some kind of release . . . but receiving neither. I continue to stare and ponder . . . dreams, smells, visual expressions that once were, laughter from family who just left, hugs and kisses radiating love. Then a doe and her twins come frisking down the hill to play and interrupt my thoughts. And I hear God's voice. "I love you. See, I sent wild ones to demonstrate my love for you." And I whisper, "Thanks God. I like that."

I miss holding her hand as we shuffle through fallen leaves on the trail below the side hill as our family chatters happily. I miss picking up leaves to save for Lori's crafts. "Here," you'd say, "she needs more red ones." And I'd put them in the bag. I miss searching for those first black-eyed Susans as we drove slowly past Dick Brown's farm.

I miss the wonderful smells of cooking and baking as I stepped inside after a hard day's work and you greeted me with that special sweet smile and a kiss. It didn't matter how tired or lousy you felt or how dirty and greasy I was, the smile and kiss were always ready just the same. I miss the attractive, tasty, candle-lit "supper for eight" you'd spend hours preparing even though it

As seen from our bedroom with binoculars.

was . . . just us. I miss washing the dishes for you and helping to put them away while you sat at the table writing cards to so many people.

I miss proudly telling people at fellowship meals . . . "That's Susan's dish." I miss watching our favorite TV shows or specials at night. I miss getting ready for our favorite time of the day after a busy hard day . . . when we'd crawl into bed to snuggle. I miss "the kiss" and "Goodnight honey, I love you." And your sweet whisper to me, "I love you too, goodnight."

I miss your elbow poking my ribs to make me stop snoring. I miss our early morning devotions together in the living room in our recliners separated by an antique stand you refinished in home ec. class in high school. I even miss our many trips to Williamsport for appointments and shopping . . . usually with a long list of stops. And, I miss those little pleasures of eating at Ruby Tuesday's, Perkins or our favorite—the Lobster Lounge. I miss your "pleasant chatter" as I drove those 40 miles each way. I wasn't always a real good listener. I'm sorry honey. If I had it to do over, I'd listen and digest every word you had to say . . . and even try to respond thoughtfully and intelligently.

I miss seeing you dress up to go away and your regular questions of "Which looks better, this one or this one?" I'm sure you knew the answer better than I did, but you still wanted my opinion. I had one, "You look good in either one." I really miss telling you how good you look and how wonderful you smell . . . all the time, anywhere, in anything or nothing. I still spray your Eternity perfume on your favorite prayer shawl that I wrap around my neck at night.

I really miss sitting across the table from you at home or a restaurant, looking into your eyes and telling you how beautiful you are and "There is NO one else I'd rather have than you." And you'd just smile at me.

I even miss hearing you say, "Are you coming?" "We're going to be late." or, "What are you doing?" "We're going to be late." You were always ready before me no matter what either of us were doing. You always knew exactly how much time to figure on to get us there ahead of time . . . not just on time. I miss hearing you ask me, "Why don't you just put your seat belt on before you start instead of waiting till you drive?" I had no good answer and still don't.

I miss the Hampton experiences, watching anything or nothing before bedtime. I miss the smell and sound of the ocean from our balcony, reading our books dressed in night robes . . . or not.

My gut has a knot in it and my throat a huge lump just reminiscing. Those were the things that helped us get through our trials. But at least I have the memories . . . I guess.

You spent half your life on the phone, or so it seemed to me. I miss seeing you in the kitchen with a phone growing out of your shoulder as you cooked and baked, washed or rested. I miss seeing and hearing you read Bible stories to the grandkids. I miss seeing your happy sweet smile when they entered the room wherever you were. They were such a joy to you. I wondered why you needed to keep every single letter, card or picture they ever wrote or drew for you.

Now I wish I could watch you stuff more of them into drawers or boxes. And . . . why do we need so many pictures? I would wonder. Now they are all treasures.

Then there were those snowy winter nights when we relaxed in the hot tub scented with fragrance. Sometimes the sky was crystal clear as God displayed His magnificent glory in the Milkyway. I miss pointing out the constellations as we sat close in the hot tub up to our necks and in our birthday suits. I miss that. Oh how I miss you . . .

I even miss driving you to your doctor and dentist appointments to be certain you got there and back safely. I miss opening the door for you. Now it's just for Toby.

I miss your generous heart. You were first to suggest that we give something to our family or those in need. And usually, you wanted to give more than me. Now, lest I miss a blessing, I listen for your nudging voice in my heart.

I miss reading Rudy's Place guestbook to you. I miss telling you what people said and liked. I miss telling you what I did today. I miss, I miss, I miss, oh how I miss . . . YOU.

Time for a four-wheeler ride with Toby before I recall what I DON'T miss. *(Sunday, November 28, 2010)*

Topping the list for what I DON'T miss, overall it has to be the pain and suffering from cancer. I don't miss hearing Dr. C.'s negative tone saying that he doesn't like the looks of that cat-scan. Nor the emotional feelings and stress that followed as we awaited the outcome of the biopsy. I don't miss the first or the last diagnosis given us by Dr. L.,

Toby waiting for Poppie.

Dr. S., Dr. H., Dr. A., Dr. N. and others. I don't miss dealing with all the unanswered questions and feelings as we so wanted to trust God for our way through the fog of doubt and fear.

I don't miss watching countless nurses sticking you seven, yes seven times trying to find a good vein to take, give, or treat your blood; holding your hand as they try again and again. I'm so glad you don't have to hear that you need another surgery or more radiation or chemo. Never again will you writhe in pain after what they called a simple procedure as an *embolization* on your poor arm or thigh to stop the cancer from progressing, yet without success. And you never exaggerated the level of your pain like others did, why would I miss watching you sob with pain when once, you labeled the pain a #12 (out of a 1 to 10). Never, no never will **we** miss that.

I don't miss the nights during chemo when your fever spiked, one in particular when we called the on-call doctor and he responded like we were bothering him. Dear God. I don't miss all the nausea, the quick stops along the highway to let you throw up for relief, the terrific struggle to get into and out of the car yet without complaining once. I don't miss the nasty, long waits in doctors' waiting rooms. I don't miss watching you be prepped for surgery and having to sign your name on so many papers waiving their responsibility if you didn't make it. I don't miss all the sad sights and cases over all the years in the hospital.

I don't miss seeing Dr. S., whom I originally called the big bad wolf, come in, sit down and deliver more bad news day after day until it couldn't get any worse. I don't miss trying to comfort you when I was in the bottom of the pit too. I don't miss trying to sleep in the hospital bed next to you while you were in far too much pain to sleep at all.

When anyone entered the room to visit you, I'll never understand how you overlooked your own pain and were first to ask "How are you doing today?" And you were genuinely interested in their life.

I'm glad I don't have to hear you ask, "Is it time for my next meds?" or if I could help you get out of bed to use the commode since the nurses were too busy. Neither do I miss having to see you propped up with six pillows and four towel rolls in hopes of easing the discomfort.

As much as I loved and appreciated Dr. Nisbet at The Gatehouse and all the nurses, I don't miss seeing you there anymore. Though there is an endless list of things I miss and don't miss one thing is certain—You aren't missing a thing now that you're in the presence of Jesus. No, it's we who are missing you. But "thanks be to God who has given us a living Hope that cannot be taken from us." We will see you soon, honey. Save a place for me, I'll be there soon. I love you . . . and I can hear you whisper back like every night so long ago . . . "I love you too."

Once again, I'm hearing Laura Story's Blessing song. You may want to read it again.

CHAPTER 86

Thinking, Pondering, Wondering . . . .

Written December 26, 2010

S ometimes I just sit and stare into space and THINK. Our minds are an incredibly intricate wonder designed by The Almighty, Creative, God of eternity. How could we begin to comprehend our own minds let alone, His?

But I can't help but wonder—now that Susan's gone to heaven and I have to "do" life without her . . . what was my purpose in life? What was Susan's purpose in life? Did we find it? Did we carry out His plan and purpose for our lives?

What kept us plowing ahead when everything kept pulling us behind? Why in the world did we stay in Sullivan County? It made more common sense to move our family back to our roots where our families could interact and physically touch each other. Certainly it would have been much easier to make a living.

Why did I insist on farming those rocky mountain fields where wildlife stole more than their portion? A land with very limited productive potential . . . a portion of Pennsylvainia where the sun refuses to shine but a third of most anywhere else.

Then I remember my childhood and youth; the days where God began to stir the ingredients of faith, hope and compassion into our hearts. Those days when He whispered His plan and calling into our minds and hearts. It is that factor which mushroomed and motivated us to keep going and keep focus.

Once again I hear that still small voice; *"For I know the plans I have for you says the Lord, plans to prosper you and not to harm you, plans to give you a future and a hope. Then you will call upon me, and come and pray to me and I will listen to you. You will seek me and find me when you seek me with all your heart. I will be found by you, declares the Lord."* Jeremiah 29: 11-14

Over and again, this verse comes to mind and renews our hope. It has become a favorite if not *the* favorite verse of mine.

Still I ponder and wonder about . . . life . . . children . . . grandchildren . . . love . . . sickness . . . health . . . pain . . . suffering . . . death?

About heaven . . . hell . . . angels . . . demons . . . eternity . . . redemption . . . the cross . . . His pain . . . His suffering . . . for me!

And it's all so mysterious and beyond comprehension . . . mind boggling. Then I recall *His ways are higher than our ways* . . . and I have Hope. And I'm content.

So much to ponder.

CHAPTER 87

Light Will Rise

"A time for everything under heaven . . . " Solomon's decree in Ecclesiastes.

It's been a long, dark season of clouds and shadows on my journey of grief this past year. Not just for me, but my entire family and many brothers and sisters in Christ. It's true; there is a time for everything under Heaven. We all encounter many different seasons in life. Some cannot be avoided. Death is one of them, though we try hard to evade it.

The Bible gives us many promises of hope for a better future coupled with conditions. I was reading in Isaiah this week and *logos* (a word of God to me), jumped off the page.

. . . "if you spend yourselves in behalf of the hungry and satisfy the needs of the oppressed, then your light will rise in the darkness and your night will become like the
noonday. The Lord will guide you always;
he will satisfy your needs in a sun-scorched land and will strengthen
your frame. You will be like a well-watered garden,
like a spring whose waters never fail." Can you grasp the picture?
Isaiah 58: 10-12

Max Lucado reminded me of the following scripture this week:

*"Do nothing from selfishness or empty conceit, but with humility
of mind regard one another as more important than yourselves; do not
merely look out for your own personal interests, but also for the interests of
others."* Phil. 2:3-4 NASB

This was the epitome of Susan; always more interested in the welfare of others. Spending her days thinking of others and how she could bring cheer to their lives and encourage them. No wonder she wore such a beautiful smile. No wonder she survived 16 years with cancer. No wonder her legacy radiates with a

Christ-like example. I'm not surprised that her doctors and nurses marveled at her patience, her countenance, her endurance and attitude.

Read those verses again and ponder them. I have. I am. "Spend yourself on the needs of others." Not a hint of selfishness there.

Result—"Your light will rise in the darkness and your night will become like the noonday."

I realized that this darkness we are encountering will dispel as we begin to spend ourselves on others needs. I get that. I've experienced it. Susan lived it and I have tried to live it.

High noon is on its way . . . this sun-scorched season of life WILL become "like a well watered garden." Hope and Light, dispelling darkness and barrenness.

As we visit our dear friends in Honduras and spend our time exploring their needs, and enjoying their country, I pray God can use this time to dispel some of the cloudy skies of grief, and replace it with bright Sonshine. The sunglasses and sunscreen are waiting.

For everything . . . a season. I think Spring is coming. Our assignment is clear. Spend—focus not only on ourselves, but the needs of others. Like Susan did. Her darkness is gone; totally and eternally gone as she reflects the brightness of the SON. She is a tree planted by the waters of life, blooming in its eternal season.

Friday night, I woke up with a childhood chorus on my mind. The words came clearly to me, "Heavenly Sunlight." Have you heard it? I got out all my hymnals and song books and found it. . . . .flooding my soul with Glory divine. And it does.

- Written just a year after Susan's death.

CHAPTER 88

Full Moon Rising

Written April 17, 2011

As I sat down to write tonight, the words surfaced again . . . *Full moon rising.* I turned my head to look at the April calendar to see just when "full moon" would be. To my delight, it is tonight. Up from my chair and to the front door I went to see for myself.

Across the field just above Bob's barn roof rose a large and full-faced moon brightly beaming its clear spring light on the field and onto our house.

My astonishment and sense of awe not quite satisfied with a peek through the living room window, I picked up the binoculars and headed for the deck. Dressed only in pj's and t-shirt, I stood shivering on the deck with the binoculars steadied between the branches of the ol' apple tree next to the playhouse. Hmmmmm, what a miracle God placed in the sky to reflect light from the sun back to earth at nighttime.

Good things and sometimes weird things happen at full moon. Susan used to say the patients at the nursing home acted strange at full moon. "Be prepared for the unexpected during full moon," she'd say.

The weather generally changes around full moon. If you get past full moon in late Spring or early Fall, you will generally evade frost. It's one of those *Farmers' Almanac* sayings you can really count on.

Lovers like to be alone under the full moon; by the beach, in a canoe on the lake, or a mountain pasture. It sets the stage for romance and opens communication of the heart.

People talk about "the man in the moon." It only takes a wee imagination to see that. But tonight . . . tonight, I saw something else. Sometimes you just have to be silent. Be still. Just look . . . and think . . . and pray . . . and wait. And listen. God doesn't always speak in the thunder, wind or storm. Often He speaks or gives visions in a whisper. I heard the whisper tonight.

My little binoculars have produced many moments of pleasure watching turkey gobblers strut and stride as they woo their harem of hens on the side hill

413

field. I've counted a dozen or more deer feeding on the same hill as two buck duel for courtship rights. Hawks have been identified through those little 8 x 21 glasses.

Not tonight. Tonight it was something much larger. Something 250,000 miles away from the side hill field. But it was as clear as those turkeys. The picture inside the full moon reminded me of a human—an unborn human. A fetus. It looked like an unborn child fully formed ready for birth. It was in the fetal position, encircled by a pure light reflected from the sun. Not all its features were visible but like an ultrasound on a pregnant woman, there was no doubt it was a perfectly formed miracle. A child with all the potential of any other human if given birth. Made in His likeness, His image. Perfect and protected. Waiting for birth at the right moment and season in time.

I went back out to see it. Clouds darkened my view. It was gone. But no, there it comes. I mean there go the clouds. It was always there, but for the clouds covering it. It's too cold to stand out there in night clothes. But it will continue its path across the night sky nevertheless . . . with the imagine intact.

"What did it whisper to me?" I wondered when you'd ask . . . or if you forgot.

Here's what I heard and thought: Seasons come and seasons go. We are consumed with daily life in each season. Before we know it, the next season is here, ready or not. The full moon makes its appearance once each month, unless the clouds obscure it. But it's there none the less. We can enjoy it or wish it wasn't so. But full moon happens.

Susan's life and mine was full of bright light for an entire season of life. We enjoyed it immensely, to put it mildly. It was so enjoyable and full of good things that before we were ready, it was over. Our season has come and gone. Ready or not, good and bad, it is now history . . . a memory. Except for the years of pain and suffering, it is a wonderful memory. Although I wanted an extended season, God had other plans. (Jer. 29:11-14)

The full moon rising . . . oh yes, what did I see and hear?

It's been over a year since that season ended. I've kept it alive, but only in memory. And I will always keep that season alive and well in my memory. I will think, dream and talk about it. We will laugh and cry over it. No one can take that from me nor should they. It is sacred and precious to all of us. Thank you God for that sweet season of life. I Praise you!

The "ultrasound" of the full moon tonight revealed a new life to be birthed. It will be a totally new and special gift from God formed in His image. Created for His pleasure (as well as ours) and for His Glory. It is His idea, His creation, invented before time existed. He knew us before we were formed in our Mothers' wombs. His plan is to prosper us and not to harm us . . . to give us a future and a hope. He said it was not good for man to be alone, so He made a helpmate for him. Woman. He said man should leave Mom and Dad and cleave to his woman. And He said when He was finished with His creation that "IT IS GOOD."

Susan, your wish is about to come true. Just before leaving us, you said "that you hoped that I would find someone, that I don't do well alone" . . .

"THE FULL MOON RISING" is about to birth a new season of life for me and Marliss. In fact it already has. After tonight the full moon begins to wane. So the birth is here. We only need to wait to celebrate its life.

And so we will wait and plan and pray. And what I hope is that all of our families and friends can rejoice with us in this new, fresh, uncharted season of life. A future season Susan had hoped and prayed for. One she knew needed to come sooner than later so my life would once again be complete and "Full" of life and joy. She knew so much better than I did. But then, why am I surprised. Wasn't she usually a step or two ahead of me?

Thanks, honey for caring for me even on your death bed. Guess you still look out for me. You're my angel now.

And thanks so much dear God, for planning yet another season of "life" for me . . . and Marliss. You are so good. You are so trustworthy. How could we have ever guessed this was in your plan?

Who would have "thunk" it? Not I. Not Marliss. Who? You dear God. You!!

CHAPTER 89

Peace in Prescot Valley

Wednesday, May 4, 2011

*B**e still and know that I am God . . . I will be exalted above the heavens . . . and as truly as I live all the earth shall be filled with the Glory of the Lord . . . The Lord is my shepherd, I shall not want, he makes me to lie down in green pastures. He leads me besides still waters. He restores my soul, he guides me in paths of righteousness for his names sake. Even though I walk through the valley of the shadow of death, I will fear no evil, for you are with me. Your rod and your staff, they comfort me. You (even) prepare a table for me in the presence of my enemies—(cancer, then loneliness). You anoint my head with oil and my cup (life) overflows. Surely goodness and mercy will follow me all the days of my life, and I will dwell in the house of the Lord forever.* (With Jesus, Susan, Chuck and loved ones.)

Ever since last summer, I've been planning to visit Lowell and Lois near Phoenix, AZ. It didn't work out until the end of April. But God had the right time planned all along. Here it is again . . . *"I know the plans I have for you, plans to prosper you and not to harm you, plans to give you a future and a hope . . . "* This we have always claimed for ourselves and our kids and grandkids.

416

But only God knows how to make it happen. He brought Marliss and I together in miraculous manner. Even if we had tried to arrange the circumstances of this relationship, it could not compare to the way He did it. Incident upon another almost daily continues to confirm and strengthen our commitment to each other.

By April 27th, the day of my flight departure, my heart was sad to be flying alone. One year and two months since my sweet Susan left us for her eternal home in Heaven, my broken heart was healing and even rejoicing as God began to establish a new relationship in a fresh, springtime of life.

"Weeping shall endure for a night, but joy comes in the morning." Joy has arrived in grand style for me and Marliss. Our cup is overflowing. Day after day we're amazed at the oneness He gives us. Daily we look longingly for the moment when we can be ONE. We wait on Him to give us His answer for "that day."

Months ago, I settled on a week for my visit with my best friend, Lowell and his wife Lois. I wanted plenty of time to visit. God is using this time to settle my spirit and emotions and confirm to me and Marliss over and again that He is ordering our steps.

A great sense of PEACE and JOY has settled into my being during this time here in Prescott Valley with the Goshows. Thank you, God for leading me besides still waters and green pastures . . . though they may not be literal. I have had time to "be still and know that YOU are GOD." You, God have arranged this time to relax, listen, laugh and enjoy friends and creation. The Bullock

JM and best friend, Lowell.

Orioles, the quail, the doves and finch display your awesome handiwork. What wonders you flaunt even in the desert. Not a drop of rain nor a gallon of water have I seen in this valley. Yet the cactus produce flowers, and the birds find food in this dry and thirsty land.

A *table* in the presence of my enemies . . . (loneliness and anxiety) lavished with peace in your presence. Peace displayed in the mother quail leading her thumb-size chicks across a highway to safety under a hedge. Peace and contentment exhibited by the family of Cooper hawks high in the ponderosa pine tree. I watched the male hawk fly to the nest with a small animal in its claws. Breakfast for Mom and babies secure in the huge nest of sticks 40 feet above threatening ground creatures. A snapshot of God's promise for provision for all of creation, including us.

"So why do you worry about what you will wear or what you will eat? Does not your heavenly Father feed the birds of the air and the fish of the sea? Consider the lily of the field in all its grandeur. Does it worry about what it will wear or what it will eat? How much more shall our Heavenly Father care for us and supply our needs? So do not worry about all these things, He knows that we need them all." (Paraphrased by me from Mt. 6.)

I am at peace as I ponder His future plans for Marliss and me. I trust His sovereignty for the future of my children and grandchildren. I trust Him to lead and direct our paths. Though I have unanswered questions about our future, about our children and grandchildren and how their lives will interact with ours, I am convinced that His plans hold blessing and prosperity (far more than financially).

I am convinced that He has ordained and ordered our steps. We need only to listen, to discern through wise counsel, to rest in His presence by still waters and obey His voice. *"For [we] are confident of this . . . that we will see the goodness of the Lord in the land of the living."*

And I am thankful that He . . . *"has turned my mourning into dancing, he has put off my sackcloth, and clothed me with gladness. To the end I shall sing praises to Him, and not be silent, Oh Lord my God, I will give thanks unto you forever."*

Peace, perfect peace, in this dark world of sin . . . the kind that passes understanding, freely given to all who accept His free gift through the cross. It floods my soul as I reflect on His goodness in the land of the living. *Joy unspeakable and full of glory . . . the half has not yet been told.* (a line from an old chorus)

Thank you Lord for the possibility of peace in a world of chaos. Thank you that our steps do not just imprint randomly. Thank you for the awesome surprises of beauty replacing the ashes of sadness. Thanks for giving the oil of joy in exchange for mourning, and the garment of praise for the spirit of heaviness in order for us to be strong, healthy trees of righteousness, planted by You, Lord, so that You are glorified.

SHALOM and Amen.

CHAPTER 90

Officially Welcomed — Marliss Ann Berke

As written to my family, Friday, July 1, 2011

I want to formally and officially welcome and introduce to you one of MawMaw's dearest and treasured friends. She called to encourage Mom/MawMaw to the very end. She is the one whom MawMaw would call several times a week after she lost her precious husband (Chuck) of 36 years, now over five years ago.

All but the very young in our family know her quite well—Marliss Ann Berke—Lori's girls call her Marly. You may hear me call her *Honey* or *Love.*

She kept contact with me as I grieved Mom's loss. Neither of us suspected a relationship like this to develop. But God did.

Down by the sea we all love.

Mom/MawMaw got her wish, Poppie found a new soul mate. And Poppie is not lonely or sad anymore. I want you to know that I plan to treat Marliss like I treated MawMaw . . . like a queen. I will not take her for granted. She can never take MawMaw's place nor would she try to. I can never take Chuck's place, nor would I try.

But she will help to fill the huge hole in Poppie's heart left when MawMaw went to be with Jesus. And Poppie is helping to fill the empty place in her heart.

We will always have wonderful lasting memories of our first love and speak often and highly of those years gone by. Their pictures will be on our walls and dressers.

She loves me with her whole heart and I love her the same. So if you see us holding hands or smiling and talking sweetly to each other, it's ok.

You will see her around me a lot now because we have a lot to do to get ready before the wedding in September, like getting her house cleaned out and ready to sell. Moving her stuff up here takes time too.

You can be sure that MawMaw and Chuck are very happy for us, though maybe a bit surprised.

> With all my heart, I love you.
> Poppie

Marliss, Chuck and JM playing pingpong.

CHAPTER 91

Hurricane Ponderings

Written Sunday, August 28, 2011

The past summer seems a blur. Just like our Mike prophesied when he said, "Dad, September 3rd will be here before you know it, just you wait."

"Yes, Mike. You're probably right," I said. "It just seems so long to wait."

Now with less than a week to go, we wonder where the time went. When I was young and "full of myself," old age and the end of life for me looked like an eternity away, and a waste of time to think about. And certainly, anyone getting married at age 68 must have dementia. How foolish a thought.

The old timers—over 50—had a saying about *time speeding up as you get older.* They were right. Anyone over 60 or even 50 can identify.

I think of myself like 30 years younger but wonder why I get tired midday. Trying to accomplish as much as that "30-something" year old man I dream myself to be, gets me in trouble most days. But I still attempt the impossible, like playing ice hockey with teenagers. Oh, well, better that way then to give in to an old age philosophy of despair.

So . . . here I sit in my same ol' chair writing while my "new honey" chooses to snooze a bit and regenerate before we attack the music list for our wedding in five days. Practicing what she preached as a good guidance counselor—think or rest before you act.

Outer band winds of Hurricane Irene still lash our landscape today, and the lights continue to blink. It was a bad storm with flooding and wind damage. In fact, I just heard that *all* of Sullivan County's main roads are closed due to flooding.

Our church service was cut short by someone popping in the back door as Scot was preaching, to inform us of imminent road closings. Rt. 87 and 154 were about to close.

Anybody needing to get home had better leave immediately. Scot reluctantly closed the service. After a quick drive to check out the rising Loyalsock around Forksville, we dodged downed trees and branches arriving home safely.

Bethy, Leah and Kaiti were here last night till late while Mike and Lori shopped in Williamsport. We had fun riding our bikes before the rain hit.

The paths through our house amidst multitudes of boxed items, is getting much wider as we work to put things in place. Actually, there are no paths now. It's beginning to look like a normal house . . . almost. After going through what seems like hundreds of boxes, order has come to the downstairs. The daily yard sale was a good idea.

"Don't you miss Susan?" you ask. "Does she still miss Chuck?"

"Can anyone forget his first love, particularly when you have spent many long wonderful years together?" I ask you.

Of course we miss our spouses. We have many great memories to enjoy as we continue to live and love each other one day at a time. We will never forget, nor would we want to.

A sense of contentment envelopes me as I write tonight—two pups are stretched out next to my new love sound asleep. The wind is howling, plants are soaking wet and swinging in the wind as others lay flat on the deck waiting to be rescued. But peace and comfort rule in the house. It's good.

Milton Henry, our gray heron, stands on the dock fishing. We named him Milton Henry because my white imitation heron is named Gracie. Marliss' Mom's name was Grace and her Dad's name was Milton. I used to call the *real* heron, Henry. But when Marliss came into my life, we added Milton.

I wonder many things lately: *How many years will God give us to enjoy together? Where will we travel to—together? Will our kids be patient with us as we try hard to divide our time with them and each other? Will we get to see our grandchildren often enough to suit everybody—us included? After all the planning, will the wedding be a blessing to us and everyone else that comes? Will the weather be good? Will our pups behave . . . especially Toby with his "Kingly" high-horse episodes? Will Noah be able to keep the pups for almost a month? Anyone want a pup for a week or three weeks?? I figured!*

So many questions, thoughts and imaginations as we enter this new life together. I am so looking forward to being married once again and done with loneliness. Mom and Chuck are already shouting, and celebrating our love and companionship in fancy fashion with the angels.

"Hey, honey, come quick and get your binoculars. It's a bear or a turkey on the side hill," I said reaching for mine. By the time she got here a deer had joined the black blob.

"It's a tom turkey," we both agreed as two more deer munched the lush grass. Then more turkeys joined in from above and more deer from below. They grazed close to each other as we lamented the fact that it was not a black bear. Maybe tomorrow. And so, we chug away at preparations, plans, and creating our home.

Why is it so hard to give up our stuff? My stuff? It's only stuff. But a lot of it holds such precious memories. I guess that's the answer. Cleaning out the drawers of the walnut desk that I made in shop in my junior year in high school exposed mounds of papers from my accounting class with Richard Detweiler. Why? Why did I keep them? I hated doing those papers. I needed Mae Reinford (R sits next to S) to help me get it right. There they were, staring in my face from the bottom of the drawer. Time to let go.

I found many letters, cards and papers from everyone. Autographed pictures of most of my classmates—do I trash them? Why keep them? But what to do with those connected with Susan? Most had to go. I kept some, actually . . . a lot. Why? Emotions, sentimental feelings, nostalgia, whatever . . . it makes us horders, keepers. And so we pile it up for someone else to dispose of when we are gone. And then, we even have trouble disposing of their stuff. Obviously, some is for historical purposes.

The desk is now in the shop awaiting restoration . . . for historical purposes. :>) I ponder if that is why the shop and other buildings house more stuff.

So I encourage each of you to "try" to hold more loosely, the "stuff" we call our possessions. Some day, sooner rather than later, we will give them all up in exchange for mansions on streets of real gold . . . imperishable "stuff!"

I truly treasure each of you as "our" own. I promise now to continue to treasure and nurture all of you the best I/we can until Jesus returns.

See y'all at the wedding. :>)

CHAPTER 92

Beauty for Ashes

JOHN'S VOWS

It is with a sense of God's miraculous mercy, grace and providence that I stand here today supported, loved and blessed by family and friends. No one but God alone knew the plans that He had for us; plans to prosper, not to harm us; plans to give us a future and a hope. It is because of those divine plans that I take you, Marliss to be my wife and best friend.

By now, you know that what you see is what you get . . . one who has experienced pain and suffering few can fathom. But I know you can. I offer to share with you the joy God has restored in me through mourning, the new life He has created out of ashes and the garment of praise that has replaced a heavy spirit.

As I fulfilled my promise to Susan those 47 years, I now happily promise to be faithful to you. I will lovingly care for you in sickness and in health as I did for her. You and I have experienced green pastures and the valley of the shadow of death. I promise to partner with you in our pursuit to know God more deeply and to follow the path of Jesus wherever He leads us.

I will try not to take myself too seriously but to nurture a "merry heart" with you. I will even try to care for Crosby as I do Toby. I expect our differences to complement each other. I love to laugh with you and promise not to laugh at you. I will weep with you when you weep. I will always try to be a good listener.

JM at age 67.

425

I promise to pick up my socks and undies and maybe even yours. I promise not to make light of your gluten-free diet as I eat my breakfast cake and ice cream. I'm happy to let you sleep in and will likely serve you coffee and premasole in bed. I will even paint your toenails.

I hope to encourage us to live for the wellbeing of others and not just ourselves. Service is my motivational gift as you know. I will endeavor to love your kids and grandkids—and their pets as my own.

Since Susan and Chuck and many more of our friends and family are dancing on golden streets, by the grace of God, we may as well enjoy the time He gives us here on earth. I'm so ready to be dancing instead of weeping. I give you all my imperfections as well as my abilities and I accept all yours as well.

Together we will gratefully and creatively exude every day that He gives us breath. How could we ever keep from singing His praise since we know we are so loved by the King of Kings.

All that I was, all that I am and hope to be, I surrender to God and share with you.

I love you.

MARLISS' VOWS

My loving John,

Standing here before all of these beloved family members and friends, I thank you for giving this fading Autumn woman a new sense of Spring and all the hope and joy that it brings. With the new buds of love bursting open in my heart, I give to you my faithfulness emotionally, physically, and spiritually as we become one before Jesus. As your wife and best friend, I pledge to love and cherish you with encouragement, patience, forgiveness, kindness, hopefulness, humility, trust, truthfulness, and perseverance. I will love and journey with you now and as you continue to grow and travel where God intends, especially in writing your life story. I will treasure you when we are together

and when we are enjoying our separate times; when our lives are at peace and when they are challenged; when you are relaxed and peaceful and when you have worked so hard and long that fatigue invades your mind and body—then I will feed you, kiss you, and put you to bed! I will honor your goals and dreams and help you to fulfill them, always encouraging your spunky and creative side! I will seek to be lovingly honest and open as we communicate, assured that God will draw us closer through that communication. I will love your children and grandchildren as my own and work hard to preserve their precious memories of MawMaw. I will love and protect Toby even at his most cantankerous times with Crosby!

Ready and eager for our new adventure together, I close with the words of one of my favorite poets, Chuck Berke: "These moments, oh that they would stay with us forever! Perhaps they will and live on in our . . . children."

TROPICAL STORM LEE ANNOUNCES:
MR. JOHN M. SOUDER & MS. MARLISS ANN BERKE

Monday afternoon, September 5, 2011.

Everyone had gone home following the celebration of our marriage with family and friends. It was wonderful. The two families blended like melted butter on mashed potatoes. Such fun. Many tears and much joy captured on camera only like Jenna could do.

Her sneak peak emailed to us was like sampling homemade ice cream—you want more but have to wait.

We lay exhausted on our bed resting peacefully after the whirlwind of activity over the past week. Our pups, Toby and Crosby, cuddled closely affirming a time to rest.

"Guess what honey, we're married!" Marliss said.

"Can you believe it? Seems like it was just yesterday when we said we didn't know if we could wait the summer to be married," I said smiling.

In no time I felt a nudge—"turn over, you're snoring."

My cell phone buzzed and I picked it up to see who it was. Brenda was texting the words, "We're in Harrisonburg, heavy rain and hard to see but we're almost home." PTL.

Tropical Storm "Lee" was raging a destructive path up through the southern states headed for the Northeast. The National Weather Service out of State College (NOAA) was calling for heavy rain for several days and local flooding. Pictures of flooded areas in the south were stunning.

Tuesday morning dawned a reddish pink sunrise to our delight. But its beauty was short-lived as angry clouds began to darken the eastern sky. Oh well, we'll unpack some more boxes, and clean up a bit today before packing up for our honeymoon to Florida tomorrow.

After more sorting, making lists, paying bills and catching up on emails most of the day, I went to the garage to mount the bicycle rack and load up the bikes. I packed some things in *Ruby*, our new Subaru Outback. Our Raleigh hybrid bikes should give us some great rides along the coast on Sanibel and Captiva Islands.

All night long heavy rain beat on the house creating a pond out front. We woke to pouring rain and wind pounding our deck and porch plants. I quickly moved the plants back onto the porch out of the weather and brought the storage boxes indoors that were on the porch.

"Wow, this is *not* looking good for driving today. Honey, look behind the playhouse. It's like a river building just from road water."

"Good day! The rain gauge is almost full. Five inches," I said heading out to empty it.

"We better get packing and get out of here," Marliss commented.

About 11:00, the phone rang and it was Lucy.

"Hi guys, just thought you should know that Elk Creek Road is closed due to flooding." (This was our normal route to Williamsport.) She said in a rather alarmed voice, "And the radio and TV are advising people to stay home unless it's an emergency because of flooding."

"Wow," I said, "we better get serious and get out of here." We had hoped to get off early afternoon but still had things to take care of. I quickly packed the rest of our pups' stuff, grabbed some boots, hats, raincoats and umbrellas and stashed it into the car.

The phone rang again. Our neighbor Bob, was on the phone. He wasted no words. "Hey, if you guys are still planning on leaving today, you'll want to go right now or stay put. I just got word that Rt. 87 to Dushore is flooded and closed as is Route 220. Route 154 is about to be closed leaving 87 South the only way out of the County. Reports are out saying all roads in Sullivan County will close imminently. The forecast calls for 3 to 6" more rain," he said.

"Wow, I had no idea it was that severe. Ok, we're outta here real soon," I said. "But we were planning on taking the pups to Noah in Dushore. But Dushore is flooded again. The third time in one year! Now what will we do?" I blurted, thinking out loud.

"I can take care of them. Just leave them here and we'll watch them. They know their boundaries by now and should stay behind the underground fence," he said reassuringly.

"Well, that sure would be great since we're out of options anyhow," I said. "If you could feed them morning and evening in their pens (houses) inside the back room and leave their doggie door open, they should be fine. I'll ask friends and Lori and Mike to stop in now and then to love on them."

"No problem . . . really. I'll be happy to care for them. Just get going ASAP," Bob said. "Have a great time but drive carefully."

"We couldn't ask for better neighbors. Thanks Bob."

By now there was a small lake by the horsey swings from rainwater streaming in from all directions. Hopefully, the 6" pipe will adequately drain it to behind the house. I asked Mike and Bob to keep watch on it. In the basement a steady strong stream of water gushed from the stone wall, flowing across the floor and into the drain. So far so good.

We picked up our pace and packed the car with everything we could remember and headed out in pouring rain. The newly ground up road bed in front of our house created by *Chief Oil & Gas*, had turned into a muddy stream bed as we sloshed along. It looked like "Agnes" in the 1972 flood all over again. Maybe it will be worse by the looks of it.

"Thank God we live up on the mountain," I said. Praying that God would send angels to guard us, we drove slowly down Route 154 and approached the intersection of 87 at Forksville, our mouths opened in amazement. The muddy torrents of angry floodwaters were already surrounding Myers' house and trailers and were within four feet of the bridge crossing the Little Loyalsock Creek . . . what we call the *Little Sock*. Large trees and trash crashed wildly down the creek and lots got caught high in trees along the bank.

"My gosh," I said, "we really *do* need to move. That is wild! Forksville will soon be underwater and I wonder about the bridges?"

We drove South on 87 speechless for a moment while the rain pounded our windshield. As we passed Forksville Inn, we noticed deep muddy water flowing through the cornfield and coming within inches of the road. Yes, inches.

The word "Wow" kept coming out of my mouth. This was serious if not tragic for lowland dwellings.

"Honey, do you think we should keep going? The road has lots of low areas which will certainly soon, if not already, be flooded," I said softly and uncertain.

Almost without hesitation she said, "Go, just keep going. If we turn back, we will not make our train tomorrow and I really want to do this trip."

I kept going. Faster, as fast as I could possibly drive in the heavy rain.

"Ok," I said. "I know where the low trouble spots are. If we make it through the next low one, we should be good."

We made it past that one. At the first bridge in Hillsgrove, Elk Creek was already over its bank and into the fields. We crossed with trepidation and amazement.

Whew, this is a real live scene out of the movie "Perfect Storm," I thought.

"The next bridge below Hillsgrove should be ok," I said. "It's higher above the creek." As we approached the bridge, on the left side down near the creek was a man frantically working to get stuff out of his cabin. Sadly, we discovered later that his entire house was swept away.

Below Hillsgrove were large fields of corn and soybeans. The water would soon be drowning all those fields. It was already into the fields.

At each low-lying area along 87, the raging floodwaters were threatening the road and many houses. Incredibly, cars and trucks were actually heading north for who knows what reason.

"Those guys will be stranded by tonight if not sooner," I said.

We knew there was no turning back now so we kept driving as fast as possible.

At Pier 87 Bar, the creek—now a raging torrent—was almost ready to break over the bank and into the restaurant. The next landmark in jeopardy was the Slabtown Bridge. The water was approaching the bridge.

Sadly to say, it was only a matter of hours that would seal the fate of that bridge, the restaurant and many, many other properties in the Northeast. We just could hardly believe the eerie pictures coming from news reporters and everywhere.

We safely reached Montoursville noting that floodwaters were threatening every low-lying area if not already done so. After picking up some medication for my sinus headache, we headed south on 180. Thinking ahead as far as possible, I knew we would not make it through Northumberland as the railroad underpass would certainly be flooded and the road closed. So we crossed over on Rt. 80 to Rt. 15 South commenting on the rising Susquehanna as we went. No problem going down 15. Only water flowing lightly across the roadway now and then. The heavy rain continued.

All the way down along the raging, muddy Susquehanna to Harrisburg, we did not encounter any flooding . . . yet.

Channel 16 TV—A view from their helicopter. Snyder's Farm in Montoursville.

Our plan was to stay with Susannah Wednesday night in Baltimore, and then head out Thursday morning to reach our destination at Lorton, Virginia, where we would load our car onto the Auto Train.

All was going well until close to York on Rt. 83. The traffic slowed and then stopped. We went two miles in a half hour and were still miles from York but close to an exit. We exited and pulled into a gas station with many other weary confused travelers. After talking with several people, some locals, we concluded there was no way through York following Route 83. The road was flooded. In fact, many local roads were already closed. One person suggested we find a motel for the night and hope for the best tomorrow.

Marliss, being the optimist she is, suggested we turn around and head back north on 83.

"Why should we do that?" I asked not knowing her strategy yet.

"Well, the forecast maps all showed the storm heading up across the eastern part of the state and north. So if we hurry and head north to the turnpike, head west and then down toward Gettysburg, we should get out of the center of the storm and traffic. I think we should try it," she said confidently.

"Sounds like a plan to me," I said and off we went, all gassed up and ready for the adventure.

A long line of cars still sat waiting for who knows what and how long. Very little traffic was heading north and we sailed along nicely. She was right, once again, and the skies actually opened up and the rain subsided until we reached Baltimore. For the last 20 minutes it dumped on us with fury, even small hail balls. Thankfully, we arrived at the Amtrak station safely.

We called home to get a flood report. All roads in the northern tier of Pennsylvania, all schools and most businesses were closed. Thousands were already in shelters and loss of life was increasing by the hour. It would go down in history as the flood of the century.

We stayed with Susannah in Baltimore overnight. The heavy rain continued all night filling every low-lying area, and flooding streets.

Early next morning we are headed south towards southern Florida. As we boarded the Auto train, the sun peeked though the clouds and bright blue sky appeared as if to say, "Everything will be okay, relax." We found our coach and sleeping berth, dropped our bags and collapsed on the bunks.

With a huge sigh and big smiles, we looked at each other and said, "Whoa! Thank you God, we made it!"

It had been a whirlwind wedding week with family, friends, celebrating, packing and finally, beating out the floodwaters heading south. Our farm and most friends were high and dry. Our lives were intact, our hearts bonded, our families connected and the future is in God's hands.

There are many questions to be answered. There are hearts and emotions that need healing from the great void of Susan and Chuck and the blending of our families. Will all the transitions be difficult? How will we find time to visit everyone fairly? These and a mountain of thoughts have been entertained and discussed over the past six months.

We are certain that as with the disciples in the boat on the Sea of Galilee, Jesus did not bring us this far to let us drown . . . or falter in our case. He will be true to all His promises to guide us and help us work though our challenges.

Can we count on . . . *"surely goodness and mercy to follow us all the days of the rest of our lives?"* If God said it, then we'll believe it.

I close this chapter of our lives with a great hymn of the Mennonite faith. Although I cannot claim to have accomplished this, it is my goal to live and have lived a life that blesses God *every day*. Feel free to hum or sing along in four-part harmony.

EVERY DAY WILL I BLESS THEE

I will extol you, O my God, and praise you, O my King;
 yea, every day and evermore your praises I will sing.

Refrain

Great is the Lord, our mighty God, and greatly to be praised;
 his greatness is unsearchable, above all glory raised.

Refrain

Each generation to the next shall testimony bear,
and to your praise, from age to age, your wondrous acts declare.

Refrain

Upon your glorious majesty and honor I will dwell,
and all your grand and glorious works and greatness I will tell.

Refrain

Your mighty acts and glorious deeds we shall with awe confess
and sing of your great goodness and your perfect righteousness.

Refrain

Most gracious and compassionate is God, who reigns above;
 his wrath is ever slow to rise, unbounded is his love.

Refrain

"Every day will I bless thee! Every day will I bless thee!
And I will praise will praise thy Name . . . For ever and ever!"

Afterword

It's over three years now that Susan went to be with Jesus. So hard to believe. It's already 20 months since I married Marliss. God is so good . . . and has such a sense of humor. Me married to Marliss? She is so different than Susan in many ways. But she loves the Lord with her whole heart, has a great sense of self worth and humor, enjoys retirement life, loves dogs, plants, and people, birds, animals, wildlife, herbs, salmon, biking, seashells and sunshine.

Likewise, I am different than Chuck, her first husband and my good friend. Yet Marliss loves me just the way I am and encourages me to be all I can be. I love her for that.

We enjoy living life together, doing what we want to, going where and when we want, and okay, I'll admit it . . . I still like to work a wee bit too much. But I'll get over it. Marliss is really good for me and I like to think . . . and believe that I'm good for her.

We do travel quite a bit and intend to do so as God gives us health. After all, Marliss has a daughter, Susannah and husband, Damon (both dermatologists) and sons Jack and Alexander in N.C., her son, Brian (an electrical engineer) and wife Jenny and little Mikayla in Pittsburgh and her son Bruce (high school PE teacher) and wife Karen, and Connor and Natalie living near Lansdale, Pa. And I have three of my kids, Renee, Brenda and Mike and nine grandkids living in Central Virginia, and another daughter and husband and their three girls living near us . . . whew!! There are plenty of places and families to go visit. And so we go.

As of this writing, May 12, 2013, here's a very short summary of my kids and grandkids:

Renee is a retired kindergarten teacher and Rod is part owner and administrator of a retirement community in Waynesboro, VA. Their kids are: Rachael, who graduates from JMU this coming December with a nursing degree and will likely spend her first year on the mission field in Zambia. I will be taking Susan's

434

place with the honor of doing the "Pinning" at graduation. Bekah has one more year at JMU with a major in education. Rayah will be a senior at Stuarts Draft High School. All three are dedicated to advancing *Young Life Club*. Rissa will be in eighth grade at the same school and loves soccer like her sisters.

Brenda is the beautician at the retirement community and Eugene is the Supervising Loan analyst. Their daughter, Ciara, married Joseph Steinburg last June and they live near D.C. Ciara will be teaching second grade this fall and Joseph is employed with Freddie Mac as a computer programmer. Tyler will be a senior at Stuarts Draft High School, loves baseball and basketball and golf and is interested in business. He too is involved with *Young Life Club*.

Mike is the outreach Pastor at Grace Covenant Church in Harrisonburg and Mercy is a family life counselor. Their son, Emmett is eight and a whiz at math, Jude is six and excels in sports, and Evangeline is a charming and active three year old.

Lori and Mike still live near us just above Estella, Pa. Lori is an itinerate hearing impaired schoolteacher and Mike farms, buys and sells machinery, and they own and operate an adjoining sports camp, Camp Maple Lake. Kaiti is fourteen, Leah is twelve and Bethany is ten. They are all athletic and excel in school.

So there's the clan. Fortunately, all of them love the Lord and want to follow His path.

The noise of 16 huge diesel generators coming from across the field at a natural gas well fracking site sounds like an enormous army of bees. But once again, as I sit writing, our dogs are asleep on the bed next to me oblivious to any noise. They are content. So am I.

God has been so good to me. Here I am, 70 years old. Just writing that number jars me a bit. You know that song . . . *Where have all the flowers gone, long time passing* . . . ? My parents, your parents, their parents were right in saying, life goes by so quickly and then it's over.

According to scripture, I have maybe 10 or so more years to live . . . if the Lord wills. Toby, stop snoring! Sorry, my dog does that when he sleeps. So there you go, it takes a lot of humor to live a good life and enjoy it. God sure had some when he made us. Think about it.

But seriously, what would I, what would you do differently if you had to live your life over? There's probably a barn full of baled ideas we could come up with but it's a moot question.

Remember the motto above your bedroom door? *Only one life, twill soon be past, only what's done for Christ will last.* It's true. But I still find myself working too hard sometimes on stuff that won't last. How 'bout you?

I stopped by Susan's grave tonight. Pulled some weeds and reset the solar light. I don't go often because I know she's not there but in Heaven. But when I do, I stare and ponder things. Like . . . what is she doing? Where exactly is Heaven? When Jesus comes back, how will all these bones come to life? They will, you know! What might that look like? What does Susan think IF she can see me working hard and for what?

My mind goes off on funny bunny trails which seem to come back around and start all over. In the end of my staring and pondering, I really do believe I have lived a good life; we have followed the path of Jesus . . . most of the time, to the best of our ability. Only eternity will tell what value our lives accomplished.

Hopefully, our legacy was not how much money or earthly possessions we passed on to our kids, or even the church. But that we lived our lives according to the plan God had for us and to extend His kingdom by being channels of His grace.

Written in the margin of my Bible in Colossians 3:23 are the words **my motto for life.** Here is what it says: *Whatever you do, work at it with all your heart, as working for the Lord, not for human masters, since you know that you will receive an inheritance from the Lord as a reward. It is the Lord Christ you are serving.*

Let me encourage you with another favorite scripture of mine for you to ponder before you close this book:

I pray that out of his glorious riches he may strengthen you with power through his Spirit in your inner being, [17] so that Christ may dwell in your hearts through faith. And I pray that you, being rooted and established in love, [18] may have power, together with all the Lord's holy people, to grasp how wide and long and high and deep is the love of Christ, [19] and to know this love that surpasses knowledge—that you may be filled to the measure of all the fullness of God.

[20] Now to him who is able to do immeasurably more than all we ask or imagine, according to his power that is at work within us,[21] to him be glory in the church and in Christ Jesus throughout all generations, for ever and ever! Amen.

To my children, grandchildren and generations to come, I pray this book has helped you to see the incredible value of following the path of Jesus at all cost and dedicating your life to His purposes. Seek first His kingdom and His righteousness and all your needs will be supplied. You will never be sorry if you do so. Hopefully, our "Song of Love" has inspired *you* to live for HIM too.

May God bless you as you seek to follow His plan.

"Big Much" Love,
Poppie.